Chambers

BIBLE QUOTATIONS

Compiled by

Martin H. Manser

Published 1989 by W & R Chambers Ltd,
43–45 Annandale Street, Edinburgh EH7 4AZ

First paperback edition published 1990

British Library Cataloguing in Publication Data

Manser, Martin H.
 Chambers book of Bible quotations.
 1. Title
200.5'2036

ISBN 0-550-21011-3

ACKNOWLEDGEMENT

The compiler wishes to express his gratitude to Rosalind Desmond
for her help in preparing the material for publication.

Cover design by Keith Kail

Typeset by Impact Repro, Edinburgh
Printed in England by Clays Ltd, St Ives plc

CONTENTS

The Books of the Prophets

THE APOCRYPHA 108

INTRODUCTION

Quotations from the Bible are among the most well-known quotations in the language. A group of people may be said to be *the salt of the earth*; the authorities are sometimes referred to as *the powers that be*; we may escape something *by the skin of our teeth*; and something that spoils may be described as *a fly in the ointment*. All these expressions, and many more, have their origins in the Bible. In fact, the style of the Authorized (King James) Version is often highly valued as significant in our national cultural heritage.

This selection of quotations from the Bible includes over 4000 quotations – from the Old Testament, the Apocrypha, and the New Testament. The biblical quotations are supplemented by quotations from the 1662 Book of Common Prayer, itself also formative in the development of the English language.

Within the text about 80 different quotations, allusions, etc., are discussed in a more detailed way, to comment on their importance.

The quotations are arranged according to the order in which they appear in the Bible. Each entry consists of the book number (1 for Genesis, 2 for Exodus, etc.) followed by the particular entry number of that quotation within that book. Following the actual quotation comes the chapter and verse location in the Bible. The index lists extracts from the quotations according to keywords, with reference to the book and entry numbers featured before each quotation in the main text.

It is hoped that readers will come across new, unfamiliar quotations as well as being reminded of those that are more generally known ... and those that are remembered only in part. Readers may find it helpful to look up the quotations in the Bible (in the Authorized Version or a more modern version) to see the fuller context of the quoted extracts. Indeed, this selection has been compiled with the intention that it will lead to a greater reading of the Bible itself, and a response to its message.

Martin H. Manser

THE
OLD TESTAMENT

THE BOOKS OF THE LAW

The first five books of the Bible describe the origin of the Jewish people and culture. *Genesis*, the book of beginnings, goes back to the creation and describes the first disobedience towards God and God's choosing of Abraham and his descendants. *Exodus* shows God's rescue of his people from slavery in Egypt under Moses' leadership. God gave Moses the laws for the new nation. *Leviticus* contains laws for the Israelites' worship especially about the sacrifices that were to be made to the holy God. *Numbers* describes the story of the Israelites' wanderings in the wilderness for 40 years. *Deuteronomy* records Moses' speeches to the Israelites, when they were just about to enter the promised land.

GENESIS

1.1   In the beginning God created the heaven and the earth. And the earth was without form, and void; and darkness was upon the face of the deep. And the Spirit of God moved upon the face of the waters.   *1:1-2*

1.2   And God said, Let there be light: and there was light.   *1:3*

1.3   And God called the light Day and the darkness he called Night. And the evening and the morning were the first day.   *1:5*

1.4   And God saw that it was good.   *1:10*

1.5   And God made two great lights; the greater light to rule the day, and the lesser light to rule the night: he made the stars also.   *1:16*

1.6   And God said, Let us make man in our image, after our likeness: and let them have dominion over the fish of the sea, and over the fowl of the air, and over the cattle, and over all the earth, and over every creeping thing that creepeth upon the earth. So God created man in his own image, in the image of God created he him; male and female created he them. And God blessed them, and God said unto them, Be fruitful, and multiply, and replenish the earth, and subdue it: and have dominion over the fish of the sea, and over the fowl of the air, and over every living thing that moveth upon the earth.   *1:26-28*

1.7   And God saw every thing that he had made, and, behold, it was very good. And the evening and the morning were the sixth day.   *1:31*

1.8   And on the seventh day God ended his work which he had made; and he rested on the seventh day from all his work which he had made. And God blessed the seventh day, and sanctified it: because that in it he had rested from all his work which God created and made. *2:2-3*

1.9   And the LORD God formed man of the dust of the ground, and breathed into his nostrils the breath of life; and man became a living soul.   *2:7*

1.10   And the LORD God planted a garden eastward in Eden; and there he put the man whom he had formed. And out of the ground made the LORD God to grow every tree that is pleasant to the sight, and good for food; the tree of life also in the midst of the garden, and the tree of knowledge of good and evil. *2:8-9*

1.11   And the LORD God took the man and put him into the garden of Eden to dress it and to keep it. And the LORD God commanded the man, saying, Of every tree of the garden thou mayest freely eat: But of the tree of the knowledge of good and evil, thou shalt not eat of it: for in the day that thou eatest thereof thou shalt surely die.   *2:15-17*

1.12   And the LORD God said, It is not good that the man should be alone; I will make him an help meet for him.   *2:18*

1.13   And out of the ground the LORD God formed every beast of the field, and every fowl of the air; and brought them unto Adam to see what he would call them: and whatsoever Adam called every living creature, that was the name thereof.   *2:19*

1.14   And the LORD God caused a deep sleep to fall upon Adam, and he slept: and

he took one of his ribs, and closed up the flesh instead thereof; And the rib, which the LORD God had taken from man, made he a woman, and brought her unto the man. And Adam said, This is now bone of my bones, and flesh of my flesh: she shall be called Woman, because she was taken out of Man. Therefore shall a man leave his father and his mother, and shall cleave unto his wife: and they shall be one flesh. And they were both naked, the man and his wife, and were not ashamed. *2:21-25*

1.15   Now the serpent was more subtil than any beast of the field which the LORD God has made. And he said unto the woman, Yea, hath God said, Ye shall not eat of every tree of the garden?   *3:1*

1.16   And the woman said unto the serpent, We may eat of the fruit of the trees of the garden: But of the fruit of the tree which is in the midst of the garden, God hath said, ye shall not eat of it, neither shall ye touch it, lest ye die. *3:2-3*

1.17   And the serpent said unto the woman, Ye shall not surely die: For God doth know that in the day ye eat thereof, then your eyes shall be opened, and ye shall be as gods, knowing good and evil.   *3:4-5*

1.18   And when the woman saw that the tree was good for food, and that it was pleasant to the eyes, and a tree to be desired to make one wise she took of the fruit thereof, and did eat, and gave also unto her husband with her; and he did eat. And the eyes of them both were opened, and they knew that they were naked; and they sewed fig leaves together, and made themselves aprons. And they heard the voice of the LORD God walking in the garden in the cool of the day: and Adam and his wife hid themselves from the presence of the LORD God amongst the trees of the garden.   *3:6-8*

1.19   And he said, I heard thy voice in the garden, and I was afraid, because I was naked; and I hid myself. And he said, Who told thee that thou wast naked? Hast thou eaten of the tree, whereof I commanded thee that thou shouldest not eat?   *3:10-11*

1.20   And the man said, The woman whom thou gavest to be with me, she gave me of the tree, and I did eat. And the LORD God said unto the woman, what is this that thou hast done? And the woman said, The serpent beguiled me, and I did eat.   *3:12-13*

1.21   And the LORD God said unto the serpent, Because thou hast done this, thou art cursed above all cattle, and above every beast of the field; upon thy belly shalt thou go, and dust shalt thou eat all the days of thy life: And I will put enmity between thee and the woman, and between thy seed and her seed; it shall bruise thy head, and thou shalt bruise his heel.   *3:14-15*

1.22   Unto the woman he said, I will greatly multiply thy sorrow and thy conception; in sorrow thou shalt bring forth children; and thy desire shall be to thy husband, and he shall rule over thee.   *3:16*

1.23   And unto Adam he said, Because thou hast hearkened unto the voice of thy wife, and hast eaten of the tree, of which I commanded thee, saying, Thou shalt not eat of it: cursed is the ground for thy sake; in sorrow shalt thou eat of it all the days of thy life.   *3:17*

1.24   In the sweat of thy face shalt thou eat bread, till thou return unto the ground; for out of it wast thou taken: for dust thou art, and unto dust shalt thou return.   *3:19*

1.25   And Adam called his wife's name Eve; because she was the mother of all living.   *3:20*

1.26   Unto Adam also and to his wife did the LORD God make coats of skins, and clothed them. And the LORD God said,

Behold, the man is become as one of us, to know good and evil: and now, lest he put forth his hand, and take also of the tree of life, and eat, and live for ever: Therefore the LORD God sent him forth from the garden of Eden, to till the ground from whence he was taken. So he drove out the man; and he placed at the east of the garden of Eden Cherubims, and a flaming sword which turned every way, to keep the way of the tree of life. *3:21-24*

1.27   And Adam knew Eve his wife; and she conceived, and bare Cain, and said, I have gotten a man from the LORD.   *4:1*

1.28   And the LORD said unto Cain, Where is Abel thy brother? And he said, I know not: Am I my brother's keeper? And he said, What hast thou done? the voice of thy brother's blood crieth unto me from the ground.   *4:9-10*

My brother's keeper

The phrase to be someone's or one's brother's keeper is used in contemporary English to mean that one accepts responsibility for another's behaviour or well-being. The phrase derives from Cain's reply, 'Am I my brother's keeper?' to God after Cain had killed his brother Abel.

1.29   And the LORD said unto him, Therefore whosoever slayeth Cain, vengeance shall be taken on him sevenfold. And the LORD set a mark upon Cain lest any finding him should kill him.   *4:15*

1.30   And Cain went out from the presence of the LORD, and dwelt in the land of Nod, on the east of Eden.   *4:16*

1.31   And Adah bare Jabal: he was the father of such as dwell in tents, and of such as have cattle.   *4:20*

1.32   And all the days of Methuselah were nine hundred sixty and nine years: and he died.   *5:27*

1.33   And Noah was five hundred years old: and Noah begat Shem, Ham, and Japheth. *5:32*

1.34   That the sons of God saw the daughters of men that they were fair; and they took them wives of all which they chose. And the LORD said, My spirit shall not always strive with man, for that he also is flesh: yet his days shall be an hundred and twenty years. There were giants in the earth in those days; and also after that, when the sons of God came in unto the daughters of men, and they bare children to them, the same became mighty men which were of old, men of renown. *6:2-4*

1.35   And it repented the LORD that he had made man on the earth, and it grieved him at his heart. *6:6*

1.36   But Noah found grace in the eyes of the LORD. *6:8*

1.37   These are the generations of Noah: Noah was a just man and perfect in his generations, and Noah walked with God. *6:9*

1.38   And, behold, I, even I, do bring a flood of waters upon the earth, to destroy all flesh, wherein is the breath of life, from under heaven; and every thing that is in the earth shall die. But with thee will I establish my covenant; and thou shalt come into the ark, thou and thy sons, and thy wife, and thy sons' wives with thee. And of every living thing of all flesh, two of every sort shalt thou bring into the ark, to keep them alive with thee; they shall be male and female. *6:17-19*

1.39   For yet seven days, and I will cause it to rain upon the earth forty days and forty nights; and every living substance that I have made will I destroy from off the face of the earth. *7:4*

1.40   There went in two and two unto Noah into the ark, the male and the female, as God had commanded Noah. *7:9*

1.41   In the six hundredth year of Noah's life, in the second month, the seventeenth day of the month, the same day were all the fountains of the great deep broken up, and the windows of heaven were opened. And the rain was upon the earth forty days and forty nights. *7:11-12*

1.42   They, and every beast after his kind, and all the cattle after their kind, and every creeping thing that creepeth upon the earth after his kind, and every fowl after his kind, every bird of every sort. And they went in unto Noah into the ark, two and two of all flesh, wherein is the breath of life. And they that went in, went in male and female of all flesh, as God had commanded him: and the LORD shut him in. *7:14-16*

1.43   And the dove came in to him in the evening; and, lo, in her mouth was an olive leaf pluckt off: so Noah knew that the waters were abated from off the earth. *8:11*

1.44   And Noah builded an altar unto the LORD; and took of every clean beast, and of every clean fowl, and offered burnt offerings on the altar. And the LORD smelled a sweet savour; and the LORD said in his heart, I will not again curse the ground any more for man's sake; for the imagination of man's heart is evil from his youth; neither will I again smite any more every thing living, as I have done. While the earth remaineth, seedtime and harvest, and cold and heat, and summer and winter, and day and night shall not cease. *8:20-22*

1.45   And surely your blood of your lives will I require; at the hand of every beast will I require it, and at the hand of man; at the hand of every man's brother will I require the life of man. Whoso sheddeth man's blood, by man shall his blood be shed: for in the image of God made he man. *9:5-6*

1.46   I do set my bow in the cloud, and it shall be for a token of a covenant between me and the earth. *9:13*

1.47   He was a mighty hunter before the LORD: wherefore it is said, Even as Nimrod the mighty hunter before the LORD. *10:9*

1.48   And the whole earth was of one language, and of one speech. *11:1*

1.49   And they said, Go to let us build us a city and a tower, whose top may reach unto heaven; and let us make us a name, lest we be scattered abroad upon the face of the whole earth. And the LORD came down to see the city and the tower, which the children of men builded. And the LORD said, Behold, the people is one, and they have all one language; and this they begin to do: and now nothing will be restrained from them, which they have imagined to do. Go to, let us go down, and there confound their language, that they may not understand one another's speech. So the LORD scattered them abroad from thence upon the face of all the earth: and they left off to build the city. Therefore is the name of it called Babel; because the LORD did there confound the language of all the earth: and from thence did the LORD scatter them abroad upon the face of all the earth. *11:4-9*

A babel of voices

A babel in modern English is a confusion of sounds or voices or a noisy or confused scene. The expression comes from the biblical tower of Babel, built with the intention of reaching to heaven. God confounded the builders' efforts by causing them to speak different languages so that they could not understand one another.

1.50   Now the LORD had said unto Abram, Get thee out of thy country, and from thy kindred, and from thy father's house, unto a land that I will shew thee: And I will make of thee a great nation, and I will bless thee, and make thy name great; and thou shalt be a blessing: And I will bless them that bless thee, and curse him that curseth thee: and in thee shall all families of the earth be blessed. *12:1-3*

1.51   So Abram departed, as the LORD had spoken unto him; and Lot went with him: and Abram was seventy and five years old when he departed out of Haran. *12:4*

1.52 And Abram passed through the land unto the place of Sichem, unto the plain of Moreh. And the Canaanite was then in the land. And the LORD appeared unto Abram, and said Unto thy seed will I give this land: and there builded he an altar unto the LORD, who appeared unto him. *12:6-7*

1.53   But the men of Sodom were wicked and sinners before the LORD exceedingly. *13:13*

1.54   And Melchizedek king of Salem brought forth bread and wine: and he was the priest of the most high God. And he blessed him, and said, Blessed be Abram of the most high God, possessor of heaven and earth: And blessed be the most high God, which hath delivered thine enemies into thy hand. And he gave him tithes of all. *14:18-20*

1.55   After these things the word of the LORD came unto Abram in a vision, saying, Fear not, Abram: I am thy shield, and thy exceeding great reward. *15:1*

1.56   And he *[Abram]* believed in the LORD; and he counted it to him for righteousness. *15:6*

1.57   And when the sun was going down, a deep sleep fell upon Abram; and, lo, an horror of great darkness fell upon him. *15:12*

1.58   And thou shalt go to thy fathers in peace; thou shalt be buried in a good old age. *15:15*

1.59   And the angel of the LORD said unto her, Behold, thou art with child, and shalt bear a son, and shalt call his name Ishmael; because the LORD hath heard thy affliction. And he will be a wild man; his hand will be against every man, and every man's hand against him; and he shall dwell in the presence of all his brethren.   *16:11-12*

1.60   And when Abram was ninety years old and nine, the LORD appeared to Abram, and said unto him, I am the Almighty God; walk before me, and be thou perfect.   *17:1*

1.61   And I will establish my covenant between me and thee and thy seed after thee in their generations for an everlasting covenant, to be a God unto thee, and to thy seed after thee. And I will give unto thee, and to thy seed after thee, the land wherein thou art a stranger, all the land of Canaan, for an everlasting possession; and I will be their God. And God said unto Abraham, Thou shalt keep my covenant therefore, thou, and thy seed after thee in their generations. This is my covenant, which ye shall keep, between me and you and thy seed after thee; Every man child among you shall be circumcised.   *17:7-10*

1.62   Now Abraham and Sarah were old and well stricken in age; and it ceased to be with Sarah after the manner of women.   *18:11*

1.63   And the LORD said unto Abraham, Wherefore did Sarah laugh, saying, Shall I of a surety bear a child, which am old? Is any thing too hard for the LORD? At the time appointed I will return unto thee, according to the time of life, and Sarah shall have a son.   *18:13-14*

1.64   And Abraham drew near, and said Wilt thou also destroy the righteous with the wicked? Peradventure there be fifty righteous within the city: wilt thou also destroy and not spare the place for the fifty righteous that are therein? That be far from thee to do after this manner, to slay the righteous with the wicked: and

that the righteous should be as the wicked, that be far from thee: Shall not the Judge of all the earth do right? *18:23-25*

1.65   And Abraham answered and said, Behold now, I have taken upon me to speak unto the Lord, which am but dust and ashes.   *18:27*

1.66   Then the LORD rained upon Sodom and upon Gomorrah brimstone and fire from the LORD out of heaven; And he overthrew those cities, and all the plain, and the inhabitants of the cities, and that which grew upon the ground. *19:24-25*

1.67   But his wife looked back from behind him, and she became a pillar of salt.   *19:26*

1.68   And it came to pass after these things, that God did tempt Abraham, and said unto him, Abraham: and he said, Behold here I am. And he said, Take now thy son, thine only son Isaac, whom thou lovest, and get thee into the land of Moriah; and offer him there for a burnt offering upon one of the mountains which I will tell thee of.   *22:1-2*

1.69   And Abraham said, My son, God will provide himself a lamb for a burnt offering: so they went both of them together.   *22:8*

1.70   And Abraham lifted up his eyes, and looked, and behold behind him a ram caught in a thicket by his horns: and Abraham went and took the ram, and offered him up for a burnt offering in the stead of his son.   *22:13*

1.71   And Abraham called the name of that place Jehovahjireh: as it is said to this day, In the mount of the LORD it shall be seen.   *22:14*

1.72   That in blessing I will bless thee, and in multiplying I will multiply thy seed as the stars of the heaven, and as the sand which is upon the sea shore; and thy seed shall possess the gate of his enemies; And in thy seed shall all the nations of the earth be blessed; because thou hast obeyed my voice. *22:17-18*

1.73   And the boys grew: and Esau was a cunning hunter, a man of the field; and Jacob was a plain man, dwelling in tents. *25:27*

1.74   And Esau said to Jacob, Feed me I pray thee, with that same red pottage; for I am faint: therefore was his name called Edom. And Jacob said, sell me this day thy birthright. And Esau said, Behold, I am at the point to die: and what profit shall this birthright do to me? And Jacob said, Swear to me this day; and he sware unto him: and he sold his birthright unto Jacob. Then Jacob gave Esau bread and pottage of lentiles; and he did eat and drink, and rose up, and went his way thus Esau despised his birthright. *25:30-34*

A mess of pottage

The saying Esau sold his birthright for a mess of pottage *is an inaccurate rendering of the original. The misquotation derives from the story of Esau giving up his birthright to his brother Jacob for a meal (Genesis 25:30-34 and Hebrews 12:16-17). The actual expression does not, however, appear in the Bible text.*

1.75   And Jacob said to Rebekah his mother, Behold, Esau my brother is a hairy man, and I am a smooth man. *27:11*

1.76   And Jacob went near unto Isaac his father; and he felt him, and said, The voice is Jacob's voice, but the hands are the hands of Esau. *27:22*

1.77   And he came near, and kissed him: and he smelled the smell of his raiment, and he blessed him, and said, See, the smell of my son is as the smell of a field which the LORD has blessed: Therefore God give thee of the dew of heaven, and

the fatness of the earth, and plenty of corn and wine. *27:27-28*

1.78   And he said, Thy brother came with subtilty, and hath taken away thy blessing. And he said, Is not he rightly named Jacob? for he hath supplanted me these two times: he took away my birthright; and, behold, now he hath taken away my blessing. And he said, Hast thou not reserved a blessing for me? *27:35-36*

1.79   And he dreamed and behold a ladder set up on the earth, and the top of it reached to heaven: and behold the angels of God ascending and descending on it. *28:12*

1.80   And Jacob awaked out of his sleep, and he said, Surely the LORD is in this place; and I knew it not. *28:16*

1.81   And Jacob served seven years for Rachel; and they seemed unto him but a few days, for the love he had to her. *29:20*

1.82   And Jacob was left alone; and there wrestled a man with him until the breaking of the day. And when he saw that he prevailed not against him, he touched the hollow of his thigh; and the hollow of Jacob's thigh was out of joint, as he wrestled with him. And he said, Let me go, for the day breaketh. And he said, I will not let thee go, except thou bless me. And he said unto him, What is thy name? And he said, Jacob. And he said, Thy name shall be called no more Jacob, but Israel: for as a prince hast thou power with God and with men, and hast prevailed. And Jacob asked him, and said, Tell me, I pray thee, thy name. And he said, Wherefore is it that thou dost ask after my name? And he blessed him there. And Jacob called the name of the place Peniel: for I have seen God face to face, and my life is preserved. *32:24-30*

1.83   Now Israel loved Joseph more than all his children, because he was the son of his old age: and he made him a coat of many colours.   *37:3*

1.84   For, behold, we were binding sheaves in the field, and, lo, my sheaf arose, and also stood upright; and, behold, your sheaves stood round about, and made obeisance to my sheaf.   *37:7*

1.85   And they said one to another, Behold, this dreamer cometh. Come now therefore, and let us slay him, and cast him into some pit, and we will say, Some evil beast hath devoured him: and we shall see what will become of his dreams.   *37:19-20*

1.86   And all his sons and all his daughters rose up to comfort him; but he refused to be comforted; and he said, For I will go down into the grave unto my son mourning. Thus his father wept for him.   *37:35*

1.87   And Onan knew that the seed should not be his; and it came to pass, when he went in unto his brother's wife, that he spilled it on the ground, lest that he should give seed to his brother.   *38:9*

1.88   And she caught him by his garment, saying, Lie with me: and he left his garment in her hand, and fled, and got him out.   *39:12*

1.89   And the seven thin ears devoured the seven rank and full ears. And Pharaoh awoke, and, behold, it was a dream. *41:7*

1.90   And the lean and the ill favoured kine did eat up the first seven fat kine. *41:20*

1.91   And the thin ears devoured the seven good ears: and I told this unto the magicians; but there was none that could declare it to me.   *41:24*

1.92   And Joseph said unto Pharaoh, The dream of Pharaoh is one: God hath shewed Pharaoh what he is about to do. The seven good kine are seven years; and

the seven good ears are seven years: the dream is one. And the seven thin and ill favoured kine that came up after them are seven years; and the seven empty ears blasted with the east wind shall be seven years of famine.   *41:25-27*

1.93   Now when Jacob saw that there was corn in Egypt, Jacob said unto his sons, Why do ye look one upon another?   *42:1*

1.94   And Joseph knew his brethren, but they knew not him. And Joseph remembered the dreams which he dreamed of them, and said unto them, Ye are spies; to see the nakedness of the land ye are come.   *42:8-9*

1.95   And he said, My son shall not go down with you; for his brother is dead, and he is left alone: if mischief befall him by the way in the which ye go, then shall ye bring down my gray hairs with sorrow to the grave.   *42:38*

1.96   And the famine was sore in the land.   *43:1*

1.97   Then Joseph could not refrain himself before all them that stood by him; and he cried, Cause every man to go out from me. And there stood no man with him, while Joseph made himself known unto his brethren. And he wept aloud: and the Egyptians and the house of Pharaoh heard. And Joseph said unto his brethren, I am Joseph; doth my father yet live? And his brethren could not answer him; for they were troubled at his presence. And Joseph said unto his brethren, Come near to me, I pray you. And they came near. And he said, I am Joseph your brother, whom ye sold into Egypt. Now therefore be not grieved, nor angry with yourselves, that ye sold me hither: for God did send me before you to preserve life.   *45:1-5*

1.98   And take your father and your households, and come unto me: and I will give you the good of the land of Egypt, and ye shall eat the fat of the land.   *45:18*

1.99   So he sent his brethren away, and they departed: and he said unto them, See that ye fall not out by the way.   *45:24*

1.100   And Jacob said unto Pharaoh, The days of the years of my pilgrimage are an hundred and thirty years: few and evil have the days of the years of my life been, and have not attained unto the days of the years of the life of my fathers in the days of their pilgrimage.   *47:9*

1.101   The sceptre shall not depart from Judah, nor a lawgiver from between his feet, until Shiloh come; and unto him shall the gathering of the people be.   *49:10*

1.102   Benjamin shall ravin as a wolf: in the morning he shall devour the prey, and at night he shall divide the spoil.   *49:27*

1.103   But as for you, ye thought evil against me; but God meant it unto good, to bring to pass, as it is this day, to save much people alive.   *50:20*

EXODUS

2.1   And the children of Israel were fruitful, and increased abundantly, and multiplied, and waxed exceeding mighty; and the land was filled with them.   *1:7*

2.2   Now there arose up a new king over Egypt, which knew not Joseph.   *1:8*

2.3   And the Egyptians made the children of Israel to serve with rigour: And they made their lives bitter with hard bondage, in morter, and in brick, and in all manner of service in the field: all their service, wherein they made them serve, was with rigour.   *1:13-14*

2.4   And Pharaoh charged all his people, saying, Every son that is born ye shall cast into the river, and every daughter ye shall save alive.   *1:22*

2.5   And the woman conceived, and bare a son: and when she saw him that he was a goodly child, she hid him three months. And when she could not longer hide him, she took for him an ark of bulrushes, and daubed it with slime and with pitch, and put the child therein; and she laid it in the flags by the river's brink.   *2:2-3*

2.6   And the child grew, and she brought him unto Pharaoh's daughter, and he became her son. And she called his name Moses: and she said, Because I drew him out of the water.   *2:10*

2.7   And he said, Who made thee a prince and a judge over us? intendest thou to kill me, as thou killedst the Egyptian? And Moses feared, and said, Surely this thing is known.   *2:14*

2.8   And she bare him a son, and he called his name Gershom: for he said, I have been a stranger in a strange land.   *2:22*

2.9   And God heard their groaning, and God remembered his covenant with Abraham, with Isaac, and with Jacob. And God looked upon the children of Israel, and God had respect unto them.   *2:24-25*

2.10   And the angel of the LORD appeared unto him in a flame of fire out of the midst of a bush: and he looked, and, behold, the bush burned with fire, and the bush was not consumed.   *3:2*

2.11   And he said, Draw not nigh hither: put off thy shoes from off thy feet, for the place whereon thou standest is holy ground. Moreover he said, I am the God of thy father, the God of Abraham, the God of Isaac, and the God of Jacob. And Moses hid his face; for he was afraid to look upon God.   *3:5-6*

2.12   And I am come down to deliver them out of the hand of the Egyptians, and to bring them up out of that land unto a good land and a large, unto a land flowing with milk and honey; unto the place of the Canaanites, and the Hittites, and the Amorites, and the Perizzites, and the Hivites, and the Jebusites.   *3:8*

A land flowing with milk and honey

The expression a land flowing with milk and honey *is used to refer to a place or state that promises to provide plentiful resources, great happiness and security, and abundant fulfilment of all one's hopes. The phrase has a similar meaning to the expression* the promised land, *originally the land of Canaan promised by God to the Israelites.*

2.13   And God said unto Moses, I AM THAT I AM: and he said, Thus shalt thou say unto the children of Israel, I AM hath sent me unto you.   *3:14*

2.14   And Moses answered and said, But, behold, they will not believe me, nor hearken unto my voice: for thy will say, The LORD hath not appeared unto thee. And the LORD said unto him, What is that in thine hand? And he said, A rod. And he said, Cast it on the ground. And he cast it on the ground, and it became a serpent; and Moses fled from before it. And the LORD said unto Moses, Put forth thine hand, and take it by the tail. And he put forth his hand, and caught it, and it became a rod in his hand.   *4:1-4*

2.15   And Moses said unto the LORD, O my Lord, I am not eloquent, neither heretofore, nor since thou hast spoken unto thy servant: but I am slow of speech, and of a slow tongue.   *4:10*

2.16   And the LORD said unto him, Who hath made man's mouth? or who maketh the dumb, or deaf, or the seeing, or the blind? have not I the LORD?   *4:11*

2.17   And Pharaoh said, Who is the LORD, that I should obey his voice to let Israel go? I know not the LORD, neither will I let Israel go.   *5:2*

2.18   And Pharaoh commanded the same day the taskmasters of the people, and their officers saying, Ye shall no more give the people straw to make brick, as heretofore: let them go and gather straw for themselves.   *5:6-7*

2.19   Wherefore say unto the children of Israel, I am the LORD, and I will bring you out from under the burdens of the Egyptians, and I will rid you out of their bondage, and I will redeem you with a stretched out arm, and with great judgments.   *6:6*

2.20   And Moses spake so unto the children of Israel: but they hearkened not unto Moses for anguish of spirit, and for cruel bondage.   *6:9*

2.21   And I will harden Pharaoh's heart, and multiply my signs and my wonders in the land of Egypt.   *7:3*

2.22   And the Egyptians shall know that I am the LORD. when I stretch forth mine hand upon Egypt, and bring out the children of Israel from among them.   *7:5*

2.23   For they cast down every man his rod, and they became serpents: but Aaron's rod swallowed up their rods.   *7:12*

2.24   And Aaron stretched out his hand over the waters of Egypt; and the frogs came up, and covered the land of Egypt.   *8:6*

2.25   Then the magicians said unto Pharaoh, This is the finger of God: and Pharaoh's heart was hardened, and he hearkened not unto them; as the LORD had said.   *8:19*

2.26   And Pharaoh's servants said unto him, How long shall this man be a snare unto us? let the men go, that they may serve the LORD their God: knowest thou not yet that Egypt is destroyed?   *10:7*

2.27 And the LORD said unto Moses, Stretch out thine hand toward heaven, that there may be darkness over the land of Egypt, even darkness which may be felt. *10:21*

2.28 And there shall be a great cry throughout all the land of Egypt, such as there was none like it, nor shall be like it any more. *11:6*

2.29 Your lamb shall be without blemish, a male of the first year: ye shall take it out from the sheep, or from the goats. *12:5*

2.30 And thus shall ye eat it; with your loins girded, your shoes on your feet, and your staff in your hand; and ye shall eat it in haste: it is the LORD'S passover. For I will pass through the land of Egypt this night, and will smite all the firstborn in the land of Egypt, both man and beast; and against all the gods of Egypt I will execute judgment: I am the LORD. And the blood shall be to you for a token upon the houses where ye are: and when I see the blood, I will pass over you, and the plague shall not be upon you to destroy you, when I smite the land of Egypt. *12:11-13*

2.31 And Pharaoh rose up in the night, he and all his servants, and all the Egyptians; and there was a great cry in Egypt; for there was not a house where there was not one dead. *12:30*

2.32 And the Egyptians were urgent upon the people, that they might send them out of the land in haste; for they said, We be all dead men. *12:33*

2.33 And the LORD spake unto Moses, saying, Sanctify unto me all the firstborn, whatsoever openeth the womb among the children of Israel, both of man and of beast: it is mine. *13:1-2*

2.34 And the LORD went before them by day in a pillar of a cloud, to lead them the way; and by night in a pillar of fire, to give them light; to go by day and night. *13:21*

2.35 And Moses stretched out his hand over the sea; and the LORD caused the sea to go back by a strong east wind all that night, and made the sea dry land, and the waters were divided. And the children of Israel went into the midst of the sea upon the dry ground: and the waters were a wall unto them on their right hand, and on their left. And the Egyptians pursued, and went in after them to the midst of the sea, even all Pharaoh's horses, his chariots, and his horsemen. *14:21-23*

2.36 Then sang Moses and the children of Israel this song unto the LORD, and spake, saying, I will sing unto the LORD for he hath triumphed gloriously: the horse and his rider hath he thrown into the sea. The LORD is my strength and song, and he is become my salvation: he is my God, and I will prepare him an habitation; my father's God, and I will exalt him. *15:1-2*

2.37 The LORD is a man of war: the LORD is his name. *15:3*

2.38 Who is like unto thee, O LORD, among the gods? who is like thee, glorious in holiness, fearful in praises, doing wonders? *15:11*

2.39 And the children of Israel said unto them, Would to God we had died by the hand of the LORD in the land of Egypt, when we sat by the flesh pots, and when we did eat bread to the full; for ye have brought us forth into this wilderness, to kill this whole assembly with hunger. *16:3*

2.40 And when the dew that lay was gone up, behold, upon the face of the wilderness there lay a small round thing, as small as the hoar frost on the ground. And when the children of Israel saw it, they said one to another, It is manna: for they wist not what it was. And Moses said unto them, This is the bread which the LORD hath given you to eat. *16:14-15*

2.41 Behold, I will stand before thee there upon the rock in Horeb; and thou shalt smite the rock, and there shall come water out of it, that the people may drink. And Moses did so in the sight of the elders of Israel. *17:6*

Where manna came from

The food that was the Israelites' main food during their wanderings in the wilderness was known as manna. The word derives from the people's question, 'What (Hebrew, man) is it?', the Israelites calling it man. Speculation continues on the exact nature of the food that was miraculously provided by God.

2.42 And it came to pass, when Moses held up his hand, that Israel prevailed: and when he let down his hand, Amalek prevailed. *17:11*

2.43 Ye have seen what I did unto the Egyptians, and how I bare you on eagles' wings, and brought you unto myself. Now therefore, if ye will obey my voice indeed, and keep my covenant, then ye shall be a peculiar treasure unto me above all people: for all the earth is mine. *19:4-5*

2.44 And God spake all these words, saying, I am the LORD thy God, which have brought thee out of the land of Egypt, out of the house of bondage. Thou shalt have no other gods before me. Thou shalt not make unto thee any graven image, or any likeness of any thing that is in heaven above, or that is in the earth beneath, or that is in the water under the earth: Thou shalt not bow down thyself to them, nor serve them: for I the LORD thy God am a jealous God, visiting the iniquity of the fathers upon the children unto the third and fourth generation of them that hate me; And shewing mercy unto thousands of them that love me, and keep my commandments. Thou shalt not take the name of the LORD thy God in vain; for the LORD will not hold him guiltless that taketh his name in vain.

Remember the sabbath day, to keep in holy. Six days shalt thou labour and do all thy work: But the seventh day is the sabbath of the LORD thy God: in it thou shalt not do any work, thou, nor thy son, nor thy daughter, thy manservant, nor thy maidservant, nor thy cattle, nor thy stranger that is within thy gates: For in six days the LORD made heaven and earth, the sea, and all that in them is, and rested the seventh day: wherefore the LORD blessed the sabbath day, and hallowed it. Honour thy father and thy mother: that thy days may be long upon the land which the LORD thy God giveth thee. Thou shalt not kill. Thou shalt not commit adultery. Thou shalt not steal. Thou shalt not bear false witness against thy neighbour. Thou shalt not covet thy neighbour's house, thou shalt not covet thy neighbour's wife, nor his manservant, nor his maidservant, nor his ox, nor his ass, nor any thing that is thy neighbour's. *20:1-17*

2.45 And they said unto Moses, Speak thou with us, and we will hear: but let not God speak with us, lest we die. *20:19*

2.46 And the people stood afar off, and Moses drew near unto the thick darkness where God was. *20:21*

2.47 And if any mischief follow, then thou shalt give life for life, Eye for eye, tooth for tooth, hand for hand, foot for foot. *21:23-24*

2.48 The first of the firstfruits of thy land thou shalt bring into the house of the LORD thy God. *23:19*

2.49 And the LORD said unto Moses, Come up to me into the mount, and be there: and I will give thee tables of stone, and a law, and commandments which I have written; that thou mayest teach them. *24:12*

2.50 And the glory of the LORD abode upon the mount Sinai, and the cloud covered it six days: and the seventh day he called unto Moses out of the midst of the cloud. And the sight of the glory of the

LORD was like devouring fire on the top of the mount in the eyes of the children of Israel. And Moses went into the midst of the cloud, and gat him up into the mount: and Moses was in the mount forty days and forty nights. *24:16-18*

2.51 And thou shalt hang up the vail under the taches, that thou mayest bring in thither within the vail the ark of the testimony: and the vail shall divide unto you between the holy place and the most holy. *26:33*

2.52 And thou shalt put the two stones upon the shoulders of the ephod for stones of memorial unto the children of Israel: and Aaron shall bear their names before the LORD upon his two shoulders for a memorial. *28:12*

2.53 And the stones shall be with the names of the children of Israel, twelve, according to their names, like the engravings of a signet; every one with his name shall they be according to the twelve tribes. *28:21*

2.54 And thou shalt put in the breastplate of judgment the Urim and the Thummim; and thy shall be upon Aaron's heart, when he goeth in before the LORD: and Aaron shall bear the judgment of the children of Israel upon his heart before the LORD continually. *28:30*

2.55 Then shalt thou take the anointing oil, and pour it upon his head, and anoint him. *29:7*

2.56 Then shalt thou kill the ram, and take of his blood, and put it upon the tip of the right ear of Aaron, and upon the tip of the right ear of his sons, and upon the thumb of their right hand, and upon the great toe of their right foot, and sprinkle the blood upon the altar round about. *29:20*

2.57 And Aaron shall make an atonement upon the horns of it once in a year with the blood of the sin offering of atonements: once in the year shall he make atonement upon it throughout your generations: it is most holy unto the LORD. *30:10*

2.58 And thou shalt anoint Aaron and his sons, and consecrate them, that they may minister unto me in the priest's office. *30:30*

2.59 And he received them at their hand, and fashioned it with a graving tool, after he had made it a molten calf: and they said, These be thy gods, O Israel, which brought thee up out of the land of Egypt. *32:4*

2.60 And they rose up early on the morrow, and offered burnt offerings, and brought peace offerings; and the people sat down to eat and to drink, and rose up to play. *32:6*

2.61 And the LORD said unto Moses, I have seen this people, and, behold, it is a stiffnecked people. *32:9*

2.62 And it came to pass, as soon as he came nigh unto the camp, that he saw the calf and the dancing: and Moses anger waxed hot, and he cast the tables out of his hands, and brake them beneath the mount. *32:19*

2.63 Then Moses stood in the gate of the camp, and said, Who is on the LORD'S side? let him come unto me. And all the sons of Levi gathered themselves together unto him. *32:26*

2.64 Yet now, if thou wilt forgive their sin; and if not, blot me, I pray thee, out of thy book which thou hast written. And the LORD said unto Moses, Whosoever hath sinned against me, him will I blot out of my book. *32:32-33*

2.65 Unto a land flowing with milk and honey: for I will not go up in the midst of thee; for thou art a stiffnecked people: lest I consume thee in the way. *33:3*

2.66 And the LORD spake unto Moses face to face, as a man speaketh unto his friend. And he turned again into the camp: but his servant Joshua, the son of Nun, a young man, departed not out of the tabernacle. *33:11*

2.67   And he said, My presence shall go with thee, and I will give thee rest. And he said unto him, If thy presence go not with me carry us not up hence. *33:14-15*

2.68   And he said, I beseech thee, shew me thy glory. *33:18*

2.69   And he said, I will make all my goodness pass before thee, and I will proclaim the name of the LORD before thee; and will be gracious to whom I will be gracious, and will shew mercy on whom I will shew mercy. And he said, Thou canst not see my face: for there shall no man see me, and live. And the LORD said, Behold, there is a place by me, and thou shalt stand upon a rock: And it shall come to pass, while my glory passeth by, that I will put thee in a clift of the rock, and will cover thee with my hand while I pass by: And I will take away mine hand, and thou shalt see my back parts: but my face shall not be seen. *33:19-23*

2.70   And the LORD descended in the cloud, and stood with him there, and proclaimed the name of the LORD. And the LORD passed by before him, and proclaimed, The LORD, The LORD God, merciful and gracious, longsuffering, and abundant in goodness and truth, Keeping mercy for thousands, forgiving iniquity and transgression and sin, and that will by no means clear the guilty; visiting the iniquity of the fathers upon the children, and upon the children's children, unto the third and to the fourth generation. And Moses made haste, and bowed his head toward the earth, and worshipped. *34:5-8*

2.71   And they came, every one whose heart stirred him up, and every one whom his spirit made willing, and they brought the LORD'S offering to the work of the tabernacle of the congregation, and

for all his service, and for the holy garments. *35:21*

2.72   And they spake unto Moses, saying, The people bring much more than enough for the service of the work, which the LORD commanded to make. *36:5*

2.73   Then a cloud covered the tent of the congregation, and the glory of the LORD filled the tabernacle. *40:34*

2.74   For the cloud of the LORD was upon the tabernacle by day, and fire was on it by night, in the sight of all the house of Israel, throughout all their journeys. *40:38*

LEVITICUS

3.1   And he shall put his hand upon the head of the burnt offering; and it shall be accepted for him to make atonement for him. *1:4*

3.2   If the priest that is anointed do sin according to the sin of the people; then let him bring for his sin, which he hath sinned, a young bullock without blemish unto the LORD for a sin offering. *4:3*

3.3   And he shall burn all his fat upon the altar, as the fat of the sacrifice of peace offerings: and the priest shall make an atonement for him as concerning his sin, and it shall be forgiven him. *4:26*

3.4   And he shall take away all the fat thereof, as the fat of the lamb is taken away form the sacrifice of the peace offerings; and the priest shall burn them upon the altar, according to the offerings made by fire unto the LORD: and the priest shall make an atonement for his sin that he hath committed, and it shall be forgiven him. *4:35*

3.5   And Moses and Aaron went into the tabernacle of the congregation, and came out, and blessed the people: and the glory of the LORD appeared unto all the people.   *9:23*

3.6   For I am the LORD your God: ye shall therefore sanctify yourselves, and ye shall be holy; for I am holy: neither shall ye defile yourselves with any manner of creeping thing that creepeth upon the earth.   *11:44*

3.7   And the leper in whom the plague is, his clothes shall be rent, and his head bare, and he shall put a covering upon his upper lip, and shall cry, Unclean, unclean.   *13:45*

3.8   But the goat, on which the lot fell to be the scapegoat, shall be presented alive before the LORD, to make an atonement with him, and to let him go for a scapegoat into the wilderness.   *16:10*

The scapegoat

Someone who is made to take the blame for the actions of other people is called a scapegoat. *The English word was coined from the words* escape *and* goat. *A scapegoat was originally the goat that symbolically carried all the sins of Israel and was sent off into the wilderness.*

3.9   And he shall take of the blood of the bullock, and sprinkle it with his finger upon the mercy seat eastward; and before the mercy seat shall he sprinkle of the blood with his finger seven times. Then shall he kill the goat of the sin offering, that is for the people, and bring his blood within the vail, and do with that blood as he did with the blood of the bullock, and sprinkle it upon the mercy seat, and before the mercy seat.   *16:14-15*

3.10   And when he hath made an end of reconciling the holy place, and the tabernacle of the congregation, and the altar, he shall bring the live goat: And Aaron shall lay both his hands upon the head of the live goat, and confess over him all the iniquities of the children of Israel, and all their transgressions in all their sins, putting them upon the head of the goat, and shall send him away by the hand of a fit man into the wilderness.   *16:20-21*

3.11   For the life of the flesh is in the blood: and I have given it to you upon the altar to make an atonement for your souls: for it is the blood that maketh an atonement for the soul.   *17:11*

3.12   Thou shalt not avenge, nor bear any grudge against the children of thy people, but thou shalt love thy neighbour as thyself: I am the LORD.   *19:18*

3.13   And ye shall be holy unto me: for I the LORD am holy, and have severed you from other people, that ye should be mine.   *20:26*

3.14   And ye shall take you on the first day the boughs of goodly trees, branches of palm trees, and the boughs of thick trees, and willows of the brook; and ye shall rejoice before the LORD your God seven days.   *23:40*

3.15   Breach for breach, eye for eye, tooth for tooth: as he hath caused a blemish in a man, so shall it be done to him again.   *24:20*

3.16   And ye shall hallow the fiftieth year, and proclaim liberty throughout all the land unto all the inhabitants thereof: it shall be a jubilee unto you; and ye shall return every man unto his possession, and ye shall return every man unto his family. A jubilee shall that fiftieth year be unto you: ye shall not sow, neither reap that which groweth of itself in it, nor gather the grapes in it of thy vine undressed.   *25:10-11*

3.17   And I will set my tabernacle among you: and my soul shall not abhor you. And I will walk among you, and will be your God, and ye shall be my people,   *26:11-12*

3.18   And that I also have walked contrary unto them, and have brought them into the land of their enemies; if then their uncircumcised hearts be humbled, and they then accept of the punishment of their iniquity.   *26:41*

NUMBERS

4.1   These are those which were numbered of the children of Israel by the house of their fathers: all those that were numbered of the camps throughout their hosts were six hundred thousand and three thousand and five hundred and fifty.   *2:32*

4.2   The LORD bless thee, and keep thee: The LORD make his face shine upon thee, and be gracious unto thee: The LORD lift up his countenance upon thee, and give thee peace.   *6:24-26*

4.3   And Aaron shall offer the Levites before the LORD for an offering of the children of Israel, that they may execute the service of the LORD.   *8:11*

4.4   So it was alway: the cloud covered it by day, and the appearance of fire by night. And when the cloud was taken up from the tabernacle, then after that the children of Israel journeyed: and in the place where the cloud abode, there the children of Israel pitched their tents. *9:16-17*

4.5   Or whether it were two days, or a month, or a year, that the cloud tarried upon the tabernacle, remaining thereon, the children of Israel abode in their tents, and journeyed not: but when it was taken up, they journeyed.   *9:22*

4.6   And when it rested, he said, Return, O LORD, unto the many thousands of Israel.   *10:36*

4.7   And when the people complained, it displeased the LORD: and the LORD heard it; and his anger was kindled; and the fire of the LORD burnt among them, and consumed them that were in the uttermost parts of the camp.   *11:1*

4.8   I am not able to bear all this people alone, because it is too heavy for me. And if thou deal thus with me, kill me, I pray thee, out of hand, if I have found favour in thy sight; and let me not see my wretchedness.   *11:14-15*

4.9   And Moses said unto him, Enviest thou for my sake? would God that all the LORD'S people were prophets, and that the LORD would put his spirit upon them!   *11:29*

4.10   (Now the man Moses was very meek, above all the men which were upon the face of the earth)   *12:3*

4.11   These are the names of the men which Moses sent to spy out the land. And Moses called Oshea the son of Nun Jehoshua.   *13:16*

4.12   And they brought up an evil report of the land which they had searched unto the children of Israel, saying, The land through which we have gone to search it, is a land that eateth up the inhabitants thereof; and all the people that we saw in it are men of a great stature. And there we saw the giants, the sons of Anak, which come of the giants: and we were in our own sight as grasshoppers, and so we were in their sight.   *13:32-33*

4.13   But my servant Caleb, because he had another spirit with him, and hath followed me fully, him will I bring into the land whereinto he went; and his seed shall possess it.   *14:24*

4.14   Speak unto the children of Israel, and bid them that they make them fringes in the borders of their garments throughout their generations, and that they put upon the fringe of the borders a ribband of blue.   *15:38*

4.15   Is it a small thing that thou hast brought us up out of a land that floweth with milk and honey, to kill us in the wilderness, except thou make thyself altogether a prince over us?   *16:13*

4.16   And it came to pass, that on the morrow Moses went into the tabernacle of witness; and behold, the rod of Aaron for the house of Levi was budded, and brought forth buds, and bloomed blossoms, and yielded almonds.   *17:8*

Aaron's rod

Aaron's rod *is a plant, especially a mullein,* Verbascum thapsus, *that has tall stems and spikes of yellow flowers. The name comes from one of the 12 rods that were placed in the tabernacle. The next day Aaron's rod budded, blossomed, and produced almonds.*

4.17   And Moses and Aaron gathered the congregation together before the rock, and he said unto them, Hear now, ye rebels; must we fetch you water out of this rock?   *20:10*

4.18   And Moses lifted up his hand, and with his rod he smote the rock twice: and the water came out abundantly, and the congregation drank, and their beasts also.   *20:11*

4.19   And the LORD spake unto Moses and Aaron, Because ye believed me not, to sanctify me in the eyes of the children of Israel, therefore ye shall not bring this congregation into the land which I have given them.   *20:12*

4.20   And the LORD said unto Moses, Make thee a fiery serpent, and set it upon a pole: and it shall come to pass, that every one that is bitten, when he looketh upon it, shall live. And Moses made a serpent of brass, and put it upon a pole, and it came to pass, that if a serpent had bitten any man, when he beheld the serpent of brass, he lived.   *21:8-9*

4.21   And the LORD opened the mouth of the ass, and she said unto Balaam, What have I done unto thee, that thou hast smitten me these three times?   *22:28*

4.22   And Balak said unto Balaam, What hast thou done unto me? I took thee to curse mine enemies, and, behold, thou hast blessed them altogether.   *23:11*

4.23   God is not a man, that he should lie; neither the son of man, that he should repent: hath he said, and shall he not do it? or hath he spoken, and shall he not make it good?   *23:19*

4.24   How goodly are thy tents, O Jacob, and thy tabernacles, O Israel!   *24:5*

4.25   And Balak's anger was kindled against Balaam, and he smote his hands together: and Balak said unto Balaam, I called thee to curse mine enemies, and, behold, thou hast altogether blessed them these three times.   *24:10*

4.26   I shall see him, but not now: I shall behold him, but not nigh: there shall come a Star out of Jacob, and a Sceptre shall rise out of Israel, and shall smite the corners of Moab, and destroy all the children of Sheth.   *24:17*

4.27   Be sure your sin will find you out.   *32:23*

DEUTERONOMY

5.1   Also the LORD was angry with me for your sakes, saying, Thou also shalt not go in thither. But Joshua the son of Nun, which standeth before thee, he shall go in thither: encourage him: for he shall cause Israel to inherit it. Moreover your little ones, which ye said should be a prey, and your children, which in that day had not knowledge between good and evil, they shall go in thither, and unto them will I give it, and they shall possess it. But as for you, turn you, and take your journey into the wilderness by the way of the Red sea.   *1:37-40*

5.2   Now therefore hearken, O Israel, unto the statutes and unto the judgments, which I teach you, for to do them, that ye may live, and go in and possess the land which the LORD God of your fathers giveth you.   *4:1*

5.3   Keep therefore and do them; for this is your wisdom and your understanding in the sight of the nations, which shall hear all these statutes, and say, Surely this great nation is a wise and understanding people.   *4:6*

5.4   I call heaven and earth to witness against you this day, that ye shall soon utterly perish from off the land whereunto ye go over Jordan to possess it; ye shall not prolong your days upon it, but shall utterly be destroyed. And the LORD shall scatter you among the nations, and ye shall be left few in number among the heathen, whither the LORD shall lead you.   *4:26-27*

5.5   But if from thence thou shalt seek the LORD thy God, thou shalt find him, if thou seek him with all thy heart and with all thy soul.   *4:29*

5.6   (For the LORD thy God is a merciful God;) he will not forsake thee, neither destroy thee, nor forget the covenant of thy fathers which he sware unto them.   *4:31*

5.7   O that there were such and heart in them, that they would fear me, and keep all my commandments always, that it might be well with them, and with their children for ever!   *5:29*

5.8   Hear, O Israel: The LORD our God is one LORD: And thou shalt love the LORD thy God with all thy soul, and with all thy might. And these words, which I command thee this day, shall be in thine heart: And thou shalt teach them diligently unto thy children, and shalt

talk of them when thou sittest in thine house, and when thou walkest by the way, and when thou liest down, and when thou risest up. And thou shalt bind them for a sign upon thine hand, and they shall be as frontlets between thine eyes. And thou shalt write them upon the posts of thy house, and on thy gates.   *6:4-9*

5.9   Then beware lest thou forget the LORD, which brought thee forth out of the land of Egypt, from the house of bondage.   *6:12*

5.10   Ye shall not go after other gods, of the gods of the people which are round about you; (For the LORD thy God is a jealous God among you) lest the anger of the LORD thy God be kindled against thee, and destroy thee from off the face of the earth.   *6:14-15*

5.11   Ye shall not tempt the LORD your God as ye tempted him in Massah.   *6:16*

5.12   For thou art an holy people unto the LORD thy God: the LORD thy God hath chosen thee to be a special people unto himself, above all people that are upon the face of the earth. The LORD did not set his love upon you, nor choose you, because ye were more in number than any people; for ye were the fewest of all people: But because the LORD loved you, and because he would keep the oath which he had sworn unto your fathers, hath the LORD brought you out with a mighty hand, and redeemed you out of the house of bondmen, from the hand of Pharaoh king of Egypt. Know therefore that the LORD thy God, he is God, the faithful God, which keepeth covenant and mercy with them that love him and keep his commandments to a thousand generations.   *7:6-9*

5.13   And he humbled thee, and suffered thee to hunger, and fed thee with manna, which thou knewest not, neither did thy fathers know; that he might make thee know that man doth not live by bread only, but by every word that proceedeth out of the mouth of the LORD doth man live.   *8:3*

5.14   For the LORD thy God bringeth thee into a good land, a land of brooks of water, of fountains and depths that spring out of valleys and hills; A land of wheat, and barley, and vines, and fig trees, and pomegranates; a land of oil olive, and honey; A land wherein thou shalt eat bread without scarceness, thou shalt not lack any thing in it; a land whose stones are iron, and out of whose hills thou mayest dig brass. When thou hast eaten and art full, then thou shalt bless the LORD thy God for the good land which he hath given thee.   *8:7-10*

5.15   Beware that thou forget not the LORD thy God, in not keeping his commandments, and his judgments, and his statutes, which I command thee this day: Lest when thou hast eaten and art full, and hast built goodly houses, and dwelt therein; And when thy herds and thy flocks multiply, and thy silver and thy gold is multiplied; and all that thou hast is multiplied; Then thine heart be lifted up, and thou forget the LORD thy God, which brought thee forth out of the land of Egypt, from the house of bondage; Who led thee through that great and terrible wilderness, wherein were fiery serpents, and scorpions, and drought, where there was no water; who brought thee forth water out of the rock of flint; Who fed thee in the wilderness with manna, which thy fathers knew not, that he might humble thee, and that he might prove thee, to do thee good at thy latter end; And thou say in thine heart, My power and the might of mine hand hath gotten me this wealth. But thou shalt remember the LORD thy God: for it is he that giveth thee power to get wealth, that he may establish his covenant which he sware unto thy fathers, as it is this day.   *8:11-18*

5.16   Speak not thou in thine heart, after that the LORD thy God hath cast them out from before thee, saying, For my righteousness the LORD hath brought me in to possess this land: but for the wicked-

ness of these nations the LORD doth drive them out from before thee.   *9:4*

5.17   Take heed to yourselves, that your heart be not deceived, and ye turn aside, and serve other gods, and worship them.   *11:16*

5.18   Therefore shall ye lay up these my words in your heart and in your soul, and bind them for a sign upon your hand, that they may be as frontlets between your eyes.   *11:18*

5.19   Ye shall utterly destroy all the places, wherein the nations which ye shall possess served their gods, upon the high mountains, and upon the hills, and under every green tree.   *12:2*

5.20   Observe and hear all these words which I command thee, that it may go well with thee, and with thy children after thee for ever, when thou doest that which is good and right in the sight of the LORD thy God.   *12.28*

5.21   If there arise among you a prophet, or a dreamer of dreams, and giveth thee a sign or a wonder.   *13:1*

5.22   Thou shalt not hearken unto the words of that prophet, or that dreamer of dreams: for the LORD you God proveth you, to know whether ye love the LORD your God with all your heart and with all your soul.   *13:3*

5.23   If thy brother, the son of thy mother, or thy son, or thy daughter, or the wife of thy bosom, or thy friend, which is as thine own soul, entice thee secretly, saying, Let us go and serve other gods, which thou hast not known, thou, nor thy fathers.   *13:6*

5.24   For thou art an holy people unto the LORD thy God, and the LORD hath chosen thee to be a peculiar people unto himself, above all the nations that are upon the earth.   *14:2*

5.25   At the end of three years thou shalt bring forth all the tithe of thine increase the same year, and shalt lay it up within thy gates. *14:28*

5.26   Thou shalt in any wise set him king over thee, whom the LORD thy God shall choose: one from among thy brethren shalt thou set king over thee: thou mayest not set a stranger over thee, which is not thy brother. *17:15*

5.27   When thou art come into the land which the LORD thy God giveth thee, thou shalt not learn to do after the abominations of those nations. *18:9*

5.28   The LORD thy God will raise up unto thee a Prophet from the midst of thee, of thy brethren, like unto me; unto him ye shall hearken. *18:15*

5.29   I will raise them up a Prophet from among their brethren, like unto thee, and will put my words in his mouth; and he shall speak unto them all that I shall command him. *18:18*

5.30   And thine eye shall not pity; but life shall go for life, eye for eye, tooth for tooth, hand for hand, foot for foot. *19:21*

5.31   When thou cuttest down thine harvest in thy field, and hast forgot a sheaf in the field, thou shalt not go again to fetch it: it shall be for the stranger, for the fatherless, and for the widow: that the LORD thy God may bless thee in all the work of thine hands. *24:19*

5.32   Thou shalt not muzzle the ox when he treadeth out the corn. *25:4*

5.33   Cursed be he that removeth his neighbour's landmark. And all the people shall say, Amen. *27:17*

5.34   And all these blessings shall come on thee, and overtake thee, if thou shalt hearken unto the voice of the LORD thy God. Blessed shalt thou be in the city, and blessed shalt thou be in the field. Blessed

shall be the fruit of thy body, and the fruit of thy ground, and the fruit of thy cattle, the increase of thy kine, and the flocks of thy sheep. *28:2-4*

5.35   But it shall come to pass, if thou wilt not hearken unto the voice of the LORD thy God, to observe to do all his commandments and his statutes which I command thee this day; that all theses curses shall come upon thee, and overtake thee: Cursed shalt thou be in the city, and cursed shalt thou be in the field. *28:15-16*

5.36   Because thou servedst not the LORD thy God with joyfulness, and with gladness of heart, for the abundance of all things; Therefore shalt thou serve thine enemies which the LORD shall send against thee, in hunger, and in thirst, and in nakedness, and in want of all things: and he shall put a yoke of iron upon thy neck, until he have destroyed thee. *28:47-48*

5.37   The secret things belong unto the LORD our God; but those things which are revealed belong unto us and our children for ever, that we may do all the words of this law. *29:29*

5.38   I call heaven and earth to record this day against you, that I have set before you life and death, blessing and cursing: therefore choose life, that both thou and thy seed may live. *30:19*

5.39   Be strong and of a good courage, fear not, nor be afraid of them: for the LORD thy God, he it is that doth go with thee: he will not fail thee, nor forsake thee. *31:6*

5.40   Give ear, O ye heavens, and I will speak: and hear, O earth, the words of my mouth. My doctrine shall drop as the rain, my speech shall distil as the dew, as the small rain upon the tender herb, and as the showers upon the grass. *32:1-2*

5.41   He is the Rock, his work is perfect: for all ways are judgment: a God of truth

without iniquity, just and right is he.
32:4

5.42   He found him in a desert land, and in the waste howling wilderness; he led him about, he instructed him, he kept him as the apple of his eye.   *32:10*

The apple of his eye

The apple of one's eye *is a person that one treasures as precious. The phrase comes from this verse, describing God's tender love for his people. The apple was originally a metaphor for the pupil of the eye, since an apple and a pupil are both round. The phrase was applied to someone who was as valuable to a person as his or her own eyes.*

5.43   As an eagle stirreth up her nest, fluttereth over her young, spreadeth abroad her wings, taketh them, beareth them on her wings: So the Lord alone did lead him, and there was no strange god with him.   *32:11-12*

5.44   But Jeshurun waxed fat, and kicked: thou art waxen fat, thou art grown thick, thou art covered with fatness; then he forsook God which made him, and lightly esteemed the Rock of his salvation.   *32:15*

5.45   O that they were wise, that they understood this, that they would consider their latter end!   *32:39*

5.46   To me belongeth vengeance and recompence; their foot shall slide in due time: for the day of their calamity is at hand, and the things that shall come upon them make haste.   *32:35*

5.47   As thy days, so shall thy strength be.   *33:25*

5.48   The eternal God is thy refuge, and underneath are the everlasting arms: and he shall thrust out the enemy from before thee; and shall say, Destroy them.   *33:27*

5.49   And Moses went up from the plains of Moab unto the mountain of Nebo, to the top of Pisgah, that is over against Jericho. And the LORD shewed him all the land of Gilead, unto Dan.   *34:1*

5.50   And the LORD said unto him, This is the land which I sware unto Abraham, unto Issac, and unto Jacob saying, I will give it unto thy seed: I have caused thee to see it with thine eyes, but thou shalt not go over thither.   *34:4*

5.51   So Moses the servant of the LORD died there in the land of Moab, according to the word of the LORD. And he buried him in a valley in the land of Moab, over against Bethpeor: but no man knoweth of his sepulchre unto this day.   *34:5-6*

5.52   And Joshua the son of Nun was full of the spirit of wisdom; for Moses had laid his hands upon him: and the children of Israel hearkened unto him, and did as the LORD commanded Moses.   *34:9*

5.53   And there arose not a prophet since in Israel like unto Moses, whom the LORD knew face to face.   *34:10*

THE HISTORICAL BOOKS

This section covers 12 books concerned with the history of the Israelites from about 1200-400 BC. *Joshua* shows how the Israelites, led by Joshua, took possession of the promised land after Moses' death. *Judges* describes how the new nation was constantly disobedient to God and how God chose leaders or 'judges'. *Ruth,* a story of love and loyalty, is followed by *1 and 2 Samuel,* a history of Israel from the last of the judges through the transitional leader Samuel and Israel's first king, Saul, to King David, 'a man after God's own heart'. *1 and 2 Kings* describe the reign of Solomon, and the later division into the northern kingdom (Israel) and the southern kingdom (Judah). Eventually Israel fell to the Assyrians, Judah (Jerusalem) to the Babylonians.

1 and 2 Chronicles mostly parallel the events of 2 Samuel and the books of Kings. *Ezra* tells of the rebuilding of the Temple in Jerusalem; Ezra himself was amongst the refugees from exile in Babylon. *Nehemiah* describes his leadership in rebuilding the walls round Jerusalem. *Esther* was a Jew who became queen of Persia and was able to save her people from a plot to exterminate them.

JOSHUA

6.1 There shall not any man be able to stand before thee all the days of thy life: as I was with Moses, so I will be with thee: I will not fail thee, nor forsake thee. Be strong and of a good courage: for unto this people shalt thou divide for an inheritance the land, which I sware unto their fathers to give them. Only be thou strong and very courageous, that thou mayest observe to do according to all the law, which Moses my servant commanded thee: turn not from it to the right hand or to the left, that thou mayest prosper whithersoever thou goest. This book of the law shall not depart out of thy mouth; but thou shalt meditate therein day and night, that thou mayest observe to do according to all that is written therein: for then thou shalt make thy way

prosperous, and then thou shalt have good success. Have not I commanded thee? Be strong and of a good courage: be not afraid, neither be thou dismayed: for the LORD thy God is with thee whithersoever thou goest.   *1:5-9*

6.2   And they answered Joshua, saying, All that thou commandest us we will do, and whithersoever thou sendeth us, we will go.   *1:16*

6.3   Now therefore, I pray you, swear unto me by the LORD, since I have shewed you kindness, that ye will also shew kindness unto my father's house, and give me a true token.   *2:12*

6.4   Behold, when we come into the land, thou shalt bind this line of scarlet thread in the window which thou didst let us down by: and thou shalt bring thy father, and thy mother, and thy brethren, and all thy father's household, home unto thee.   *2:18*

6.5   And Joshua said unto the people, Sanctify yourselves: for to morrow the LORD will do wonders among you.   *3:5*

6.6   And it came to pass, when Joshua was by Jericho, that he lifted up his eyes and looked, and, behold, there stood a man over against him with his sword drawn in his hand: and Joshua went unto him, and said unto him, Art thou for us, or for our adversaries?   *5:13*

6.7   So the people shouted when the priests blew with the trumpets: and it came to pass, when the people heard the sound of the trumpet, and the people shouted with a great shout, that the wall fell down flat, so that the people went up into the city, every man straight before him, and they took the city.   *6:20*

6.8   And Joshua said, Alas, O Lord GOD, wherefore hast thou at all brought this people over Jordan, to deliver us into the hand of the Amorites, to destroy us? would to God we had been content, and dwelt on the other side Jordan!   *7:7*

6.9   And the princes said unto them, Let them live; but let them be hewers of wood and drawers of water unto all the congregation; as the princes had promised them.   *9:21*

6.10   Then spake Joshua to the LORD in the day when the LORD delivered up the Amorites before the children of Israel, and he said in the sight of Israel, Sun, stand thou still upon Gibeon; and thou, Moon, in the valley of Ajalon. And the sun stood still, and the moon stayed, until the people had avenged themselves upon their enemies, Is not this written in the book of Jasher? So the sun stood still in the midst of heaven, and hasted not to go down about a whole day.   *10:12-13*

6.11   And the LORD said unto Joshua, Be not afraid because of them: for to morrow about this time will I deliver them up all slain before Israel: thou shalt hough their horses, and burn their chariots with fire.   *11:6*

6.12   And Joshua said unto the children of Israel, How long are ye slack to go to possess the land, which the LORD God of your fathers hath given you?   *18:3*

6.13   Speak to the children of Israel, saying, Appoint out for you cities of refuge, whereof I spake unto you by the hand of Moses.   *20:2*

6.14   There failed not ought of any good thing which the LORD had spoken unto the house of Israel; all came to pass.   *21:45*

6.15   And, behold, this day I am going the way of all the earth: and ye know in all your hearts and in all your souls, that not one thing hath failed of all the good things which the LORD your God spake concerning you; all are come to pass unto you, and not one thing hath failed thereof.   *23:14*

6.16   And if it seem evil unto you to serve the LORD, choose you this day whom ye will serve; whether the gods which your fathers served that were on the other side of the flood, or the gods of the Amorites, in whose land ye dwell: but as for me and my house, we will serve the LORD.   *24:15*

6.17   And Israel served the LORD all the days of Joshua, and all the days of the elders that overlived Joshua, and which had known all the works of the LORD, that he had done for Israel.   *24:31*

JUDGES

7.1   And the children of Israel did evil in the sight of the LORD, and served Baalim: And they forsook the LORD God of their fathers, which brought them out of the land of Egypt, and followed other gods of the gods of the people that were round about them, and bowed themselves unto them, and provoked the LORD to anger. And they forsook the LORD, and served Baal and Ashtaroth. And the anger of the LORD was hot against Israel, and he delivered them into the hands of spoilers that spoiled them, and he sold them into the hands of their enemies round about, so that they could not any longer stand before their enemies.　*2:11-14*

7.2　And when the LORD raised them up judges, then the LORD was with the judge, and delivered them out of the hand of their enemies all the days of the judge: for it repented the LORD because of their groanings by reason of them that oppressed them and vexed them.　*2:18*

7.3　And the Spirit of the LORD came upon him *[Othniel]*, and he judged Israel, and went out to war: and the LORD delivered Chushanrishathaim king of Mesopotamia into his hand; and his hand prevailed against Chushanrishathaim.　*3:10*

7.4　And she said, I will surely go with thee: notwithstanding the journey that thou takest shall not be for thine honour; for the LORD shall sell Sisera into the hand of a woman. And Deborah arose, and went with Barak to Kedesh.　*4:9*

7.5　Then Jael Heber's wife took a nail of the tent, and took an hammer in her hand, and went softly unto him and smote the nail into his temples, and fastened it into the ground: for he was fast asleep and weary. So he died.　*4:21*

7.6　The inhabitants of the villages ceased, they ceased in Israel, until that I Deborah arose, that I arose a mother in Israel.　*5:7*

7.7　Why abodest thou among the sheepfolds, to hear the bleatings of the flocks? For the divisions of Reuben there were great searchings of heart.　*5:16*

7.8　They fought from heaven; the stars in their courses fought against Sisera.　*5:20*

7.9　He asked water, and she brought him milk; she brought forth butter in a lordly dish. She put her hand to the nail, and her right hand to the workmen's hammer; and with the hammer she smote Sisera, she smote off his head, when she had pierced and stricken through his temples. At her feet he bowed, he fell, he lay down: at her feet he bowed he fell: where he bowed, there he fell down dead. The mother of Sisera looked out at a window, and cried through the lattice, Why is his chariot so long in coming? why tarry the wheels of his chariots?　*5:25-28*

7.10　And the angel of the LORD appeared unto him, and said unto him, The LORD is with thee, thou mighty man of valour.　*6:12*

7.11　And the LORD said unto him, Peace be unto thee; fear not: thou shalt not die.　*6:23*

7.12　Behold, I will put a fleece of wool in the floor; and if the dew be on the fleece only, and it be dry upon all the earth beside, then shall I know that thou wilt save Israel by mine hand, as thou hast said. And it was so: for he rose up early on the morrow, and thrust the fleece together, and wringed the dew out of the fleece, a bowl of water.　*6:37-38*

7.13　So the people took victuals in their hand, and their trumpets: and he sent all the rest of Israel every man unto his tent, and retained those three hundred men: and the host of Midian was beneath him in the valley.　*7:8*

7.14　When I blow with a trumpet, I and all that are with me, then blow ye the trumpets also on every side of all the camp, and say, The sword of the LORD, and of Gideon.　*7:18*

7.15   And he said unto them, What have I done now in comparison of you? Is not the gleaning of the grapes of Ephraim better than the vintage of Abiezer?   *8:2*

7.16   And Gideon came to Jordan, and passed over, he, and the three hundred men that were with him, faint yet pursuing them.   *8:4*

7.17   Then said they unto him, Say now Shibboleth: and he said Sibboleth: for he could not frame to pronounce it right. Then they took him, and slew him at the passages of Jordan: and there fell at that time of the Ephraimites forty and two thousand.   *12:6*

The first shibboleth

A shibboleth is a use of language, or a saying or custom, especially one that distinguishes members of a certain group. The origin of the word lies in Judges 12:4-6. In a battle between the Gileadites and Ephraimites, the Gileadites captured the fords. When any of the Ephraimite survivors wanted to cross, they would be asked if they were Ephraimites. If the answer was no, they would then be asked to say the word shibboleth. *Anyone who gave the incorrect pronunciation of* shibboleth *was killed.*

7.18   And Manoah said unto the angel of the LORD, What is thy name, that when thy sayings come to pass we may do thee honour? And the angel of the LORD said unto him, Why askest thou thus after my name, seeing it is secret?   *13:17-18*

7.19   And the Spirit of the LORD began to move him *[Samson]* at times in the camp of Dan between Zorah and Eshtaol.   *13:25*

7.20   And he came up, and told his father and his mother, and said, I have seen a woman in Timnath of the daughters of the Philistines: now therefore get her for me to wife.   *14:2*

7.21   And he said unto them, Out of the eater came forth meat, and out of the strong came forth sweetness. And they could not in three days expound the riddle.   *14:14*

7.22   And the men of the city said unto him on the seventh day before the sun went down, What is sweeter than honey? and what is stronger than a lion? And he said unto them, If ye had not plowed with my heifer, ye had not found out my riddle.   *14:18*

7.23   And he smote them hip and thigh with a great slaughter: and he went down and dwelt in the top of the rock Etam.   *15:8*

7.24   And he found a new jawbone of an ass, and put forth his hand, and took it, and slew a thousand men therewith. And Samson said, With the jawbone of an ass, heaps upon heaps, with the jaw of an ass have I slain a thousand men.   *15:15-16*

7.25   Now there were men lying in wait, abiding with her in the chamber. And she said unto him, The Philistines be upon thee, Samson. And he brake the withs, as a thread of tow is broken when it toucheth the fire. So his strength was not known.   *16:9*

7.26   *[Samson to Delilah]* He told her all his heart, and said unto her, There hath not come a rasor upon mine head; for I have been a Nazarite unto God from my mother's womb: if I be shaven, then my strength will go from me, and I shall become weak, and be like any other man.   *16:17*

7.27   And she made him sleep upon her knees; and she called for a man, and she caused him to shave off the seven locks of his head; and she began to afflict him, and his strength went from him. And she said, The Philistines be upon thee, Samson. And he awoke out of his sleep, and said, I will go out as at other times before, and shake myself. And he wist not that the LORD was departed from him. But the

Philistines took him, and put out his eyes, and brought him down to Gaza, and bound him with fetters of brass; and he did grind in the prison house.   *16:19-21*

7.28   And Samson took hold of the two middle pillars upon which the house stood, and on which it was borne up, of the one with his right hand, and of the other with his left. And Samson said, Let me die with the Philistines. And he bowed himself with all his might; and the house fell upon the lords, and upon all the people that were therein. So the dead which he slew at his death were more than they which he slew in his life.   *16:29-30*

7.29   In those days there was no king in Israel, but every man did that which was right in his own eyes.   *17:6*

7.30   Then all the children of Israel went out, and the congregation was gathered together as one man, from Dan even to Beersheba, with the land of Gilead, unto the LORD in Mizpeh.   *20:1*

7.31   And all the people arose as one man, saying, We will not any of us go to his tent, neither will we any of us turn into his house.   *20:8*

RUTH

8.1   And Naomi said unto her two daughters in law, Go, return each to her mother's house: the LORD deal kindly with you, as ye have dealt with the dead, and with me.   *1:8*

8.2   And Ruth said, Intreat me not to leave thee, or to return from following after thee: for whither thou goest, I will go; and where thou lodgest, I will lodge: thy people shall be my people, and thy God my God: Where thou diest, will I die, and there will I be buried: the LORD do so to me, and more also, if ought but death part thee and me.   *1:16-17*

8.3   So they two went until they came to Bethlehem. And it came to pass, when they were come to Bethlehem, that all the city was moved about them, and they said, Is this Naomi? And she said unto them, Call me not Naomi, call me Mara: for the Almighty hath dealt very bitterly with me. I went out full, and the LORD hath brought me home again empty: why then call ye me Naomi, seeing the LORD hath testified against me, and the Almighty hath afflicted me?   *1:19-21*

8.4   And she went, and came, and gleaned in the field after the reapers: and her hap was to light on a part of the field belonging unto Boaz, who was of the kindred of Elimelech.   *2:3*

8.5   So she gleaned in the field until even, and beat out that she had gleaned: and it was about an ephah of barley.   *2:17*

8.6   And Naomi said unto her daughter in law, Blessed be he of the LORD, who hath not left off his kindness to the living and to the dead. And Naomi said unto her, The man is near of kin unto us, one of our next kinsmen.   *2:20*

8.7   And she lay at his feet until morning: and she rose up before one could know another. And he said, Let it not be known that a woman came into the floor. Also he said, Bring the vail that thou hast upon thee, and hold it. And when she held it, he measured six measures of barley, and laid it on her: and she went into the city.   *4:14-15*

1 SAMUEL

9.1   Now the sons of Eli were sons of Belial: they knew not the LORD.   *2:12*

9.2   But Samuel ministered before the LORD, being a child, girded with a linen ephod.   *2:18*

9.3 Wherefore the LORD God of Israel saith, I said indeed that thy house, and the house of thy father, should walk before me for ever: but now the Lord saith, Be it far from me; for them that honour me I will honour, and they that despise me shall be lightly esteemed. *2:30*

9.4 And the man of thine, whom I shall not cut off from mine altar, shall be to consume thine eyes, and to grieve thine heart: and all the increase of thine house shall die in the flower of their age. *2:33*

9.5 That the LORD called Samuel: and he answered, Here am I. And he ran unto Eli, and said, Here am I; for thou calledst me. And he said, I called not; lie down again. And he went and lay down. *3:45*

9.6 Therefore Eli said unto Samuel, Go, lie down: and it shall be, if he call thee, that thou shalt say, Speak, LORD; for thy servant heareth. So Samuel went and lay down in his place. And the LORD came, and stood, and called as at other times, Samuel, Samuel. Then Samuel answered, Speak; for thy servant heareth. *3:9-10*

9.7 And the LORD said to Samuel, Behold, I will do a thing in Israel, at which both the ears of every one that heareth it shall tingle. *3:11*

9.8 Be strong, and quit yourselves like men, O ye Philistines, that ye be not servants unto the Hebrews, as they have been to you: quit yourselves like men, and fight. *4:9*

9.9 And it came to pass, when he made mention of the ark of God, that he fell from off the seat backward by the side of the gate, and his neck brake, and he died: for he was an old men, and heavy. And he had judged Israel forty years. *4:18*

9.10 And she named the child Ichabod, saying, The glory is departed from Israel: because the ark of God was taken, and because of her father in law and her husband. *4:21*

9.11 Then Samuel took a stone, and set it between Mizpeh and Shen, and called the name of it Ebenezer, saying, Hitherto hath the LORD helped us. *7:12*

9.12 And said unto him, Behold, thou art old, and thy sons walk not in thy ways: now make us a king to judge us like all the nations. *8:5*

9.13 After that thou shalt come to the hill of God, where is the garrison of the Philistines: and it shall come to pass, when thou art come thither to the city, that thou shalt meet a company of prophets coming down from the high place with a psaltery, and tabret, and a pipe, and a harp, before them; and they shall prophesy. *10:5*

9.14 And it came to pass, when all that knew him beforetime saw that, behold, he prophesied among the prophets, then the people said one to another, What is this that is come unto the son of Kish? Is Saul also among the prophets? *10:11*

9.15 And said unto the children of Israel, Thus saith the LORD God of Israel, I brought up Israel out of Egypt, and delivered you out of the hand of the Egyptians, and out of the hand of all kingdoms, and of them that oppressed you: And ye have this day rejected your God, who himself saved you out of all your adversities and your tribulations; and ye have said unto him, Nay, but set a king over us. Now therefore present yourselves before the LORD by your tribes, and by your thousands. *10:18-19*

9.16 And Samuel said to all the people, See ye him whom the LORD hath chosen, that there is none like him among all the people? And all the people shouted, and said, God save the king. *10:24*

9.17 If ye will fear the LORD, and serve him, and obey his voice, and not rebel against the commandment of the LORD, then shall both ye and also the king that reigneth over you continue following the LORD your God: But if ye will not obey

the voice of the LORD, but rebel against
the commandment of the LORD, then
shall the hand of the LORD be against you,
as it was against your fathers.   *12:14-15*

9.18   But now thy kingdom shall not
continue: the LORD hath sought him a
man after his own heart, and the LORD
hath commanded him to be captain over
his people, because thou hast not kept that
which the LORD commanded thee.
13:14

A man after his own heart

A person who is after someone's own
heart *is one who is exactly the kind that
someone likes most, because they share the
same ideals. The source of this phrase is
this verse: God was seeking the kind of
man he wanted - one who would closely
follow his ways.*

9.19   And the people said unto Saul,
Shall Jonathan die, who hath wrought
this great salvation in Israel? God forbid:
as the LORD liveth, there shall not one hair
of his head fall to the ground; for he hath
wrought with God this day. So the people
rescued Jonathan, that he died not.
14:45

9.20   And Samuel said, What meaneth
then this bleating of the sheep in mine
ears, and the lowing of the oxen which I
hear?   *15:14*

9.21   And Samuel said, Hath the LORD
as great delight in burnt offerings and
sacrifices, as in obeying the voice of the
LORD? Behold, to obey is better than
sacrifice, and to hearken than the fat of
rams.   *15:22*

9.22   For rebellion is as the sin of
witchcraft, and stubbornness is as
iniquity and idolatry. Because thou hast
rejected the word of the LORD, he hath
also rejected thee from being king.
15:23

9.23   But the LORD said unto Samuel,
Look not on his countenance, or on the
height of his stature; because I have
refused him: for the LORD seeth not as
man seeth; for man looketh on the
outward appearance, but the LORD
looketh on the heart.   *16:7*

9.24   And he *[Samuel]* sent, and brought
him *[David]* in. Now he was ruddy, and
withal of a beautiful countenance, and
goodly to look to. And the LORD said,
Arise, anoint him: for this is he.   *16:12*

9.25   And there went out a champion
out of the camp of the Philistines, named
Goliath, of Gath, whose height was six
cubits and a span. And he had an helmet
of brass upon his head, and he was armed
with a coat of mail; and the weight of the
coat was five thousand shekels of brass.
And he had greaves of brass upon his legs,
and a target of brass between his
shoulders. And the staff of his spear was
like a weaver's beam; and his spear's head
weighed six hundred shekels of iron: and
one bearing a shield went before him.
17:4-7

9.26   And Eliab his eldest brother heard
when he spake unto the men; and Eliab's
anger was kindled against David, and he
said, Why camest thou down hither? and
with whom hast thou left those few sheep
in the wilderness? I know thy pride, and
the naughtiness of thine heart; for thou
art come down that thou mightest see the
battle. And David said, What have I now
done? Is there not a cause?   *17:28-29*

9.27   David said moreover, The LORD
that delivered me out of the paw of the
lion, and out of the paw of the bear, he
will deliver me out of the hand of this
Philistine. And Saul said unto David, Go,
and the LORD be with thee.   *17:37*

9.28   And he took his staff in his hand,
and chose him five smooth stones out of
the brook, and put them in a shepherd's
bag which he had, even in a scrip; and his
sling was in his hand: and he drew near to
the Philistine.   *17:40*

9.29   And the Philistine said unto David, Am I a dog, that thou comest to me with staves? And the Philistine cursed David by his gods.   *17:43*

9.30   And the women answered one another as they played, and said, Saul hath slain his thousands, and David his ten thousands.   *18:7*

9.31   And the priest answered David, and said, There is no common bread under mine hand, but there is hallowed bread; if the young men have kept themselves at least from women.   *21:4*

9.32   Moreover, my father, see, yea, see the skirt of thy robe in my hand: for in that I cut off the skirt of thy robe, and killed thee not, know thou and see that there is neither evil nor transgression in mine hand, and I have not sinned against thee; yet thou huntest my soul to take it. The LORD judge between me and thee, and the LORD avenge me of thee: but mine hand shall not be upon thee.   *24:11-12*

9.33   Then said Saul, I have sinned: return, my son David: for I will no more do thee harm, because my soul was precious in thine eyes this day: behold, I have played the fool, and have erred exceedingly.   *26:21*

---

2 SAMUEL

10.1   The beauty of Israel is slain upon thy high places: how are the mighty fallen! Tell it not in Gath, publish it not in the streets of Askelon; lest the daughters of the Philistines rejoice, lest the daughters of the uncircumcised triumph.   *1:19-20*

10.2   Saul and Jonathan were lovely and pleasant in their lives, and in their death they were not divided: they were swifter than eagles, they were stronger than lions. Ye daughters of Israel, weep over Saul, who clothed you in scarlet, with other delights, who put on ornaments of gold upon your apparel. How are the mighty fallen in the midst of the battle! O Jonathan, thou wast slain in thine high places. I am distressed for thee, my brother Jonathan: very pleasant hast thou been unto me: thy love to me was wonderful, passing the love of women. How are the mighty fallen, and the weapons of war perished!   *1:23-27*

10.3   And David danced before the LORD with all his might; and David was girded with a linen ephod.   *6:14*

10.4   Now therefore so shalt thou say unto my servant David, Thus saith the LORD of hosts, I took thee from the sheepcote, from following the sheep, to be ruler over my people, over Israel.   *7:8*

10.5   And thine house and thy kingdom shall be established for ever before thee: thy throne shall be established for ever.   *7:16*

10.6   And it came to pass in an eveningtide, that David arose from off his bed, and walked upon the roof of the king's house: and from the roof he saw a woman washing herself; and the woman was very beautiful to look upon.   *11:2*

10.7   And he wrote in the letter, saying, Set ye Uriah in the forefront of the hottest battle, and retire ye from him, that he may be smitten, and die.   *11:15*

10.8   But the poor man had nothing, save one little ewe lamb, which he had bought and nourished up: and it grew up together with him, and with his children; it did eat of his own meat, and drank of his own cup, and lay in his bosom, and was unto him as a daughter.   *12:3*

10.9   And David's anger was greatly kindled against the man; and he said to Nathan, As the LORD liveth, the man that hath done this thing shall surely die: And he shall restore the lamb fourfold, because he did this thing, and because he had no pity.   *12:5-6*

10.10   And Nathan said to David, Thou art the man. Thus saith the LORD God of Israel, I anointed thee king over Israel, and I delivered thee out of the hand of Saul; And I gave thee thy master's house, and thy master's wives into thy bosom, and gave thee the house of Israel and of Judah: and if that had been too little, I would moreover have given unto thee such and such things. Wherefore hast thou despised the commandment of the LORD to do evil in his sight? thou hast killed Uriah the Hittite with the sword, and hast taken his wife to be thy wife, and hast slain him with the sword of the children of Ammon.   *12:7-9*

10.11   For we must needs die, and are as water spilt on the ground, which cannot be gathered up again: neither doth God respect any person: yet doth he devise means, that his banished be not expelled from him.   *14:14*

10.12   And thus said Shimei when he cursed, Come out, come out, thou bloody man, and thou man of Belial.   *16:7*

10.13   And the king was much moved, and went up to the chamber over the gate, and wept: and as he went, thus he said, O my son Absalom, my son, my son Absalom! would God I had died for thee, O Absalom, my son, my son!   *18:33*

10.14   And he said, The LORD is my rock, and my fortress, and my deliverer: The God of my rock; in him will I trust, he is my shield, and the horn of my salvation, my high tower, and my refuge, my saviour; thou savest me from violence.   *22:2-3*

10.15   For thou art my lamp, O LORD: and the LORD will lighten my darkness.   *22:29*

10.16   As for God, his way is perfect; the word of the LORD is tried: he is a buckler to all them that trust in him. For who is God, save the LORD? and who is a rock, save our God? God is my strength and power: and he maketh my way perfect. He maketh my feet like hinds' feet: and setteth me upon my high places.   *22:31-34*

10.17   Now these be the last words of David. David the son of Jesse said, and the man who was raised up on high, the anointed of the God of Jacob, and the sweet psalmist of Israel, said.   *23:1*

10.18   And he said, Be it far from me, O Lord, that I should do this: is not this the blood of the men that went in jeopardy of their lives? therefore he would not drink it. These things did these three mighty men.   *23:17*

10.19   And the king said unto Araunah, Nay: but I will surely buy it of thee at a price: neither will I offer burnt offerings unto the Lord my God of that which dost cost me nothing. So David bought the threshingfloor and the oxen for the fifty shekels of silver.   *24:24*

1 KINGS

11.1   Now king David was old and stricken in years; and they covered him with clothes, but he gat no heat.   *1:1*

11.2   I go the way of all the earth: be thou strong therefore, and shew thyself a man.   *2:2*

To go the way of all flesh

The expression to go the way of all flesh *means to die or disappear finally. The phrase is in fact an alteration of the Bible narrative of David's dying words to Solomon. The actual phrase* go the way of all flesh *is not part of the Bible text.*

11.3   And keep the charge of the LORD thy God, to walk in his ways, to keep his statutes, and his commandments, and his judgments, and his testimonies, as it is

11.4   written in the law of Moses, that thou mayest prosper in all that thou doest, and whithersoever thou turnest thyself.   *2:3*

11.4   He said moreover, I have somewhat to say unto thee. And she said, Say on. *2:14*

11.5   In Gibeon the LORD appeared to Solomon in a dream by night: and God said, Ask what I shall give thee.   *3:5*

11.6   And now, O LORD my God, thou hast made thy servant king instead of David my father: and I am but a little child: I know not how to go out or come in.   *3:7*

11.7   Give therefore thy servant an understanding heart to judge thy people, that I may discern between good and bad: for who is able to judge this thy so great a people?   *3:9*

11.8   And the king said, Divide the living child in two, and give half to the one, and half to the other.   *3:25*

11.9   Then the king answered and said, Give her the living child, and in no wise slay it: she is the mother thereof. And all Israel heard of the judgment which the king had judged; and they feared the king: for they saw that the wisdom of God was in him, to do judgment.   *3:27-28*

11.10   And God gave Solomon wisdom and understanding exceeding much, and largeness of heart, even as the sand that is on the sea shore. And Solomon's wisdom excelled the wisdom of all the children of the east country, and all the wisdom of Egypt.   *4:29-20*

11.11   So that the priests could not stand to minister because of the cloud: for the glory of the LORD had filled the house of the LORD.   *8:11*

11.12   I have surely built thee an house to dwell in, a settled place for thee to abide in for ever.   *8:13*

11.13   But will God indeed dwell on the earth? behold, the heaven and heaven of heavens cannot contain thee; how much less this house that I have builded.   *8:27*

11.14   The LORD our God be with us, as he was with our fathers: let him not leave us, nor forsake us: That he may incline our hearts unto him, to walk in all his ways, and to keep his commandments, and his statutes, and his judgments, which he commanded our fathers. *8:57-58*

11.15   Let your heart therefore be perfect with the LORD our God, to walk in his statutes, and to keep his commandments, as at this day.   *8:61*

11.16   And the LORD said unto him, I have heard thy prayer and thy supplication, that thou hast made before me: I have hallowed this house, which thou hast built, to put my name there for ever; and mine eyes and mine heart shall be there perpetually.   *9:3*

11.17   But if ye shall at all turn from following me, ye or your children, and will not keep my commandments and my statutes which I have set before you, but go and serve other gods, and worship them: Then will I cut off Israel out of the land which I have given them; and this house, which I have hallowed for my name, will I cast out of my sight; and Israel shall be a proverb and a byword among all people.   *9:6-7*

11.18   And when the queen of Sheba heard of the fame of Solomon concerning the name of the LORD, she came to prove him with hard questions.   *10:1*

11.19   Howbeit I believed not the words, until I came, and mine eyes had seen it: and, behold, the half was not told me: thy wisdom and prosperity exceedeth the fame which I heard.   *10:7*

11.20   For the king had at sea a navy of Tharshish with the navy of Hiram: once in three years came the navy of Tharshish, bringing gold, and silver, ivory, and apes, and peacocks.   *10:22*

11.21   But king Solomon loved many strange women, together with the daughter of Pharaoh, women of the Moabites, Ammonites, Edomites, Zidonians, and Hittites.   *11.1*

11.22   For it came to pass, when Solomon was old, that his wives turned away his heart after other gods: and his heart was not perfect with the LORD his God, as was the heart of David his father.   *11:4*

11.23   And the man Jeroboam was a mighty man of valour: and Solomon seeing the young man that he was industrious, he made him ruler over all the charge of the house of Joseph.   *11:28*

11.24   And the young men that were grown up with him spake unto him, saying Thus shalt thou speak unto this people that spake unto thee, saying, Thy father made our yoke heavy, but make thou it lighter unto us; thus shalt thou say unto them, My little finger shall be thicker than my father's loins. And now whereas my father did lade you with a heavy yoke, I will add to your yoke: my father hath chastised you with whips, but I will chastise you with scorpions. *12:10-11*

11.25   So when all Israel saw that the king hearkened not unto them, the people answered the king, saying, What portion have we in David? neither have we inheritance in the son of Jesse: to your tents, O Israel: now see to thine own house, David. So Israel departed unto their tents.   *12:16*

11.26   And he shall give Israel up because of the sins of Jeroboam, who did sin, and who made Israel to sin.   *14:16*

11.27   And there was war between Rehoboam and Jeroboam all their days.   *14:30*

11.28   The rest of all the acts of Asa, and all his might, and all that he did, and the cities which he built, are they not written in the book of the chronicles of the kings of Judah? Nevertheless in the time of his old age he was diseased in his feet.   *15:23*

11.29   Get thee hence, and turn thee eastward, and hide thyself by the brook Cherith, that is before Jordan. And it shall be, that thou shalt drink of the brook; and I have commanded the ravens to feed thee there.   *17:3-4*

11.30   And the ravens brought him *[Elijah]* bread and flesh in the morning, and bread and flesh in the evening; and he drank of the brook. And it came to pass after a while, that the brook dried up, because there had been no rain in the land.   *17:6-7*

11.31   *[The widow at Zarephath]* she said, As the LORD thy God liveth, I have not a cake, but an handful of meal in a barrel, and a little oil in a cruse: and, behold, I am gathering two sticks, that I may go in and dress it for me and my son, that we may eat it, and die. And Elijah said unto her, Fear not; go and do as thou hast said: but make me thereof a little cake first, and bring it unto me, and after make for thee and for thy son. For thus saith the LORD thy God of Israel, The barrel of meal shall not waste, neither shall the cruse of oil fail, until the day that the LORD sendeth rain upon the earth. And she went and did according to the saying of Elijah: and she, and he, and her house, did eat many days. And the barrel of meal wasted not, neither did the cruse of oil fail, according to the word of the LORD, which he spake unto Elijah.   *17:12-16*

11.32   And he stretched himself upon the child three times, and cried unto the LORD, and said, O LORD my God, I pray thee, let this child's soul come into him again. And the Lord heard the voice of Elijah: and the soul of the child came into him again, and he revived.   *17:21-22*

11.33   And the woman said unto Elijah, Now by this I know that thou art a man of God, and that the word of the LORD in thy mouth is truth.   *17:24*

11.34   And Elijah came unto all the people, and said, How long halt ye between two opinions? if the LORD be God, follow him: but if Baal, then follow him. And the people answered him not a word.   *18:21*

11.35   And call ye on the name of your gods, and I will call on the name of the LORD: and the God that answereth by fire, let him be God. And all the people answered and said, It is well spoken. *18:24*

11.36   And it came to pass at noon, that Elijah mocked them, and said, Cry aloud: for he is a god; either he is talking, or he is pursuing, or he is in a journey, or peradventure he sleepeth, and must be wakened.   *18:27*

11.37   Hear me, O LORD, hear me, that this people may know that thou art the LORD God, and that thou hast turned their heart back again. Then the fire of the LORD fell, and consumed the burnt sacrifice, and the wood, and the stones, and the dust, and licked up the water that was in the trench. And when all the people saw it, they fell on their faces: and they said, The LORD, he is the God; the LORD, he is the God. And Elijah said unto them, Take the prophets of Baal; let not one of them escape. And they took them: and Elijah brought them down to the brook Kishon, and slew them there. *18:37-40*

11.38   And Elijah said unto Ahab, Get thee up, eat and drink; for there is a sound of abundance of rain.   *18:41*

11.39   And it came to pass at the seventh time, that he said, Behold, there ariseth a little cloud out of the sea, like a man's hand. And he said, Go up, say unto Ahab, Prepare thy chariot, and get thee down, that the rain stop thee not.   *18:44*

11.40   And the hand of the LORD was on Elijah; and he girded up his loins, and ran before Ahab to the entrance of Jezreel. *18:46*

11.41   And when he saw that, he arose, and went for his life, and came to Beersheba, which belongeth to Judah, and left his servant there. But he himself went a day's journey into the wilderness, and came and sat down under a juniper tree: and he requested for himself that he might die; and said, It is enough, now, O LORD, take away my life; for I am not better than my fathers.   *19:3-4*

11.42   And he said, I have been very jealous for the LORD God of hosts: for the children of Israel have forsaken thy covenant, thrown down thine altars, and slain thy prophets with the sword; and I, even I only, am left; and they seek my life, to take it away.   *19:10*

11.43   And he said, Go forth, and stand upon the mount before the LORD. And, behold, the LORD passed by, and a great and strong wind rent the mountains, and brake in pieces the rocks before the LORD; but the LORD was not in the wind: and after the wind an earthquake; but the LORD was not in the earthquake: And after the earthquake a fire; but the LORD was not in the fire: and after the fire a still small voice.   *19:11-12*

The still small voice

A still small voice *is sometimes used in modern English to stand for the 'voice' of one's conscience, one's inner sense of right and wrong, an expression of a calm and sensible viewpoint. The phrase comes from the quiet gentle means with which God spoke to Elijah after he had fled to Horeb.*

11.44   So he departed thence and found Elisha the son of Shaphat, who was plowing with twelve yoke of oxen before him, and he with the twelfth: and Elijah passed by him and cast his mantle upon him.   *19:19*

11.45   And the king of Israel answered and said, Tell him, Let not him that girdeth on his harness boast himself as he that putteth it off.   *20:11*

11.46   And it came to pass after these things, that Naboth the Jezreelite had a vineyard, which was in Jezreel, hard by the palace of Ahab king of Samaria. And Ahab spake unto Naboth, saying, Give me thy vineyard, that I may have it for a garden of herbs, because it is near unto my house: and I will give thee for it a better vineyard than it; or, if it seem good to thee, I will give thee the worth of it in money. And Naboth said to Ahab, The LORD forbid it me, that I should give the inheritance of my fathers unto thee. *21:1-3*

11.47   And thou shalt speak unto him, saying, Thus saith the LORD, Hast thou killed, and also taken possession? And thou shalt speak unto him, saying, Thus saith the LORD, In the place where dogs licked the blood of Naboth shall dogs lick thy blood, even thine. And Ahab said to Elijah, Hast thou found me, O mine enemy? And he answered, I have found thee: because thou hast sold thyself to work evil in the sight of the LORD. *21:19-20*

11.48   And he said, I saw all Israel scattered upon the hills, as sheep that have not a shepherd: and the LORD said, These have no master: let them return every man to his house in peace.   *22:17*

11.49   And say, Thus saith the king, Put this fellow in the prison, and feed him with bread of affliction and with water of affliction, until I come in peace.   *22:27*

11.50   And a certain man drew a bow at a venture, and smote the king of Israel between the joints of the harness: wherefore he said unto the driver of his chariot, Turn thine hand, and carry me out of the host; for I am wounded.   *22:34*

11.51   And he *[Ahaziah]* did evil in the sight of the LORD, and walked in the way

of his father, and in the way of his mother, and in the way of Jeroboam the son of Nebat, who made Israel to sin.   *22:52*

---

2 KINGS

12.1   And it came to pass, when they were gone over, that Elijah said unto Elisha, Ask what I shall do for thee, before I be taken away from thee. And Elisha said, I pray thee, let a double portion of thy spirit be upon me.   *2:9*

12.2   And it came to pass, as they still went on, and talked, that, behold there appeared a chariot of fire, and horses of fire, and parted them both asunder; and Elijah went up by a whirlwind into heaven. And Elisha saw it, and he cried, My father, my father, the chariot of Israel, and the horsemen thereof, And he saw him no more: and he took hold of his own clothes, and rent them in two pieces. *2:11-12*

12.3   And when the sons of the prophets which were to view at Jericho saw him, they said, The spirit of Elijah doth rest on Elisha. And they came to meet him, and bowed themselves to the ground before him.   *2:15*

12.4   And he went up from thence unto Bethel: and as he was going up by the way, there came forth little children out of the city, and mocked him, and said unto him, Go up, thou bald head;, go up, thou bald head.   *2:23*

12.5   And he turned back, and looked on them, and cursed them in the name of the LORD. And there came forth two she bears out of the wood, and tare forty and two children of them.   *2:24*

12.6   Run now, I pray thee, to meet her, and say unto her, Is it well with thee? is it well with thy husband? is it well with the child? And she answered, It is well.   *4:26*

12.7   And it was so, when Elisha the man of God had heard that the king of Israel had rent his clothes, that he sent to the king, saying, Wherefore hast thou rent thy clothes? let him come now to me, and he shall know that there is a prophet in Israel.   *5:8*

12.8   And Elisha sent a messenger unto him, saying, Go and wash in Jordan seven times, and thy flesh shall come again to thee, and thou shalt be clean. But Naaman was wroth, and went away, and said, Behold, I thought, He will surely come out to me, and stand, and call on the name of the LORD his God, and strike his hand over the place, and recover the leper. Are not Abana and Pharpar, rivers of Damascus, better than all the waters of Israel? may I not wash in them, and be clean? So he turned and went away in a rage. And his servants came near, and spake unto him, and said, My father, if the prophet had bid thee do some great thing, wouldest thou not have done it? how much rather then, when he saith to thee, Wash, and be clean? Then went he down, and dipped himself seven times in Jordan, according to the saying of the man of God: and his flesh came again like unto the flesh of a little child, and he was clean.   *5:10-14*

12.9   The leprosy therefore of Naaman shall cleave unto thee, and unto thy seed for ever. And he went out from his presence a leper as white as snow.   *5:27*

12.10   And Hazael said, But what, is thy servant a dog, that he should do this great thing? And Elisha answered, The LORD hath shewed me that thou shalt be king over Syria.   *8:13*

12.11   And Elisha the prophet called one of the children of the prophets, and said unto him, Gird up thy loins, and take this box of oil in thine hand, and go to Ramoth-gilead.   *9:1*

12.12   So there went one on horseback to meet him, and said, Thus saith the King, Is it peace? And Jehu said, What hast thou

to do with peace? turn thee behind me. And the watchman told, saying, The messenger came to them, but he cometh not again.   *9:18*

Gird up your loins

To gird up one's loins *means to prepare for energetic action. This rather old-fashioned idiomatic expression is said to derive from the fact that the Israelites wore loose flowing robes. These were impractical for working or travelling in unless fastened up with a girdle or belt. Girding up the loins therefore served as a means of getting ready for the difficult task about to be faced.*

12.13   And the watchman told, saying, He came even unto them, and cometh not again and the driving is like the driving of Jehu the son of Nimshi; for he driveth furiously.   *9:20*

12.14   And when Jehu was come to Jezreel, Jezebel heard of it; and she painted her face, and tired her head, and looked out at a window.   *9:30*

12.15   And he lifted up his face to the window, and said, Who is on my side? who? And there looked out to him two or three eunuchs.   *9:32*

12.16   And he said, Throw her down. So they threw her down: and some of her blood was sprinkled on the wall, and on the horses: and he trode her under foot.   *9:33*

12.17   And they went to bury her: but they found no more of her than the skull, and the feet, and the palms of her hands.   *9:35*

12.18   And he *[Azariah]* did that which was right in the sight of the LORD, according to all that his father Amaziah had done; Save that the high places were not removed: the people sacrificed and burnt incense still on the high places.   *15:3-4*

12.19   And they rejected his statutes, and his covenant that he made with their fathers, and his testimonies which he testified against them; and they followed vanity, and became vain, and went after the heathen that were round about them, concerning whom the LORD had charged them, that they should not do like them.   *17:15*

12.20   Now, behold, thou trustest upon the staff of this bruised reed, even upon Egypt, on which if a man lean, it will go into his hand, and pierce it: so is Pharaoh king of Egypt unto all that trust on him.   *18:21*

12.21   And they said unto him, Thus saith Hezekiah, This day is a day of trouble, and of rebuke, and blasphemy: for the children are come to the birth, and there is not strength to bring forth.   *19:3*

12.22   Then he turned his face to the wall, and prayed unto the LORD,   *20:2*

12.23   And the rest of the acts of Hezekiah, and all his might, and how he made a pool, and a conduit, and brought water into the city, are they not written in the book of the chronicles of the kings of Judah?   *20:20*

12.24   And it came to pass, when the king had heard the words of the book of the law, that he rent his clothes.   *22:11*

12.25   And the LORD said, I will remove Judah also out of my sight, as I have removed Israel, and will cast off this city Jerusalem which I have chosen, and the house of which I said, My name shall be there.   *23:27*

---

1 CHRONICLES

13.1   And when they came unto the threshingfloor of Chidon, Uzza put forth his hand to hold the ark; for the oxen stumbled. And the anger of the LORD was kindled against Uzza, and he smote him, because he put his hand to the ark: and there he died before God.   *13:9-10*

13.2   Give thanks unto the LORD, call upon his name, make known his deeds among the people. Sing unto him, sing psalms unto him, talk ye of all his wondrous works. Glory ye in his holy name: let the heart of them rejoice that seek the LORD. Seek the LORD and his strength, seek his face continually. Remember his marvellous works that he hath done, his wonders, and judgments of his mouth; O ye seed of Israel his servant, ye children of Jacob, his chosen ones.   *16:8-13*

13.3   Give unto the LORD, ye kindreds of the people, give unto the LORD glory and strength. Give unto the LORD the glory due unto his name: bring an offering, and come before him: worship the LORD in the beauty of holiness. *16:28-29*

13.4   Let the sea roar, and the fulness thereof: let the fields rejoice, and all that is therein.   *16:32*

13.5   O give thanks unto the LORD; for he is good; for his mercy endureth for ever.   *16:34*

13.6   And David the king came and sat before the LORD, and said, Who am I, O LORD God, and what is mine house, that thou hast brought me hitherto? And yet this was a small thing in thine eyes, O God; for thou hast also spoken of thy servant's house for a great while to come, and hast regarded me according to the estate of a man of high degree, O LORD God.   *17:16-17*

13.7   And what one nation in the earth is like thy people Israel, whom God went to redeem to be his own people, to make thee a name of greatness and terribleness, by driving out nations from before thy people, whom thou hast redeemed out of Egypt.   *17:21*

13.8   And David lifted up his eyes, and saw the angel of the LORD stand between the earth and the heaven, having a drawn sword in his hand stretched out over Jerusalem. Then David and the elders of Israel, who were clothed in sackcloth, fell upon their faces.   *21:16*

13.9   Wherefore David blessed the LORD before all the congregation: and David said, Blessed be thou, LORD God of Israel our father, for ever and ever. Thine, O LORD, is the greatness, and the power, and the glory, and the victory, and the majesty: for all that is in the heaven and in the earth is thine, thine is the kingdom, O LORD, and thou art exalted as head above all.   *29:10-11*

13.10   But who am I, and what is my people, that we should be able to offer so willingly after this sort? for all things come of thee, and of thine own have we given thee. For we are strangers before thee, and soujourners, as were all our fathers: our days on the earth are as a shadow, and there is none abiding. *29:14-15*

13.11   And give unto Solomon my son a perfect heart, to keep thy commandments, thy testimonies, and thy statutes, and to do all these things, and to build the palace, for the which I have made provision.   *29:19*

13.12   And he died in a good old age, full of days, riches, and honour: and Solomon his son reigned in his stead.   *29:28*

2 CHRONICLES

14.1   It came even to pass, as the trumpeters and singers were as one, to make one sound to be heard in praising and thanking the LORD; and when they lifted up their voice with the trumpets and cymbals and instruments of musick, and praised the LORD, saying, For he is good; for his mercy endureth for ever;

that then the house was filled with a cloud, even the house of the LORD.   *5:13*

14.2   If my people, which are called by my name, shall humble themselves, and pray, and seek my face, and turn from their wicked ways; then will I hear from heaven, and will forgive their sin and will heal their land.   *7:14*

14.3   And king Solomon gave to the queen of Sheba all her desire, whatsoever she asked, beside that which she had brought unto the king. So she turned, and went away to her own land, she and her servants.   *9:12*

14.4   And Asa cried unto the LORD his God, and said, LORD, it is nothing with thee to help, whether with many, or with them that have no power: help us, O LORD our God; for we rest on thee, and in thy name we go on against this multitude. O LORD, thou art our God; let not man prevail against thee.   *14:11*

14.5   And he went out to meet Asa, and said unto him, Hear ye me, Asa, and all Judah and Benjamin; The LORD is with you, while ye be with him; and if ye seek him, he will be found of you; but if ye forsake him, he will forsake you.   *15:2*

14.6   For the eyes of the LORD run to and fro throughout the whole earth, to shew himself strong in the behalf of them whose heart is perfect toward him. Herein thou hast done foolishly: therefore from henceforth thou shalt have wars. *16:9*

14.7   But Jehoshaphat said, Is there not here a prophet of the LORD besides, that we might inquire of him?   *18:6*

14.8   And said, O LORD God of our fathers, art not thou God in heaven? and rulest not thou over all the kingdoms of the heathen? and in thine hand is there not power and might, so that none is able to withstand thee?   *20:6*

14.9 O our God, wilt thou not judge them? for we have no might against this great company that cometh against us; neither know we what to do: but our eyes are upon thee. *20:12*

Our eyes are upon thee

Bible commentators often point to King Jehoshaphat's prayer, recorded in 2 Chronicles 20:6-12, as a model prayer. Jehoshaphat started by praising God; he then recalled God's promises, presented the difficulty to God and humbly asked for his help.

14.10 And he said, Hearken ye, all Judah, and ye inhabitants of Jerusalem, and thou king Jehoshaphat, Thus saith the LORD unto you, Be not afraid nor dismayed by reason of this great multitude; for the battle is not yours, but God's. *20:15*

14.11 And they rose early in the morning, and went forth into the wilderness of Tekoa: and as they went forth, Jehoshaphat stood and said, Hear me, O Judah, and ye inhabitants of Jerusalem; Believe in the LORD your God, so shall ye be established; believe his prophets, so shall ye prosper. *20:20*

14.12 Be strong and courageous, be not afraid nor dismayed for the king of Assyria, for for all the multitude that is with him: for there be more with us than with him: With him is an arm of flesh; but with us is the LORD our God to help us, and to fight our battles, And the people rested themselves upon the words of Hezekiah king of Judah. *32:7-8*

14.13 And prayed unto him: and he was intreated of him, and heard his supplication, and brought him again to Jerusalem into his kingdom. Then Manasseh knew that the LORD he was God. *33:13*

EZRA

15.1 Then rose up the chief of the fathers of Judah and Benjamin, and the priests, and the Levites, with all them whose spirit God had raised, to go up to build the house of the LORD which is in Jerusalem. *1:5*

15.2 But many of the priests and Levites and chief of the fathers, who were ancient men, that had seen the first house, when the foundation of this house was laid before their eyes, wept with a loud voice; and many shouted aloud for joy. *3:12*

15.3 This Ezra went up from Babylon; and he was a ready scribe in the law of Moses, which the LORD God of Israel had given: and the king granted him all his request, according to the hand of the LORD his God upon him. *7.6*

15.4 For Ezra had prepared his heart to seek the law of the LORD, and to do it, and to teach in Israel statutes and judgments. *7:10*

15.5 Then we departed from the river of Ahava on the twelfth day of the first month, to go unto Jerusalem: and the hand of our God was upon us, and he delivered us from the hand of the enemy, and of such as lay in wait by the way. *8:31*

15.6 Now when Ezra had prayed, and when he had confessed, weeping and casting himself down before the house of God, there assembled unto him out of Israel a very great congregation of men and women and children: for the people wept very sore. *10:1*

NEHEMIAH

16.1 And it came to pass, when I heard these words, that I sat down and wept,

and mourned certain days, and fasted, and prayed before the God of heaven.
1:4

16.2   Then the king said unto me, For what dost thou make request? So I prayed to the God of heaven. And I said unto the king, If it please the king, and if thy servant have found favour in thy sight, that thou wouldest send me unto Judah, unto the city of my fathers' sepulchres, that I may build it.   *2:4-5*

16.3   Then I said unto them, Ye see the distress that we are in, how Jerusalem lieth waste, and the gates thereof are burned with fire: come, and let us build up the wall of Jerusalem, that we be no more a reproach. Then I told them of the hand of my God which was good upon me; as also the king's words that he had spoken unto me. And they said, Let us rise up and build. So they strengthened their hands for this good work.   *2:17-18*

16.4   But it came to pass, that when Sanballat, and Tobiah, and the Arabians, and the Ammonites, and the Ashdodites, heard that the walls of Jerusalem were made up, and that the breaches began to be stopped, then they were very wroth, And conspired all of them together to come and to fight against Jerusalem, and to hinder it. Nevertheless we made our prayer unto our God, and set a watch against them day and night, because of them.   *4:7-9*

16.5   And I looked, and rose up, and said unto the nobles, and to the rulers, and to the rest of the people, Be ye not afraid of them: remember the Lord, which is great and terrible, and fight for your brethren, your sons, and your daughters, your wives, and your houses.   *4:14*

16.6   They which builded on the wall, and they that bare burdens, with those that laded, every one with one of his hands wrought in the work, and with the other hand held a weapon. For the builders, every one had his sword girded by his side, and so builded. And he that

sounded the trumpet was by me.
4:17-18

16.7   And the people gathered themselves together as one man into the street that was before the water gate; and they spake unto Ezra the scribe to bring the book of the law of Moses, which the LORD had commanded to Israel. And Ezra the priest brought the law before the congregation both of men and women, and all that could hear with understanding, upon the first day of the seventh month.   *8:1-2*

16.8   And he *[Ezra]* read therein before the street that was before the water gate from the morning until midday, before the men and the women, and those that could understand; and the ears of all the people were attentive unto the book of the law.   *8:3*

16.9   And Nehemiah, which is the Tirshatha, and Ezra the priest the scribe, and the Levites that taught the people, said unto all the people, This day is holy unto the LORD your God; mourn not, nor weep. For all the people wept, when they heard the words of the law.   *8:9*

16.10   Then he said unto them, Go your way, eat the fat, and drink the sweet, and send portions unto them for whom nothing is prepared: for this day is holy unto our Lord; neither be ye sorry; for the joy of the LORD is your strength.   *8:10*

16.11   Then the Levites, Jeshua, and Kadmiel, Bani, Hashabniah, Sherebiah, Hodijah, Shebaniah, and Pethahiah, said, Stand up and bless the LORD your God for ever and ever: and blessed be thy glorious name, which is exalted above all blessing and praise. Thou, even thou, art LORD alone; thou hast made heaven, the heaven of heavens, with all their host, the earth, and all things that are therein, the seas, and all that is therein, and thou preservest them all; and the host of heaven worshippeth thee.   *9:5-6*

16.12   In those days saw I in Judah some treading wine presses on the sabbath, and bringing in sheaves, and lading asses; as also wine, grapes, and figs, and all manner of burdens, which they brought into Jerusalem on the sabbath day: and I testified against them in the day wherein they sold victuals: There dwelt men of Tyre also therein, which brought fish, and all manner of ware, and sold on the sabbath unto the children of Judah, and in Jerusalem. Then I contended with the nobles of Judah, and said unto them, What evil thing is this that ye do, and profane the sabbath day? Did not your fathers thus and did not our God bring all this evil upon us, and upon this city? yet ye bring more wrath upon Israel by profaning the sabbath. And it came to pass, that when the gates of Jerusalem began to be dark before the sabbath, I commanded that the gates should be shut, and charged that they should not be opened till after the sabbath: and some of my servants set I at the gates, that there should no burden be brought in on the sabbath day.   *13:15-19*

ESTHER

17.1   If it please the king, let there go a royal commandment from him, and let it be written among the laws of the Persians and Medes, that it be not altered, That Vashti come no more before king Ahasuerus; and let the king give her royal estate unto another that is better than she.   *1:19*

17.2   And the king loved Esther above all the women, and she obtained grace and favour in his sight more than all the virgins; so that he set the royal crown upon her head, and made her queen instead of Vashti.   *2:17*

17.3   And when Haman saw that Mordecai bowed not, nor did him reverence, then was Haman full of wrath. And he thought scorn to lay hands on

Mordecai alone; for they had shewed him the people of Mordecai: wherefore Haman sought to destroy all the Jews that were throughout the whole kingdowm of Ahasuerus, even the people of Mordecai.   *3:5-6*

> ### The providence of God
> *Strangely, the book of Esther never mentions the name of God once. The message of this book, however, is that God is sovereign 'behind the scenes', even when this is not acknowledged. The book also describes the origin of the Feast of Purim (Esther 9:18-32), to celebrate God's miraculous deliverance of his people.*

17.4   And the letters were sent by posts into all the king's provinces, to destroy, to kill, and to cause to perish, all Jews, both young and old, little children and women, in one day, even upon the thirteenth day of the twelfth month, which is the month Adar, and to take the spoil of them for a prey.   *3:13*

17.5   For if thou altogether holdest thy peace at this time, then shall there enlargement and deliverance arise to the Jews from another place; but thou and thy father's house shall be destroyed: and who knoweth whether thou art come to the kingdom for such a time as this?   *4:14*

17.6   Go, gather together all the Jews that are present in Shushan, and fast ye for me, and neither eat nor drink three days, night or day: I also and my maidens will fast likewise; and so will I go in unto the king, which is not according to the law: and if I perish, I perish.   *4:16*

17.7   So Haman came in. And the king said unto him, What shall be done unto the man whom the king delighteth to honour? Now Haman thought in his heart, To whom would the king delight to do honour more than to myself?   *6:6*

17.8   Then Esther the queen answered and said, If I have found favour in thy sight, O king, and if it please the king, let my life be given me at my petition, and my people at my request: For we are sold, I and my people, to be destroyed, to be slain, and to perish. But if we had been sold for bondmen and bondwomen, I had held my tongue, although the enemy could not countervail the king's damage.   *7:3-4*

17.9   And the Jews undertook to do as they had begun, and as Mordecai had written unto them; Because Haman the son of Hammedatha, the Agagite, the enemy of all the Jews, had devised against the Jews to destroy them, and had cast Pur, that is, the lot, to consume them, and to destroy them; But when Esther came before the king, he commanded by letters that his wicked device, which he devised against the Jews, should return upon his own head, and that he and his sons should be hanged on the gallows. Wherefore they called these days Purim after the name of Pur. Therefore for all the words of this letter, and of that which they had seen concerning this matter, and which had come unto them.   *9:23-26*

THE BOOKS OF POETRY AND WISDOM

The books of poetry and wisdom deal with important questions of life. *Job*, a good man, grappled with the vexed question, 'Why do the innocent suffer?' The *Psalms* are prayers, hymns, and poems that cover the full range of human emotions. Many of the psalms were written for public worship. *Proverbs* is a collection of wise sayings by different authors on a variety of everyday themes. *Ecclesiastes*, like the book of Job, considers the age-old question, 'What is life all about?' The *Song of Solomon* is a poem that celebrates and delights in the physical love that a couple find in each other.

JOB

18.1 There was a man in the land of Uz, whose name was Job; and that man was perfect and upright, and one that feared God, and eschewed evil. *1:1*

18.2 Now there was a day when the sons of God came to present themselves before the LORD, and Satan came also among them. And the LORD said unto Satan, Whence comest thou? Then Satan answered the LORD, and said, From going to and fro in the earth, and from walking up and down in it. And the LORD said unto Satan, Hast thou considered my servant Job, that there is none like him in the earth, a perfect and an upright man, one that feareth God, and escheweth evil? Then Satan answered the LORD, and said, Doth Job fear God for nought? Hast not thou made an hedge about him, and about his house, and about all that he hath on every side? thou hast blessed the work of his hands, and his substance is increased in the land. But put forth thine hand now, and touch all that he hath, and he will curse thee to thy face. And the LORD said unto Satan, Behold, all that he hath is in thy power, only upon himself put not forth thine hand. So Satan went forth from the presence of the LORD. *1:6-12*

18.3 And said, Naked came I out of my mother's womb, and naked shall I return thither: the LORD gave, and the LORD hath taken away; blessed be the name of the LORD. *1:21*

18.4 And Satan answered the LORD, and said, Skin for skin, yea, all that a man hath will he give for his life. But put forth thine hand now, and touch his bone and his flesh, and he will curse thee to thy face. *2:4-5*

18.5 And the LORD said unto Satan, Behold, he is in thine hand; but save his life. *2:6*

18.6 So went Satan forth from the presence of the LORD, and smote Job with sore boils from the sole of his foot unto his crown. *2:7*

18.7 And he took him a potsherd to scrape himself withal; and he sat down among the ashes. Then said his wife unto him, Dost thou still retain thine integrity? curse God, and die.　*2:8-9*

18.8　And Job spake, and said, Let the day perish wherein I was born, and the night in which it was said, There is a man child conceived.　*3:2-3*

18.9　Remember, I pray thee, who ever perished, being innocent? or where were the righteous cut off? Even as I have seen, they that plow iniquity, and sow wickedness, reap the same.　*4:7-8*

18.10　Fear came upon me, and trembling, which made all my bones to shake. Then a spirit passed before my face; the hair of my flesh stood up.　*4:14-15*

18.11　Shall mortal man be more just then God? shall a man be more than his maker?　*4:17*

18.12　Yet man is born unto trouble, as the sparks fly upward.　*5:7*

18.13　My flesh is clothed with worms and clods of dust; my skin is broken, and become loathsome.　*7:5*

18.14　Behold, God will not cast away a perfect man, neither will he help the evil doers.　*8:20*

18.15　Then Job answered and said, I know it is so of a truth: but how should man be just with God?　*9:1-2*

18.16　Which removeth the mountains, and they know not: which overturneth them in his anger. Which shaketh the earth out of her place, and the pillars thereof tremble. Which commandeth the sun, and it riseth not, and sealeth up the stars.　*9:5-7*

18.17　My soul is weary of my life; I will leave my complaint upon myself; I will speak in the bitterness of my soul.　*10:1*

18.18　Wherefore then hast thou brought me forth out of the womb? Oh that I had given up the ghost, and no eye had seen me!　*10:18*

18.19　Are not my days few? cease then, and let me alone, that I may take comfort a little, Before I go whence I shall not return, even to the land of darkness and the shadow of death; A land of darkness, as darkness itself; and of the shadow of death, without any order, and where the light is as darkness.　*10:20-22*

18.20　Canst thou by searching find out God? canst thou find out the Almighty unto perfection? It is as high as heaven; what canst thou do? deeper than hell; what canst thou know? The measure thereof is longer than the earth, and broader than the sea.　*11:7-9*

18.21　No doubt but ye are the people, and wisdom shall die with you.　*12:2*

18.22　With the ancient is wisdom; and in length of days understanding.　*12:12*

18.23　Surely I would speak to the Almighty, and I desire to reason with God. But ye are forgers of lies, ye are all physicians of no value. O that ye would altogether hold your peace! and it should be your wisdom.　*13:3-5*

18.24　Though he slay me, yet will I trust in him: but I will maintain mine own ways before him.　*13:15*

18.25　How many are mine iniquities and sins? make me to know my transgression and my sin.　*17:23*

18.26　Man that is born of a woman is of few days, and full of trouble. He cometh forth like a flower, and is cut down: he fleeth also as a shadow, and continueth not.　*14:1-2*

18.27　Then Job answered and said, I have heard many such things: miserable comforters are ye all.　*16:1-2*

18.28   My bone cleaveth to my skin and to my flesh, and I am escaped with the skin of my teeth.   *19:20*

A Job's comforter

A Job's comforter *is someone who while perhaps intending to sympathize with a person who is unhappy, in reality makes that person even more unhappy by telling him or her of the hopelessness of the situation. The expression derives from the three 'friends' of Job, who offered him miserable comfort in his affliction. Nevertheless, even in this affliction Job showed the very great patience which has become proverbially linked with his name. The expression* to escape by the skin of one's teeth, *to escape something narrowly, also has its origin in the book of Job (Job 19:20).*

18.29   Oh that my words were now written! oh that they were printed in a book!   *19:23*

18.30   For I know that my redeemer liveth, and that he shall stand at the latter day upon the earth: And though after my skin worms destroy this body, yet in my flesh shall I see God: Whom I shall see for myself, and mine eyes shall behold, and not another; though my reins be consumed within me.   *19:25-27*

18.31   But ye should say, Why persecute we him, seeing the root of the matter is found in me?   *19:28*

18.32   Oh that I knew where I might find him! that I might come even to his seat! I would order my cause before him, and fill my mouth with arguments. I would know the words which he would answer me, and understand what he would say unto me.   *23:3-5*

18.33   Oh that one would hear me! behold, my desire is, that the Almighty would answer me, and that mine adversary had written a book.   *31:35*

18.34   But there is a spirit in man: and the inspiration of the Almighty giveth them understanding. Great men are not always wise: neither do the aged understand judgment.   *32:8-9*

18.35   Yea, I attended unto you, and, behold, there was none of you that convinced Job, or that answered his words.   *32:12*

18.36   Surely thou hast spoken in mine hearing, and I have heard the voice of thy words, saying, I am clean without transgression, I am innocent; neither is there iniquity in me. Behold, he findeth occasions against me, he counteth me for his enemy, He putteth my feet in the stocks, he marketh all my paths. Behold, in this thou art not just: I will answer thee, that God is greater than man.   *33:8-12*

18.37   For God speaketh once, yea twice, yet man perceiveth it not. In a dream, in a vision of the night, when deep sleep falleth upon men, in slumberings upon the bed.   *33:14-15*

18.38   He is chastened also with pain upon his bed, and the multitude of his bones with strong pain: So that his life abhorreth bread, and his soul dainty meat. His flesh is consumed away, that it cannot be seen; and his bones that were not seen stick out. Yea, his soul draweth near unto the grave, and his life to the destroyers.   *33:19-22*

18.39   He looketh upon men, and if any say, I have sinned, and perverted that which was right, and it profited me not; He will deliver his soul from going into the pit, and his life shall see the light.   *33:27-28*

18.40   Therefore hearken unto me, ye men of understanding: far be it from God, that he should do wickedness; and from the Almighty, that he should commit iniquity.   *34:10*

18.41   Therefore doth Job open his mouth in vain; he multiplieth words without knowledge.   *35:16*

18.42   Suffer me a little, and I will shew thee that I have yet to speak on God's behalf. I will fetch my knowledge from afar, and will ascribe righteousness to my Maker. For truly my words shall not be false: he that is perfect in knowledge is with thee.   *36:2-4*

18.43   He delivereth the poor in his affliction, and openeth their ears in oppression.   *36:15*

18.44   Hearken unto this, O Job: stand still, and consider the wondrous works of God.   *37:14*

18.45   Teach us what we shall say unto him; for we cannot order our speech by reason of darkness.   *37:19*

18.46   Then the LORD answered Job out of the whirlwind, and said, Who is this that darkeneth counsel by words without knowledge? Gird up now thy loins like a man; for I will demand of thee, and answer thou me. Where wast thou when I laid the foundations of the earth? declare, if thou hast understanding. Who hath laid the measures thereof, if thou knowest? or who hath stretched the line upon it? Whereupon are the foundations thereof fastened? or who laid the corner stone thereof; When the morning stars sang together, and all the sons of God shouted for joy? Or who shut up the sea with doors, when it brake forth, as if it had issued out of the womb? When I made the cloud the garment thereof, and thick darkness a swaddlingband for it, And brake up for it my decreed place, and set bars and doors, And said, Hitherto shalt thou come, but no further: and here shall thy proud waves be stayed?   *38:1-11*

18.47   Hast thou commanded the morning since thy days; and caused the dayspring to know his place.   *38:12*

18.48   Hast thou entered into the springs of the sea? or hast thou walked in the search of the depth?   *38:16*

18.49   Hast thou entered into the treasures of the snow? or hast thou seen the treasures of the hail.   *38:22*

18.50   Hath the rain a father? or who hath begotten the drops of dew?   *38:28*

18.51   Canst thou bind the sweet influences of Pleiades, or loose the bands of Orion?   *38:31*

18.52   Hast thou given the horse strength? hast thou clothed his neck with thunder? Canst thou make him afraid as a grasshopper? the glory of his nostrils is terrible. He paweth in the valley and rejoiceth in his strength: he goeth on to meet the armed men.   *39:19-21*

18.53   He swalloweth the ground with fierceness and rage: neither believeth he that it is the sound of the trumpet. He saith among the trumpets, Ha, ha, and he smelleth the battle afar off, the thunder of the captains, and the shouting.   *39:24-25*

18.54   Moreover the LORD answered Job, and said, Shall he that contendeth with the Almighty instruct him? he that reproveth God, let him answer it.   *40:1-2*

18.55   Behold now behemoth, which I made with thee; he eateth grass as an ox.   *40:15*

18.56   He lieth under the shady trees, in the covert of the reed, and fens. The shady trees cover him with their shadow; the willows of the brook compass him about. Behold, he drinketh up a river, and hasteth not: he trusteth that he can draw up Jordan into his mouth.   *40:21-23*

18.57   Canst thou draw out leviathan with an hook? or his tongue with a cord which thou lettest down?   *41:1*

18.58   His heart is as firm as a stone; yea, as hard as a piece of the nether millstone.   *41:24*

18.59   I know that thou canst do every thing, and that no thought can be withholden from thee.   *42.2*

18.60   I have heard of thee by the hearing of the ear: but now mine eye seeth thee. Wherefore I abhor myself, and repent in dust and ashes.   *42:5-6*

18.61   And it was so, that after the LORD had spoken these words unto Job, the LORD said to Eliphaz the Temanite, My wrath is kindled against thee, and against thy two friends: for ye have not spoken of me the thing that is right, as my servant Job hath.   *42:7*

18.62   And the LORD turned the captivity of Job, when he prayed for his friends: also the LORD gave Job twice as much as he had before.   *42:10*

18.63   So the LORD blessed the latter end of Job more than his beginning: for he had fourteen thousand sheep, and six thousand camels, and a thousand yoke of oxen, and a thousand she asses.   *42:12*

PSALMS

19.1   Blessed is the man that walketh not in the counsel of the ungodly, nor standeth in the way of sinners, nor sitteth in the seat of the scornful. But his delight is in the law of the LORD; and in his law doth he meditate day and night. And he shall be like a tree planted by the rivers of water, that bringeth forth his fruit in his season; his leaf also shall not wither; and whatsoever he doeth shall prosper. The ungodly are not so: but are like the chaff which the wind driveth away.   *1:1-4*

19.2   For the LORD knoweth the way of the righteous: but the way of the ungodly shall perish.   *1:6*

19.3   Why do the heathen rage, and the people imagine a vain thing? The kings of the earth set themselves, and the rulers take counsel together, against the LORD, and against his anointed, saying, Let us break their bands asunder, and cast away their cords from us.   *2:1-3*

19.4   He that sitteth in the heavens shall laugh: the Lord shall have them in derision.   *2:4*

19.5   I will declare the decree: the LORD hath said unto me, Thou art my Son: this day have I begotten thee. Ask of me, and I shall give thee the heathen for thine inheritance, and the uttermost parts of the earth for thy possession. Thou shalt break them with a rod of iron; thou shalt dash them in pieces like a potter's vessel.   *2:7-9*

19.6   Serve the LORD with fear, and rejoice with trembling. Kiss the Son, lest he be angry, and ye perish from the way, when his wrath is kindled but a little. Blessed are all they that put their trust in him.   *2:11-12*

19.7   Stand in awe, and sin not: commune with your own heart upon your bed, and be still. Selah.   *4:4*

19.8   Lead me, O LORD, in thy righteousness because of mine enemies; make thy way straight before my face. For there is no faithfulness in their mouth; their inward part is very wickedness; their throat is an open sepulchre; they flatter with their tongue.   *5:8-9*

19.9   O LORD our Lord, how excellent is thy name in all the earth! who hast set thy glory above the heavens. Out of the mouth of babes and sucklings hast thou ordained strength because of thine enemies, that thou mightest still the enemy and the avenger.   *8:1-2*

19.10   When I consider thy heavens, the work of thy fingers, the moon and the stars, which thou hast ordained; What is man, that thou art mindful of him? and the son of man, that thou visitest him? For thou hast made him a little lower than the angels, and hast crowned him with glory and honour. Thou madest him to have dominion over the works of thy hands; thou hast put all things under his feet: All sheep and oxen, yea and the beasts of the field; The fowl of the air, and the fish of the sea, and whatsoever passeth through the paths of the seas. O LORD our Lord, how excellent is thy name in all the earth!   *8:3-9*

Out of the mouth of babes

The comment out of the mouths of babes and sucklings *is sometimes made when a young child or untaught person utters a wise and perceptive remark. The source of this quotation shows that the praise of God may come from even the youngest voice.*

19.11   In the LORD put I my trust: how say ye to my soul, Flee as a bird to your mountain?   *11:1*

19.12   The LORD is in his holy temple, the LORD'S throne is in heaven: his eyes behold, his eyelids try, the children of men.   *11:4*

19.13   The fool hath said in his heart, There is no God. They are corrupt, they have done abominable works, there is none that doeth good. The LORD looked down from heaven upon the children of men, to see if there were any that did understand, and seek God. They are all gone aside, they are all together become filthy: there is none that doeth good, no, not one.   *14:1-3*

19.14   LORD, who shall abide in thy tabernacle? who shall dwell in thy holy hill? He that walketh uprightly, and worketh righteousness, and speaketh the truth in his heart.   *15:1-2*

19.15   The LORD is the portion of mine inheritance and of my cup: thou

maintainest my lot. The lines are fallen unto me in pleasant places; yea, I have a goodly heritage.   *16:5-6*

19.16   I have set the LORD always before me: because he is at my right hand, I shall not be moved. Therefore my heart is glad, and my glory rejoiceth: my flesh also shall rest in hope.   *16:8-9*

19.17   For thou wilt not leave my soul in hell; neither wilt thou suffer thine Holy One to see corruption. Thou wilt shew me the path of life: in thy presence is fulness of joy; at thy right hand there are pleasures for evermore.   *16:10-11*

19.18   Keep me as the apple of the eye, hide me under the shadow of thy wings.   *17:8*

19.19   As for me, I will behold thy face in righteousness: I shall be satisfied, when I awake, with thy likeness.   *17:15*

19.20   I will love thee, O LORD, my strength. The LORD is my rock, and my fortress, and my deliverer; my God, my strength, in whom I will trust; my buckler, and the horn of my salvation, and my high tower. I will call upon the LORD, who is worthy to be praised: so shall I be saved from mine enemies.   *18:1-3*

19.21   The sorrows of death compassed me, and the floods of ungodly men made me afraid. The sorrows of hell compassed me about: the snares of death prevented me. In my distress I called upon the LORD, and cried unto my God: he heard my voice out of his temple, and my cry came before him, even into his ears.   *18:4-6*

19.22   For by thee I have run through a troop; and by my God have I leaped over a wall. As for God, his way is perfect: the word of the LORD is tried: he is a buckler to all those that trust in him.   *18:29-30*

19.23   He maketh my feet like hinds' feet, and setteth me upon my high places.   *18:33*

19.24   The heavens declare the glory of God; and the firmament sheweth his handywork. Day unto day uttereth speech, and night unto night sheweth knowledge. There is no speech nor language, where their voice is not heard. Their line is gone out through all the earth, and their words to the end of the world. In them hath he set a tabernacle for the sun, Which is as a bridegroom coming out of his chamber, and rejoiceth as a strong man to run a race. His going forth is from the end of the heaven, and his circuit unto the ends of it: and there is nothing hid from the heat thereof. *19:1-6*

19.25   The law of the LORD is perfect, converting the soul: the testimony of the LORD is sure, making wise the simple. The statutes of the LORD are right, rejoicing the heart: the commandment of the LORD is pure, enlightening the eyes. The fear of the LORD is clean, enduring for ever: the judgments of the LORD are true and righteous altogether. More to be desired are they than gold, yea, than much fine gold: sweeter also than honey and the honeycomb. Moreover by them is thy servant warned: and in keeping of them there is great reward. Who can understand his errors? cleanse thou me from secret faults. Keep back thy servant also from presumptuous sins; let them not have dominion over me: then shall I be upright, and I shall be innocent from the great transgression. Let the words of my mouth, and the meditation of my heart, be acceptable in thy sight, O LORD, my strength, and my redeemer.   *19:7-14*

19.26   Some trust in chariots, and some in horses: but we will remember the name of the LORD our God.   *20:7*

19.27   My God, my God, why hast thou forsaken me? why art thou so far from helping me, and from the words of my roaring?   *22:1*

19.28   But thou art holy, O thou that inhabitest the praises of Israel.   *22:3*

19.29   But I am a worm, and no man; a reproach of men, and despised of the people. All they that see me laugh me to scorn: they shoot out the lip, they shake the head, saying, He trusted on the LORD that he would deliver him: let him deliver him, seeing he delighted in him.   *22:6-8*

19.30   They gaped upon me with their mouths, as a ravening and a roaring lion. I am poured out like water, and all my bones are out of joint: my heart is like wax; it is melted in the midst of my bowels. My strength is dried up like a potsherd; and my tongue cleaveth to my jaws; and thou hast brought me into the dust of death. For dogs have compassed me: the assembly of the wicked have inclosed me: they pierced my hands and my feet. I may tell all my bones: they look and stare upon me. They part my garments among them, and cast lots upon my vesture. But be not thou far from me, O LORD: O my strength, haste thee to help me.   *22:13-19*

All the days of my life

Psalm 23 is amongst the most well-known portions of the Bible and it has given the English language a number of idiomatic expressions. These include all the days of one's life, *for as long as one lives, and* the valley of the shadow of death, *the dark circumstances in which one finds oneself facing death. The psalm goes on to show that knowing the Shepherd's presence means that death can be faced without fear.*

19.31   The LORD is my shepherd; I shall not want. He maketh me to lie down in green pastures: he leadeth me beside the still waters. He restoreth my soul: he leadeth me in the paths of righteousness for his name's sake. Yea, though I walk through the valley of the shadow of death, I will fear no evil: for thou art with me; thy rod and thy staff they comfort me. Thou preparest a table before me in the presence of mine enemies: thou anointest my head with oil; my cup runneth over. Surely goodness and mercy shall follow me all the days of my life: and I will dwell in the house of the LORD for ever.   *23:1-6*

19.32   The earth is the LORD'S, and the fulness thereof; the world, and they that dwell therein.   *24:1*

19.33   Who shall ascend into the hill of the LORD? or who shall stand in his holy place? He that hath clean hands, and a pure heart; who hath not lifted up his soul unto vanity, nor sworn deceitfully. *24:3-4*

19.34   Lift up your heads, O ye gates; and be ye lift up, ye everlasting doors; and the King of glory shall come in. Who is this King of glory? The LORD strong and mighty, the LORD mighty in battle. Lift up your heads, O ye gates; even lift them up, ye everlasting doors; and the King of glory shall come in. Who is this King of glory? The LORD of hosts, he is the King of glory. Selah.   *24:7-10*

19.35   Unto thee, O LORD, do I lift up my soul. O my God, I trust in thee: let me not be ashamed, let not mine enemies triumph over me.   *25:1-2*

19.36   Shew me thy ways, O LORD; teach me thy paths. Lead me in thy truth, and teach me: for thou art the God of my salvation; on thee do I wait all the day. Remember, O LORD, thy tender mercies and thy loving kindnesses; for thy have been ever of old. Remember not the sins of my youth, nor my transgressions: according to thy mercy remember thou me for thy goodness' sake, O LORD. *25:4-7*

19.37   Good and upright is the LORD: therefore will he teach sinners in the way. The meek will he guide in judgment: and the meek will he teach his way. All the paths of the LORD are mercy and truth unto such as keep his covenant and his testimonies.   *25:8-10*

19.38   The secret of the LORD is with them that fear him; and he will shew them his covenant.   *25:14*

19.39   Redeem Israel, O God, out of all his troubles.   *25:22*

19.40   Examine me, O LORD and prove me; try my reins and my heart.   *26:2*

19.41   The LORD is my light and my salvation; whom shall I fear? the LORD is the strength of my life; of whom shall I be afraid?   *27:1*

19.42   Though an host should encamp against me, my heart shall not fear: though war should rise against me, in this will I be confident. One thing have I desired of the LORD, that will I seek after; that I may dwell in the house of the LORD all the days of my life, to behold the beauty of the LORD, and to inquire in his temple.   *27:3-4*

19.43   When thou saidst, Seek ye my face; my heart said unto thee, **Thy** face, LORD will I seek.   *27:8*

19.44   Teach me thy way, O LORD, and lead me in a plain path, because of mine enemies.   *27:11*

19.45   Wait on the LORD: be of good courage, and he shall strengthen thine heart: wait, I say, on the LORD.   *27:14*

19.46   Give unto the LORD, O ye mighty, give unto the LORD glory and strength. Give unto the LORD the glory due unto his name; worship the LORD in the beauty of holiness.   *29:1-2*

19.47   O LORD, thou hast brought up my soul from the grave: thou hast kept me alive, that I should not go down to the pit.   *30:3*

19.48   Thou hast turned for me my mourning into dancing: thou hast put off my sackcloth, and girded me with gladness.   *30:11*

19.49   In thee, O LORD, do I put my trust; let me never be ashamed: deliver me in thy righteousness.   *31:1*

19.50   Into thine hand I commit my spirit: thou hast redeemed me, O LORD God of truth.   *31:5*

19.51   My times are in thy hand: deliver me from the hand of mine enemies, and from them that persecute me. Make thy face to shine upon thy servant: save me for thy mercies' sake.   *31:15-16*

19.52   O love the LORD, all ye his saints: for the LORD preserveth the faithful, and plentifully rewardeth the proud doer. *31:23*

19.53   Blessed is he whose transgression is forgiven, whose sin is covered. Blessed is the man unto whom the LORD imputeth not iniquity, and in whose spirit there is no guile. When I kept silence, my bones waxed old through my roaring all the day long.   *32:1-3*

19.54   I acknowledged my sin unto thee, and mine iniquity have I not hid. I said, I will confess my transgressions unto the LORD; and thou forgavest the iniquity of my sin. Selah. For this shall every one that is godly pray unto thee in a time when thou mayest be found: surely in the floods of great waters they shall not come nigh unto him. Thou art my hiding place; thou shalt preserve me from trouble; thou shalt compass me about with songs of deliverance. Selah.   *32:5-7*

19.55   I will instruct thee and teach thee in the way which thou shalt go: I will guide thee with mine eye. Be ye not as the horse, or as the mule, which have no understanding: whose mouth must be held in with bit and bridle, lest they come near unto thee.   *32:8-9*

19.56   Blessed is the nation whose God is the LORD; and the people whom he hath chosen for his own inheritance. *33:12*

19.57   I will bless the LORD at all times: his praise shall continually be in my mouth. My soul shall make her boast in the LORD: the humble shall hear thereof, and be glad. O magnify the LORD with me, and let us exalt his name together. I sought the LORD, and he heard me, and delivered me from all my fears.   *34:1-4*

19.58   They looked unto him, and were lightened: and their faces were not ashamed. This poor man cried, and the LORD heard him, and saved him out of all his troubles.   *34:5-6*

19.59   O taste and see that the LORD is good: blessed is the man that trusteth in him. O fear the LORD, ye his saints: for there is no want to them that fear him. The young lions do lack, and suffer hunger: but they that seek the LORD shall not want any good thing.   *34:8-10*

19.60   Come, ye children, hearken unto me: I will teach you the fear of the LORD. What man is he that desireth life, and loveth many days, that he may see good? Keep thy tongue from evil, and thy lips from speaking guile. Depart from evil, and do good; seek peace, and pursue it. The eyes of the LORD are upon the righteous, and his ears are open unto their cry.   *34:11-15*

19.61   How excellent is thy loving kindness, O God! therefore the children of men put their trust under the shadow of thy wings.   *36:7*

19.62   For with thee is the fountain of life: in thy light shall we see light.   *36:9*

19.63   Fret not thyself because of evildoers, neither be thou envious against the workers of iniquity.   *37:1*

19.64   Trust in the LORD, and do good; so shalt thou dwell in the land, and verily thou shalt be fed. Delight thyself also in the LORD, and he shall give thee the desires of thine heart. Commit thy way unto the LORD; trust also in him; and he shall bring it to pass.   *37:3-5*

19.65   But the meek shall inherit the earth; and shall delight themselves in the abundance of peace.   *37:11*

19.66   I have been young and now am old; yet have I not seen the righteous forsaken, nor his seed begging bread. *37:25*

19.67   Hear my prayer, O LORD, and give ear unto my cry; hold not thy peace at my tears: for I am a stranger with thee, and a sojourner, as all my fathers were. *39:12*

19.68   I waited patiently for the LORD, and he inclined unto me, and heard my cry. He brought me up also out of an horrible pit, out of the miry clay, and set my feet upon a rock, and established my goings.   *40:1-2*

19.69   And he hath put a new song in my mouth, even praise unto our God: many shall see it, and fear, and shall trust in the LORD.   *40:3*

19.70   Sacrifice and offering thou didst not desire; mine ears hast thou opened: burnt offering and sin offering hast thou not required.   *40:6*

19.71   Then said I, Lo, I come: in the volume of the book it is written of me, I delight to do thy will, O my God: yea, thy law is within my heart. I have preached righteousness in the great congregation: lo, I have not refrained my lips, O LORD, thou knowest. I have not hid thy righteousness within my heart; I have declared thy faithfulness and thy salvation: I have not concealed thy lovingkindness and thy truth from the great congregation.   *40:7-10*

19.72   Be pleased, O LORD, to deliver me: O LORD, make haste to help me. *40:13*

19.73   Let all those that seek thee rejoice and be glad in thee: let such as love thy salvation say continually, The LORD be magnified. But I am poor and needy; yet the Lord thinketh upon me: thou art my help and my deliverer; make no tarrying, O my God.   *40:16-17*

19.74   Yea, mine own familiar friend, in whom I trusted, which did eat of my bread, hath lifted up his heel against me.   *41:9*

19.75   As the hart panteth after the water brooks, so panteth my soul after thee, O God. My soul thirsteth for God, for the living God: when shall I come and appear before God? My tears have been my meat day and night, while they continually say unto me, Where is thy God? When I remember these things, I pour out my soul in me: for I had gone with the multitude, I went with them to the house of God, with the voice of joy and praise, with a multitude that kept holyday. Why art thou cast down, O my soul? and why art thou disquieted in me? hope thou in God: for I shall yet praise him for the help of his countenance.   *42:1-5*

19.76   Deep calleth unto deep at the noise of thy waterspouts: all thy waves and thy billows are gone over me.   *42:7*

19.77   Why art thou cast down, O my soul? and why art thou disquieted within me? hope thou in God: for I shall yet praise him, who is the health of my countenance, and my God.   *42:11*

19.78   Yea, for thy sake are we killed all the day long; we are counted as sheep for the slaughter.   *44:22*

19.79   My heart is inditing a good matter: I speak of the things which I have made touching the king: my tongue is the pen of a ready writer. Thou art fairer than the children of men: grace is poured into thy lips: therefore God hath blessed thee for ever.   *45:1-2*

19.80   Thy throne, O God, is for ever and ever: the sceptre of thy kingdom is a right sceptre. Thou lovest righteousness, and hatest wickedness: therefore God, thy

God, hath anointed thee with the oil of gladness above thy fellows.   *45:6-7*

19.81   God is our refuge and strength, a very present help in trouble. Therefore will not we fear, though the earth be removed, and though the mountains be carried into the midst of the sea; Though the waters thereof roar and be troubled, though the mountains shake with the swelling thereof. Selah. There is a river, the streams whereof shall make glad the city of God, the holy place of the tabernacles of the most High. God is in the midst of her; she shall not be moved: God shall help her, and that right early. *46:1-5*

19.82   The heathen raged, the kingdoms were moved: he uttered his voice, the earth melted. The LORD of hosts is with us; the God of Jacob is our refuge. Selah.   *46:6-7*

19.83   Come, behold the works of the LORD, what desolations he hath made in the earth. He maketh wars to cease unto the end of the earth; he breaketh the bow, and cutteth the spear in sunder; he burneth the chariot in the fire. Be still, and know that I am God: I will be exalted among the heathen, I will be exalted in the earth. The LORD of hosts is with us; the God of Jacob is our refuge. Selah. *46:8-11*

19.84   O Clap your hands, all ye people; shout unto God with the voice of triumph.   *47:1*

19.85   God is gone up with a shout, the LORD with the sound of a trumpet.   *47:5*

19.86   Great is the LORD, and greatly to be praised in the city of our God, in the mountain of his holiness. Beautiful for situation, the joy of the whole earth, is mount Zion, on the sides of the north, the city of the great King.   *48:1-2*

19.87   The mighty God, even the LORD, hath spoken, and called the earth from the rising of the sun unto the going down thereof.   *50:1*

We will remember them

This verse is known for its rendering in the poem 'For the Fallen' by the English poet Laurence Binyon (1869-1943), used in remembrance services:
They shall not grow old, as we that are left grow old:
Age shall not weary them, nor the years condemn.
At the going down of the sun and in the morning
We will remember them.

19.88   I will take no bullock out of thy house, nor he goats out of thy folds. For every beast of the forest is mine, and the cattle upon a thousand hills.   *50:9-10*

19.89   Offer unto God thanksgiving; and pay thy vows unto the most High: And call upon me in the day of trouble: I will deliver thee, and thou shalt glorify me.   *50:14-15*

19.90   Have mercy upon me, O God, according to thy lovingkindness: according unto the multitude of thy tender mercies blot out my transgressions. Wash me throughly from mine iniquity, and cleanse me from my sin.   *51:1-2*

19.91   For I acknowledge my transgressions: and my sin is ever before me. Against thee, thee only, have I sinned, and done this evil in thy sight: that thou mightest be justified when thou speakest, and be clear when thou judgest. Behold, I was shapen in iniquity; and in sin did my mother conceive me.   *51:3-5*

19.92   Behold, thou desirest truth in the inward parts: and in the hidden part thou shalt make me to know wisdom. Purge me with hyssop, and I shall be clean: wash me, and I shall be whiter than snow. Make me to hear joy and gladness; that the bones which thou hast broken may rejoice. Hide thy face from my sins, and blot out all mine iniquities.   *57:6-9*

19.93   Create in me a clean heart, O God; and renew a right spirit within me. Cast me not away from thy presence; and take not thy holy spirit from me. Restore unto me the joy of thy salvation; and uphold me with thy free spirit. Then will I teach transgressors thy ways; and sinners shall be converted unto thee.   *51:10-13*

19.94   Deliver me from bloodguiltiness, O God, thou God of my salvation: and my tongue shall sing aloud of thy righteousness. O Lord, open thou my lips; and my mouth shall shew forth thy praise. For thou desirest not sacrifice; else would I give it: thou delightest not in burnt offering. The sacrifices of God are a broken spirit: a broken and a contrite heart, O God, thou wilt not despise. *51:14-17*

19.95   Do good in thy good pleasure unto Zion: build thou the walls of Jerusalem. Then shalt thou be pleased with the sacrifices of righteousness, with burnt offering and whole burnt offering: then shall they offer bullocks upon thine altar.   *51:18-19*

19.96   And I said, Oh that I had wings like a dove! for then would I fly away, and be at rest.   *55:6*

19.97   Cast thy burden upon the LORD, and he shall sustain thee: he shall never suffer the righteous to be moved.   *55:22*

19.98   Lead me to the rock that is higher than I.   *61:2*

19.99   Truly my soul waiteth upon God: from him cometh my salvation. He only is my rock and my salvation; he is my defence; I shall not be greatly moved. *62:1-2*

19.100   He only is my rock and my salvation: he is my defence; I shall not be moved. In God is my salvation and my glory: the rock of my strength, and my

refuge, is in God. Trust in him at all times; ye people, pour out your heart before him: God is a refuge for us. Selah. *62:6-8*

19.101   O God, thou art my God; early will I seek thee: my soul thirsteth for thee, my flesh longeth for thee in a dry and thirsty land, where no water is; To see thy power and thy glory, so as I have seen thee in the sanctuary. Because thy lovingkindness is better than life, my lips shall praise thee. Thus will I bless thee while I live: I will lift up my hands in thy name.   *63:1-4*

19.102   My soul shall be satisfied as with marrow and fatness; and my mouth shall praise thee with joyful lips: When I remember thee upon my bed, and meditate on thee in the night watches. Because thou hast been my help, therefore in the shadow of thy wings will I rejoice. My soul followeth hard after thee: thy right hand upholdeth me. *63:5-8*

19.103   Thou visitest the earth, and waterest it: thou greatly enrichest it with the river of God, which is full of water: thou preparest them corn, when thou hast so provided for it. Thou waterest the ridges thereof abundantly: thou settlest the furrows thereof: thou makest it soft with showers: thou blessest the springing thereof. Thou crownest the year with thy goodness; and thy paths drop fatness. They drop upon the pastures of the wilderness: and the little hills rejoice on every side. The pastures are clothed with flocks; the valleys also are covered over with corn; they shout for joy, they also sing.   *65:9-13*

19.104   Make a joyful noise unto God, all ye lands: Sing forth the honour of his name: make his praise glorious. Say unto God, How terrible art thou in thy works! through the greatness of thy power shall thine enemies submit themselves unto thee. All the earth shall worship thee, and shall sing unto thee; they shall sing to thy name. Selah. Come and see the works of

God: he is terrible in his doing toward the children of men.   *66:1-5*

19.105   Come and hear, all ye that fear God, and I will declare what he hath done for my soul.   *66:16*

19.106   God be merciful unto us, and bless us; and cause his face to shine upon us; Selah. That thy way may be known upon earth, thy saving health among all nations. Let the people praise thee, O God; let all the people praise thee. *67:1-3*

19.107   Sing unto God, sing praises to his name: extol him that rideth upon the heavens by his name JAH, and rejoice before him. A father of the fatherless, and a judge of the widows, is God in his holy habitation. God setteth the solitary in families: he bringeth out those which are bound with chains: but the rebellious dwell in a dry land.   *68:4-6*

19.108   Thou hast ascended on high, thou hast led captivity captive: thou hast received gifts for men; yea, for the rebellious also, that the LORD God might dwell among them.   *68:18*

19.109   Blessed be the Lord, who daily loadeth us with benefits, even the God of our salvation. Selah.   *68:19*

19.110   He that is our God is the God of salvation; and unto GOD the Lord belong the issues from death.   *68:20*

19.111   I am weary of my crying: my throat is dried: mine eyes fail while I wait for my God. They that hate me without a cause are more than the hairs of mine head: they that would destroy me, being mine enemies wrongfully, are mighty: then I restored that which I took not away.   *69:3-4*

19.112   For the zeal of thine house hath eaten me up; and the reproaches of them that reproached thee are fallen upon me.   *69:9*

19.113   But as for me, my prayer is unto thee, O LORD, in an acceptable time: O God, in the multitude of thy mercy hear me, in the truth of thy salvation.   *69:13*

The suffering of a righteous man

Psalm 69 is quoted several times in the New Testament as a foreshadowing of Jesus. For example, verse 4 is quoted in John 15:25, verse 9 in John 2:17 and Romans 15:3, and verse 21 in John 19:28. Not every part of the psalm is followed, however. In place of the curses directed towards the psalmist's enemies, Jesus prayed that those who crucified him would be forgiven.

19.114   Reproach hath broken my heart; and I am full of heaviness: and I looked for some to take pity, but there was none; and for comforters, but I found none. They gave me also gall for my meat; and in my thirst they gave me vinegar to drink. *69:20-21*

19.115   Let them be blotted out of the book of the living, and not be written with the righteous. But I am poor and sorrowful: let thy salvation, O God, set me up on high.   *69:28-29*

19.116   Let them be turned back for a reward of their shame that say, Aha, aha.   *70:3*

19.117   In thee, O LORD, do I put my trust: let me never be put to confusion. *71:1*

19.118   O God, thou hast taught me from my youth: and hitherto have I declared thy wondrous works. Now also when I am old and grayheaded, O God, forsake me not; until I have shewed thy strength unto this generation, and thy power to every one that is to come. *71:17-18*

19.119   He shall come down like rain upon the mown grass: as showers that water the earth. In his days shall the righteous flourish; and abundance of peace so long as the moon endureth. *72:6-7*

19.120   He shall have dominion also from sea to sea, and from the river unto the ends of the earth. They that dwell in the wilderness shall bow before him; and his enemies shall lick the dust. The kings of Tarshish and of the isles shall bring presents: the kings of Sheba and Seba shall offer gifts. Yea, all kings shall fall down before him: all nations shall serve him.   *72:8-11*

19.121   And he shall live, and to him shall be given of the gold of Sheba; prayer also shall be made for him continually; and daily shall he be praised.   *72:15*

19.122   His name shall endure for ever: his name shall be continued as long as the sun: and men shall be blessed in him: all nations shall call him blessed.   *72:17*

19.123   Truly God is good to Israel, even to such as are of a clean heart. But as for me, my feet were almost gone; my steps had well nigh slipped. For I was envious at the foolish, when I saw the prosperity of the wicked.   *73:1-3*

19.124   When I thought to know this, it was too painful for me; Until I went into the sanctuary of God; then understood I their end.   *73:16-17*

19.125   Nevertheless I am continually with thee: thou hast holden me by my right hand. Thou shalt guide me with thy counsel, and afterward receive me to glory. Whom have I in heaven but thee? and there is none upon earth that I desire beside thee. My flesh and my heart faileth: but God is the strength of my heart, and my portion for ever.   *73:23-26*

19.126   I have considered the days of old, the years of ancient times. I call to remembrance my song in the night: I commune with mine own heart: and my spirit made diligent search.   *77:5-6*

19.127   I will remember the works of the LORD: surely I will remember thy wonders of old. I will meditate also of all thy work, and talk of thy doings. *77:11-12*

19.128   I am the LORD thy God, which brought thee out of the land of Egypt: open thy mouth wide, and I will fill it. *81:10*

19.129   How amiable are thy tabernacles, O LORD of hosts! My soul longeth, yea, even fainteth for the courts of the LORD: my heart and my flesh crieth out for the living God. Yea, the sparrow hath found an house, and the swallow a nest for herself, where she may lay her young, even thine altars, O LORD of hosts, my King, and my God.   *84:1-3*

19.130   They go from strength to strength, every one of them in Zion appeareth before God.   *84:7*

19.131   For a day in thy courts is better than a thousand. I had rather be a doorkeeper in the house of my God, than to dwell in the tents of wickedness. *84:10*

19.132   For the LORD God is a sun and shield: the LORD will give grace and glory: no good thing will he withhold from them that walk uprightly.   *84:11*

19.133   Teach me thy way, O LORD; I will walk in thy truth: unite my heart to fear thy name.   *86:11*

19.134   But thou, O Lord, art a God full of compassion, and gracious, longsuffering, and plenteous in mercy and truth.   *86:15*

19.135   His foundation is in the holy mountains. The LORD loveth the gates of Zion more than all the dwellings of Jacob. Glorious things are spoken of thee, O city of God. Selah.   *87:1-3*

19.136   I have made a covenant with my chosen, I have sworn unto David my servant.   *89:3*

19.137   For who in the heaven can be compared unto the LORD? who among the sons of the mighty can be likened unto the LORD?   *89:6*

19.138   Lord, thou hast been our dwelling place in all generations. Before the mountains were brought forth, or ever thou hadst formed the earth and the world, even from everlasting to everlasting, thou art God.   *90:1-2*

19.139   For a thousand years in thy sight are but as yesterday when it is past, and as a watch in the night.   *90:4*

19.140   The days of our years are threescore years and ten; and if by reason of strength they be fourscore years, yet is their strength labour and sorrow; for it is soon cut off, and we fly away.   *90:10*

Three score years and ten

Three score years and ten *is 70 years, the period of time that people may be expected to live, or* four score, *80 years, if given the strength. The fine-sounding biblical* threescore years and ten *and* fourscore *still linger on in the English language. It is interesting to note, however, that the original Hebrew had just simply 'seventy'... 'eighty'.*

19.141   So teach us to number our days that we may apply our hearts unto wisdom   *90:12*

19.142   He that dwelleth in the secret place of the most High shall abide under the shadow of the Almighty. I will say of the LORD, He is my refuge and my fortress: my God; in him will I trust.   *91:1-2*

19.143   Surely he shall deliver thee from the snare of the fowler, and from the noisome pestilence. He shall cover thee with his feathers, and under his wings shalt thou trust: his truth shall be thy shield and buckler Thou shalt not be afraid for the terror by night; nor for the arrow that flieth by day; Nor for the pestilence that walketh in darkness; nor for the destruction that wasteth at noonday. A thousand shall fall at thy side, and ten thousand at thy right hand, but it shall not come nigh thee.   *91:3-7*

19.144   Because thou hast made the LORD, which is my refuge, even the most High, thy habitation; There shall no evil befall thee, neither shall any plague come nigh thy dwelling. For he shall give his angels charge over thee, to keep thee in all thy ways. They shall bear thee up in their hands, lest thou dash thy foot against a stone. Thou shalt tread upon the lion and adder: the young lion and the dragon shalt thou trample under feet. Because he hath set his love upon me, therefore will I deliver him: I will set him on high, because he hath known my name. He shall call upon me, and I will answer him: I will be with him in trouble; I will deliver him, and honour him. With long life will I satisfy him, and shew him my salvation.   *91:9-16*

19.145   It is a good thing to give thanks unto the LORD, and to sing praises unto thy name, O most High: To shew forth thy lovingkindness in the morning, and thy faithfulness every night, Upon an instrument of ten strings, and upon the psaltery; upon the harp with a solemn sound.   *92:1-3*

19.146   For thou, LORD, hast made me glad through thy work: I will triumph in the works of thy hands. O LORD, how great are thy works! and thy thoughts are very deep.   *92:4-5*

19.147   The righteous shall flourish like the palm tree: he shall grow like a cedar in Lebanon.   *92:12*

19.148   They shall still bring forth fruit in old age; they shall be fat and flourishing.   *92:14*

19.149   The LORD reigneth, he is clothed with majesty; the LORD is clothed with strength, wherewith he hath girded himself: the world also is stablished, that it cannot be moved. Thy throne is established of old: thou art from everlasting.   *93:1-2*

19.150   He that planted the ear, shall he not hear? he that formed the eye, shall he not see?   *94:9*

19.151   O come let us sing unto the LORD: let us make a joyful noise to the rock of our salvation. Let us come before his presence with thanksgiving, and make a joyful noise unto him with psalms.   *95:1-2*

19.152   For the LORD is a great God, and a great King above all gods. In his hand are the deep places of the earth: the strength of the hills is his also. The sea is his, and he made it: and his hands formed the dry land. O come, let us worship and bow down: let us kneel before the LORD our maker. For he is our God; and we are the people of his pasture, and the sheep of his hand.   *95:3-7*

19.153   Harden not your heart, as in the provocation, and as in the day of temptation in the wilderness: When your fathers tempted me, proved me, and saw my work. Forty years long was I grieved with this generation, and said, It is a people that do err in their heart, and they have not known my ways: Unto whom I sware in my wrath that they should not enter into my rest.   *95:8-11*

19.154   O sing unto the LORD a new song: sing unto the LORD, all the earth. Sing unto the LORD, bless his name; shew forth his salvation from day to day. Declare his glory among the heathen, his wonders among all people. For the LORD is great, and greatly to be praised: he is to be feared above all gods.   *96:1-4*

19.155   O worship the LORD in the beauty of holiness: fear before him, all the earth.   *96:9*

19.156   O sing unto the LORD a new song; for he hath done marvellous things: his right hand, and his holy arm, hath gotten him the victory. The LORD hath made known his salvation: his righteousness hath he openly shewed in the sight of the heathen.   *98:1-2*

19.157   He hath remembered his mercy and his truth toward the house of Israel: all the ends of the earth have seen the salvation of our God. Make a joyful noise unto the LORD, all the earth: make a loud noise, and rejoice, and sing praise. *98:3-4*

19.158   Make a joyful noise unto the LORD, all ye lands. Serve the LORD with gladness: come before his presence with singing. Know ye that the LORD he is God: it is he that hath made us, and not we ourselves; we are his people, and the sheep of his pasture. Enter into his gates with thanksgiving, and into his courts with praise: be thankful unto him, and bless his name. For the LORD is good; his mercy is everlasting; and his truth endureth to all generations.   *100:1-5*

19.159   Bless the LORD, O my soul: and all that is within me, bless his holy name. Bless the LORD, O my soul, and forget not all his benefits: Who forgiveth all thine iniquities; who healeth all thy diseases; Who redeemeth thy life from destruction; who crowneth thee with lovingkindness and tender mercies; Who satisfieth thy mouth with good things; so that thy youth is renewed like the eagle's.   *103:1-5*

19.160   The LORD is merciful and gracious, slow to anger, and plenteous in mercy. He will not always chide: neither will he keep his anger for ever. He hath not dealt with us after our sins; nor rewarded us according to our iniquities.   *103:8-10*

19.161   For as the heaven is high above the earth, so great is his mercy toward them that fear him. As far as the east is from the west, so far hath he removed our transgressions from us. *103:11-12*

19.162   Like as a father pitieth his children, so the LORD pitieth them that fear him. For he knoweth our frame; he remembereth that we are dust. *103:13-14*

19.163   As for man, his days are as grass: as a flower of the field, so he flourisheth. For the wind passeth over it, and it is gone; and the place thereof shall know it no more. *103:15-16*

19.164   Bless the LORD, O my soul. O LORD my God, thou art very great; thou art clothed with honour and majesty. Who coverest thyself with light as with a garment: who stretchest out the heavens like a curtain: Who layeth the beams of his chambers in the waters: who maketh the clouds his chariot: who walketh upon the wings of the wind: Who maketh his angels spirits; his ministers a flaming fire: Who laid the foundations of the earth, that it should not be removed for ever. Thou coveredst it with the deep as with a garment: the waters stood above the mountains. At thy rebuke they fled; at the voice of thy thunder they hasted away. *104:1-7*

19.165   He causeth the grass to grow for the cattle, and herb for the service of man: that he may bring forth food out of the earth; And wine that maketh glad the heart of man, and oil to make his face to shine, and bread which strengtheneth man's heart. *104:14-15*

19.166   Man goeth forth unto his work and to his labour until the evening. O LORD, how manifold are thy works! in wisdom hast thou made them all: the earth is full of thy riches. *104:23-24*

19.167   So is this great and wide sea, wherein are things creeping innumerable, both small and great beasts. There go the ships: there is that leviathan, whom thou hast made to play therein.

These wait all upon thee; that thou mayest give them their meat in due season. *104:25-27*

19.168   I will sing unto the LORD as long as I live: I will sing praise to my God while I have my being. *104:33*

19.169   Seek the LORD, and his strength: seek his face evermore. *105:4*

19.170   He hath remembered his covenant for ever, the word which he commanded to a thousand generations. *105:8*

19.171   Praise ye the LORD. O give thanks unto the LORD; for he is good: for his mercy endureth for ever. *106:1*

19.172   They wandered in the wilderness in a solitary way; they found no city to dwell in. Hungry and thirsty, their soul fainted in them. Then they cried unto the LORD in their trouble, and he delivered them out of their distresses. And he led them forth by the right way, that they might go to a city of habitation. Oh that men would praise the LORD for his goodness, and for his wonderful works to the children of men! *107:4-8*

19.173   For he satisfieth the longing soul, and filleth the hungry soul with goodness. *107:9*

19.174   Then they cried unto the LORD in their trouble, and he saved them out of their distresses. *107:13*

19.175   They that go down to the sea in ships, that do business in great waters; These see the works of the LORD, and his wonders in the deep. *107:23-24*

19.176   They reel to and fro, and stagger like a drunken man, and are at their wit's end. Then they cry unto the LORD in their trouble, and he bringeth them out of their distresses. *107:27-28*

19.177　Whoso is wise, and will observe these things, even they shall understand the lovingkindness of the LORD.　*107:43*

19.178　O God, my heart is fixed; I will sing and give praise, even with my glory.　*108:1*

19.179　The LORD said unto my Lord, Sit thou at my right hand, until I make thine enemies thy footstool.　*110:1*

David's Lord

This verse is the Old Testament verse that is most frequently quoted in the New Testament. The psalmist, David, describes the coming king as 'my Lord' - not only pointing to the Messiah but also honouring him with great respect. The psalmist goes on to show the Messiah's authority and power. The New Testament writers see the fulfilment of this verse in the person of Jesus Christ.

19.180　The LORD hath sworn, and will not repent, Thou art a priest for ever after the order of Melchizedek.　*110:4*

19.181　The fear of the LORD is the beginning of wisdom: a good understanding have all they that do his commandments: his praise endureth forever.　*111:10*

19.182　Praise ye the LORD. Praise, O ye servants of the LORD, praise the name of the LORD. Blessed be the name of the LORD from this time forth and for evermore. From the rising of the sun unto the going down of the same the LORD's name is to be praised.　*113:1-3*

19.183　Not unto us, O LORD, not unto us, but unto thy name give glory, for thy mercy, and for thy truth's sake.　*115:1*

19.184　Their idols are silver and gold, the work of men's hands. They have mouths but they speak not: eyes have they, but they see not: They have ears, but they hear not: noses have they, but they smell not: They have hands, but they handle not: feet have they, but they walk not: neither speak they through their throat.　*115:4-7*

19.185　I love the LORD, because he hath heard my voice and my supplications.　*116:1*

19.186　For thou hast delivered my soul from death, mine eyes from tears, and my feet from falling. I will walk before the LORD in the land of the living. I believed, therefore have I spoken: I was greatly afflicted: I said in my haste, All men are liars.　*116:8-11*

19.187　What shall I render unto the LORD for all his benefits toward me? I will take the cup of salvation, and call upon the name of the LORD. I will pay my vows unto the LORD now in the presence of all his people.　*116:12-14*

19.188　Precious in the sight of the LORD is the death of his saints.　*116:15*

19.189　O give thanks unto the LORD; for he is good: because his mercy endureth for ever.　*118:1*

19.190　The right hand of the LORD is exalted: the right hand of the LORD doeth valiantly. I shall not die, but live, and declare the works of the LORD.　*118:16-17*

19.191　The stone which the builders refused is become the head stone of the corner. This is the LORD's doing; it is marvellous in our eyes. This is the day which the LORD hath made; we will rejoice and be glad in it.　*118:22-24*

19.192　Blessed be he that cometh in the name of the LORD: we have blessed you out of the house of the LORD.　*118:26*

19.193　Wherewithal shall a young man cleanse his way? by taking heed thereto according to thy word.　*119:9*

19.194   Thy word have I hid in mine heart, that I might not sin against thee.
119:11

19.195   Open thou mine eyes, that I may behold wondrous things out of thy law.
119:18

19.196   Teach me, O LORD, the way of thy statutes; and I shall keep it unto the end. Give me understanding, and I shall keep thy law; yea, I shall observe it with my whole heart. Make me to go in the path of thy commandments; for therein do I delight. Incline my heart unto thy testimonies; and not to covetousness. Turn away mine eyes from beholding vanity; and quicken thou me in thy way.
119:33-37

19.197   My hands also will I lift up unto thy commandments, which I have loved; and I will meditate in thy statutes.
119:48

19.198   It is good for me that I have been afflicted; that I might learn thy statutes.
119:71

19.199   O how love I thy law! it is my meditation all the day.   *119:97*

19.200   I have more understanding than all my teachers: for thy testimonies are my meditation.   *119:99*

19.201   How sweet are thy words unto my taste! yea, sweeter than honey to my mouth!   *119:103*

19.202   Thy word is a lamp unto my feet, and a light unto my path.   *119:105*

19.203   Uphold me according unto thy word, that I may live: and let me not be ashamed of my hope.   *119:116*

19.204   The entrance of thy words giveth light; it giveth understanding unto the simple.   *119:130*

19.205   Great peace have they which love thy law: and nothing shall offend them.
119:165

19.206   I will lift up mine eyes unto the hills, from thence cometh my help. My help cometh from the LORD, which made heaven and earth. He will not suffer thy foot to be moved: he that keepeth thee will not slumber. Behold, he that keepeth Israel shall neither slumber nor sleep. The LORD is thy keeper: the LORD is thy shade upon thy right hand. The sun shall not smite thee by day, nor the moon by night. The LORD shall preserve thee from all evil: he shall preserve thy soul. The LORD shall preserve thy going out and thy coming in from this time forth, and even for evermore.   *121:1-8*

Love for God's law

Psalm 119 is the longest psalm, with 176 verses. It is an acrostic poem - each of the 22 letters of the Hebrew alphabet is the initial letter of the eight verses in the consecutive stanzas. The psalm is a meditative love poem to God and his law - his guidelines for right living.

19.207   I was glad when thy said unto me, Let us go into the house of the LORD.   *122:1*

19.208   Jerusalem is builded as a city that is compact together.   *122:3*

19.209   Pray for the peace of Jerusalem: they shall prosper that love thee. Peace be within thy walls, and prosperity within thy palaces.   *122:6-7*

19.210   Unto thee lift I up mine eyes, O thou that dwellest in the heavens. Behold, as the eyes of servants look unto the hand of their masters, and as the eyes of a maiden unto the hand of her mistress; so our eyes wait upon the LORD our God, until that he have mercy upon us.
123:1-2

19.211   They that trust in the LORD shall be as mount Zion, which cannot be removed, but abideth for ever.   *125:1*

19.212   When the LORD turned again the captivity of Zion, we were like them that dream. Then was our mouth filled with laughter, and our tongue with singing: then said they among the heathen, The LORD hath done great things for them. The LORD hath done great things for us; whereof we are glad. *126:1-3*

19.213 They that sow in tears shall reap in joy. He that goeth forth and weepeth, bearing precious seed, shall doubtless come again with rejoicing, bringing his sheaves with him. *126:5-6*

19.214 Except the LORD build the house, they labour in vain that build it: except the LORD keep the city, the watchman waketh but in vain. It is vain for you to rise up early, to sit up late, to eat the bread of sorrows: for so he giveth his beloved sleep. *127:1-2*

19.215 Lo, children are an heritage of the LORD: and the fruit of the womb is his reward. As arrows are in the hand of a mighty man; so are children of the youth. Happy is the man that hath his quiver full of them: they shall not be ashamed, but they shall speak with the enemies in the gate. *127:3-5*

19.216 Thy wife shall be as a fruitful vine by the sides of thine house: thy children like olive plants round about thy table. *128:3*

19.217 Out of the depths have I cried unto thee, O LORD. Lord, hear my voice: let thine ears be attentive to the voice of my supplications. If thou, LORD, shouldest mark iniquities, O Lord, who shall stand? But ,there is forgiveness with thee, that thou mayest be feared. *130:1-4*

19.218 My soul waiteth for the Lord more than they that watch for the morning: I say, more than they that watch for the morning. *130:6*

19.219 Let Israel hope in the LORD: for with the LORD there is mercy, and with him is plenteous redemption. And he shall redeem Israel from all his iniquities. *130:7-8*

19.220 Behold, how good and how pleasant it is for brethren to dwell together in unity! It is like the precious ointment upon the head, that ran down upon the beard, even Aaron's beard: that went down to the skirts of his garments; As the dew of Hermon, and as the dew that descended upon the mountains of Zion: for there the LORD commanded the blessing, even life for evermore. *133:1-3*

19.221 O give thanks unto the LORD; for he is good: for his mercy endureth for ever. *136:1*

19.222 By the rivers of Babylon, there we sat down, yea, we wept, when we remembered Zion. We hanged our harps upon the willows in the midst thereof. For there they that carried us away captive required of us a song; and they that wasted us required of us mirth, saying, Sing us one of the songs of Zion. How shall we sing the LORD'S song in a strange land? *137:1-4*

19.223 O daughter of Babylon, who art to be destroyed; happy shall he be, that rewardeth thee as thou hast served us. Happy shall he be, that taketh and dasheth thy little ones against the stones. *137:8-9*

19.224 O LORD, thou hast searched me, and known me. Thou knowest my downsitting and mine uprising, thou understandest my thought afar off Thou compassest my path and my lying down, and art acquainted with all my ways. For there is not a word in my tongue, but, lo, O LORD, thou knowest it altogether. Thou hast beset me behind and before, and laid thine hand upon me. Such knowledge is too wonderful for me; it is high, I cannot attain unto it. *139:1-6*

19.225 Whither shall I go from thy spirit? or whither shall I flee from thy presence? If I ascend up into heaven, thou art there: if I make my bed in hell, behold, thou art there. If I take the wings of the morning, and dwell in the uttermost parts of the sea; Even there shall thy hand lead me, and thy right hand shall hold me. If I say, Surely the darkness shall cover me; even the night shall be light about me. Yea, the darkness hideth not from thee; but the night shineth as the day: the darkness and the light are both alike to thee.   *139:7-12*

19.226   I will praise thee; for I am fearfully and wonderfully made: marvellous are thy works; and that my soul knoweth right well. My substance was not hid from thee, when I was made in secret, and curiously wrought in the lowest parts of the earth. Thine eyes did see my substance, yet being unperfect; and in thy book all my members were written, which in continuance were fashioned, when as yet there was none of them.   *139:14-16*

19.227   How precious also are thy thoughts unto me, O God! how great is the sum of them! If I should count them, they are more in number than the sand: when I awake, I am still with thee. *139:17-18*

19.228   Search me, O God, and know my heart: try me, and know my thoughts: And see if there be any wicked way in me, and lead me in the way everlasting. *139:23-24*

19.229   Set a watch, O LORD, before my mouth; keep the door of my lips.   *141:3*

19.230   Hear my prayer, O LORD, give ear to my supplications: in thy faithfulness answer me, and in thy righteousness. And enter not into judgment with thy servant: for in thy sight shall no man living be justified. *143:1-2*

19.231   The LORD is gracious, and full of compassion; slow to anger, and of great mercy. The LORD is good to all: and his tender mercies are over all his works. All thy works shall praise thee, O LORD; and thy saints shall bless thee.   *145:8-10*

19.232   The eyes of all wait upon thee; and thou givest them their meat in due season. Thou openest thine hand, and satisfiest the desire of every living thing.   *145:15-16*

19.233   The LORD is nigh unto all them that call upon him, to all that call upon him in truth. He will fulfil the desire of them that fear him: he also will hear their cry, and will save them.   *145:18-19*

19.234   Praise ye the LORD. Praise the LORD, O my soul.   *146:1*

19.235   While I live will I praise the LORD: I will sing praises unto my God while I have any being.   *146:2*

19.236   Put not your trust in princes nor in the son of man, in whom there is no help.   *146:3*

19.237   He telleth the number of the stars; he calleth them all by their names. *147:4*

19.238   Great is our Lord, and of great power: his understanding is infinite. *147:5*

19.239   Praise ye the LORD. Praise ye the LORD from the heavens: praise him in the heights. Praise ye him, all his angels: praise ye him, all his hosts. Praise ye him, sun and moon: praise him, all ye stars of light. Praise him, ye heavens of heavens, and ye waters that be above the heavens. *148:1-4*

19.240   Praise the LORD from the earth, ye dragons, and all deeps: Fire, and hail: snow, and vapour; stormy wind fulfilling his word: Mountains, and all hills; fruitful trees, and all cedars: Beasts, and all cattle; creeping things, and flying fowl: Kings of the earth, and all people; princes, and all judges of the earth: Both young men, and maidens; old men, and children: Let them praise the name of the LORD: for his name alone is excellent; his glory is above the earth and heaven.   *148:7-13*

19.241   Praise ye the LORD. Sing unto the LORD a new song, and his praise in the congregation of saints.   *149:1*

19.242   For the LORD taketh pleasure in his people: he will beautify the meek with salvation.   *149:4*

19.243   Let the high praises of God be in their mouth, and a two-edged sword in their hand.   *149:6*

19.244   Praise ye the LORD. Praise God in his sanctuary: praise him in the firmament of his power. Praise him for his mighty acts: praise him according to his excellent greatness. Praise him with the sound of the trumpet: praise him with the psaltery and harp. Praise him with the timbrel and dance: praise him with stringed instruments and organs. Praise him upon the loud cymbals: praise him upon the high sounding cymbals. Let every thing that hath breath praise the LORD. Praise ye the LORD.   *150:1-6*

PROVERBS

20.1   The proverbs of Solomon the son of David, king of Israel; To know wisdom and instruction; to perceive the words of understanding.   *1:1-2*

The fear of the LORD

'*The fear of the LORD* is the beginning of knowledge.' This is the general motto of the Wisdom writings. The fundamental principle of this wise way to live is a relationship of reverence and submission to the LORD.

20.2   A wise men will hear, and will increase learning; and a man of understanding shall attain unto wise counsels: To understand a proverb, and the interpretation; the words of the wise, and their dark sayings. The fear of the LORD is the beginning of knowledge: but fools despise wisdom and instruction.   *1:5-7*

20.3   Wisdom crieth without; she uttereth her voice in the streets.   *1:20*

20.4   Yea, if thou criest after knowledge, and liftest up thy voice for understanding; If thou seekest her as silver, and searchest for her as for hid treasures; Then shalt thou understand the fear of the LORD, and find the knowledge of God.   *2:3-5*

20.5   Trust in the LORD with all thine heart; and lean not unto thine own understanding. In all thy ways acknowledge him, and he shall direct thy paths.   *3:56*

20.6   Be not wise in thine own eyes: fear the LORD, and depart from evil. It shall be health to thy navel, and marrow to thy bones. Honour the LORD with thy substance, and with the firstfruits of all thine increase: So shall thy barns be filled with plenty, and thy presses shall burst out with new wine.   *3:7-10*

20.7   My son, despise not the chastening of the LORD; neither be weary of his correction: For whom the LORD loveth he correcteth; even as a father the son in whom he delighteth.   *3:11-12*

20.8   Happy is the man that findeth wisdom, and the man that getteth understanding. For the merchandise of it is better than the merchandise of silver, and the gain thereof than fine gold. She is more precious than rubies: and all the things thou canst desire are not to be compared unto her. Length of days is in her right hand; and in her left hand riches and honour. Her ways are ways of pleasantness, and all her paths are peace. She is a tree of life to them that lay hold upon her: and happy is evey one that retaineth her.   *3:13-18*

20.9   The LORD by wisdom hath founded the earth; by understanding hath he established the heavens.   *3:19*

20.10   Wisdom is the principal thing; therefore get wisdom: and with all thy getting get understanding.   *4:7*

20.11   But the path of the just is as the shining light, that shineth more and more unto the perfect day.   *14:18*

20.12   For the lips of a strange woman drop as an honeycomb, and her mouth is smoother than oil: But her end is bitter as wormwood, sharp as a two-edged sword. Her feet go down to death; her steps take hold on hell.   *5:3-5*

20.13   Let thy fountain be blessed: and rejoice with the wife of thy youth. Let her be as the loving hind and pleasant roe; let her breasts satisfy thee at all times; and be thou ravished always with her love. *5:18-19*

20.14   Go to the ant, thou sluggard; consider her ways, and be wise.   *6:6*

20.15   Yet a little sleep, a little slumber, a little folding of the hands to sleep: So shall thy poverty come as one that travelleth, and thy want as an armed man.   *6:10-11*

20.16   These six things doth the LORD hate: yea, seven are an abomination unto him: A proud look, a lying tongue, and hands that shed innocent blood, An heart that deviseth wicked imaginations, feet that be swift in running to mischief, A false witness that speaketh lies, and he that soweth discord among brethren. *6:16-19*

20.17   Lust not after her beauty in thine heart; neither let her take thee with her eyelids.   *6:25*

20.18   Can a man take fire in his bosom, and his clothes not be burned? Can one go upon hot coals, and his feet not be burned?   *6:27-28*

20.19   For wisdom is better than rubies; and all the things that may be desired are not to be compared to it.   *8:11*

20.20   The fear of the LORD is to hate evil: pride, and arrogancy, and the evil way, and the froward mouth, do I hate. *8:13*

20.21   The LORD possessed me in the beginning of his way, before his works of old. I was set up from everlasting, from the beginning, or ever the earth was. When there were no depths, I was brought forth; when there were no fountains abounding with water. Before the mountains were settled, before the hills was I brought forth: While as yet he had not made the earth, not the fields, nor the highest part of the dust of the world. When he prepared the heavens, I was there: when he set a compass upon the face of the depth: When he established the clouds above: when he strengthened the fountains of the deep: When he gave to the sea his decree, that the waters should not pass his commandment: when he appointed the foundations of the earth: Then I was by him, as one brought up with him: and I was daily his delight, rejoicing always before him; Rejoicing in the habitable part of his earth; and my delights were with the sons of men. *8:22-31*

20.22   For whoso findeth me findeth life, and shall obtain favour of the LORD.   *8:35*

20.23   Wisdom hath builded her house, she hath hewn out her seven pillars.   *9:1*

20.24   The fear of the LORD is the beginning of wisdom: and the knowledge of the holy is understanding.   *9:10*

20.25   Stolen waters are sweet, and bread eaten in secret is pleasant.   *9:17*

20.26   A wise son maketh a glad father: but a foolish son is the heaviness of his mother.   *10:1*

20.27   The memory of the just is blessed: but the name of the wicked shall rot.   *10:7*

20.28   Hatred stirreth up strifes: but love covereth all sins.   *10:12*

20.29   The rich man's wealth is his strong city: the destruction of the poor is their poverty.   *10:15*

20.30   In the multitude of words there wanteth not sin: but he that refraineth his lips is wise.   *10:19*

20.31   The tongue of the just is as choice silver: the heart of the wicked is little worth.   *10:20*

20.32   The blessing of the LORD, it maketh rich, and he addeth no sorrow with it.   *10:22*

20.33   A false balance is abomination to the LORD: but a just weight is his delight.   *11:1*

20.34   Riches profit not in the day of wrath: but righteousness delivereth from death.   *11:4*

20.35   Where no counsel is, the people fall: but in the multitude of counsellers there is safety.   *11:14*

20.36   He that is surety for a stranger shall smart for it: and he that hateth suretiship is sure.   *11:15*

20.37   A virtuous woman is a crown to her husband: but she that maketh ashamed is as rottenness in his bones. *12:4*

20.38   A righteous man regardeth the life of his beast: but the tender mercies of the wicked are cruel.   *12:10*

20.39   The way of a fool is right in his own eyes: but he that hearkeneth unto counsel is wise.   *12:15*

20.40   A wise son heareth his father's instruction: but a scorner heareth not rebuke.   *13:1*

20.41   Hope deferred maketh the heart sick: but when the desire cometh, it is a tree of life.   *13:12*

20.42   Good understanding giveth favour: but the way of transgressors is hard.   *13:15*

20.43   The desire accomplished is sweet to the soul: but it is abomination to fools to depart from evil.   *13:19*

20.44   He that walketh with wise men shall be wise: but a companion of fools shall be destroyed.   *13:20*

20.45   He that spareth his rod hateth his son: but he that loveth him chasteneth him betimes.   *13:24*

Spare the rod

Spare the rod and spoil the child *is a saying that comes from Proverbs. The expression is often used to support physical punishment so that a child will learn to behave properly and know the difference between right and wrong.*

20.46   There is a way which seemeth right unto a man, but the end thereof are the ways of death.   *14:12*

20.47   The poor is hated even of his own neighbour: but the rich hath many friends.   *14:20*

20.48   In all labour there is profit: but the talk of the lips tendeth only to penury.   *14:23*

20.49   A sound heart is the life of the flesh: but envy the rottenness of the bones.   *14:30*

20.50   Righteousness exalteth a nation: but sin is a reproach to any people.   *14:34*

20.51   A soft answer turneth away wrath: but grievous words stir up anger.   *15:1*

20.52   The sacrifice of the wicked is an abomination to the LORD: but the prayer of the upright is his delight.   *15:8*

20.53   A merry heart maketh a cheerful countenance: but by sorrow of the heart the spirit is broken.   *15:13*

20.54   Better is little with the fear of the LORD than great treasure and trouble therewith. Better is a dinner of herbs where love is, than a stalled ox and hatred therewith.   *15:16-17*

20.55   A man hath joy by the answer of his mouth: and a word spoken in due season, how good is it!   *15:23*

20.56   The light of the eyes rejoiceth the heart: and a good report maketh bones fat.   *15:30*

20.57   Commit thy works unto the LORD, and thy thoughts shall be established.   *16:3*

20.58   Pride goeth before destruction, and an haughty spirit before a fall.   *16:18*

Pride goes before a fall

The English proverb pride goes before a fall *means that a person who behaves in an over-confident and vain manner is soon likely to suffer misfortune. The expression is a rendering of this verse.*

20.59   The hoary head is a crown of glory, if it be found in the way of righteousness.   *16:31*

20.60   He that is slow to anger is better than the mighty; and he that ruleth his spirit than he that taketh a city.   *16:32*

20.61   The lot is cast into the lap; but the whole disposing thereof is of the LORD.   *16.33*

20.62   Children's children are the crown of old men; and the glory of children are their fathers.   *17:6*

20.63   He that covereth a transgression seeketh love; but he that repeateth a matter separateth very friends.   *17:9*

20.64   Whoso rewardeth evil for good, evil shall not depart from his house.   *17:13*

20.65   A friend loveth at all times, and a brother is born for adversity.   *17:17*

20.66   A merry heart doeth good like a medicine: but a broken spirit drieth the bones.   *17:22*

20.67   The name of the LORD is a strong tower: the righteous runneth into it, and is safe.   *18:10*

20.68   The spirit of a man will sustain his infirmity; but a wounded spirit who can bear?   *18:14*

20.69   A man that hath friends must shew himself friendly: and there is a friend that sticketh closer than a brother.   *18:24*

20.70   Wealth maketh many friends; but the poor is separated from his neighbour.   *19:4*

20.71   He that hath pity upon the poor lendeth unto the LORD; and that which he hath given will he pay him again.   *19:17*

20.72   There are many devices in a man's heart; nevertheless the counsel of the LORD, that shall stand.   *19:21*

20.73   The king's heart is in the hand of the LORD, as the rivers of water: he turneth it whithersoever he will.   *20:1*

20.74   To do justice and judgment is more acceptable to the LORD than sacrifice.   *20:3*

20.75   The spirit of man is the candle of the LORD, searching all the inward parts of the belly.   *20.27*

20.76   Every way of a man is right in his own eyes: but the LORD pondereth the hearts.   *21:2*

20.77   It is better to dwell in a corner of the housetop, than with a brawling woman in a wide house.   *21:9*

20.78   Train up a child in the way he should go: and when he is old, he will not depart from it.   *22:6*

20.79   Wilt thou set thine eyes upon that which is not? for riches certainly make themselves wings; they fly away as an eagle toward heaven.   *23:5*

20.80   Remove not the old landmark; and enter not into the fields of the fatherless.   *23:10*

20.81   Apply thine heart unto instruction, and thine ears to the words of knowledge.   *23:12*

20.82   A wise man is strong; yea, a man of knowledge increaseth strength.   *24:5*

20.83   If thou faint in the day of adversity, thy strength is small.   *24:10*

20.84   Yet a little sleep, a little slumber, a little folding of the hands to sleep. *24:33*

20.85   It is the glory of God to conceal a thing: but the honour of kings is to search out a matter.   *25:2*

20.86   A word fitly spoken is like apples of gold in pictures of silver.   *25:11*

20.87   Confidence in an unfaithful man in time of trouble is like a broken tooth, and a foot out of joint.   *25:19*

20.88   If thine enemy be hungry, give him bread to eat; and if he be thirsty, give him water to drink: For thou shalt heap coals of fire upon his head, and the LORD shall reward thee. *25:21-2*

20.89   As cold waters to a thirsty soul, so is good news from a far country. *25:25*

20.90   Answer a fool according to his folly, lest he be wise in his own conceit. *26:5*

20.91   As a dog returneth to his vomit, so a fool returneth to his folly.   *26:11*

20.92   The slothful man saith, There is a lion in the way; a lion is in the streets. *26:13*

20.93   The sluggard is wiser in his own conceit than seven men that can render a reason.   *26:16*

20.94   Where no wood is, there the fire goeth out: so where there is no talebearer, the strife ceaseth.   *26:20*

20.95   Boast not thyself of to morrow; for thou knowest not what a day may bring forth.   *27:1*

20.96   Wrath is cruel, and anger is outrageous; but who is able to stand before envy?   *27:4*

20.97   Open rebuke is better than secret love. Faithful are the wounds of a friend; but the kisses of an enemy are deceitful. *27:5-6*

20.98   A continual dropping in a very rainy day and a contentious woman are alike.   *27:15*

20.99   Iron sharpeneth iron; so a man sharpeneth the contenance of his friend.   *27:17*

20.100   Hell and destruction are never full; so the eyes of man are never satisfied.   *27:20*

20.101   A fool uttereth all his mind: but a wise man keepeth it in till afterwards. *29:11*

20.102   Where there is no vision, the people perish: but he that keepeth the law, happy is he.   *29:18*

20.103   Who can find a virtuous woman? for her price is far above rubies.   *31:10*

20.104   She perceiveth that her merchandise is good: her candle goeth not out by night.   *31:18*

20.105   She maketh fine linen, and selleth it; and delivereth girdles unto the merchant. Strength and honour are her clothing; and she shall rejoice in time to come. She openeth her mouth with wisdom; and in her tongue is the law of kindness. She looketh well to the ways of her household, and eateth not the bread of idleness. Her children arise up, and call her blessed; her husband also, and he praiseth her.   *31:24-28*

20.106   Favour is deceitful, and beauty is vain: but a woman that feareth the LORD, she shall be praised.   *31:30*

ECCLESIASTES

21.1   Vanity of vanities, saith the Preacher, vanity of vanities; all is vanity. What profit hath a man of all his labour which he taketh under the sun? One generation passeth away, and another generation cometh: but the earth abideth for ever.   *1:2-4*

21.2   All the rivers run into the sea; yet the sea is not full; unto the place from whence the rivers come, thither they return again.   *1:7*

21.3   All things are full of labour; man cannot utter it: the eye is not satisfied with seeing, nor the ear filled with hearing. *1:8*

21.4   The thing that hath been, it is that which shall be; and that which is done is that which shall be done: and there is no new thing under the sun.   *1:9*

> ### Nothing new under the sun
> *The proverbial expression* there is nothing new under the sun *is applied to something that looks original and novel but in fact is not. The saying has its source in this verse.*

21.5   There is no remembrance of former things; neither shall there be any remembrance of things that are to come with those that shall come after.   *1:11*

21.6   And I gave my heart to seek and search out by wisdom concerning all things that are done under heaven: this sore travail hath God given to the sons of man to be exercised therewith. I have seen all the works that are done under the sun; and, behold, all is vanity and vexation of spirit.   *1:13-14*

21.7   That which is crooked cannot be made straight: and that wh.. .h is wanting cannot be numbered.   *1:15*

21.8   For in much wisdom is much grief: and he that increaseth knowledge increaseth sorrow.   *1:18*

21.9   I said of laughter, It is mad: and of mirth, What doeth it?   *2:2*

21.10   Then I saw that wisdom excelleth folly, as far as light excelleth darkness. The wise man's eyes are in his head; but the fool walketh in darkness: and I myself perceived also that one event happeneth to them all.   *2:13-14*

21.11   To every thing there is a season, and a time to every purpose under the heaven: A time to be born, and a time to die; a time to plant, and a time to pluck up that which is planted; A time to kill, and a time to heal; a time to break down, and a time to build up; A time to weep, and a time to laugh; a time to mourn, and a time to dance: A time to cast away stones, and a time to gather stones together; a time to embrace, and a time to refrain from embracing; A time to get, and a time to lose; a time to keep, and a time to cast away; A time to rend, and a time to sew; a time to keep silence, and a time to speak; A time to love, and a time to hate; a time of war, and a time of peace. *3:1-8*

A time and a place for everything

The expression there's a time and a place for everything *means that there are certain circumstances when a particular action is appropriate. It is often used with the implication that a particular action may not be done at any time or in any place. The origin of the expression lies in the Preacher's statement of the varying seasons of human existence.*

21.12   He hath made every thing beautiful in his time: also he hath set the world in their heart, so that no man can find out the work that God maketh from the beginning to the end. *3:11*

21.13   I know that there is no good in them, but for a man to rejoice, and to do good in his life. And also that every man should eat and drink, and enjoy the good of all his labour, it is the gift of God. I know that, whatsoever God doeth, it shall be for ever: nothing can be put to it, nor any thing taken from it: and God doeth it, that men should fear before him. That which hath been is now; and that which is to be hath already been; and God requireth that which is past. *3:12-15*

21.14   I said in mine heart, God shall judge the righteous and the wicked: for there is a time there for every purpose and for every work. *3:17*

21.15   All go unto one place; all are of the dust, and all turn to dust again. *3:20*

21.16   Wherefore I perceive that there is nothing better, than that a man should rejoice in his own works; for that is his

portion: for who shall bring him to see what shall be after him? *3:22*

21.17   Wherefore I praise the dead which are already dead more than the living which are yet alive. *4:2*

21.18   Better is an handful with quietness, than both the hands full with travail and vexation of spirit. *4:6*

21.19   Two are better than one; because they have a good reward for their labour. For if they fall, the one will lift up his fellow: but woe to him that is alone when he falleth; for he hath not another to help him up. *4:9-10*

21.20   And if one prevail against him, two shall withstand him; and a threefold cord is not quickly broken. *4:12*

21.21   Better is a poor and a wise child than an old and foolish king, who will no more be admonished. *4:13*

21.22   Keep thy foot when thou goest to the house of God, and be more ready to hear, than to give the sacrifice of fools: for they consider not that they do evil. *5:1*

21.23   Be not rash with thy mouth, and let not thine heart be hasty to utter any thing before God: for God is in heaven, and thou upon earth: therefore let thy words be few. *5:2*

21.24   The sleep of a labouring man is sweet, whether he eat little or much: but the abundance of the rich will not suffer him to sleep. *5:12*

21.25   Behold that which I have seen: it is good and comely for one to eat and to drink, and to enjoy the good of all his labour that he taketh under the sun all the days of his life, which God giveth him: for it is his portion. *5:18*

21.26   Better is the sight of the eyes than the wandering of the desire: this is also vanity and vexation of spirit. *6:9*

21.27   A good name is better than precious ointment; and the day of death than the day of one's birth.   *7:1*

21.28   For as the crackling of thorns under a pot, so is the laughter of a fool: this also is vanity.   *7:6*

21.29   Better is the end of a thing than the beginning thereof: and the patient in spirit is better than the proud in spirit.   *7:8*

21.30   Say not thou, What is the cause that the former days were better than these? for thou dost not inquire wisely concerning this.   *7:10*

21.31   Wisdom is good with an inheritance: and by it there is profit to them that see the sun.   *7:11*

21.32   In the day of prosperity be joyful, but in the day of adversity consider; God also hath set the one over against the other, to the end that man should find nothing after him. All things have I seen in the days of my vanity: there is a just man that perisheth in his righteousness, and there is a wicked man that prolongeth his life in his wickedness. Be not righteous over much; neither make thyself over wise: why shouldest thou destroy thyself?   *7:14-16*

21.33   Which yet my soul seeketh, but I find not: one man among a thousand have I found; but a woman among all those have I not found. Lo, this only have I found, that God hath made man upright; but they have sought out many inventions.   *7:28-29*

21.34   There is no man that hath power over the spirit to retain the spirit; neither hath he power in the day of death: and there is no discharge in that war; neither shall wickedness deliver those that are given to it.   *8:8*

21.35   Though a sinner do evil an hundred times, and his days be prolonged, yet surely I know that it shall be well with them that fear God, which fear before him: But it shall not be well with the wicked, neither shall he prolong his days, which are as a shadow; because he feareth not before God.   *8:12-13*

21.36   Then I commended mirth, because a man hath no better thing under the sun, than to eat, and to drink, and to be merry: for that shall abide with him of his labour the days of his life, which God giveth him under the sun.   *8:15*

21.37   When I applied mine heart to know wisdom, and to see the business that is done upon the earth: (for also there is that neither day nor night seeth sleep with his eyes:) Then I beheld all the work of God, that a man cannot find out the work that is done under the sun: because though a man labour to seek it out, yet he shall not find it; yea further; though a wise man think to know it, yet shall he not be able to find it.   *8:16-17*

21.38   For to him that is joined to all the living there is hope: for a living dog is better than a dead lion. For the living know that they shall die: but the dead know not any thing, neither have they any more a reward; for the memory of them is forgotten.   *9:4-5*

21.39   Go thy way, eat thy bread with joy, and drink thy wine with a merry heart; for the God now accepteth thy works.   *9:7*

21.40   Whatsoever thy hand findeth to do; do it with thy might; for there is no work, nor device, nor knowledge, nor wisdom, in the grave, whither thou goest.   *9:10*

21.41   I returned, and saw under the sun, that the race is not to the swift, nor the battle to the strong, neither yet bread to the wise, nor yet riches to men of understanding, nor yet favour to men of skill; but time and chance happeneth to them all.   *9:11*

21.42   For man also knoweth not his time: as the fishes that are taken in an evil net, and as the birds that are caught in the snare; so are the sons of men snared in an evil time, when it falleth suddenly upon them.   *9:12*

21.43   The words of wise men are heard in quiet more than the cry of him that ruleth among fools.   *9:17*

21.44   Dead flies cause the ointment of the apothecary to send forth a stinking savour: so doth a little folly him that is in reputation for wisdom and honour.   *10.1*

A fly in the ointment

The expression a fly in the ointment *is used to refer to a person or thing that spoils a situation which is perfect in every other way. The source of the expression shows that as dead flies give even sweet-smelling perfume a bad odour, so a little folly spoils the virtues of wisdom and honour.*

21.45   He that diggeth a pit shall fall into it; and whoso breaketh an hedge, a serpent shall bite him.   *10:8*

21.46   A feast is made for laughter, and wine maketh merry: but money answereth all things.   *10:19*

21.47   Curse not the king, no not in thy thought; and curse not the rich in thy bedchamber: for a bird of the air shall carry the voice, and that which hath wings shall tell the matter.   *10:20*

21.48   Cast thy bread upon the waters: for thou shalt find it after many days.   *11:1*

21.49   If the clouds be full of rain, they empty themselves upon the earth: and if the tree fall toward the south, or toward the north, in the place where the tree falleth, there it shall be.   *11:3*

21.50   In the morning sow thy seed, and in the evening withhold not thine hand: for thou knowest not whether shall prosper, either this or that, or whether they both shall be alike good.   *11:6*

21.51   Truly the light is sweet, and a pleasant thing it is for the eyes to behold the sun.   *11:7*

21.52   Rejoice, O young man, in thy youth; and let thy heart cheer thee in the days of thy youth, and walk in the ways of thine heart, and in the sight of thine eyes: but know thou, that for all these things God will bring thee into judgment.   *11:9*

21.53   Remember now thy Creator in the days of thy youth, while the evil days come not, nor the years draw nigh, when thou shalt say, I have no pleasure in them; While the sun, or the light, or the moon, or the stars, be not darkened, nor the clouds return after the rain: In the day when the keepers of the house shall tremble, and the strong men shall bow themselves, and the grinders cease because they are few, and those that look out of the windows be darkened, And the doors shall be shut in the streets, when the sound of the grinding is low, and he shall rise up at the voice of the bird, and all the daughters of musick shall be brought low; Also when they shall be afraid of that which is high, and fears shall be in the way, and the almond tree shall flourish, and the grasshopper shall be a burden, and desire shall fail: because man goeth to his long home, and mourners go about the streets: Or ever the silver cord be loosed, or the golden bowl be broken, or the pitcher be broken at the fountain, or the wheel broken at the cistern. Then shall the dust return to the earth as it was: and the spirit shall return unto God who gave it.   *12:1-7*

21.54   And further, by these, my son, be admonished: of making many books there is no end; and much study is a weariness of the flesh.   *12:12*

21.55   Let us hear the conclusion of the whole matter: Fear God, and keep his commandments: for this is the whole duty of man.   *12:13*

SONG OF SOLOMON

22.1   The song of songs, which is Solomon's.   *1:1*

22.2   Draw me, we will run after thee: the king hath brought me into his chambers: we will be glad and rejoice in thee, we will remember thy love more than wine: the upright love thee. I am black, but comely, O ye daughters of Jerusalem, as the tents of Kedar, as the curtains of Solomon.   *1:4-5*

22.3   If thou know not, O thou fairest among women, go thy way forth by the footsteps of the flock, and feed thy kids beside the shepherds' tents.   *1:8*

22.4   A bundle of myrrh is my wellbeloved unto me; he shall lie all night betwixt my breasts.   *1:13*

22.5   I am the rose of Sharon, and the lily of the valleys. As the lily among thorns, so is my love among the daughters. *2:1-2*

22.6   As the apple tree among the trees of the wood, so is my beloved among the sons. I sat down under his shadow with great delight, and his fruit was sweet to my taste   *2:3*

22.7   He brought me to the banqueting house, and his banner over me was love. *2:4*

22.8   Stay me with flagons, comfort me with apples: for I am sick of love.   *2:5*

22.9   I charge you, O ye daughters of Jerusalem, by the roes, and by the hinds of the field, that ye stir not up, nor awake my love, till he please.   *2:7*

22.10   The voice of my beloved! behold, he cometh leaping upon the mountains, skipping upon the hills.   *2:8*

22.11   My beloved spake, and said unto me, Rise up, my love, my fair one, and come away. For lo, the winter is past, the rain is over and gone.   *2:10-11*

22.12   My beloved is mine, and I am his: he feedeth among the lilies.   *2:16*

22.13   By night on my bed I sought him whom my soul loveth: I sought him, but I found him not.   *3:1*

22.14   I charge you, O ye daughters of Jerusalem, by the roes, and by the hinds of the field, that ye stir not up, nor awake my love, till he please.   *3:5*

22.15   Behold, thou art fair, my love; behold, thou art fair; thou hast doves' eyes within thy locks: thy hair is as a flock of goats, that appear from mount Gilead. Thy teeth are like a flock of sheep that are even shorn, which came up from the washing; whereof every one bear twins, and none is barren among them. Thy lips are like a thread of scarlet, and thy speech is comely: thy temples are like a piece of a pomegranate within thy locks. Thy neck is like the tower of David builded for an armoury, whereon there hang a thousand bucklers, all shields of mighty men. Thy two breasts are like two young roes that are twins, which feed among the lilies. Until the day break, and the shadows flee away, I will get me to the mountain of myrrh, and to the hill of frankincense. Thou art all fair, my love; there is no spot in thee.   *4:1-7*

22.16   A garden inclosed is my sister, my spouse; a spring shut up, a fountain sealed.   *4:12*

22.17   Let my beloved come into his garden, and eat his pleasant fruits.   *4:16*

22.18   I am come into my garden, my sister, my spouse: I have gathered my myrrh with my spice; I have eaten my honeycomb with my honey; I have drunk my wone with my milk: eat, O friends; drink, yea, drink abundantly, O beloved. I sleep, but my heart waketh: it is the voice of my beloved that knocketh, saying, Open to me, my sister, my love, my dove, my undefiled: for my head is filled with dew, and my locks with the drops of the night.   *5:1-2*

22.19   My beloved put in his hand by the hole of the door, and my bowels were moved for him.   *5:4*

22.20   I opened to my beloved; but my beloved had withdrawn himself, and was gone: my soul failed when he spake: I sought him, but I could not find him; I called him, but he gave me no answer. *5:6*

22.21   What is thy beloved more than another beloved, O thou fairest among women? what is thy beloved more than another beloved, that thou dost so charge us? My beloved is white and ruddy, the chiefest among ten thousand. His head is as the most fine gold, his locks are bushy, and black as a raven. His eyes are as the eyes of doves by the rivers of waters, washed with milk, and fitly set. His cheeks are as a bed of spices, as sweet flowers; his lips like lilies, dropping sweet smelling myrrh. His hands are as gold rings set with the beryl: his belly is as bright ivory overlaid with sapphires. His legs are as pillars of marble, set upon

sockets of fine gold: his countenance is as Lebanon, excellent as the cedars. His mouth is most sweet: yea, he is altogether lovely. This is my beloved, and this is my friend, O daughters of Jerusalem. *5:9-16*

22.22   I am my beloved's, and my beloved is mine: he feedeth among the lilies.   *6:3*

22.23   How beautiful are thy feet with shoes, O prince's daughter! the joints of thy thighs are like jewels, the work of the hands of a cunning workmen.   *7:1*

22.24   Thy neck is as a tower of ivory; thine eyea like the fishpools in Heshbon, by the gate of Bathrabbim: thy nose is as the tower of Lebanon which looketh toward Damascus.   *7:4*

22.25   How fair and how pleasant art thou, O love, for delights!   *7:6*

22.26   I am my beloved's and his desire is toward me.   *7:10*

22.27   Love is strong as death; jealousy is cruel as the grave: the coals thereof are coals of fire, which hath a most vehement flame. Many waters cannot quench love, neither can the floods drown it: if a man would give all the substance of his house for love, it would utterly be contemned.   *8:6-7*

THE BOOKS OF THE PROPHETS

The prophets predicted future events, especially about the coming Messiah, but their main task was to call God's people back to their God. *Isaiah* describes the threat of the Assyrian conquest, promises to exiles in Babylon, and a message of hope to the Jews after they had returned from the exile. The warning messages of *Jeremiah* came in the closing years of Judah. The book of *Lamentations* is a song of sorrow about the destruction of Jerusalem by the Babylonians. *Ezekiel* records the visions and prophecies of the prophet in exile in Babylon. *Daniel*, captive in Babylon, lived a life of integrity and faithfulness to God; the second part of this book gives visions of the future.

Hosea records prophecies to the northern kingdom of Israel in its closing years: even though the people were faithless, God was still faithful. *Joel* describes a devastating plague of locusts that is seen as a sign of the coming final 'day of the Lord': the people should therefore turn back to God. *Amos* preached a message of social justice to the materialist, affluent society of Israel. *Obadiah*, the shortest book in the Old Testament, is a prophecy against Edom, a country bordering Judah. *Jonah* describes the prophet's reluctance to go to preach in Nineveh, the capital of Assyria, Israel's enemy. *Micah* records prophecies against injustices in society yet also contains a message of hope, forgiveness, and restoration. *Nahum* foretells the destruction of Nineveh. In *Habakkuk* the prophet questioned God about how he could use the wicked Babylon to punish people who were better than them. *Zephaniah* prophesied against Judah; *Haggai* urged the people on in their commitment to God and to rebuild the temple; *Zechariah*, like Haggai, encouraged the people to rebuild the temple; *Malachi*, the last Old Testament prophet, questioned the people's religious apathy and challenged them to wholehearted obedience to God.

ISAIAH

23.1   The ox knoweth his owner, and the ass his master's crib: but Israel doth not know, my people doth not consider.   *1:3*

23.2   Why should ye be stricken any more? ye will revolt more and more: the whole head is sick, and the whole heart faint. From the sole of the foot even unto the head there is no soundness in it; but wounds, and bruises, and putrifying sores: they have not been closed, neither bound up, neither mollified with ointment.   *1:5-6*

23.3   And the daughter of Zion is left as a cottage in a vineyard, as a lodge in a garden of cucumbers, as a besieged city.   *1:8*

23.4   Bring no more vain oblations; incense is an abomination unto me; the new moons and sabbaths, the calling of assemblies, I cannot away with; it is iniquity, even the solemn meeting.   *1:13*

23.5   Learn to do well; seek judgment, relieve the oppressed, judge the fatherless, plead for the widow. Come now, and let us reason together, saith the LORD: though your sins be as scarlet, they shall be as white as snow; though they be red like crimson. they shall be as wool.   *1:17-18*

23.6   And he shall judge among the nations, and shall rebuke many people: and they shall beat their swords into plowshares, and their spears into pruninghooks: nation shall not lift up sword against nation, neither shall they learn war any more.   *2:4*

23.7   O house of Jacob, come ye, and let us walk in the light of the LORD.   *2:5*

23.8   And they shall go into the holes of the rocks, and into the caves of the earth, for fear of the LORD, and for the glory of his majesty, when he ariseth to shake terribly the earth.   *2:19*

23.9   What mean ye that ye beat my people to pieces, and grind the faces of the poor? saith the Lord GOD of hosts.   *3:15*

Grind the faces of the poor

The expression to grind the faces of the poor *means to govern someone cruelly or cause him or her suffering by unjust treatment. This rather old-fashioned expression has its origin in Isaiah's prophecy to cruel rulers.*

23.10   Now will I sing to my wellbeloved a song of my beloved touching his vineyard. My wellbeloved hath a vineyard in a very fruitful hill: And he fenced it, and gathered out the stones thereof, and planted it with the choicest vine, and built a tower in the midst of it, and also made a winepress therein: and he looked that it

should bring forth grapes, and it brought forth wild grapes.   *5:1-2*

23.11   And now, O inhabitants of Jerusalem, and men of Judah, judge, I pray you, betwixt me and my vineyard. What could have been done more to my vineyard, that I have not done in it? wherefore, when I looked that it should bring forth grapes, brought is forth wild grapes? And now go to; I will tell you what I will do to my vineyard: I will take away the hedge thereof, and it shall be eaten up; and break down the wall thereof, and it shall be trodden down: And I will lay it waste: it shall not be pruned, nor digged; but there shall come up briers and thorns: I will also command the clouds that they rain no rain upon it. For the vineyard of the LORD of hosts is the house of Israel, and the men of Judah his pleasant plant: and he looked for judgment, but behold oppression; for righteousness, but behold a cry.   *5:3-7*

23.12   Woe unto them that rise up early in the morning, that they may follow strong drink; that continue until night, till wine inflame them!   *5:11*

23.13   In the year that king Uzziah died I saw also the Lord sitting upon a throne, high and lifted up, and his train filled the temple. Above it stood the seraphims: each one had six wings; with twain he covered his face, and with twain he covered his feet, and with twain he did fly. And one cried unto another, and said, Holy, holy, holy, is the LORD of hosts: the whole earth is full of his glory. And the posts of the door moved at the voice of him that cried, and the house was filled with smoke.   *6:1-4*

23.14   Then said I, Woe is me! for I am undone; because I am a man of unclean lips, and I dwell in the midst of a people of unclean lips; for mine eyes have seen the King, the LORD of hosts. Then flew one of the seraphims unto me, having a live coal in his hand, which he had taken with the tongs from off the altar: And he laid it upon my mouth, and said, Lo, this hath touched thy lips; and thine iniquity is taken away, and thy sin purged. Also I heard the voice of the Lord, saying, Whom shall I send, and who will go for us? Then said I, Here am I; send me. *6:5-8*

23.15   And he said, Go, and tell this people, Hear ye indeed, but understand not; and see ye indeed, but perceive not. Make the heart of this people fat, and make their ears heavy, and shut their eyes; lest they see with their eyes, and hear with their ears, and understand with their heart, and convert, and be healed. Then said I, Lord, how long? And he answered, Until the cities be wasted without inhabitant, and the houses without man, and the land be utterly desolate, And the LORD have removed men far away, and there be a great forsaking in the midst of the land. But yet in it shall be a tenth, and it shall return, and shall be eaten: as a teil tree, and as an oak, whose substance is in them, when they cast their leaves: so the holy seed shall be the substance therefore.   *6:9-13*

23.16   Therefore the Lord himself shall give you a sign; Behold, a virgin shall conceive, and bear a son, and shall call his name Immanuel.   *7:14*

23.17   And he shall be for a sanctuary; but for a stone of stumbling and for a rock of offence to both the houses of Israel, for a gin and for a snare to the inhabitants of Jerusalem.   *8:14*

23.18   Bind up the testimony, seal the law among my disciples. And I will wait upon the LORD, that hideth his face from the house of Jacob, and I will look for him. Behold, I and the children whom the LORD hath given me are for signs and for wonders in Israel from the LORD of hosts, which dwelleth in mount Zion.   *8:16-18*

23.19   The people that walked in darkness have seen a great light: they that dwell in the land of the shadow of death, upon them hath the light shined.   *9:2*

23.20   For unto us a child is born, unto us a son is given: and the government shall be upon his shoulder: and his name shall be called Wonderful, Counseller, The mighty God, The everlasting Father, The Prince of Peace. Of the increase of his government and peace there shall be no end, upon the throne of David, and upon his kingdom, to order it, and to establish it with judgment and with justice from henceforth even for ever. The zeal of the LORD of hosts will perform this.   *9:6-7*

23.21   O Assyrian, the rod of mine anger, and the staff in their hand is mine indignation. I will send him against an hypocritical nation, and against the people of my wrath will I give him a charge, to take the spoil, and to take the prey, and to tread them down like the mire of the streets.   *10:5-6*

23.22   And it shall come to pass in that day, that the remnant of Israel, and such as are escaped of the house of Jacob, shall no more again stay upon him that smote them; but shall stay upon the LORD, the Holy One of Israel, in truth.   *10:20*

23.23   And there shall come forth a rod out of the stem of Jesse, and a Branch shall grow out of his roots: And the spirit of the LORD shall rest upon him, the spirit of wisdom and understanding, the spirit of counsel and might, the spirit of knowledge and of the fear of the LORD. *11:1-2*

23.24   The wolf also shall dwell with the lamb, and the leopard shall lie down with the kid; and the calf and the young lion and the fatling together; and a little child shall lead them. And the cow and the bear shall feed; their young ones shall lie down together: and the lion shall eat straw like the ox. And the sucking child shall play on the hole of the asp, and the weaned child shall put his hand on the cockatrice' den. They shall not hurt nor destroy in all my holy mountain for the earth shall be full of the knowledge of the LORD, as the waters cover the sea.   *11:6-9*

23.25   And in that day thou shalt say, O LORD, I will praise thee: though thou wast angry with me, thine anger is turned away, and thou comfortedst me. Behold, God is my salvation; I will trust, and not be afraid: for the LORD JEHOVAH is my strength and my song; he also is become my salvation. Therefore with joy shall ye draw water out of the wells of salvation.   *12:1-3*

23.26   Cry out and shout, thou inhabitant of Zion: for great is the Holy One of Israel in the midst of thee.   *12:6*

23.27   How art thou fallen from heaven, O Lucifer, son of the morning! how art thou cut down to the ground, which didst weaken the nations!   *14:12*

23.28   At that day shall a man look to his Maker, and his eyes shall have respect to the Holy One of Israel.   *17:7*

23.29   And behold joy and gladness, slaying oxen, and killing sheep, eating flesh, and drinking wine: let us eat and drink; for to morrow we shall die.   *22:13*

Eat, drink, and be merry

The saying eat, drink, and be merry, *sometimes followed by the additional phrase* for tomorrow we die *expresses the philosophy that one should enjoy oneself fully with worldly pleasures at the present time, because the future is uncertain. The saying is derived from two verses, Ecclesiastes 8:15 and Isaiah 22:13.*

23.30   And the key of the house of David will I lay upon his shoulder; so he shall open, and none shall shut; and he shall shut, and none shall open.   *22:22*

23.31   The earth shall reel to and fro like a drunkard, and shall be removed like a cottage; and the transgression thereof shall be heavy upon it; and it shall fall, and not rise again.   *24:20*

23.32   Then the moon shall be confounded, and the sun ashamed, when the LORD of hosts shall reign in mount Zion, and in Jerusalem, and before his ancients gloriously.   *24:23*

23.33   O LORD, thou art my God; I will exalt thee, I will praise thy name; for thou hast done wonderful things; thy counsels of old are faithfulness and truth.   *25:1*

23.34   For thou hast been a strength to the poor, a strength to the needy in his distress, a refuge from the storm, a shadow from the heat, when the blast of the terrible ones is as a storm against the wall.   *25:4*

23.35   He will swallow up death in victory; and the Lord GOD will wipe away tears from off all faces; and the rebuke of his people shall he take away from off all the earth: for the LORD hath spoken it.   *25:8*

23.36   And it shall be said in that day, Lo, this is our God; we have waited for him, and he will save us: this is the LORD; we have waited for him, we will be glad and rejoice in his salvation.   *25:9*

23.37   Thou wilt keep him in perfect peace, whose mind is stayed on thee: because he trusteth in thee. Trust ye in the LORD for ever: for in the LORD JEHOVAH is everlasting strength.   *26:3-4*

23.38   Thy dead men shall live, together with my dead body shall they arise. Awake and sing, ye that dwell in dust: for thy dew is as the dew of herbs, and the earth shall cast out the dead.   *26:19*

23.39   For precept must be upon precept, precept upon precept; line upon line, line upon line; here a little, and there a little: For with stammering lips and another tongue will he speak to this people.   *28:10-11*

23.40   Therefore thus saith the Lord GOD, Behold, I lay in Zion for a foundation a stone, a tried stone, a precious corner stone, a sure foundation: he that believeth shall not make haste. Judgment also will I lay to the line, and righteousness to the plummet: and the hail shall sweep away the refuge of lies, and the waters shall overflow the hiding place. *28:16-17*

23.41   Wherefore the Lord said, Forasmuch as this people draw near me with their mouth, and with their lips do honour me, but have removed their heart far from me, and their fear toward me is taught by the precept of men. *29:13*

23.42   Therefore, behold, I will proceed to do a marvellous work among this people, even a marvellous work and a wonder: for the wisdom of their wise men shall perish, and the understanding of their prudent men shall be hid. *29:14*

23.43   And in that day shall the deaf hear the words of the book, and the eyes of the blind shall see out of obscurity, and out of darkness. *29:18*

23.44   For thus saith the Lord GOD, the Holy One of Israel; In returning and rest shall ye be saved; in quietness and in confidence shall be your strength: and ye would not. *30:15*

23.45   And thine ears shall hear a word behind thee, saying, This is the way, walk ye in it, when ye turn to the right hand, and when ye turn to the left. *30:21*

23.46   Behold, a king shall reign in righteousness, and princes shall rule in judgment. *32:1*

23.47   And a man shall be as an hiding place from the wind, and a covert from the tempest; as rivers of water in a dry place, as the shadow of a great rock in a weary land. *32:2*

23.48   O LORD, be gracious unto us; we have waited for thee: be thou their arm every morning, our salvation also in the time of trouble. *33:2*

23.49   Thine eyes shall see the king in his beauty: they shall behold the land that is very far off. *33:17*

23.50   It shall blossom abundantly, and rejoice even with joy and singing: the glory of Lebanon shall be given unto it, the excellencey of Carmel and Sharon, they shall see the glory of the LORD, and the excellency of our God. *35:2*

23.51   Strengthen ye the weak hands, and confirm the feeble knees. *35:3*

23.52   Then the eyes of the blind shall be opened, and the ears of the deaf shall be unstopped. Then shall the lame man leap as an hart, and the tongue of the dumb sing: for in the wilderness shall waters break out, and streams in the desert. And the parched ground shall become a pool, and the thirsty land springs of water: in the habitation of dragons, where each lay, shall be grass with reeds and rushes. *35:5-7*

23.53   And an highway shall be there, and a way, and it shall be called The way of holiness; the unclean shall not pass over it; but it shall be for those: the wayfaring men, though fools shall not err therein. *35:8*

23.54   And the ransomed of the LORD shall return, and come to Zion with songs and everlasting joy upon their heads: they shall obtain joy and gladness, and sorrow and sighing shall flee away. *35:10*

23.55   I say, sayest thou, (but they are but vain words) I have counsel and strength for war: now on whom dost thou trust, that thou rebellest against me? Lo, thou trusted in the staff of this broken reed, on Egypt; whereon if a man lean, it will go into his hand, and pierce it: so is Pharaoh king of Egypt to all that trust in him. *36:5-6*

23.56   Comfort ye, comfort ye my people, saith your God. Speak ye comfortably to Jerusalem, and cry unto her, that her warfare is accomplished, that her iniquity is pardoned: for she hath received of the LORD'S hand double for all her sins. The voice of him that crieth in the wilderness, Prepare ye the way of the LORD, make straight in the desert a highway for our God. Every valley shall be exalted, and every mountain and hill shall be made low: and the crooked shall be made straight, and the rough places plain: And the glory of the LORD shall be revealed, and all flesh shall see it together: for the mouth of the LORD hath spoken it. The voice said, Cry. And he said, What shall I cry? All flesh is grass, and all the goodliness thereof is as the flower of the field: The grass withereth, the flower fadeth: because the spirit of the LORD bloweth upon it: surely the people is grass. The grass withereth, the flower fadeth: but the word of our God shall stand for ever.   *40:1-8*

23.57   O Zion, that bringest good tidings, get thee up into the high mountain; O Jerusalem, that bringest good tidings, lift up thy voice with strength; lift it up, be not afraid; say unto the cities of Judah, Behold your God! *40:9*

23.58   Behold, the Lord GOD will come with strong hand, and his arm shall rule for him: behold, his reward is with him, and his work before him. He shall feed his flock like a shepherd: he shall gather the lambs with his arm, and carry them in his bosom, and shall gently lead those that are with young.   *40:10-11*

23.59   Who hath measured the waters in the hollow of his hand, and meted out heaven with the span, and comprehended the dust of the earth in a measure, and weighed the mountains in scales, and the hills in a balance? Who hath directed the Spirit of the LORD, or being his counseller hath taught him?   *40:12-13*

23.60   With whom took he counsel, and who instructed him, and taught him in the path of judgment, and taught him knowledge, and shewed to him the way of understanding? Behold, the nations are as a drop of a bucket, and are counted as the small dust of the balance: behold, he taketh up the isles as a very little thing. *40:14-15*

A drop in the ocean

A drop in the ocean *(or* bucket*) is something very small compared with something larger that is required. For example, a tiny grant of money may be just* a drop in the ocean *when one considers the total amount that is really needed. The origin of the expression shows the insignificance of the earthly nations when compared with the greatness of God.*

23.61   To whom then will ye liken God? or what likeness will ye compare unto him?   *40:18*

23.62   Have ye not known? have ye not heard? hath it not been told you from the beginning? have ye not understood from the foundations of the earth?   *40:21*

23.63   It is he that sitteth upon the circle of the earth, and the inhabitants thereof are as grasshoppers; that stretcheth out the heavens as a curtain, and spreadeth them out as a tent to dwell in: That bringeth the princes to nothing; he maketh the judges of the earth as vanity. Yea, they shall not be planted; yea, their stock shall not take root in the earth: and he shall also blow upon them, and they shall wither, and the whirlwind shall take them away as stubble.   *40:22-24*

23.64   To whom then will ye liken me, or shall I be equal? saith the Holy One. *40:25*

23.65   Lift up your eyes on high, and behold who hath created these things, that bringeth out their host by number: he calleth them all by names by the greatness of his might, for that he is strong in power; not one faileth.   *40:26*

23.66   Why sayest thou, O Jacob, and speakest, O Israel, My way is hid from the

LORD, and my judgment is passed over from my God? *40:27*

23.67   Hast thou not known? hast thou not heard, that the everlasting God, the LORD, the Creator of the ends of the earth, fainteth not, neither is weary? there is no searching of his understanding. He giveth power to the faint; and to them that have no might he increaseth strength. Even the youths shall faint and be weary, and the young men shall utterly fall: But they that wait upon the LORD shall renew their strength; they shall mount up with wings as eagles; they shall run, and not be weary; and they shall walk, and not faint. *40:28-31*

23.68   Fear thou not; for I am with thee: be not dismayed; for I am thy God: I will strengthen thee; yea, I will help thee; yea, I will uphold thee with the right hand of my righteousness. *41:10*

23.69   A bruised reed shall he not break, and the smoking flax shall he not quench: he shall bring forth judgment unto truth. He shall not fail nor be discouraged, till he have set judgment in the earth: and the isles shall wait for his law. *42:3-4*

23.70   To open the blind eyes, to bring out the prisoners from the prison, and them that sit in darkness out of the prison house. *42:7*

23.71   But now thus saith the LORD that created thee, O Jacob, and he that formed thee, O Israel, Fear not: for I have redeemed thee, I have called thee by thy name; thou art mine. When thou passest through the waters, I will be with thee; and through the rivers, they shall not overflow thee: when thou walkest through the fire, thou shalt not be burned; neither shall the flame kindle upon thee. For I am the LORD thy God, the Holy One of Israel, thy Saviour: I gave Egypt for thy ransom, Ethiopia and Seba for thee. Since thou wast precious in my sight, thou hast been honourable, and I have loved thee: therefore will I give men for thee, and people for thy life. Fear not:

for I am with thee: I will bring thy seed from the east, and gather thee from the west; *43:1-5*

23.72   This people have I formed for myself; they shall shew forth my praise. *43:21*

23.73   For I will pour water upon him that is thirsty, and floods upon the dry ground: I will pour my spirit upon thy seed, and my blessing upon thine offspring. *44:3*

23.74   I am the LORD, and there is none else, there is no God beside me: I girded thee, though thou hast not known me: That they may know from the rising of the sun, and from the west, that there is none beside me. I am the LORD, and there is none else. *45:5-6*

23.75   Woe unto him that striveth with his Maker! Let the potsherd strive with the potsherds of the earth. Shall the clay say to him that fashioneth it, What makest thou? or thy work, He hath no hands? *45:9*

23.76   Look unto me, and be ye saved, all the ends of the earth: for I am God, and there is none else. *45:22*

23.77   Bel boweth down, Nebo stoopeth, their idols were upon the beasts, and upon the cattle: your carriages were heavy loaden; they are a burden to the weary beast. *46:1*

23.78   I bring near my righteousness; it shall not be far off, and my salvation shall not tarry: and I will place salvation in Zion for Israel my glory. *46:13*

23.79   Behold, I have refined thee, but not with silver; I have chosen thee in the furnace of affliction. *48:10*

23.80   O that thou hadst hearkened to my commandments! then had thy peace been as a river, and thy righteousness as the waves of the sea. *48:18*

23.81   There is no peace, saith the LORD, unto the wicked.   *48:22*

23.82   And he said, It is a light thing that thou shouldest be my servant to raise up the tribes of Jacob, and to restore the preserved of Israel: I will also give thee for a light to the Gentiles, that thou mayest be my salvation unto the end of the earth.   *49:6*

23.83   Thus saith the LORD, In an acceptable time have I heard thee, and in a day of salvation have I helped thee: and I will preserve thee, and give thee for a covenant of the people, to establish the earth, to cause to inherit the desolate heritages.   *49:8*

23.84   They shall not hunger nor thirst; neither shall the heat nor sun smite them: for he that hath mercy on them shall lead them, even by the springs of water shall he guide them.   *49:10*

23.85   Can a woman forget her suckling child, that she should not have compassion on the son of her womb? yea, they may forget, yet will I not forget thee.   *49:15*

23.86   Behold, I have graven thee upon the palms of my hands; thy walls are continually before me.   *49:16*

23.87   Wherefore, when I came, was there no man? when I called, was there none to answer? Is my hand shortened at all, that it cannot redeem? or have I not power to deliver? behold, at my rebuke I dry up the sea, I make the rivers a wilderness: their fish stinketh, because there is no water, and dieth for thirst. *50:2*

23.88   The Lord GOD hath given me the tongue of the learned, that I should know how to speak a word in season to him that is weary: he wakeneth morning by morning, he wakeneth mine ear to hear as the learned.   *50:4*

23.89   The Lord GOD hath opened mine ear, and I was not rebellious, neither turned away back. I gave my back to the smiters, and my cheeks to them that plucked off the hair: I hid not my face from shame and spitting. For the Lord GOD will help me; therefore shall I not be confounded: therefore have I set my face like a flint, and I know that I shall not be ashamed. He is near that justifieth me; who will contend with me? let us stand together: who is mine adversary? let him come near to me. Behold, the Lord GOD will help me; who is he that shall condemn me? lo, they all shall wax old as a garment; the moth shall eat them up. *50:5-9*

23.90   Who is among you that feareth the LORD, that obeyeth the voice of his servant, that walketh in darkness, and hath no light, let him trust in the name of the LORD, and stay upon his God. Behold, all ye that kindle a fire, that compass yourselves about with sparks: walk in the light of your fire, and in the sparks that ye have kindled. This shall ye have of mine hand; ye shall lie down in sorrow.   *50:10-11*

23.91   For the LORD shall comfort Zion: he will comfort all her waste places; and he will make her wilderness like Eden, and her desert like the garden of the LORD; joy and gladness shall be found therein, thanksgiving, and the voice of melody.   *51:3*

23.92   How beautiful upon the mountains are the feet of him that bringeth good tidings, that publisheth peace; that bringeth good tidings of good, that publisheth salvation; that saith unto Zion, Thy God reigneth! Thy watchmen shall lift up the voice; with the voice together shall they sing: for they shall see eye to eye, when the LORD shall bring again Zion.   *52:7-8*

23.93   Break forth into joy, sing together, ye waste places of Jerusalem: for the LORD hath comforted his people, he hath redeemed Jerusalem. The LORD hath

made bare his holy arm in the eyes of all the nations; and all the ends of the earth shall see the salvation of our God.
52:9-10

23.94   As many were astonied at thee; his visage was so marred more than any man, and his form more than the sons of men: So shall he sprinkle many nations; the kings shall shut their mouths at him: for that which had not been told them shall they see; and that which they had not heard shall they consider.   *52:14-15*

Like a lamb to the slaughter

The expression like a lamb to the slaughter *means quietly and without complaining. It is often used to refer to someone who is unwittingly about to go into a dangerous or difficult situation or to be the helpless victim of punishment. Sometimes the word* lamb *is replaced by* sheep. *The basis of the expression is Isaiah 53:7, which describes the sacrifice of the suffering servant, and Acts 8:32, where the prophecy is applied to Jesus.*

23.95   Who hath believed our report? and to whom is the arm of the LORD revealed? For he shall grow up before him as a tender plant, and as a root out of a dry ground: he hath no form nor comeliness; and when we shall see him, there is no beauty that we should desire him. He is despised and rejected of men; a man of sorrows, and acquainted with grief: and we hid as it were our faces from him; he was despised, and we esteemed him not. Surely he hath borne our griefs, and carried our sorrows: yet we did esteem him stricken, smitten of God, and afflicted. But he was wounded for our transgressions, he was bruised for our iniquities: the chastisement of our peace was upon him; and with his stripes we are healed. All we like sheep have gone astray; we have turned every one to his own way; and the LORD hath laid on him the iniquity of us all. He was oppressed, and he was afflicted, yet he opened not his mouth: he is brought as a lamb to the

slaughter, and as a sheep before her shearers is dumb, so he openeth not his mouth. He was taken from prison and from judgment: and who shall declare his generation? for he was cut off out of the land of the living: for the transgression of my people was he stricken. And he made his grave with the wicked, and with the rich in his death; because he had done no violence, neither was any deceit in his mouth.   *53:1-9*

23.96   Yet it pleased the LORD to bruise him: he hath put him to grief: when thou shalt make his soul an offering for sin, he shall see his seed, he shall prolong his days, and the pleasure of the LORD shall prosper in his hand. He shall see of the travail of his soul, and shall be satisfied: by his knowledge shall my righteous servant justify many; for he shall bear their iniquities. Therefore will I divide him a portion with the great, and he shall divide the spoil with the strong; because he hath poured out his soul unto death: and he was numbered with the transgressors; and he bare the sin of many, and made intercession for the transgressors.   *53:10-12*

23.97   Sing, O barren, thou that didst not bear; break forth into singing, and cry aloud that that didst not travail with child: for more are the children of the desolate than the children of the married wife, saith the LORD. Enlarge the place of thy tent, and let them stretch forth the curtains of thine habitations: spare not, lengthen thy cords, and strengthen thy stakes.   *54:1-2*

23.98   And all thy children shall be taught of the LORD; and great shall be the peace of thy children.   *54:13*

23.99   Ho, every one that thirsteth, come ye to the waters, and he that hath no money; come ye, buy, and eat; yea, come, buy wine and milk without money and without price. Wherefore do ye spend money for that which is not bread? and your labour for that which satisfieth not?

hearken diligently unto me, and eat ye that which is good, and let your soul delight itself in fatness. Incline your ear, and come unto me: hear, and your soul shall live; and I will make an everlasting convenant with you, even the sure mercies of David.   *55:1-3*

23.100   Seek ye the LORD while he may be found, call ye upon him while he is near.   *55:6*

23.101   Let the wicked forsake his way, and the unrighteous man his thoughts: and let him return unto the LORD, and he will have mercy upon him; and to our God, for he will abundantly pardon.   *55:7*

23.102   For my thoughts are not your thoughts, neither are your ways my ways, saith the LORD. For as the heavens are higher than the earth, so are my ways higher than your ways, and my thoughts than your thoughts.   *55:8-9*

23.103   For as the rain cometh down, and the snow from heaven, and returneth not thither, but watereth the earth, and maketh it bring forth and bud, that it may give seed to the sower, and bread to the eater: So shall my word be that goeth forth out of my mouth: it shall not return unto me void, but it shall accomplish that which I please, and it shall prosper in the thing whereto I sent it.   *55:10-11*

23.104   For ye shall go out with joy, and be led forth with peace: the mountains and the hills shall break forth before you into singing, and all the trees of the field shall clap their hands.   *55:12*

23.105   Instead of the thorn shall come up the fir tree, and instead of the brier shall come up the myrtle tree: and it shall be to the LORD for a name, for an everlasting sign that shall not be cut off.   *55:13*

23.106   Even unto them will I give in mine house and within my walls a place and a name better than of sons and of

daughters: I will give them an everlasting name, that shall not be cut off.   *56:5*

23.107   For thus saith the high and lofty One that inhabiteth eternity, whose name is Holy; I dwell in the high and holy place, with him also that is of a contrite and humble spirit, to revive the spirit of the humble, and to revive the heart of the contrite ones.   *57:15*

23.108   I create the fruit of the lips; Peace, peace to him that is far off, and to him that is near, saith the LORD; and I will heal him.   *57:19*

23.109   There is no peace, saith my God, to the wicked.   *57:21*

No peace for the wicked

There is no peace for the wicked *is often used ironically as a mild comment when one is under pressure or has to do something that one does not want to do. The expression comes originally from this verse in Isaiah: anxiety and fear are experienced by those who do evil.*

23.110   Is it such a fast that I have chosen? a day for a man to afflict his soul? is it to bow down his head as a bulrush, and to spread sackcloth and ashes under him? wilt thou call this a fast, and an acceptable day to the LORD?   *58:5*

23.111   Is not this the fast that I have chosen? to loose the bands of wickedness, to undo the heavy burdens, and to let the oppressed go free, and that ye break every yoke? Is it not to deal thy bread to the hungry, and that thou bring the poor that are cast out to thy house? when thou seest the naked, that thou cover him; and that thou hide not thyself from thine own flesh?   *58:6-7*

23.112   Then shall thy light break forth as the morning, and thine health shall spring forth speedily: and thy righteousness shall go before thee; the glory of the LORD shall be thy rereward.   *58:8*

23.113   And if thou draw out thy soul to the hungry, and satisfy the afflicted soul; then shall thy light rise in obscurity, and thy darkness be as the noonday: And the LORD shall guide thee continually, and satisfy thy soul in drought, and make fat thy bones: and thou shalt be like a watered garden, and like a spring of water, whose waters fail not.   *58:10-11*

23.114   If thou turn away thy foot from the sabbath, from doing thy pleasure on my holy day; and call the sabbath a delight, the holy of the LORD, honourable; and shalt honour him, not doing thine own ways, nor finding thine own pleasure, nor speaking thine own words: Then shalt thou delight thyself in the LORD; and I will cause thee to ride upon the high places of the earth, and feed thee with the heritage of Jacob thy father: for the mouth of the LORD hath spoken it.   *58:13-14*

23.115   Behold, the LORD'S hand is not shortened, that it cannot save; neither his ear heavy, that it cannot hear: But your iniquities have separated between you and your God, and your sins have hid his face from you, that he will not hear.   *59:1-2*

23.116   For he put on righteousness as a breastplate, and an helmet of salvation upon his head; and he put on the garments of vengeance for clothing, and was clad with zeal as a cloke.   *59:17*

23.117   And the Redeemer shall come to Zion, and unto them that turn from transgression in Jacob, saith the LORD. *59:20*

23.118   Arise, shine; for thy light is come, and the glory of the LORD is risen upon thee. For, behold, the darkness shall cover the earth, and gross darkness the people: but the LORD shall arise upon thee, and his glory shall be seen upon thee. And the Gentiles shall come to thy light, and kings to the brightness of thy rising.   *60:1-3*

23.119   Violence shall no more be heard in thy land, wasting nor destruction within thy borders; but thou shalt call thy walls Salvation, and thy gates Praise. The sun shall be no more thy light by day; neither for brightness shall the moon give light unto thee: but the LORD shall be unto thee an everlasting light, and thy God thy glory. Thy sun shall no more go down; neither shall thy moon withdraw itself: for the LORD shall be thine everlasting light, and the days of thy mourning shall be ended.   *60:18-20*

23.120   The Spirit of the Lord GOD is upon me; because the LORD hath anointed me to preach good tidings unto the meek; he hath sent me, to bind up the brokenhearted, to proclaim liberty to the captives, and the opening of the prison to them that are bound; To proclaim the acceptable year of the LORD, and the day of vengeance of our God; to comfort all that mourn; To appoint unto them that mourn in Zion, to give unto them beauty for ashes, the oil of joy for mourninng, the garment of praise for the spirit of heaviness; that they might be called trees of righteousness, the planting of the LORD, that he might be glorified. *61:1-3*

23.121   I will greatly rejoice in the LORD, my soul shall be joyful in my God; for he hath clothed me with the garments of salvation, he hath covered me with the robe of righteousness, as a bridegroom decketh himself with ornaments, and as a bride adorneth herself with her jewels. For as the earth bringeth forth her bud, and as the garden causeth the things that are sown in it to spring forth; so the Lord GOD will cause righteousness and praise to spring forth before all the nations. *61:10-11*

23.122   For Zion's sake will I not hold my peace, and for Jerusalem's sake I will not rest, until the righteousness thereof go forth as brightness, and that salvation thereof as a lamp that burneth. And the Gentiles shall see thy righteousness, and all kings thy glory: and thou shalt be called by a new name, which the mouth of the LORD shall name. Thou shalt also be a crown of glory in the hand of the LORD, and a royal diadem in the hand of thy God. Thou shalt no more be termed Forsaken, neither shall thy land any more be termed Desolate: but thou shalt be called Hephzibah, and thy land Beulah: for the LORD delighteth in thee, and thy land shall be married.   *62:1-4*

23.123   And they shall call them, The holy people, The redeemed of the LORD: and thou shalt be called, Sought out, A city not forsaken.   *62:12*

23.124   In all their affliction he was afflicted, and the angel of his presence saved them: in his love and in his pity he redeemed them; and he bare them, and carried them all the days of old.   *63:9*

23.125   Oh that thou wouldest rend the heavens, that thou wouldest come down, that the mountains might flow down at thy presence.   *64:1*

23.126   But we are all as an unclean thing, and all our righteousnesses are as filthy rags; and we all do fade as a leaf; and our iniquities, like the wind, have taken us away.   *64:6*

Holier than thou

People who are holier-than-thou *behave towards others in a way that shows they think they are better, especially more moral or virtuous, than others. The origin of this phrase lies in this verse. Isaiah was prophesying against the self-righteousness of some who smugly claimed to be superior to others.*

23.127   Which say, Stand by thyself, come not near to me; for I am holier than thou. These are a smoke in my nose, a fire that burneth all the day.   *65:5*

23.128   Thus saith the LORD, As the new wine is found in the cluster, and one saith, Destroy it not; for a blessing is in it: so will I do for my servants' sakes, that I may not destroy them all.   *65:8*

23.129   For, behold, I create new heavens and a new earth: and the former shall not be remembered, nor come into mind. *65:17*

23.130   The wolf and the lamb shall feed together, and the lion shall eat straw like the bullock: and dust shall be the serpent's meat. They shall not hurt nor destroy in all my holy mountain, saith the LORD. *65:25*

23.131   As one whom his mother comforteth, so will I comfort you; and ye shall be comforted in Jerusalem.   *66:13*

23.132   For, behold, the LORD will come with fire, and with his chariots like a whirlwind, to render his anger with fury, and his rebuke with flames of fire. For by fire and by his sword will the LORD plead with all flesh: and the slain of the LORD shall be many.   *66:15-16*

JEREMIAH

24.1   Then the word of the LORD came unto me, saying, Before I formed thee in the belly I knew thee; and before thou camest forth out of the womb I sanctified thee, and I ordained thee a prophet unto the nations. Then said I, Ah, Lord GOD! behold, I cannot speak: for I am a child. *1:4-6*

24.2   But the LORD said unto me, Say not, I am a child: for thou shalt go to all that I shall send thee, and whatsoever I command thee thou shalt speak. Be not afraid of their faces: for I am with thee to deliver thee, saith the LORD. Then the LORD put forth his hand, and touched my mouth. And the LORD said unto me, Behold, I have put my words in thy mouth. See, I have this day set thee over the nations and over the kingdoms, to root out, and to pull down, and to destroy, and to throw down, to build, and to plant. *1:7-10*

24.3　Then said the LORD unto me, Thou hast well seen: for I will hasten my word to perform it. *1:12*

24.4　For my people have committed two evils; they have forsaken me the fountain of living waters, and hewed them out cisterns, broken cisterns, that can hold no water. *2:13*

24.5　Thine own wickedness shall correct thee, and thy backslidings shall reprove thee: know therefore and see that it is an evil thing and bitter, that thou hast forsaken the LORD thy God, and that my fear is not in thee, saith the Lord GOD of hosts. *2:19*

24.6　But thou hast played the harlot with many lovers; yet return again to me, saith the LORD. *3:1*

24.7　Turn, O backsliding children, saith the LORD; for I am married unto you: and I will take you one of a city, and two of a family, and I will bring you to Zion: *3:14*

24.8　And thou shalt swear, The LORD liveth, in truth, in judgment, and in righteousness; and the nations shall bless themselves in him, and in him shall they glory. *4:2*

24.9　Circumcise yourselves to the LORD, and take away the foreskins of your heart, ye men of Judah and inhabitants of Jerusalem: lest my fury come forth like fire, and burn that none can quench it, because of the evil of your doings. *4:4*

24.10　Run ye to and fro through the streets of Jerusalem, and see now, and know, and seek in the broad places thereof, if ye can find a man, if there be any that executeth judgment, that seeketh the truth; and I will pardon it. *5:1*

24.11　But this people hath a revolting and a rebellious heart; they are revolted and gone. *5:23*

24.12　The prophets prophesy falsely, and the priests bear rule by their means; and my people love to have it so: and what will ye do in the end thereof? *5:31*

24.13　For from the least of them even unto the greatest of them every one is given to covetousness; and from the prophet even unto the priest every one dealeth falsely. They have healed also the hurt of the daughter of my people slightly, saying, Peace, peace; when there is no peace. *6:13-14*

24.14　Thus saith the LORD, Stand ye in the ways, and see, and ask for the old paths, where is the good way, and walk therein, and ye shall find rest for your souls. But they said, We will not walk therein. *6:16*

24.15　Is this house, which is called by my name, become a den of robbers in your eyes? Behold, even I have seen it, saith the LORD. *7:11*

24.16　We looked for peace, but no good came; and for a time of health, and behold trouble! *8:15*

24.17　The harvest is past, the summer is ended, and we are not saved. *8:20*

24.18　Is there no balm in Gilead; is there no physician there? why then is not the health of the daughter of my people recovered? *8:22*

24.19　And they will deceive every one his neighbour, and will not speak the truth: they have taught their tongue to speak lies, and weary themselves to commit iniquity. *9:5*

24.20　Thus saith the LORD, Let not the wise man glory in his wisdon, neither let the mighty man glory in his might, let not the rich man glory in his riches: But let him that glorieth glory in this, that he understandeth and knoweth me, that I am the LORD which exercise lovingkindness, judgment, and righteousness, in the earth: for in these things I delight, saith the LORD.   *9:23-24*

24.21   Can the Ethiopian change his skin, or the leopard his spots? then may ye also do good, that are accustomed to do evil.   *13:23*

The leopard cannot change his spots

The saying the leopard cannot change his spots *means that the basic character or nature of a person or institution cannot be changed. The expression derives from one of Jeremiah's warnings of judgment against Judah.*

24.22   Then the LORD said unto me, The prophets prophesy lies in my name: I sent them not, neither have I commanded them, neither spake unto them: they prophesy unto you a false vision and divination, and a thing of nought, and the deceit of their heart.   *14:14*

24.23   Woe is me, my mother, that thou hast borne me a man of strife and a men of contention to the whole earth! I have neither lent on usury, nor men have lent to me on usury; yet every one of them doth curse me.   *15:10*

24.24   The heart is deceitful above all things, and desperately wicked: who can know it? I the LORD search the heart, I try the reins, even to give every man according to his ways, and according to the fruit of his doings.   *17:9-10*

24.25   O LORD, the hope of Israel, all that forsake thee shall be ashamed, and they that depart from me shall be written in the earth, because they have forsaken the LORD, the fountain of living waters.   *17:13*

24.26   Heal me, O LORD, and I shall be healed; save me, and I shall be saved: for thou art my praise.   *17:14*

24.27   Then I said, I will not make mention of him, nor speak any more in his name: But his word was in mine heart as a burning fire shut up in my bones, and I was weary with forbearing, and I could not stay.   *20:9*

24.28   Cursed be the day wherein I was born: let not the day wherein my mother bare me be blessed. Cursed be the man who brought tidings to my father, saying, A man child is born unto thee; making him very glad.   *20:14-15*

24.29   Behold, the days come, saith the LORD, that I will raise unto David a righteous Branch, and a King shall reign and prosper, and shall execute judgment and justice in the earth. In his days Judah shall be saved, and Israel shall dwell safely: and this is his name whereby he shall be called, THE LORD OUR RIGHTEOUSNESS.   *23:5-6*

24.30   Is not my word like as a fire? saith the LORD; and like a hammer that breaketh the rock in pieces?   *23:29*

24.31   And ye shall seek me, and find me, when ye shall search for me with all your heart. And I will be found of you, saith the LORD: and I will turn away your captivity, and I will gather you from all the nations, and from all the places whither I have driven you, saith the LORD; and I will bring you again into the place whence I caused you to be carried away captive.   *29:13-14*

24.32   The LORD hath appeared of old unto me, saying, Yea, I have loved thee with an everlasting love: therefore with lovingkindness have I drawn thee.   *31:3*

24.33   Hear the word of the LORD, O ye nations, and declare it in the isles afar off, and say, He that scattered Israel will gather him, and keep him, as a shepherd doth his flock.   *31:10*

24.34   Thus saith the LORD; A voice was heard in Ramah, lamentation, and bitter weeping; Rahel weeping for her children refused to be comforted for her children, because they were not. *31:15*

24.35   Behold, the days come, saith the LORD, that I will make a new covenant with the house of Israel, and with the house of Judah: Not according to the convenant that I made with their fathers in the day that I took them by the hand to bring them out of the land of Egypt; which my convenant they brake, although I was an husband unto them saith the LORD: But this shall be the convenant that I will make with the house of Israel; After those days, saith the LORD, I will put my law in their inward parts, and write it in their hearts; and will be their God, and they shall be my people. And they shall teach no more every man his neighbour, and every man his brother, saying, Know the LORD: for they shall all know me, from the least of them unto the greatest of them, saith the LORD: for I will forgive their iniquity, and I will remember their sin no more. *31:31-34*

24.36   And I will make an everlasting covenant with them, that I will not turn away from them, to do them good; but I will put my fear in their hearts, that they shall not depart from me. *32:40*

24.37   In those days and at that time, will I cause the Branch of righteousness to grow up unto David; and he shall execute judgment and righteousness in the land. In those days shall Judah be saved, and Jerusalem shall dwell safely: and this is the name wherewith she shall be called, The LORD our righteousness. *33:15-16*

24.38   I have sent also unto you all my servants the prophets, rising up early and sending them, saying, Return ye now every man from his evil way, and amend your doings, and go not after other gods to serve them, and ye shall dwell in the land which I have given to you and to your fathers: but ye have not inclined your ear, nor hearkened unto me. *35:15*

24.39   And seekest thou great things for thyself? seek them not: for, behold, I will bring evil upon all flesh, saith the LORD: but thy life will I give unto thee for a prey in all places whither thou goest. *45:5*

24.40   How say ye, We are mighty and strong men for the war? *48:14*

24.41   In those days, and in that time, saith the LORD, the children of Israel shall come, they and the children of Judah together, going and weeping: they shall go, and seek the LORD their God. *50:4*

24.42   In those days, and in that time, saith the LORD, the iniquity of Israel shall be sought for, and there shall be none; and the sins of Judah, and they shall not be found: for I will pardon them whom I reserve. *50:20*

24.43   Their Redeemer is strong; the LORD of hosts is his name: he shall throughly plead their cause, that he may give rest to the land, and disquiet the inhabitants of Babylon. *50:34*

24.44   Thus saith the LORD; Behold, I will raise up against Babylon, and against them that dwell in the midst of them that rise up against me, a destroying wind. *51:1*

LAMENTATIONS

25.1   How doth the city sit solitary, that was full of people! how is she become as a widow! she that was great among the nations, and princess among the provinces, how is she become tributary! *1:1*

25.2   Is it nothing to you, all ye that pass by? behold, and see if there be any sorrow like unto my sorrow, which is done unto me, wherewith the LORD hath afflicted me in the day of his fierce anger. *1:12*

25.3   And thou hast removed my soul far off from peace: I forgat prosperity. *3:17*

25.4   And I said, My strength and my hope is perished from the LORD: Remembering mine affliction and my misery, the wormwood and the gall. *3:18-19*

Gall and wormwood

Something that is gall and wormwood *to someone is an experience that causes intense bitterness. The origin of the expression is Jeremiah's cry of affliction. Gall is the bitter secretion of the liver; wormwood is a plant with a very bitter taste that is used in making the liqueur absinthe.*

25.5   This I recall to my mind therefore have I hope. It is of the LORD'S mercies that we are not consumed, because his compassions fail not. They are new every morning: great is thy faithfulness. *3:21-23*

25.6   The LORD is my portion saith my soul; therefore will I hope in him. The LORD is good unto them that wait for him, to the soul that seeketh him. It is good that a man should both hope and quietly wait for the salvation of the LORD. *3:24-26*

25.7   It is good for a man that he bear the yoke in his youth. *3:27*

25.8   He giveth his cheek to him that smiteth him: he is filled full with reproach. *3:30*

25.9   For he doth not afflict willingly nor grieve the children of men. *3:33*

25.10   Waters flowed over mine head; then I said, I am cut off. *3:54*

EZEKIEL

26.1   Also out of the midst thereof came the likeness of four living creatures. And this was their appearance;they had the likeness of a man. And every one had four faces, and every one had four wings. *1:5-6*

26.2   Now as I beheld the living creatures, behold one wheel upon the earth by the living creatures, with his four faces. The appearance of the wheels and their work was like unto the colour of a beryl: and they four had one likeness: and their appearance and their work was as it were a wheel in the middle of a wheel. *1:15-16*

Wheels within wheels

The expression wheels within wheels *is used to describe a complex series of several different interrelated influences or issues. This phrase comes from the description of Ezekiel's vision of the living creatures and the glory of God.*

26.3   And above the firmament that was over their heads was the likeness of a throne, as the appearance of a sapphire stone: and upon the likeness of the throne was the likeness as the appearance of a man above upon it. And I saw as the colour of amber, as the appearance of fire round about within it, from the appearance of his loins even upward, and from the appearance of his loins even downward, I saw as it were the appearance of fire, and it had brightness round about. As the appearance of the bow that is in the cloud in the day of rain, so was the appearance of the brightness round about. This was the appearance of the likeness of the glory of the LORD. And when I saw it, I fell upon my face, and I heard a voice of one that spake. *1:26-28*

26.4   And he said unto me, Son of man, stand upon thy feet, and I will speak unto thee. And the spirit entered into me when he spake unto me, and set me upon my feet, that I heard him that spake unto me. And he said unto me, Son of man, I send thee to the children of Israel, to a rebellious nation that hath rebelled against me: they and their fathers have transgressed against me, even unto this very day. *2:1-3*

26.5 And thou, son of man, be not afraid of them, neither be afraid of their words, though briers and thorns be with thee, and thou dost dwell among scorpions: be not afraid of their words, nor be dismayed at their looks, though they be a rebellious house. And thou shalt speak my words unto them, whether they will hear, or whether they will forbear: for they are most rebellious. But thou, son of man, hear what I say unto thee; Be not thou rebellious like that rebellious house: open thy mouth, and eat that I give thee. *2:6-8*

26.6 And he said unto me, Son of man, cause thy belly to eat, and fill thy bowels with this roll that I give thee. Then did I eat it; and it was in my mouth as honey for sweetness. *3:3*

26.7 For thou art not sent to a people of a strange speech and of an hard language, but to the house of Israel; Not many people of a strange speech and of an hard language, whose words thou canst not understand. Surely, had I sent thee to them, they would have hearkened unto thee. *3:5-6*

26.8 Son of man, I have made thee a watchman unto the house of Israel: therefore hear the word at my mouth, and give them warning from me. *3:17*

26.9 And I will make thy tongue cleave to the roof of thy mouth, that thou shalt be dumb, and shalt not be to them a reprover: for they are a rebellious house. *3:26*

26.10 And I will give them one heart, and I will put a new spirit within you; and I will take the stony heart out of their flesh, and will give them an heart of flesh. *11:19*

26.11 Son of man, thou dwellest in the midst of a rebellious house, which have eyes to see, and see not; they have ears to hear, and hear not: for they are a rebellious house. *12:2*

26.12 Son of man, eat thy bread with quaking, and drink thy water with trembling and with carefulness. *12:18*

26.13 Son of man, what is that proverb that ye have in the land of Israel, saying, The days are prolonged, and every vision faileth? *12:22*

26.14 Because, even because they have seduced my people, saying, Peace; and there was no peace; and one built up a wall, and, lo, others daubed it with untempered morter. *13:10*

26.15 What mean ye, that ye use this proverb concerning the land of Israel, saying, The fathers have eaten sour grapes, and the children's teeth are set on edge? *18:2*

26.16 Behold, all souls are mine; as the soul of the father, so also the soul of the son is mine: the soul that sinneth, it shall die. *18:4*

26.17 Have I any pleasure at all that the wicked should die? saith the Lord GOD: and not that he should return from his ways, and live? *18:23*

26.18 Yet ye say, The way of the Lord is not equal. Hear now, O house of Israel; Is not my way equal? are not your ways unequal? *18:27*

26.19 Again, when the wicked man turneth away from his wickedness that he hath committed, and doeth that which is lawful and right, he shall save his soul alive. *18:27*

26.20 I will accept you with your sweet savour, when I bring you out from the people, and gather you out of the countries wherein ye have been scattered; and I will be sanctified in you before the heathen. And ye shall know that I am the LORD, when I shall bring you into the land of Israel, into the country for the which I lifted up mine hand to give it to your fathers. And there shall ye remember your ways, and all your doings, wherein ye have been defiled; and ye shall loath yourselves in your own sight for all your evils that ye have committed. _20:41-43_

26.21   And say to the land of Israel, Thus saith the LORD; Behold, I am against thee, and will draw forth my sword out of his sheath, and will cut off from thee the righteous and the wicked. _21:3_

26.22   Neither left she her whoredoms brought from Egypt: for in her youth they lay with her, and they bruised the breasts of her virginity, and poured their whoredom upon her. Wherefore I have delivered her into the hand of her lovers, into the hand of the Assyrians, upon whom she doted. _23:8-9_

26.23   It shall be a place for the spreading of nets in the midst of the sea: for I have spoken it, saith the Lord GOD: and it shall become a spoil to the nations. _26:5_

26.24   Speak, and say, Thus saith the Lord GOD; Behold, I am against thee, Pharaoh king of Egypt, the great dragon that lieth in the midst of his rivers, which hath said, My river is mine own, and I have made it for myself. _29:3_

26.25   So thou, O son of man, I have set thee a watchman unto the house of Israel; therefore thou shalt hear the word at my mouth, and warn them from me. When I say unto the wicked, O wicked man, thou shalt surely die; if thou dost not speak to warn the wicked from his way, that wicked man shall die in his iniquity; but his blood will I require at thine hand. Nevertheless, if thou warn the wicked of his way to turn from it; if he do not turn from his way, he shall die in his iniquity; but thou hast delivered thy soul. _33:7-9_

26.26   Say unto them, As I live, saith the Lord GOD, I have no pleasure in the death of the wicked; but that the wicked turn from his way and live: turn ye, turn ye from your evil ways; for why will ye die, O house of Israel? _33:11_

26.27   And they come unto thee as the people cometh, and they sit before thee as my people, and they hear thy words, but they will not do them: for with their mouth they shew much love, but their heart goeth after their covetousness. _33:31_

26.28   And the word of the LORD came unto me, saying, Son of man, prophesy against the shepherds of Israel, prophesy, and say unto them, Thus saith the Lord GOD unto the shepherds; Woe be to the shepherds of Israel that do feed themselves! should not the shepherds feed the flocks. _34:1-2_

26.29   My sheep wandered through all the mountains, and upon every high hill: yea, my flock was scattered upon all the face of the earth, and none did search or seek after them. _34:6_

26.30   For thus saith the Lord GOD; Behold, I, even I, will both search my sheep, and seek them out. As a shepherd seeketh out his flock in the day that he is among his sheep that are scattered; so will I seek out my sheep, and will deliver them out of all places where they have been scattered in the cloudy and dark day. And I will bring them out from the people, and gather them from the countries, and will bring them to their own land, and feed them upon the mountains of Israel by the rivers, and in all the inhabited places of the country. I will feed them in a good pasture, and upon the high mountains of Israel shall their fold be: there shall they lie in a good fold, and in a fat pasture shall they feed upon the mountains of Israel. I will feed my flock, and I will cause them to lie down, saith the Lord GOD. I will seek that which was lost, and bring again that which was driven away, and will bind up that which was broken, and will strengthen that which was sick: but I will destroy the fat and the strong; I will feed them with judgment. _34:11-16_

26.31   And I will set up one shepherd over them, and he shall feed them, even my servant David; he shall feed them, and he shall be their shepherd. And I the LORD will be their God, and my servant David a prince among them; I the LORD have spoken it. *34:23-24*

26.32 Then will I sprinkle clean water upon you, and ye shall be clean: from all your filthiness, and from all your idols, will I cleanse you; A new heart also will I give you, and a new spirit will I put within you: and I will take away the stony heart out of your flesh, and I will give you an heart of flesh. And I will put my spirit within you, and cause you to walk in my statutes, and ye shall keep my judgments, and do them. And ye shall dwell in the land that I gave to your fathers; and ye shall be my people, and I will be your God. *36:25-28*

26.33 The hand of the LORD was upon me, and carried me out in the spirit of the LORD, and set me down in the midst of the valley which was full of bones, And caused me to pass by them round about: and, behold, there were very many in the open valley; and, lo, they were very dry. And he said unto me, Son of man, can these bones live? And I answered, O Lord GOD, thou knowest. Again he said unto me, Prophesy upon these bones, and say unto them, O ye dry bones, hear the word of the LORD. Thus saith the Lord GOD unto these bones; Behold, I will cause breath to enter into you, and ye shall live: And I will lay sinews upon you, and will bring up flesh upon you, and cover you with skin, and put breath in you, and ye shall live; and ye shall know that I am the LORD. So I prophesied as I was commanded: and as I prophesied, there was a noise, and behold a shaking, and the bones came together, bone to his bone. And when I beheld, lo, the sinews and the flesh came up upon them, and the skin covered them above: but there was no breath in them. Then said he unto me, Prophesy unto the wind, prophesy, son of man, and say to the wind, Thus saith the Lord GOD; Come from the four winds, O breath, and breathe upon these slain, that they may live. So I prophesied

as he commanded me, and the breath came into them, and they lived, and stood up upon their feet, an exceeding great army. *37:1-10*

> ### The valley of dry bones
> *Ezekiel's vision of the valley of dry bones is a remarkable story. Israel was in a state of despair in exile, having been punished by God for sin. Yet the vision of the prophet showed a message of restoration, a promise of new life given by God's Spirit. God would revive his people.*

26.34 Then he said unto me, Son of man, these bones are the whole house of Israel: behold, they say, Our bones are dried, and our hope is lost: we are cut off for our parts. Therefore prophesy and say unto them, Thus saith the Lord GOD; Behold, O my people, I will open your graves, and cause you to come up out of your graves, and bring you into the land of Israel. And ye shall know that I am the LORD, when I have opened your graves, O my people, and brought you up out of your graves, And shall put my spirit in you, and ye shall live, and I shall place you in your own land: then shall ye know that I the LORD have spoken it, and performed it, saith the LORD. *37:11-14*

26.35 And David my servant shall be king over them; and they all shall have one shepherd: they shall also walk in my judgments, and observe my statutes, and do them. *37:24*

26.36 Afterward he brought me to the gate, even the gate that looketh toward the east: And, behold, the glory of the God of Israel came from the way of the east: and his voice was like a noise of many waters: and the earth shined with his glory. And it was according to the appearance of the vision which I saw, even according to the vision that I saw when I came to destroy the city: and the visions were like the vision that I saw by the river Chebar; and I fell upon my face. And the glory of the LORD came into the house by the way of the gate whose prospect is toward the east. So the spirit took me up, and brought me into the inner court; and, behold, the glory of the LORD filled the house.　*43:1-5*

26.37　It was round about eighteen thousand measures: and the name of the city from that day shall be, The LORD is there.　*48:35*

DANIEL

27.1　Children in whom was no blemish, but well favoured, and skilful in all wisdom, and cunning in knowledge, and understanding science, and such as had ability in them to stand in the king's palace, and whom they might teach the learning and the tongue of the Chaldeans. And the king appointed them a daily provision of the king's meat, and of the wine which he drank: so nourishing them three years, that at the end thereof they might stand before the king.　*1:4-5*

27.2　But Daniel purposed in his heart that he would not defile himself with the portion of the king's meat, nor with the wine which he drank: therefore he requested of the prince of the eunuchs that he might not defile himself.　*1:8*

27.3　As for these four children, God gave them knowledge and skill in all learning and wisdom: and Daniel had understanding in all visions and dreams.　*1:17*

27.4　Then spake the Chaldeans to the king in Syriack, O king, live for ever: tell thy servants the dream, and we will shew the interpretation.　*2:4*

27.5　Then Daniel went to his house, and made the thing known to Hananiah, Mishael, and Azariah, his companions: That they would desire mercies of the God of heaven concerning this secret; that

Daniel and his fellows should not perish with the rest of the wise men of Babylon.　*2:17-18*

27.6　Daniel answered and said, Blessed be the name of God for ever and ever: for wisdom and might are his: And he changeth the times and the seasons: he removeth kings, and setteth up kings: he giveth wisdom unto the wise, and knowledge to them that know understanding: He revealeth the deep and secret things: he knoweth what is in the darkness, and the light dwelleth with him. I thank thee, and praise thee, O thou God of my fathers, who hast given me wisdom and might, and hast made known unto me now what we desired of thee: for thou hast now made known unto us the king's matter.　*2:20-23*

27.7　Daniel answered in the presence of the king, and said, The secret which the king hath demanded cannot the wise men, the astrologers, the magicians, the soothsayers, shew unto the king; But there is a God in heaven that revealeth secrets, and maketh known to the king Nebuchadnezzar what shall be in the latter days. Thy dream, and the visions of thy head upon thy bed, are these:　*2:27-28*

27.8　Thou, O king, sawest, and behold a great image. This great image, whose brightness was excellent, stood before thee; and the form thereof was terrible. This image's head was of fine gold, his breast and his arms of silver, his belly and his thighs of brass. His legs of iron, his feet part of iron and part of clay. Thou sawest till that a stone was cut out without hands, which smote the image upon his feet that were of iron and clay, and brake them to pieces.　*2:31-34*

27.9　And in the days of these kings shall the God of heaven set up a kingdom, which shall never be destroyed: and the kingdom shall not be left to other people, but it shall break in pieces and consume all these kingdoms, and it shall stand for ever.　*2:44*

27.10   The king answered unto Daniel, and said, Of a truth it is, that your God is a God of gods, and a Lord of kings, and a revealer of secrets, seeing thou couldest reveal this secret. Then the king made Daniel a great man, and gave him many great gifts, and made him ruler over the whole province of Babylon, and chief of the governors over all the wise men of Babylon.   *2:47-48*

27.11   Then an herald cried aloud, To you it is commanded, O people, nations, and languages, That at what time ye hear the sound of the cornet, flute, harp, sackbut, psaltery, dulcimer, and all kinds of musick, ye fall down and worship the golden image that Nebuchadnezzar the king hath set up: And whoso falleth not down and worshippeth shall the same hour be cast into the midst of a burning fiery furnace.   *3:4-6*

27.12   Now if ye be ready that at what time ye hear the sound of the cornet, flute, harp, sackbut, psaltery, and dulcimer, and all kinds of musick, ye fall down and worship the image which I have made; well: but if ye worship not, ye shall be cast the same hour into the midst of a burning fiery furnace; and who is that God that shall deliver you out of my hands? Shadrach, Meshach, and Abednego, answered and said to the king, O Nebuchadnezzar, we are not careful to answer thee in this matter.   *3:15-16*

27.13   Then was Nebuchadnezzar full of fury, and the form of his visage was changed against Shadrach, Meshach, and Abednego: therefore he spake, and commanded that they should heat the furnace one seven times more than it was wont to be heated. And he commanded the most mighty men that were in his army to bind Shadrach, Meshach, and Abednego, and to cast them into the burning fiery furnace. Then these men were bound in their coats, their hosen, and their hats, and their other garments, and were cast into the midst of the burning fiery furnace. Therefore because the king's commandment was urgent,

and the furnace exceeding hot, the flame of the fire slew those men that took up Shadrach, Meshach, and Abednego. And these three men, Shadrach, Meshach, and Abednego, fell down bound into the midst of the burning fiery furnace.   *3:19-23*

27.14   Then Nebuchadnezzar the king was astonied, and rose up in haste, and spake, and said unto his counsellers, Did not we cast three men bound into the midst of the fire? They answered and said unto the king, True, O king. He answered and said, Lo, I see four men loose, walking in the midst of the fire, and they have no hurt; and the form of the fourth is like the Son of God. Then Nebuchadnezzar came near to the mouth of the burning fiery furnace, and spake, and said, Shadrach, Meshach, and Abednego, ye servants of the most high God, come forth, and come hither. Then Shadrach, Meshach, and Abednego, came forth of the midst of the fire.   *3:24-26*

27.15   Then Nebuchadnezzar spake, and said, Blessed be the God of Shadrach, Meshach, and Abednego, who hath sent his angel, and delivered his servants that trusted in him, and have changed the king's word, and yielded their bodies, that they might not serve nor worship any god, except their own God.   *3:28*

27.16   While the word was in the king's mouth, there fell a voice from heaven, saying, O king Nebuchadnezzar, to thee it is spoken; The kingdom is departed from thee. And they shall drive thee from men, and thy dwelling shall be with the beasts of the field: they shall make thee to eat grass as oxen, and seven times shall pass over thee, until thou know that the most High ruleth in the kingdom of men, and giveth it to whomsoever he will.   *4:31-32*

27.17   The same hour was the thing fulfilled upon Nebuchadnezzar: and he was driven from men, and did eat grass as oxen, and his body was wet with the dew of heaven, till his hairs were grown like eagles' feathers, and his nails like birds' claws.   *4:33*

27.18   And at the end of the days I Nebuchadnezzar lifted up mine eyes unto heaven, and mine understanding returned unto me, and I blessed the most High, and I praised and honoured him that liveth for ever, whose dominion is an everlasting dominion, and his kingdom is from generation to generation: And all the inhabitants of the earth are reputed as nothing: and he doeth according to his will in the army of heaven, and among the inhabitants of the earth: and none can stay his hand, or say unto him, What doest thou?   *4:34-35*

27.19   Belshazzar the king made a great feast to a thousand of his lords, and drank wine before the thousand.   *5:1*

The writing on the wall

The expression the writing on the wall *refers to the existence of signs that warn of imminent failure or ruin. The phrase alludes to the mysterious inscription that appeared on the wall of the royal place of King Belshazzar, interpreted as describing the king's downfall. One of the words inscribed was* Tekel, *interpreted by Daniel as referring to King Belshazzar's life, that it had been* weighed in the balances *and* found wanting. *This expression has also passed into the language to stand for something that is judged and considered not to come up to a required standard.*

27.20   Then they brought the golden vessels that were taken out of the temple of the house of God which was at Jerusalem; and the king, and his princes, his wives, and his concubines, drank in them. They drank wine, and praised the gods of gold, and of silver, of brass, of iron, of wood, and of stone. In the same hour came forth fingers of a man's hand, and wrote over against the candlestick upon the plaister of the wall of the king's

palace: and the king saw the part of the hand that wrote.   *5:3-5*

27.21   And this is he writing that was written, MENE, MENE, TEKEL, UPHARSIN. This is the interpretation of the thing: MENE; God hath numbered thy kingdom, and finished it, TEKEL; Thou art weighed in the balances, and art found wanting. PERES; Thy kingdom is divided, and given to the Medes and Persians.   *5:25-28*

27.22   Then said these man, We shall not find any occasion against this Daniel, except we find it against him concerning the law of his God.   *6:5*

27.23   Then these presidents and princes assembled together to the king, and said thus unto him, King Darius, live for ever. All the presidents of the kingdom, the governors, and the princes, the counsellers, and the captains, have consulted together to establish a royal statute, and to make a firm decree, that whosoever shall ask a petition of any God or man for thirty days, save of thee, O king, he shall be cast into the den of lions. Now, O king, establish the decree, and sign the writing, that it be not changed, according to the law of the Medes and Persians, which altereth not.   *6:6-8*

27.24   Then the king commanded, and they brought Daniel, and cast him into the den of lions. Now the king spake and said unto Daniel, Thy God whom thou servest continually, he will deliver thee.   *6:16*

27.25   My God hath sent his angel, and hath shut the lions' mouths, that they have not hurt me: forasmuch as before him innocencey was found in me; and also before thee, O king, have I done no hurt.   *6:22*

27.26   And four great beasts came up from the sea, diverse one from another.   *7:3*

27.27   I beheld till the thrones were cast down, and the Ancient of days did sit, whose garment was white as snow, and the hair of his head like the pure wool: his throne was like the fiery flame, and his wheels as burning fire. A fiery stream issued and came forth from before him: thousand thousands ministered unto him, and ten thousand times ten thousand stood before him: the judgment was set, and the books were opened. *7:9-10*

27.28   I saw in the night visions and, behold, one like the Son of man came with the clouds of heaven, and came to the Ancient of days, and they brought him near before him. And there was given him dominion, and glory, and a kingdom, that all people, nations, and languages, should serve him: his dominion is an everlasting dominion, which shall not pass away, and his kingdom that which shall not be destroyed.   *7:13-14*

27.29   Until the Ancient of days came, and judgment was given to the saints of the most High; and the time came that the saints possessed the kingdom.   *7:22*

27.30   Now therefore, O our God, hear the prayer of thy servant, and his supplications, and cause thy face to shine upon thy sanctuary that is desolate, for the Lord's sake. O my God, incline thine ear, and hear; open thine eyes, and behold our desolations, and the city which is called by thy name: for we do not present our supplications before thee for our righteousnesses, but for thy great mercies. O Lord, hear; O Lord, forgive; O Lord, hearken and do; defer not, for thine own sake, O my God: for thy city and thy people are called by thy name. *9:17-19*

27.31   Seventy weeks are determined upon thy people and upon thy holy city, to finish the transgression, and to make an end of sins, and to make reconciliation for iniquity, and to bring in everlasting righteousness, and to seal up the vision and prophecy, and to anoint the most Holy.   *9:24*

27.32   And he said unto me, O Daniel, a man greatly beloved, understand the words that I speak unto thee, and stand upright: for unto thee am I now sent. And when he had spoken this word unto me, I stood trembling.   *10:11*

27.33   And at that time shall Michael stand up, the great prince which standeth for the children of thy people: and there shall be a time of trouble, such as never was since there was a nation even to that same time: and at that time thy people shall be delivered, every one that shall be found written in the book. And many of them that sleep in the dust of the earth shall awake, some to everlasting life, and some to shame and everlasting contempt. And they that be wise shall shine as the brightness of the firmament; and they that turn many to righteousness as the stars for ever and ever. But thou, O Daniel, shut up the words, and seal the book, even to the time of the end: many shall run to and fro, and knowledge shall be increased.   *12:1-4*

HOSEA

28.1   The beginning of the word of the LORD by Hosea. And the LORD said to Hosea, Go, take unto thee a wife of whoredoms and children of whoredoms: for the land hath committed great whoredom, departing from the LORD. *1:2*

28.2   Yet the number of the children of Israel shall be as the sand of the sea, which cannot be measured nor numbered; and it shall come to pass, that in the place where it was said unto them, Ye are not my people, there it shall be said unto them, Ye are the sons of the living God.   *1:10*

28.3   And I will visit upon her the days of Baalim, wherein she burned incense to them, and she decked herself with her earrings and her jewels, and she went after her lovers, and forgat me, saith the LORD.   *2:13*

28.4 And I will betroth thee unto me for ever; yea, I will betroth thee unto me in righteousness, and in judgment, and in lovingkindness, and in mercies. I will even betroth thee unto me in faithfulness: and thou shalt know the LORD.   *2:19-20*

28.5 My people are destroyed for lack of knowledge: because thou hast rejected knowledge, I will also reject thee, that thou shalt be no priest to me: seeing thou hast forgotten the law of thy God, I will also forget thy children.   *4:6*

28.6 Come, and let us return unto the LORD: for he hath torn, and he will heal us; he hath smitten, and he will bind us up. After two days will he revive us: in the third day he will raise us up, and we shall live in his sight. Then shall we know, if we follow on to know the LORD: his going forth is prepared as the morning; and he shall come unto us as the rain, as the latter and former rain unto the earth. O Ephraim, what shall I do unto thee? O Judah, what shall I do unto thee? for your goodness is as a morning cloud, and as the early dew it goeth away.   *6:1-4*

Sow the wind and reap the whirlwind

The expression sow the wind and reap the whirlwind *means to do something that appears harmless but leads to the suffering of unforeseen disastrous consequences. The source of this expression lies in Hosea's prophecy: Israel had sowed the wind of idolatry and would reap the whirlwind of an Assyrian invasion.*

28.7 For I desired mercy, and not sacrifice; and the knowledge of God more than burnt offerings.   *6:6*

28.8 For they have sown the wind, and they shall reap the whirlwind: it hath no

stalk: the bud shall yield no meal: if so be it yield, the strangers shall swallow it up.   *8:7*

28.9 When Israel was a child, then I loved him, and called my son out of Egypt.   *11:1*

28.10 I drew them with cords of a man, with bands of love: and I was to them as they that take off the yoke on their jaws, and I laid meat unto them.   *11:4*

28.11 How shall I give thee up, Ephraim: how shall I deliver thee, Israel? how shall I make thee as Admah? how shall I set thee as Zeboim? mine heart is turned within me, my repentings are kindled together.   *11:8*

28.12 Therefore they shall be as the morning cloud, and as the early dew that passeth away, as the chaff that is driven with the whirlwind out of the floor, and as the smoke out of the chimney.   *13:3*

28.13 I will ransom them from the power of the grave; I will redeem them from death: O death, I will be thy plagues; O grave, I will be thy destruction: repentance shall be hid from mine eyes.   *13:14*

28.14 I will heal their backsliding, I will love them freely: for mine anger is turned away from him.   *14:4*

JOEL

29.1 That which the palmerworm hath left hath the locust eaten: and that which the locust hath left hath the cankerworm eaten; and that which the cankerworm hath left hath the caterpiller eaten.   *1:4*

29.2 Blow ye the trumpet in Zion, and sound an alarm in my holy mountain: let all the inhabitants of the land tremble: for the day of the LORD cometh, for it is nigh at hand.   *2:1*

29.3   A fire devoureth before them; and behind them a flame burneth: the land is as the garden of Eden before them, and behind them a desolate wilderness; yea, and nothing shall escape them.   *2:3*

29.4   The earth shall quake before them; the heavens shall tremble: the sun and the moon shall be dark, and the stars shall withdraw their shining: And the LORD shall utter his voice before his army: for his camp is very great: for he is strong that executeth his word: for the day of the LORD is great and very terrible; and who can abide it?   *2:10-11*

29.5   Therefore also now, saith the LORD, turn ye even to me with all your heart, and with fasting, and with weeping, and with mourning: And rend your heart, and not your garments, and turn unto the LORD your God: for he is gracious and merciful, slow to anger, and of great kindness, and repenteth him of the evil. Who knoweth if he will return and repent, and leave a blessing behind him; even a meat offering and a drink offering unto the LORD your God? *2:12-14*

29.6   And I will restore to you the years that the locust hath eaten, the cankerworm, and the caterpiller, and the palmerworm, my great army which I sent among you. And ye shall eat in plenty, and be satisfied, and praise the name of the LORD your God, that hath dealt wondrously with you: and my people shall never be ashamed.   *2:25-26*

29.7   And it shall come to pass afterward, that I will pour out my spirit upon all flesh, and your sons and your daughters shall prophesy, your old men shall dream dreams, your young men shall see visions: And also upon the servants and upon the handmaids in those days will I pour out my spirit. And I will shew wonders in the heavens and in the earth, blood, and fire, and pillars of smoke. The sun shall be turned into darkness, and the moon into blood, before the great and the terrible day of the LORD come. And it shall come to pass, that whosoever shall call on the name of the LORD shall be delivered: for in mount Zion and in Jerusalem shall be deliverance, as the LORD hath said, and in the remnant whom the LORD shall call. *2:28-32*

29.8   For, behold, in those days, and in that time, when I shall bring again the captivity of Judah and Jerusalem, I will also gather all nations, and will bring them down into the valley of Jehoshaphat, and will plead with them there for my people and for my heritage Israel, whom they have scattered among the nations, and parted my land. And they have cast lots for my people; and have given a boy for an harlot, and sold a girl for wine, that they might drink. Yea, and what have ye to do with me, O Tyre, and Zidon, and all the coasts of Palestine? will ye render me a recompence? and if ye recompense me, swiftly and speedily will I return your recompence upon your own head.   *3:1-4*

29.9   Beat your plowshares into swords, and your pruninghooks into spears: let the weak say, I am strong.   *3:10*

29.10   The LORD also shall roar out of Zion, and utter his voice from Jerusalem; and the heavens and the earth shall shake: but the LORD will be the hope of his people, and the strength of the children of Israel.   *3:16*

29.11   So shall ye know that I am the LORD your God dwelling in Zion, my holy mountain: then shall Jerusalem be holy, and there shall no strangers pass through her any more. And it shall come to pass in that day, that the mountains shall drop down new wine, and the hills shall flow with milk, and all the rivers of Judah shall flow with waters, and a fountain shall come forth of the house of the LORD, and shall water the valley of Shittim.   *3:17-18*

AMOS

30.1   The words of Amos, who was among the herdmen of Tekoa, which he saw concerning Israel in the days of Uzziah king of Judah, and the days of Jeroboam the son of Joash king of Israel, two years before the earthquake. And he said, The LORD will roar from Zion, and utter his voice from Jerusalem; and the habitations of the shepherds shall mourn, and the top of Carmel shall wither. *1:1-2*

30.2   That pant after the dust of the earth on the head of the poor, and turn aside the way of the meek: and a man and his father will go in unto the same maid, to profane my holy name: *2:7*

30.3   Can two walk together, except they be agreed? *3:3*

30.4   Shall a trumpet be blown in the city, and the people not be afraid? shall there be evil in a city, and the LORD hath not done it? *3:6*

30.5   Surely the Lord GOD will do nothing, but he revealeth his secret unto his servants the prophets. The lion hath roared, who will not fear? the Lord GOD hath spoken, who can but prophesy? *3:7-8*

30.6   Hear this word, ye kine of Bashan, that are in the mountain of Samaria, which oppress the poor, which crush the needy, which say to their masters, Bring, and let us drink. *4:1*

30.7   I have overthrown some of you, as God overthrew Sodom and Gomorrah, and ye were as a firebrand plucked out of the burning: yet have ye not returned unto me, saith the LORD. *4:11*

30.8   Therefore thus will I do unto thee, O Israel: and because I will do this unto thee, prepare to meet thy God, O Israel.

For, lo, he that formeth the mountains, and createth the wind, and declareth unto man what is his thought, that maketh the morning darkness, and treadeth upon the high places of the earth, The LORD, The God of hosts, is his name. *4:12-13*

30.9   For thus saith the LORD unto the house of Israel, Seek ye me, and ye shall live. *5:4*

30.10   Seek him that maketh the seven stars and Orion, and turneth the shadow of death into the morning, and maketh the day dark with night: that calleth for the waters of the sea, and poureth them out upon the face of the earth: The LORD is his name. *5:8*

30.11   Seek good, and not evil, that ye may live: and so the LORD, the God of hosts, shall be with you, as ye have spoken. Hate the evil, and love the good, and establish judgment in the gate: it may be that the LORD God of hosts will be gracious unto the remnant of Joseph. *5:14-15*

30.12   Shall not the day of the LORD be darkness, and not light? even very dark, and no brightness in it? *5:20*

30.13   I hate, I despise your feast days, and I will not smell in your solemn assemblies. Though ye offer me burnt offerings and your meat offerings, I will not accept them: neither will I regard the peace offerings of your fat beasts. Take thou away from me the noise of thy songs; for I will not hear the melody of thy viols. But let judgment run down as waters, and righteousness as a mighty stream. *5:21-24*

30.14   Woe to them that are at ease in Zion, and trust in the mountain of Samaria, which are named chief of the nations, to whom the house of Israel came! *6:1*

30.15   Ye that put far away the evil day, and cause the seat of violence to come near; That lie upon beds of ivory, and stretch themselves upon their couches, and eat the lambs out of the flock, and the calves out of the midst of the stall. *6:3-4*

30.16   Thus he shewed me: and, behold, the Lord stood upon a wall made by a plumbline, with a plumbline in his hand. And the LORD said unto me, Amos, what seest thou? And I said, A plumbline. Then said the Lord, Behold, I will set a plumbline in the midst of my people Israel: I will not again pass by them any more.   *7:7-8*

30.17   Hear this, O ye that swallow up the needy, even to make the poor of the land to fail, Saying, When will the new moon be gone, that we may sell corn? and the sabbath, that we may set forth wheat, making the ephah small, and the shekel great, and falsifying the balances by deceit? That we may buy the poor for silver, and the needy for a pair of shoes; yea, and sell the refuse of the wheat? *8:4-6*

30.18   Behold, the days come, saith the Lord GOD, that I will send a famine in the land, not a famine of bread, nor a thirst for water, but of hearing the words of the LORD: And they shall wander from sea to sea, and from the north even to the east, they shall run to and fro to seek the word of the LORD, and shall not find it. *8:11-12*

30.19   In that day will I raise up the tabernacle of David that is fallen, and close up the breaches thereof; and I will raise up his ruins, and I will build it as in the days of old.   *9:11*

30.20   Behold, the days come, saith the LORD, that the plowman shall overtake the reaper, and the treader of grapes him that soweth seed; and the mountains shall drop sweet wine, and all the hills shall melt. And I will bring again the captivity of my people of Israel, and they shall build the waste cities, and inhabit them; and they shall plant vineyards, and drink the wine thereof; they shall also make gardens, and eat the fruit of them. And I will plant them upon their land, and they

shall no more be pulled up out of their land which I have given them, saith the LORD thy God.   *9:13-15*

OBADIAH

31.1   Though thou exalt thyself as the eagle, and though thou set thy nest among the stars, thence will I bring thee down, saith the LORD.   *4*

31.2   Shall I not in that day, saith the LORD, even destroy the wise men out of Edom, and understanding out of the mount of Esau?   *8*

31.3   For the day of the LORD is near upon all the heathen: as thou hast done, it shall be done unto thee: thy reward shall return upon thine own head.   *15*

31.4   But upon mount Zion shall be deliverance, and there shall be holiness; and the house of Jacob shall possess their possessions.   *17*

31.5   And saviours shall come up on mount Zion to judge the mount of Esau; and the kingdom shall be the LORD'S. *21*

JONAH

32.1   Now the word of the LORD came unto Jonah the son of Amittai, saying, Arise, go to Nineveh, that great city, and cry against it; for their wickedness is come up before me. But Jonah rose up to flee unto Tarshish from the presence of the LORD, and went down to Joppa; and he found a ship going to Tarshish: so he paid the fare thereof, and went down into it, to go with them unto Tarshish from the presence of the LORD.   *1:1-3*

32.2   So the shipmaster came to him, and said unto him, What meanest thou, O sleeper? arise, call upon thy God, if so be that God will think upon us, that we perish not. And they said every one to his fellow, Come, and let us cast lots, that we may know for whose cause this evil is upon us. So they cast lots, and the lot fell upon Jonah.   *1:6-7*

A Jonah

Jonah *is someone who brings bad luck - from the story of the biblical Jonah. Jonah ran away from God and boarded a ship to Tarshish. He was then held responsible for the violent storm that struck the ship. Other biblical figures whose names are associated with particular character traits include:*

Delilah: *a treacherous and seductive woman*

Jeremiah: *a pessimistic person who predicts a gloomy future*

Jezebel: *a shameless, scheming, or immoral woman*

Judas: *a traitor; a person who betrays a friend*

Samson: *an immensely strong man*

32.3   Now the LORD had prepared a great fish to swallow up Jonah. And Jonah was in the belly of the fish three days and three nights.   *1:17*

32.4   Then Jonah prayed unto the LORD his God out of the fish's belly, And said, I cried by reason of mine affliction unto the LORD, and he heard me; out of the belly of hell cried I, and thou heardest my voice.   *2:1-2*

32.5   When my soul fainted within me I remembered the LORD: and my prayer came in unto thee, into thine holy temple.   *2:7*

32.6   But I will sacrifice unto thee with the voice of thanksgiving; I will pay that that I have vowed. Salvation is of the LORD.   *2:9*

32.7   And the word of the LORD came unto Jonah the second time, saying, Arise, go unto Nineveh, that great city, and preach unto it the preaching that I bid thee. So Jonah arose, and went unto Nineveh, according to the word of the LORD. Now Nineveh was an exceeding great city of three days' journey. And Jonah began to enter into the city a day's journey, and he cried, and said, Yet, forty days, and Nineveh shall be overthrown. So the people of Nineveh believed God, and proclaimed a fast, and put on sackcloth, from the greatest of them even to the least of them.   *3:1-5*

32.8   And God saw their works, that they turned from their evil way; and God repented of the evil, that he had said that he would do unto them; and he did it not.   *3:10*

32.9   But it displeased Jonah exceedingly, and he was very angry.   *4:1*

32.10   And the LORD God prepared a gourd, and made it to come up over Jonah, that it might be a shadow over his head, to deliver him from his grief. So Jonah was exceeding glad of the gourd. But God prepared a worm when the morning rose the next day, and it smote the gourd that it withered. And it came to pass, when the sun did arise, that God prepared a vehement east wind; and the sun beat upon the head of Jonah, that he fainted, and wished in himself to die, and said, It is better for me to die than to live.   *4:6-8*

32.11   And God said to Jonah, Doest thou well to be angry for the gourd? And he said, I do well to be angry, even unto death. Then said the LORD, Thou hast had pity on the gourd, for the which thou hast not laboured, neither madest it grow; which came up in a night, and perished in a night: And should not I spare Nineveh, that great city, wherein are more than sixscore thousand persons that cannot discern between their right hand and their left hand; and also much cattle?   *4:9-11*

MICAH

33.1   For, behold, the LORD cometh forth out of his place, and will come down, and tread upon the high places of the earth. And the mountains shall be molten under him, and the valleys shall be cleft, as wax before the fire, and as the waters that are poured down a steep place.   *1:3-4*

33.2   Woe to them that devise iniquity, and work evil upon their beds! when the morning is light, they practise it, because it is in the power of their hand.   *2:1*

33.3   And many nations shall come, and say, Come, and let us go up to the mountain of the LORD, and to the house of the God of Jacob; and he will teach us of his ways, and we will walk in his paths: for the law shall go forth of Zion, and the word of the LORD from Jerusalem. And he shall judge among many people, and rebuke strong nations afar off; and they shall beat their swords into plowshares, and their spears into pruninghooks: nation shall not lift up a sword against nation, neither shall they learn war any more. But they shall sit every man under his vine and under his fig tree; and none shall make them afraid: for the mouth of the LORD of hosts hath spoken it.   *4:2-4*

33.4   But thou, Bethlehem Ephratah, though thou be little among the thousands of Judah, yet out of thee shall he come forth unto me that is to be ruler in Israel; whose goings forth have been from of old, from everlasting.   *5:2*

33.5   Therefore will he give them up, until the time that she which travaileth hath brought forth: then the remnant of his brethren shall return unto the children of Israel. And he shall stand and feed in the strength of the LORD, in the majesty of the name of the LORD his God; and they shall abide: for now shall he be great unto the ends of the earth.   *5:3-4*

33.6   And the remnant of Jacob shall be in the midst of many people as a dew from the LORD, as the showers upon the grass, that tarrieth not for man, nor waiteth for the sons of men.   *5:7*

33.7   He hath shewed thee, O man, what is good; and what doth the LORD require of thee, but to do justly, and to love mercy, and to walk humbly with thy God?   *6:8*

What is important to God

This verse is a reminder to the people of God of the kind of life that he requires of them. The qualities that are important to God are just behaviour, constant committed love, and humble fellowship with himself.

33.8   Who is a God like unto thee, that pardoneth iniquity, and passeth by the transgression of the remnant of his heritage? he retaineth not his anger for ever, because he delighteth in mercy. He will turn again, he will have compassion upon us; he will subdue our iniquities; and thou wilt cast all their sins into the depths of the sea.   *7:18-19*

NAHUM

34.1   The burden of Nineveh. The book of the vision of Nahum the Elkoshite. God is jealous, and the LORD revengeth; the LORD revengeth, and is furious; the LORD will take vengeance on his adversaries, and he reserveth wrath for his enemies. The LORD is slow to anger, and great in power, and will not at all acquit the wicked: the LORD hath his way in the whirlwind and in the storm, and the clouds are the dust of his feet.   *1:1-3*

34.2   Who can stand before his indignation? and who can abide in the fierceness of his anger? his fury is poured out like fire, and the rocks are thrown down by him. The LORD is good, a strong hold in the day of trouble; and he knoweth them that trust in him.   *1:6-7*

34.3   Behold, upon the mountains the feet of him that bringeth good tidings, that publisheth peace! O Judah, keep thy solemn feasts, perform thy vows: for the wicked shall no more pass through thee; he is utterly cut off.   *1:15*

34.4   The shield of his mighty men is made red, the valiant men are in scarlet: the chariots shall be with flaming torches in the day of his preparation, and the fir trees shall be terrribly shaken. The chariots shall rage in the streets, they shall justle one against another in the broad ways: they shall seem like torches, they shall run like the lightnings.   *2:3-4*

34.5   Behold, I am against thee, saith the LORD of hosts, and I will burn her chariots in the smoke, and the sword shall devour thy young lions: and I will cut off thy prey from the earth, and the voice of thy messengers shall no more be heard. *2:13*

34.6   Woe to the bloody city! it is all full of lies and robbery; the prey departeth not.   *3:1*

HABAKKUK

35.1   Behold ye among the heathen, and regard, and wonder marvellously: for I will work a work in your days, which ye will not believe, though it be told you. For, lo, I raise up the Chaldeans, that bitter and hasty nation, which shall march through the breadth of the land, to possess the dwellingplaces that are not theirs.   *1:5-6*

35.2   Art thou not from everlasting, O LORD my God, mine Holy One? we shall not die. O LORD, thou hast ordained

them for judgment; and, O mighty God, thou hast established them for correction. Thou art of purer eyes than to behold evil, and canst not look on iniquity: wherefore lookest thou upon them that deal treacherously, and holdest thy tongue when the wicked devoureth the man that is more righteous then he?   *1:12-13*

35.3   I will stand upon my watch, and set me upon the tower, and will watch to see what he will say unto me, and what I shall answer when I am reproved. And the LORD answered me, and said, Write the vision, and make it plain upon tables, that he may run that readeth it. For the vision is yet for an appointed time, but at the end it shall speak, and not lie: though it tarry, wait for it; because it will surely come, it will not tarry. Behold, his soul which is lifted up is not upright in him: but the just shall live by his faith.   *2:1-4*

35.4   But the LORD is in his holy temple: let all the earth keep silence before him. *2:20*

35.5   O LORD, I have heard thy speech,, and was afraid: O LORD, revive thy work in the midst of the years, in the midst of the years make known; in wrath remember mercy.   *3:2*

35.6   When I heard, my belly trembled; my lips quivered at the voice: rottenness entered into my bones, and I trembled in myself, that I might rest in the day of trouble: when he cometh up unto the people, he will invade them with his troops.   *3:16*

35.7   Although the fig tree shall not blossom, neither shall fruit be in the vines; the labour of the olive shall fail, and the fields shall yield no meat; the flock shall be cut off from the fold, and there shall be no herd in the stalls: Yet I will rejoice in the LORD. I will joy in the God of my salvation.   *3:17-18*

35.8   The LORD God is my strength, and he will make my feet like hinds' feet, and he will make me to walk upon mine high places. To the chief singer on my stringed instruments.   *3:19*

ZEPHANIAH

36.1   I will utterly consume all things from off the land, saith the LORD. I will consume man and beast; I will consume the fowls of the heaven, and the fishes of the sea, and the stumblingblocks with the wicked; and I will cut off man from off the land, saith the LORD.   *1:2-3*

36.2   I will also stretch out mine hand upon Judah, and upon all the inhabitants of Jerusalem; and I will cut off the remnant of Baal from this place, and the name of the Chemarims with the priests; And them that worship the host of heaven upon the housetops; and them that worship and that swear by the LORD, and that swear by Malcham; And them that are turned back from the LORD; and those that have not sought the LORD, nor inquired for him.   *1:4-6*

36.3   Hold thy peace at the presence of the Lord GOD: for the day of the LORD is at hand: for the LORD hath prepared a sacrifice, he hath bid his guests.   *1:7*

36.4   The great day of the LORD is near, it is near, and hasteth greatly, even the voice of the day of the LORD: the mighty man shall cry there bitterly. That day is a day of wrath, a day of trouble and distress, a day of wasteness and desolation, a day of darkness and gloominess, a day of clouds and thick darkness.   *1:14-15*

36.5   Seek ye the LORD, all ye meek of the earth, which have wrought his judgment; seek righteousness, seek meekness: it may be ye shall be hid in the day of the LORD'S anger.   *2:3*

36.6   For then will I turn to the people a pure language, that they may all call upon the name of the LORD, to serve him with one consent.   *3:9*

36.7   I will also leave in the midst of thee an afflicted and poor people, and they shall trust in the name of the LORD. The remnant of Israel shall not do iniquity, nor speak lies; neither shall a deceitful tongue be found in their mouth: for they shall feed and lie down, and none shall make them afraid.   *3:12-13*

36.8   The LORD thy God in the midst of thee is mighty; he will save, he will rejoice over thee with joy; he will rest in his love, he will joy over thee with singing.   *3:17*

36.9   At that time will I bring you again, even in the time that I gather you: for I will make you a name and a praise among all people of the earth, when I turn back your captivity before your eyes, saith the LORD.   *3:20*

HAGGAI

37.1   Thus speaketh the LORD of hosts, saying, This people say, The time is not come, the time that the LORD'S house should be built. Then came the word of the LORD by Haggai the prophet, saying, Is it time for you, O ye, to dwell in your cieled houses, and this house lie waste? Now therefore thus saith the LORD of hosts; Consider your ways. Ye have sown much, and bring in little; ye eat, but ye have not enough; ye drink, but ye are not filled with drink; ye clothe you, but there is none warm; and he that earneth wages earneth wages to put it into a bag with holes.   *1:2-6*

37.2   Then Zerubbabel the son of Shealtiel, and Joshua the son of Josedech, the high priest, with all the remnant of the people, obeyed the voice of the LORD their God, and the words of Haggai the prophet, as the LORD their God had sent him, and the people did fear before the LORD.   *1:12*

37.3   Yet now be strong, O Zerubbabel, saith the LORD; and be strong, O Joshua, son of Josedech, the high priest; and be strong, all ye people of the land, saith the LORD, and work: for I am with you, saith the LORD of hosts: According to the word that I covenanted with you when ye came out of Egypt, so my spirit remaineth among you: fear ye not. For thus saith the LORD of hosts; Yet once, it is a little while, and I will shake the heavens, and the earth, and the sea, and the dry land. *2:4-6*

37.4   And I will shake all nations, and the desire of all nations shall come: and I will fill this house with glory, saith the LORD of hosts. The silver is mine, and the gold is mine, saith the LORD of hosts. The glory of this latter house shall be greater than of the former, saith the LORD of hosts: and in this place will I give peace, saith the LORD of hosts.   *2:7-9*

ZECHARIAH

38.1   Be ye not as your fathers, unto whom the former prophets have cried, saying, Thus saith the LORD of hosts; Turn ye now from your evil ways, and from your evil doings: but they did not hear, nor hearken unto me, saith the LORD. Your fathers, where are they? and the prophets, do they live for ever?   *1:4-5*

38.2   And they answered the angel of the LORD that stood among the myrtle trees, and said, We have walked to and fro through the earth, and, behold, all the earth sitteth still, and is at rest.   *1:11*

38.3   So the angel that communed with me said unto me, Cry thou, saying, Thus saith the LORD of hosts; I am jealous for Jerusalem and for Zion with a great jealousy. And I am very sore displeased with the heathen that are at ease: for I was but a little displeased, and they helped forward the affliction. Therefore thus saith the LORD; I am returned to Jerusalem with mercies: my house shall be built in it, saith the LORD of hosts, and

a line shall be stretched forth upon Jerusalem.   *1:14-16*

38.4   I lifted up mine eyes again, and looked, and behold a man with a measuring line in his hand. Then said I, Whither goest thou? And he said unto me, To measure Jerusalem, to see what is the breadth thereof, and what is the length thereof.   *2:1-2*

38.5   For thus saith the LORD of hosts; After the glory hath he sent me unto the nations which spoiled you: for he that toucheth you toucheth the apple of his eye.   *2:8*

38.6   Hear now, O Joshua the high priest, thou, and thy fellows that sit before thee: for they are men wondered at: for, behold, I will bring forth my servant the BRANCH.   *3:8*

38.7   Then he answered and spake unto me, saying, This is the word of the LORD unto Zerubbabel, saying, Not by might, nor by power, but by my spirit, saith the LORD of hosts.   *4:6*

38.8   For who hath despised the day of small things? for they shall rejoice, and shall see the plummet in the hand of Zerubbabel with those seven; they are the eyes of the LORD, which run to and fro through the whole earth.   *4:10*

38.9   And speak unto him, saying, Thus speaketh the LORD of hosts, saying, Behold the man whose name is The BRANCH; and he shall grow up out of his place, and he shall build the temple of the LORD: Even he shall build the temple of the LORD; and he shall bear the glory, and shall sit and rule upon his throne; and he shall be a priest upon his throne: and the counsel of peace shall be between them both.   *6:12-13*

38.10   And the word of the LORD came unto Zechariah, saying, Thus speaketh the LORD of hosts, saying, Execute true judgment, and shew mercy and compassions every man to his brother:

And oppress not the widow, nor the fatherless, the stranger, nor the poor; and let none of you imagine evil against his brother in your heart.   *7:8-10*

38.11   Rejoice greatly, O daughter of Zion; shout, O daughter of Jerusalem: behold, thy King cometh unto thee: he is just, and having salvation; lowly, and riding upon an ass, and upon a colt the foal of an ass.   *9:9*

Prophecies of the Messiah

A number of prophecies of the Messiah come in the book of Zechariah. Such prophecies include the triumphal entry of the King into Jerusalem (9:9), the betrayal of Christ for thirty pieces of silver (11:12), the piercing of his side (12:10), the pouring of his blood as a cleansing from sin (13:1), and the scattering of his followers (13:7).

38.12   Turn you to the strong hold, ye prisoners of hope: even to day do I declare that I will render double unto thee.   *9:12*

38.13   And I said unto them, If ye think good, give me my price; and if not, forbear. So they weighed for my price thirty pieces of silver.   *11:12*

38.14   And I will pour upon the house of David, and upon the inhabitants of Jerusalem, the spirit of grace and of supplications: and they shall look upon me whom they have pierced, and they shall mourn for him, as one mourneth for his only son, and shall be in bitterness for him, as one that is in bitterness for his firstborn.   *12:10*

38.15   In that day there shall be a fountain opened to the house of David and to the inhabitants of Jerusalem for sin and for uncleanness.   *13:1*

38.16   And one shall say unto him, What are these wounds in thine hands? Then he shall answer, Those with which I was wounded in the house of my friends. Awake, O sword, against my shepherd,

and against the man that is my fellow, saith the LORD of hosts: smite the shepherd, and the sheep shall be scattered: and I will turn mine hand upon the little ones.   *13:6-7*

38.17   And it shall be in that day, that living waters shall go out from Jerusalem; half of them toward the former sea, and half of them toward the hinder sea: in summer and in winter shall it be. And the LORD shall be king over all the earth: in that day shall there be one LORD, and his name one.   *14:8-9*

38.18   Yea, every pot in Jerusalem and in Judah shall be holiness unto the LORD of hosts: and all they that sacrifice shall come and take of them, and seethe therein: and in that day there shall be no more the Canaanite in the house of the LORD of hosts.   *14:21*

MALACHI

39.1   A son honoureth his father, and a servant his master: if then I be a father, where is mine honour? and if I be a master, where is my fear? saith the LORD of hosts unto you, O priests, that despise my name. And ye say, Wherein have we despised thy name?   *1:6*

39.2   For from the rising of the sun even unto the going down of the same my name shall be great among the Gentiles; and in every place incense shall be offered unto my name, and a pure offering: for my name shall be great among the heathen, saith the LORD of hosts.   *1:11*

39.3   The law of truth was in his mouth, and iniquity was not found in his lips: he walked with me in peace and equity, and did turn many away from iniquity.   *2:6*

39.4   Have we not all one father, hath not one God created us? why do we deal treacherously every man against his brother, by profaning the covenant of our fathers?   *2:10*

39.5   Ye have wearied the LORD with your words. Yet ye say, Wherein have we wearied him? When ye say, Every one that doeth evil is good in the sight of the LORD, and he delighteth in them; or, Where is the God of judgment?   *2:17*

39.6   Behold, I will send my messenger, and he shall prepare the way before me: and the Lord, whom ye seek, shall suddenly come to his temple, even the messenger of the covenant, whom ye delight in: behold, he shall come, saith the LORD of hosts. But who may abide the day of his coming? and who shall stand when he appeareth? for his is like a refiner's fire, and like fullers' soap: And he shall sit as a refiner and purifier of silver: and he shall purify the sons of Levi, and purge them as gold and silver, that they may offer unto the LORD an offering in righteousness.   *3:1-3*

39.7   For I am the LORD, I change not; therefore ye sons of Jacob are not consumed.   *3:6*

39.8   Bring ye all the tithes into the storehouse, that there may be meat in mine house, and prove me now herewith, saith the LORD of hosts, if I will not open you the windows of heaven, and pour you out a blessing, that there shall not be room enough to receive it.   *3:10*

39.9   Then they that feared the LORD spake often one to another: and the LORD hearkened, and heard it, and a book of remembrance was written before him for them that feared the LORD, and that thought upon his name.   *3:16*

39.10   For, behold, the day cometh, that shall burn as an oven; and all the proud, yea, and all that do wickedly, shall be stubble: and the day that cometh shall burn them up, saith the LORD of hosts, that it shall leave them neither root nor branch. But unto you that fear my name shall the Sun of righteousness arise with healing in his wings; and ye shall go forth, and grow up as calves of the stall.   *4:1-2*

39.11   Behold, I will send you Elijah the prophet before the coming of the great and dreadful day of the LORD: And he shall turn the heart of the fathers to the children, and the heart of the children to their fathers, lest I come and smite the earth with a curse.   *4:5-6*

THE APOCRYPHA

The Apocrypha consists of a varied collection of Jewish writings from the period between about 300 BC and AD 100. *Apocrypha*, a Greek word meaning 'hidden things' is used to describe certain books that were included in early Latin and Greek versions of the Scriptures but were excluded from the Hebrew Scriptures.

The Council of Trent (1548) of the Roman Catholic Church accepted the books, apart from 1 and 2 Esdras and the Prayer of Manasses, as part of the Scriptures. According to the Thirty-Nine Articles of the Church of England, the books of the Apocrypha should be read 'for example of life and instruction of manners', but not used to establish doctrine.

1 ESDRAS

40.1   The first wrote, Wine is the strongest. The second wrote, The king is strongest. The third wrote, Women are strongest: but above all things Truth beareth away the victory.   *3:10-12*

40.2   And he said thus, O ye men, how exceeding strong is wine! it causeth all men to err that drink it: It maketh the mind of the king and of the fatherless child to be all one; of the bondman and of the freeman, of the poor man and of the rich: It turneth also every thought into jollity and mirth, so that a man remembereth neither sorrow nor debt: *3:18-20*

40.3   And when they are in their cups, they forget their love both to friends and brethren, and a little after draw out swords: But when they are form the wine, they remember not what they have done.   *3:22-23*

40.4   O ye men, do not men excel in strength, that bear rule over sea and land, and all things in them?   *4:2*

40.5   Yea, and if men have gathered together gold and silver, or any other goodly thing, do they not love a woman which is comely in favour and beauty?   *4:18*

40.6   By this also ye must know that women have dominion over you: do ye not labour and toil, and give and bring all to the woman? Yea, a man taketh his sword, and goeth his way to rob and to steal, to sail upon the sea and upon rivers; And looketh upon a lion, and goeth in the darkness; and when he hath stolen, spoiled, and robbed, he bringeth it to his love.   *4:22-24*

40.7   And with that he held his peace. And all the people then shouted, and said, Great is Truth, and mighty above all things.   *4:41*

40.8   And said, From thee cometh victory, from thee cometh wisdom, and thine is the glory, and I am thy servant. Blesed art thou, who hast given me wisdom: for to thee I give thanks, O Lord of our fathers.   *4:59-60*

40.9   And by their secret plots, and popular persuasions and commotions, they hindered the finishing of the building all the time that king Cyrus lived: so they were hindered from building for the space of two years, until the reign of Darius.   *5:73*

40.10   Go then, and eat the fat, and drink the sweet, and send part to them that have nothing; For this day is holy unto the Lord: and be not sorrowful; for the Lord will bring you to honour.

---

2 ESDRAS

41.1   I Esdras saw upon the mount Sion a great people, whom I could not number, and they all praised the Lord with songs. And in the midst of them there was a young man of a high stature, taller than all the rest, and upon every one of their heads he set crowns, and was more exalted; which I marvelled at greatly. So I asked the angel, and said, Sir, what are these? He answered and said unto me, These be they that have put off the mortal clothing, and put on the immortal, and have confessed the name of God: now are they crowned, and receive palms. Then said I unto the angel, What young person is it that crowneth them, and giveth them palms in their hands? So he answered and said unto me, It is the Son of God, whom they have confessed in the world. Then began I greatly to commend them that stood so stiffly for the name of the Lord.   *2:42-47*

41.2   And he said unto me, If I should ask thee how great dwellings are in the midst of the sea, or how many springs are in the beginning of the deep, or how many springs are above the firmament, or which are the outgoings of paradise:

Peradventure thou wouldest say unto me, I never went down into the deep, nor as yet into hell, neither did I ever climb up into heaven.   *4:7-8*

41.3   He answered me, and said, I went into a forest into a plain, and the trees took counsel, And said, Come, let us go and make war against the sea, that it may depart away before us, and that we may make us more woods. The floods of the sea also in like manner took counsel, and said, Come, let us go up and subdue the woods of the plain, that there also we may make us another country. The thought of the wood was in vain, for the fire came and consumed it. The thought of the floods of the sea came likewise to nought, for the sand stood up and stopped them.   *4:13-17*

41.4   Then were the entrances of this world made narrow, full of sorrow and travail: they are but few and evil, full of perils, and very painful. For the entrances of the elder world were wide and sure, and brought immortal fruit. If then they that live labour not to enter these strait and vain things, they can never receive those that are laid up for them.   *7:12-14*

41.5   For the world hath lost his youth, and the times begin to wax old.   *14:10*

41.6   And come hither, and I shall light a candle of understanding in thine heart, which shall not be put out, till the things be performed which thou shalt begin to write.   *14:25*

TOBIT

42.1   O Lord, thou art just, and all thy works and all thy ways are mercy and truth, and thou judgest truly and justly for ever. Remember me, and look on me, punish me not for my sins and ignorances, and the sins of my fathers, who have sinned before thee.   *3:2-3*

42.2   Be not greedy to add money to money: but let it be as refuse in respect of our child.   *5:18*

42.3   Be of good comfort, my daughter; the Lord of heaven and earth give thee joy for this thy sorrow: be of good comfort, my daughter.   *7:18*

42.4   If ye turn to him with your whole heart, and with your whole mind, and deal uprightly before him, then will he turn unto you, and will not hide his face from you. Therefore see what he will do with you, and confess him with your whole mouth, and praise the Lord of might, and extol the everlasting King. In the land of my captivity do I praise him, and declare his might and majesty to a sinful nation. O ye sinners, turn and do justice before him: who can tell if he will accept you, and have mercy on you? I will extol my God, and my soul shall praise the King of heaven, and shall rejoice in his greatness.   *13:6-7*

JUDITH

43.1   So all went forth, and none was left in the bedchamber, neither little nor great. Then Judith, standing by his bed, said in her heart, O Lord God of all power, look at this present upon the works of mine hands for the exaltation of Jerusalem.   *13:4*

43.2   And she *[Judith]* smote twice upon his neck with all her might, and she took away his head from him.   *13:8*

43.3   Then she said to them with a loud voice, Praise, praise God, praise God, I say, for he hath not taken away his mercy from the house of Israel, but hath destroyed our enemies by mine hands this night. So she took the head out of the bag, and shewed it, and said unto them, Behold the head of Holofernes, the chief captain of the army of Assur, and behold the canopy, wherein he did lie in his

drunkeness; and the Lord hath smitten him by the hand of a woman.   *13:14-15*

43.4   And Judith said, Begin unto my God with timbrels, sing unto my Lord with cymbals: tune unto him a new psalm: exalt him, and call upon his name. For God breaketh the battles: for among the camps in the midst of the people he hath delivered me out of the hands of them that persecuted me.   *16:2-3*

ADDITIONS TO ESTHER

44.1   Then Mardocheus said, God hath done these things. For I remember a dream which I saw concerning these matters, and nothing thereof hath failed. A little fountain became a river, and there was light, and the sun, and much water: this river is Esther, whom the king married, and made queen: And the two dragons are I and Aman. And the nations were those that were assembled to destroy the name of the Jews: And my nation is this Israel, which cried to God, and were saved: for the Lord hath saved his people, and the Lord hath delivered us from all those evils, and God hath wrought signs and great wonders, which have not been done among the Gentiles.   *10:4-9*

44.2   Then Mardocheus thought upon all the works of the Lord, and made his prayer unto him, Saying, O Lord, Lord, the King Almighty: for the whole world is in thy power, and if thou hast appointed to save Israel, there is no man that can gainsay thee: For thou hast made heaven and earth, and all the wondrous things under the heaven. Thou art Lord of all things, and there is no man that can resist thee, which art the Lord. Thou knowest all things, and thou knowest, Lord, that it was neither in contempt nor pride, nor for any desire of glory, that I did not bow down to proud Aman. For I could have been content with good will for the salvation of Israel to kiss the soles of his feet. But I did this, that I might not prefer the glory of man above the glory of God: neither will I worship any but thee, O God, neither will I do it in pride. And now, O Lord God and King, spare thy people: for their eyes are upon us to bring us to nought; yea, they desire to destroy the inheritance, that hath been thine from the beginning. Despise not the portion, which thou hast delivered out of Egypt for thine own self. Hear my prayer, and be merciful unto thine inheritance: turn our sorrow into joy, that we may live, O Lord, and praise thy name: and destroy not the mouths of them that praise thee, O Lord. All Israel in like manner cried most earnestly unto the Lord, because their death was before their eyes.   *13:8-18*

WISDOM OF SOLOMON

45.1   Love righteousness, ye that be judges of the earth: think of the Lord with a good (heart,) and in simplicity of heart seek him. For he will be found of them that tempt him not; and sheweth himself unto such as do not distrust him.   *1:1-2*

The Wisdom of Solomon

The Wisdom of Solomon is a sublime collection of moral teachings, written under the influence of Greek thought. The author of the book is unknown: a Greek-speaking Jew of first-century BC Alexandria is a possibility.

45.2   For the holy spirit of discipline will flee deceit, and remove from thoughts that are without understanding, and will not abide when unrighteousness cometh in.   *1:5*

45.3   For the ear of jealousy heareth all things: and the noise of murmurings is not hid.   *1:10*

45.4   Nevertheless through envy of the devil came death into the world: and they that do hold of his side do find it.   *2:24*

45.5   But the souls of the righteous are in the hand of God, and there shall no torment touch them. In the sight of the unwise they seemed to die: and their departure is taken for misery, And their going from us to be utter destruction: but they are in peace. For though they be punished in the sight of men, yet is their hope full of immortality. And having been a little chastised, they shall be greatly rewarded: for God proved them, and found them worthy for himself.   *3:1-5*

45.6   And in the time of their visitation they shall shine, and run to and fro like sparks among the stubble.   *3:7*

45.7   For the bewitching of naughtiness doth obscure things that are honest; and the wanderings of concupiscence doth undermine the simple mind. He being made perfect in a short time, fulfilled a long time.   *4:12-13*

45.8   Even so we in like manner, as soon as we were born, began to draw to our end, and had no sign of virtue to shew; but were consumed in our own wickedness. For the hope of the ungodly is like dust that is blown away with the wind; like a thin froth that is driven away with the storm; like as the smoke which is dispersed here and there with a tempest, and passeth away as the remembrance of a guest that tarrieth but a day.   *5:13-14*

45.9   For all men have one entrance into life, and the like going out.   *7:6*

45.10   For wisdom is more moving than any motion: she passeth and goeth through all things by reason of her pureness. For she is the breath of the power of God, and a pure influence flowing from the glory of the Almighty: therefore can no defiled thing fall into her. For she is the brightness of the everlasting light, the unspotted mirror of the power of God, and the image of his goodness.

And being but one, she can do all things: and remaining in herself, she maketh all things new: and in all ages entering into holy souls, she maketh them friends of God, and prophets. For God loveth none but him that dwelleth with wisdom. *7:24-28*

45.11   Wisdom reacheth from one end to another mightily: and sweetly doth she order all things.   *8:1*

45.12   But thou sparest all: for they are thine, O Lord, thou lover of souls. *11:26*

45.13   Also the singular diligence of the artificer did help to set forward the ignorant to more superstition. For he, peradventure willing to please one in authority, forced all his skill to make the resemblance of the best fashion. And so the multitude, allured by the grace of the work, took him now for a god, which a little before was but honoured as a man. And this was an occasion to deceive the world: for men, serving either calamity or tyranny, did ascribe unto stones and stocks the incommunicable name. *14:18-21*

45.14   For thou hast power of life and death: thou leadest to the gates of hell, and bringest up again.   *16:13*

ECCLESIASTICUS

46.1   My son, if thou come to serve the Lord, prepare thy soul for temptation. *2:1*

46.2   Ye that fear the Lord, believe him; and your reward shall not fail.   *2:8*

46.3   For the Lord is full of compassion and mercy, longsuffering, and very pitiful, and forgiveth sins, and saveth in time of affliction.   *2:11*

46.4   Saying, We will fall into the hands of the Lord, and not into the hands of men: for as his majesty is, so is his mercy.   *2:18*

46.5   Be not curious in unnecessary matters: for more things are shewed unto thee than men understand.   *3:23*

46.6   If thou hast understanding, answer thy neighbour; if not, lay thy hand upon thy mouth. Honour and shame is in talk: and the tongue of man is his fall.   *5:12-13*

46.7   Be not ignorant of any thing in a great matter or a small.   *5:15*

46.8   A faithful friend is the medicine of life; and they that fear the Lord shall find him.   *6:16*

46.9   Laugh no man to scorn in the bitterness of his soul: for there is one which humbleth and exalteth.   *7:11*

46.10   Miss not the discourse of the elders: for they also learned of their fathers, and of them thou shalt learn understanding, and to give answer as need requireth.   *8:9*

46.11   Open not thine heart to every man, lest he requite thee with a shrewd turn.   *8:19*

46.12   Give not thy soul unto a woman to set her foot upon thy substance.   *9:2*

46.13   Forsake not an old friend; for the new is not comparable to him: a new friend is as new wine; when it is old, thou shalt drink it with pleasure.   *9:10*

46.14   Many kings have sat down upon the ground; and one that was never thought of hath worn the crown.   *11:5*

46.15   Judge none blessed before his death: for a man shall be known in his children.   *11:28*

46.16   He that toucheth pitch shall be defiled therewith; and he that hath fellowship with a proud man shall be like unto him. *13:1*

46.17   Burden not thyself above thy power while thou livest; and have no fellowship with one that is mightier and richer that thyself: for how agree the kettle and the earthen pot together? for if the one be smitten against the other, it shall be broken. *13:2*

46.18   All flesh waxeth old as a garment: for the covenant from the beginning is, Thou shalt die the death. *14:17*

46.19   Desire not a multitude of unprofitable children, neither delight in ungodly sons. *16:1*

46.20   Be not made a beggar by banqueting upon borrowing, when thou hast nothing in thy purse: for thou shalt lie in wait for thine own life, and be talked on. *18:33*

46.21   A labouring man that is given to drunkenness shall not be rich: and he that contemneth small things shall fall by little and little. *19:1*

46.22   Wine and women will make men of understanding to fall away: and he that cleaveth to harlots will become impudent. *19:2*

46.23   If thou hast heard a word, let it die with thee; and be bold, it will not burst thee. *19:10*

46.24   If thou hast gathered nothing in thy youth, how canst thou find any thing in thine age? *25:3*

46.25   All wickedness is but little to the wickedness of a woman: let the portion of a sinner fall upon her. *25:19*

46.26   As the climbing up a sandy way is to the feet of the aged, so is a wife full of words to a quiet man. *25:20*

46.27   The stroke of the whip maketh marks in the flesh: but the stroke of the tongue breaketh the bones. Many have fallen by the edge of the sword: but not so many as have fallen by the tongue. *28:17-18*

46.28   Envy and wrath shorten the life, and carefulness bringeth age before the time. *30:24*

46.29   Leave off first for manners' sake; and be not unsatiable, lest thou offend. *31:17*

46.30   Wine is a good as life to a man, if it be drunk moderately: what life is then to a man that is without wine? for it was made to make men glad. *31:27*

46.31   Let thy speech be short, comprehending much in few words; be as one that knoweth and yet holdeth his tongue. *32:8*

46.32   In all thy works keep to thyself the preeminence; leave not a stain in thine honour. *33:22*

46.33   Honour a physician with the honour due unto him for the uses which ye may have of him: for the Lord hath created him. For of the most High cometh healing, and he shall receive honour of the king. *38:1-2*

46.34   The wisdom of a learned man cometh by opportunity of leisure: and he that hath little business shall become wise. How can he get wisdom that holdeth the plough, and that glorieth in the goad, that driveth oxen, and is occupied in their labours, and whose talk is of bullocks? *38:24-25*

46.35   But they will maintain the state of the world, and (all) their desire is in the work of their craft. *38:34*

46.36   Let us now praise famous men, and our fathers that begat us. *44:1*

46.37   Such as did bear rule in their kingdoms, men renowned for their power, giving counsel by their understanding, and declaring prophecies: Leaders of the people by their counsels, and by their knowledge of learning meet for the people, wise and eloquent in their instructions: Such as found out musical tunes, and recited verses in writing: Rich men furnished with ability, living peaceably in their habitations: All these were honoured in their generations, and were the glory of their times. There be of them, that have left a name behind them, that their praises might be reported. And some there be, which have no memorial; who are perished, as though they had never been; and are become as though they had never been born; and their children after them. But these were merciful men, whose righteousness hath not been forgotten.   *44:3-10*

46.38   Their bodies are buried in peace; but their name liveth for evermore.
44:14

46.39   When I was yet young, or ever I went abroad, I desired wisdom openly in my prayer. I prayed for her before the temple, and will seek her out even to the end. Even from the flower till the grape was ripe hath my heart delighted in her: my foot went the right way, from my youth up sought I after her. I bowed down mine ear a little, and received her, and gat much learning.   *51:13-16*

BARUCH

47.1   Learn where is wisdom, where is strength, where is understanding; that thou mayest know also where is length of days, and life, where is the light of the eyes, and peace.   *3:14*

47.2   Ye were sold to the nations, not for (your) destruction: but because ye moved God to wrath, ye were delivered unto the enemies. For ye provoked him that made you by sacrificing unto devils, and not to God. Ye have forgotten the everlasting

God, that brought you up; and ye have grieved Jerusalem, that nursed you.
4:6-8

EPISTLE OF JEREMY

48.1   Sometimes also the priests convey from their gods gold and silver, and bestow it upon themselves. Yea, they will give thereof to the common harlots, and deck them as men with garments, (being) gods of silver, and gods of gold, and wood. Yet cannot these gods save themselves from rust and moths, though they be covered with purple raiment.
6:10-12

SONG OF THE THREE HOLY CHILDREN

49.1   And they walked in the midst of the fire, praising God, and blessing the Lord.   *1*

49.2   O all ye works of the Lord, bless ye the Lord: praise and exalt him above all for ever.   *35*

49.3   O Ananias, Azarias, and Misael, bless ye the Lord: praise and exalt him above all for ever: for he hath delivered us from hell, and saved us from the hand of death, and delivered us out of the midst of the furnace and burning flame: even out of the midst of the fire hath he delivered us. O give thanks unto the Lord, because he is gracious: for his mercy endureth for ever. O all ye that worship the Lord, bless the God of gods, praise him, and give him thanks: for his mercy endureth for ever.
66-68

HISTORY OF SUSANNA

50.1   Behold, the garden doors are shut, that no man can see us, and we are in love with thee; therefore consent unto us, and lie with us. If thou wilt not, we will bear witness against thee, that a young men was with thee: and therefore thou didst send away thy maids from thee. Then Susanna sighed, and said, I am straitened on every side: for if I do this thing, it is death unto me: and if I do it not, I cannot escape your hands.   *20-22*

50.2   Then Susanna cried out with a loud voice, and said, O everlasting God, that knowest the secrets, and knowest all things before they be: Thou knowest that they have borne false witness against me, and, behold, I must die, whereas I never did such things as these men have maliciously invented against me. And the Lord heard her voice.   *42-44*

50.3   So when they were put asunder one from another, he called one of them, and said unto him, O thou that art waxen old in wickedness, now thy sins which thou hast committed aforetime are come to light: *52*

A Daniel come to judgment

The expression a Daniel come to judgment *is used to refer to an upright person who makes a wise decision about a matter that has puzzled others, The allusion is to the Daniel of the Old Testament and the apocryphal History of Susanna. The source of the phrase itself is Shakespeare's* Merchant of Venice *(Act 4, Scene 1).*

50.4   And they arose against the two elders, for Daniel had convicted them of false witness by their own mouth: And according to the law of Moses they did unto them is such sort as they maliciously

intended to do to their neighbour: and they put them to death. Thus the innocent blood was saved the same day. Therefore Chelcias and his wife praised God for their daughter Susanna, with Joacim her husband, and all the kindred, because there was no dishonesty found in her. From that day forth was Daniel had in great reputation in the sight of the people.   *61-64*

BEL AND THE DRAGON

51.1   Now the priests of Bel were threescore and ten, beside their wives and children. And the king went with Daniel into the temple of Bel. So Bel's priests said, Lo, we go out: but thou, O king, set on the meat, and make ready the wine, and shut the door fast, and seal it with thine own signet; And to morrow when thou comest in, if thou findest not that Bel hath eaten up all, we will suffer death: or else Daniel, that speaketh falsely against us. And they little regarded it: for under the table they had made a privy entrance, whereby they entered in continually, and consumed those things.   *10-13*

51.2   And Daniel said, Thou hast remembered me, O God: neither hast thou forsaken them that seek thee and love thee.   *38*

PRAYER OF MANASSES

52.1   I have sinned above the number of the sands of the sea. My transgressions, O Lord, are multiplied: my transgressions are multiplied, and I am not worthy to behold and see the height of heaven for the multitude of mine iniquities. I am bowed down with many iron bands, that I cannot lift up mine head, neither have any release: for I have provoked thy wrath, and done evil before thee: I did not thy will, neither kept I thy commandments: I have set up abominations, and have multiplied offences. Now therefore I bow the knee of mine heart, beseeching thee of grace. I have sinned, O Lord, I have sinned, and I acknowledge mine iniquities: wherefore, I humbly beseech thee, forgive me, O Lord, forgive me, and destroy me not with mine iniquities. Be not angry with me for ever, by reserving evil for me; neither condemn me into the lower parts of the earth. For thou art the God, even the God of them that repent; and in me thou wilt shew all thy goodness: for thou wilt save me, that am unworthy, according to thy great mercy;. Therefore I will praise thee for ever all the days of my life: for all the powers of the heavens do praise thee, and thine is the glory; for ever and ever. Amen.

1 MACCABEES

53.1   Now the fifteenth day of the month Casleu, in the hundred forty and fifth year, they set up the abomination of desolation upon the altar, and builded idol altars throughout the cities of Juda on every side.   *1:54*

53.2   I perceive therefore that for this cause these troubles are come upon me, and, behold, I perish through great grief in a strange land.   *6:13*

53.3   Then Judas said, God forbid that I should do this thing, and flee away from them: if our time be come, let us die manfully for our brethren, and let us not stain our honour.   *9:10*

53.4   As concerning the rest of the acts of John, and his wars, and worthy deeds which he did, and the building of the walls which he made, and his doings,

Behold, these are written in the chronicles of his priesthood, from the time he was made high priest after his father.   *16:23-24*

2 MACCABEES

54.1   Here then will we begin the story: only adding thus much to that which hath been said, that it is a foolish thing to make a long prologue, and to be short in the story itself.   *2:32*

54.2   And when he was at the last gasp, he said, Thou like a fury takest us out of this present life, but the King of the world shall raise us up, who have died for his laws, unto everlasting life.   *7:9*

At the last gasp

The expression at the *(or* one's*)* last gasp, *meaning at the point when one is just about to die, collapse, or give up, has its origin in this verse. The last gasp refers here to the final few breaths taken by one of the Jewish believers before he was tortured.*

54.3   For if he had not hoped that they that were slain should have risen again, it had been superfluous and vain to pray for the dead. And also in that he perceived that there was great favour laid up for those that died godly, it was an holy and good thought. Whereupon he made a reconciliation for the dead, that they might be delivered from sin. *12:44-45*

54.4   And if I have done well, and as is fitting the story, it is that which I desired: but if slenderly and meanly, it is that which I could attain unto. For as it is hurtful to drink wine or water alone; and as wine mingled with water is pleasant, and delighteth the taste: even so speech finely framed delighteth the ears of them that read the story. And here shall be an end.   *15:38-39*

THE
NEW TESTAMENT

THE GOSPELS AND ACTS

The word *gospel* means 'good news'. Nearly half of the New Testament consists of four accounts of Jesus' life and the good news that he brought to the world. The Gospels particularly emphasize the events of the last week of Jesus' life, his death, and his resurrection.

Each of the four Gospels has its own emphasis. *Matthew* shows a particular interest in Jewish Christians: Jesus is the Messiah long-expected by the Jews. *Mark* is a brief, action-packed, fast-moving account of Jesus' life and work. The Gospel of *Luke* and the Acts of the Apostles are two parts of one work. Luke records several incidents concerning Jesus' birth and early life. He emphasizes Jesus as the Saviour of all different kinds of people, especially the poor and needy. The Gospel of *John* is different from the other three: seven signs (miracles) and seven sayings (the 'I am' sayings), point to Jesus as the Son of God. John's purpose in writing was to encourage personal belief.

The *Acts of the Apostles* takes the story on from Jesus' ascension into heaven and the gift of the Holy Spirit at Pentecost. The church was born. Peter and, later, Paul emerged as leaders, and the message of Jesus spread rapidly from Jerusalem throughout the eastern Roman Empire.

ST MATTHEW

55.1   The book of the generation of Jesus Christ, the son of David, the son of Abraham.   *1:1*

55.2   And she shall bring forth a son, and thou shalt call his name JESUS: for he shall save his people from their sins. *1:21*

55.3   Now all this was done, that it might be fulfilled which was spoken of the Lord by the prophet, saying, Behold, a virgin shall be with child, and shall bring forth a son, and they shall call his name Emmanuel, which being interpreted is, God with us.   *1:22-23*

55.4   Now when Jesus was born in Bethlehem of Judaea in the days of Herod the king, behold, there came wise men from the east to Jerusalem, Saying, Where is he that is born King of the Jews? for we have seen his star in the east, and are come to worship him. *2:1-2*

55.5   And when they were come into the house, they saw the young child with Mary his mother, and fell down, and worshipped him: and when they had opened their treasures, they presented unto him gifts; gold, and frankincense, and myrrh. *2:11*

55.6   And saying, Repent ye: for the kingdom of heaven is at hand. For this is he that was spoken of by the prophet Esaias, saying, The voice of one crying in the wilderness, Prepare ye the way of the Lord, make his paths straight. *3:2-3*

55.7   And the same John had his raiment of camel's hair, and a leathern girdle about his loins; and his meat was locusts and wild honey. *3:4*

55.8   But when he saw many of the Pharisees and Sadducees come to his baptism, he said unto them, O generation of vipers, who hath warned you to flee from the wrath to come? *3:7*

55.9   I indeed baptize you with water unto repentance: but he that cometh after me is mightier than I, whose shoes I am not worthy to bear: he shall baptize you with the Holy Ghost, and with fire. *3:11*

55.10   And Jesus, when he was baptized, went up straightway out of the water: and, lo, the heavens were opened unto him, and he saw the Spirit of God descending like a dove, and lighting upon him: And lo a voice from heaven, saying, This is my beloved Son, in whom I am well pleased. *3:16-17*

55.11   Then was Jesus led up of the Spirit into the wilderness to be tempted of the devil. And when he had fasted forty days and forty nights, he was afterward an hungred. And when the tempter came to him, he said, If thou be the Son of God, command that these stones be made

bread. But he answered and said, It is written, Man shall not live by bread alone, but by every word that proceedeth out of the mouth of God. *4:1-4*

55.12   Jesus said unto him, It is written again, Thou shalt not tempt the Lord thy God. *4:7*

55.13   Again, the devil taketh him up into an exceeding high mountain, and sheweth him all the kingdoms of the world, and the glory of them; And saith unto him, All these things will I give thee, if thou wilt fall down and worship me. Then saith Jesus unto him, Get thee hence, Satan: for it is written, Thou shalt worship the Lord thy God, and him only shalt thou serve. *4:8-10*

55.14   The people which sat in darkness saw great light; and to them which sat in the region and shadow of death light is sprung up. *4:16*

55.15   From that time Jesus began to preach, and to say, Repent: for the kingdom of heaven is at hand. *4:17*

55.16   And he saith unto them, Follow me, and I will make you fishers of men. *4:19*

55.17   And seeing the multitudes, he went up into a mountain: and when he was set, his disciples came unto him: And he opened his mouth, and taught them, saying, Blessed are the poor in spirit: for theirs is the kingdom of heaven. Blessed are they that mourn: for they shall be comforted. Blessed are the meek: for they shall inherit the earth. Blessed are they which do hunger and thirst after righteousness: for they shall be filled. Blessed are the merciful: for they shall obtain mercy. Blessed are the pure in heart: for they shall see God. Blessed are the peacemakers: for they shall be called the children of God. Blessed are they which are persecuted for righteousness' sake: for theirs is the kingdom of heaven. Blessed are ye, when men shall revile you, and persecute you, and shall say all manner of evil against you falsely, for my sake. Rejoice, and be exceeding glad: for great is your reward in heaven: for so persecuted they the prophets which were before you.   *5:1-12*

55.18   Ye are the salt of the earth: but if the salt have lost his savour, wherewith shall it be salted? it is thenceforth good for nothing, but to be cast out, and to be trodden under foot of men.   *5:13*

A well-known sermon

Many of the expressions found in Jesus' Sermon on the Mount (Matthew 5-7) have become well-known idiomatic phrases in the English language. Such expressions include the following:
the salt of the earth, *people thought to have an admirable character and to be of great value;*
hide one's light under a bushel, *to conceal or be modest about one's talents or abilities;*
an eye for an eye, *punishment or retaliation that is expressed in the same way as the offence that was committed, originally a reference to Exodus 21:24;*
turn the other cheek, *to refuse to retaliate when provoked, sometimes also to be ready to be humiliated further;*
the left hand does not know what the right hand is doing, *applied, for example, to the lack of communication between departments in a large organization;*
cast pearls before swine, *to waste something of quality or value on those who cannot appreciate it;*
the straight and narrow, *the upright, moral, and correct way to behave;*
a wolf in sheep's clothing, *someone who seems friendly and harmless but in reality is dangerous and ruthless.*

55.19   Ye are the light of the world. A city that is set on an hill cannot be hid. Neither do men light a candle, and put it under a bushel, but on a candlestick; and it giveth

light unto all that are in the house. Let your light so shine before men, that they may see your good works and glorify your Father which is in heaven.   *5:14-16*

55.20   Think not that I am come to destroy the law, or the prophets: I am not come to destroy, but to fulfil. For verily I say unto you, Till heaven and earth pass, one jot or one tittle shall in no wise pass from the law, till all be fulfilled.   *5:17-18*

55.21   For I say unto you, That except your righteousness shall exceed the righteousness of the scribes and Pharisees, ye shall in no case enter into the kingdom of heaven.   *5:20*

55.22   But I say unto you, That whosoever is angry with his brother without a cause shall be in danger of the judgment: and whosoever shall say to his brother, Raca, shall be in danger of the council: but whosoever shall say, Thou fool, shall be in danger of hell fire.   *5:22*

55.23   Ye have heard that it was said by them of old time. Thou shall not commit adultery: But I say unto you. That whosoever looketh on a woman to lust after her hath committed adultery with her already in his heart.   *5:27–28*

55.24   And if thy right eye offend thee, pluck it out, and cast it from thee: for it is profitable for thee that one of thy members should perish, and not that thy whole body should be cast into hell. And if thy right hand offend thee, cut it off, and cast it from thee: for it is profitable for thee that one of thy members should perish, and not that thy whole body should be cast into hell.   *5:29-30*

55.25   Ye have heard that it hath been said, An eye for an eye, and a tooth for a tooth: But I say unto you, That ye resist not evil: but whosoever shall smite thee on thy right cheek, turn to him the other also.   *5:38-39*

55.26   And whosoever shall compel thee to go a mile, go with him twain.   *5:41*

55.27   Ye have heard that it hath been said, Thou shalt love thy neighbour, and hate thine enemy. But I say unto you, Love your enemies, bless them that curse you, do good to them that hate you, and pray for them which despitefully use you, and persecute you.   *5:43-44*

55.28   That ye may be the children of your Father which is in heaven: for he maketh his sun to rise on the evil and on the good, and sendeth rain on the just and on the unjust.   *5:45*

55.29   Be ye therefore perfect, even as your Father which is heaven is perfect. *5:48*

55.30   Therefore when thou doest thine alms, do not sound a trumpet before thee, as the hypocrites do in the synagogues and in the streets, that they may have glory of men, Verily I say unto you, They have their reward. But when thou doest alms, let not thy left hand know what thy right hand doeth: That thine alms may be in secret: and thy Father which seeth in secret himself shall reward thee openly. *6:2-4*

55.31   And when thou prayest, thou shalt not be as the hypocrites are: for they love to pray standing in the synagogues and in the corners of the streets, that they may be seen of men. Verily I say unto you, They have their reward.   *6:5*

55.32   But thou, when thou prayest, enter into thy closet, and when thou hast shut thy door, pray to thy Father which is in secret; and thy Father which seeth in secret shall reward thee openly. But when ye pray, use not vain repetitions, as the heathen do: for they think that they shall be heard for their much speaking.   *6:6-7*

55.33   After this manner therefore pray ye: Our Father which art in heaven, Hallowed be thy name. Thy kingdom come. Thy will be done in earth, as it is in heaven. Give us this day our daily bread. And forgive us our debts, as we forgive our debtors. And lead us not into temptation, but deliver us from evil: For thine is the kingdom, and the power, and the glory, for ever. Amen.   *6:9-13*

55.34   Lay not up for yourselves treasures upon earth, where moth and rust doth corrupt, and where thieves break through and steal: But lay up for yourselves treasures in heaven, where neither moth nor rust doth corrupt, and where thieves do not break through nor steal: For where your treasure is, there will your heart be also.   *6:19-21*

55.35   No man can serve two masters: for either he will hate the one, and love the other; or else he will hold to the one, and despise the other. Ye cannot serve God and mammon.   *6:24*

55.36   Behold the fowls of the air: for they sow not, neither do they reap, nor gather into barns; yet your heavenly Father feedeth them. Are ye not much better than they? Which of you by taking thought can add one cubit unto his stature? And why take ye thought for raiment? Consider the lilies of the field, how they grow; they toil not, neither do they spin: And yet I say unto you, That even Solomon in all his glory was not arrayed like one of these.   *6:26-29*

55.37   But seek ye first the kingdom of God, and his righteousness; and all these things shall be added unto you. Take therefore no thought for the morrow: for the morrow shall take thought for the things of itself. Sufficient unto the day is the evil thereof.   *6:33-34*

55.38   Judge not, that ye be not judged. For with what judgment ye judge, ye shall be judged: and with what measure ye mete, it shall be measured to you again.   *7:1-2*

55.39   And why beholdest thou the mote that is in thy brother's eye, but considerest not the beam that is in thine own eye?   *7:3*

55.40   Give not that which is holy unto the dogs, neither cast ye your pearls before swine, lest they trample them under their feet, and turn again and rend you.   *7:6*

55.41   Ask, and it shall be given you; seek, and ye shall find; knock, and it shall be opened unto you: For every one that asketh receiveth; and he that seeketh findeth; and to him that knocketh it shall be opened.   *7:7-8*

55.42   Or what man is there of you, whom if his son ask bread, will he give him a stone? Or if he ask a fish, will he give him a serpent? If ye then, being evil, know how to give good gifts unto your children, how much more shall your Father which is in heaven give good things to them that ask him?   *7:9-11*

55.43   Therefore all things whatsoever ye would that men should do to you, do ye even so to them: for this is the law and the prophets.   *7:12*

55.44   Enter ye in at the strait gate: for wide is the gate, and broad is the way, that leadeth to destruction, and many there be which go in thereat: Because strait is the gate, and narrow is the way, which leadeth unto life, and few there be that find it.   *7:13-14*

55.45   Beware of false prophets, which come to you in sheep's clothing, but inwardly they are ravening wolves.   *7:15*

55.46   Wherefore by their fruits ye shall know them.   *7:20*

55.47   Not every one that saith unto me, Lord, Lord, shall enter into the kingdom of heaven; but he that doeth the will of my Father which is in heaven.   *7:21*

55.48   Therefore whosoever heareth these sayings of mine, and doeth them, I will liken him unto a wise man, which built his house upon a rock: And the rain descended, and the floods came, and the winds blew, and beat upon that house;

and it fell not: for it was founded upon a rock. And every one that heareth these sayings of mine, and doeth them not, shall be likened unto a foolish man, which built his house upon the sand: And the rain descended, and the floods came, and the winds blew, and beat upon that house; and it fell: and great was the fall of it. *7:24-27*

55.49   The centurion answered and said, Lord, I am not worthy that thou shouldest come under my roof: but speak the word only, and my servant shall be healed. For I am a man under authority, having soldiers under me: and I say to this man, Go, and he goeth; and to another, Come, and he cometh; and to my servant, Do this, and he doeth it. When Jesus heard it, he marvelled, and said to them that followed, Verily I say unto you, I have not found so great faith, no, not in Israel.   *8:8-10*

Say the word

The expression say the word, *to state one's intentions to someone who is willing to fulfil them immediately, has its basis in this verse. The centurion had such faith that he believed that Jesus only had to speak the word of healing and his servant would be completely well again.*

55.50   But the children of the kingdom shall be cast out into outer darkness: there shall be weeping and gnashing of teeth. *8:12*

55.51   And Jesus saith unto him, The foxes have holes, and the birds of the air have nests; but the Son of man hath not where to lay his head.   *8:20*

55.52   But Jesus said unto him, Follow me; and let the dead bury their dead. *8:22*

55.53   And his disciples came to him, and awoke him, saying, Lord, save us: we perish. And he saith unto them, Why are ye fearful, O ye of little faith? Then he arose, and rebuked the winds and the sea; and there was a great calm. But the men marvelled, saying, What manner of man is this, that even the winds and the sea obey him!   *8:25-27*

55.54   And he said unto them, Go. And when they were come out, they went into the herd of swine: and, behold, the whole herd of swine ran violently down a steep place into the sea, and perished in the waters.   *8:32*

55.55   And as Jesus passed forth from thence, he saw a man, named Matthew, sitting at the receipt of custom: and he saith unto him, Follow me. And he arose, and followed him.   *9:9*

55.56   And when the Pharisees saw it, they said unto his disciples, Why eateth your Master with publicans and sinners?   *9:11*

55.57   But when Jesus heard that, he said unto them, They that be whole need not a physician, but they that are sick. But go ye and learn what that meaneth, I will have mercy, and not sacrifice: for I am not come to call the righteous, but sinners to repentance.   *9:12-13*

55.58   No man putteth a piece of new cloth unto an old garment, for that which is put in to fill it up taketh from the garment, and the rent is made worse. Neither do men put new wine into old bottles: else the bottles break, and the wine runneth out, and the bottles perish: but they put new wine into new bottles, and both are preserved.   *9:16-17*

55.59   And, behold, a woman, which was diseased with an issue of blood twelve years, came behind him, and touched the hem of his garment: For she said within herself, If I may but touch his garment, I shall be whole. But Jesus turned him about, and when he saw her, he said, Daughter, be of good comfort; thy faith hath made thee whole. And the woman was made whole from that hour. *9:20-22*

55.60   But the Pharisees said, He casteth out devils through the prince of the devils.   *9:34*

55.61   But when he saw the multitudes, he was moved with compassion on them, because they fainted, and were scattered abroad, as sheep having no shepherd. Then saith he unto his disciples, The harvest truly is plenteous, but the labourers are few: Pray ye therefore the Lord of the harvest, that he will send forth labourers into his harvest.   *9:36-38*

55.62   Now the names of the twelve apostles are these; The first, Simon, who is called Peter, and Andrew his brother; James the son of Zebedee, and John his brother; Philip, and Bartholomew; Thomas, and Matthew the publican; James the son of Alphaeus, and Lebbaeus, whose surname was Thaddaeus; Simon the Canaanite, and Judas Iscariot, who also betrayed him.   *10:2-4*

55.63   But go rather to the lost sheep of the house of Israel.   *10:6*

55.64   Heal the sick, cleanse the lepers, raise the dead, cast out devils: freely ye have received, freely give.   *10:8*

55.65   And whosoever shall not receive you, nor hear your words, when ye depart out of that house or city, shake off the dust of your feet.   *10:14*

55.66   Behold, I send you forth as sheep in the midst of wolves: be ye therefore wise as serpents, and harmless as doves. *10:16*

55.67   And ye shall be hated of all men for my name's sake: but he that endureth to the end shall be saved.   *10:22*

55.68   The disciple is not above his master, nor the servant above his lord. *10:24*

55.69   Are not two sparrows sold for a farthing? and one of them shall not fall on the ground without your Father. But the very hairs of your head are all numbered. Fear ye not therefore, ye are of more value than many sparrows.   *10:29-31*

55.70   Think not that I am come to send peace on earth: I came not to send peace, but a sword.   *10:34*

55.71   He that loveth father or mother more than me is not worthy of me: and he that loveth son or daughter more than me is not worthy of me. And he that taketh not his cross, and followeth after me, is not worthy of me. He that findeth his life shall lose it: and he that loseth his life for my sake shall find it.   *10:37-39*

55.72   He that receiveth you receiveth me, and he that receiveth me receiveth him that sent me.   *10:40*

55.73   And whosoever shall give to drink unto one of these little ones a cup of cold water only in the name of a disciple, verily I say unto you, he shall in no wise lose his reward.   *10:42*

55.74   And said unto him, Art thou he that should come, or do we look for another?   *11:3*

55.75   Jesus answered and said unto them, Go and shew John again those things which ye do hear and see: The blind receive their sight, and the lame walk, the lepers are cleansed, and the deaf hear, the dead are raised up, and the poor have the gospel preached to them. *11:4-5*

55.76   And as they departed, Jesus began to say unto the multitudes concerning John, What went ye out into the wilderness to see A reed shaken with the wind? But what went ye out for to see? A man clothed in soft raiment? behold, they that wear soft clothing are in kings' houses. But what went ye out for to see? A prophet? yea, I say unto you, and more than a prophet. For this is he, of whom it is written, Behold, I send my messenger before thy face, which shall prepare thy way before thee.   *11:7-10*

55.77   Verily I say unto you, Among them that are born of women there hath not risen a greater than John the Baptist: notwithstanding he that is least in the kingdom of heaven is greater than he. *11:11*

55.78   He that hath ears to hear, let him hear.   *11:15*

55.79   And saying, We have piped unto you, and ye have not danced; we have mourned unto you, and ye have not lamented.   *11:17*

55.80   The Son of man came eating and drinking, and they say, Behold a man gluttonous, and winebibber, a friend of publicans and sinners. But wisdom is justified of her children.   *11:19*

55.81   Woe unto thee, Chorazin! woe unto thee, Bethsaida! for if the mighty works, which were done in you, had been done in Tyre and Sidon, they would have repented long ago in sackcloth and ashes.   *11:21*

55.82   All things are delivered unto me of my Father: and no man knoweth the Son, but the Father; neither knoweth any man the Father, save the Son, and he to whomsoever the Son will reveal him. *11:27*

55.83   Come unto me, all ye that labour and are heavy laden, and I will give you rest. Take my yoke upon you, and learn of me; for I am meek and lowly in heart: and ye shall find rest unto your souls. For my yoke is easy, and my burden is light. *11:28-30*

55.84   A bruised reed shall he not break, and smoking flax shall he not quench, till he send forth judgment unto victory. *12:20*

55.85   He that is not with me is against me: and he that gathereth not with me scattereth abroad.   *12:30*

55.86   Wherefore I say unto you, All manner of sin and blasphemy shall be forgiven unto men: but the blasphemy against the Holy Ghost shall not be forgiven unto men.   *12:31*

55.87   O generation of vipers, how can ye, being evil, speak good things? for out of the abundance of the heart the mouth speaketh.   *12:34*

55.88   But he answered and said unto them, An evil and adulterous generation seeketh after a sign; and there shall no sign be given to it, but the sign of the prophet Jonas: For Jonas was three days and three nights in the whale's belly; so shall the Son of man be three days and three nights in the heart of the earth.   *12:39-40*

55.89   The queen of the south shall rise up in the judgment with this generation, and shall condemn it: for she came from the uttermost parts of the earth to hear the wisdom of Solomon; and, behold, a greater than Solomon is here.   *12:42*

55.90   When the unclean spirit is gone out of a man, he walketh through dry places, seeking rest, and findeth none. Then he saith, I will return into my house from whence I came out; and when he is come, he findeth it empty, swept, and garnished. Then goeth he, and taketh with himself seven other spirits more wicked than himself, and they enter in and dwell there: and the last state of that man is worse than the first. Even so shall it be also unto this wicked generation. *12:43-45*

55.91   And he stretched forth his hand toward his disciples, and said, Behold my mother and my brethren! For whosoever shall do the will of my Father which is in heaven, the same is my brother, and sister, and mother.   *12:49-50*

55.92   And he spake many things unto them in parables, saying, Behold, a sower went forth to sow; And when he sowed, some seeds fell by the wayside, and the fowls came and devoured them up: Some fell upon stony places, where they had not much earth: and forthwith they sprung up, because they had no deepness of earth: And when the sun was up, they were scorched; and because they had no root, they withered away. And some fell among thorns; and the thorns sprung up, and choked them: But other fell into good ground, and brought forth fruit, some an hundredfold, some sixtyfold, some thirtyfold.   *13:3-8*

55.93   He also that received seed among the thorns is he that heareth the word; and the care of this world, and the deceitfulness of riches, choke the word, and he becometh unfruitful.   *13:22*

55.94   But he that received seed into the good ground is he that heareth the word, and understandeth it; which also beareth fruit, and bringeth forth, some an hundredfold, some sixty, some thirty. *13:23*

55.95   But while men slept, his enemy came and sowed tares among the wheat, and went his way.   *13:25*

55.96   He said unto them, An enemy hath done this. The servants said unto him, Wilt thou then that we go and gather them up?   *13:28*

55.97   Another parable put he forth unto them, saying, The kingdom of heaven is like to a grain of mustard seed which a man took, and sowed in his field: Which indeed is the least of all seeds: but when it is grown, it is the greatest among herbs, and becometh a tree, so that the birds of the air come and lodge in the branches thereof.   *13:31-32*

55.98   Again the kingdom of heaven is like unto a merchant man, seeking goodly pearls: Who, when he had found one pearl of great price, went and sold all that he had, and bought it.   *13:45-46*

55.99   And they were offended in him. But Jesus said unto them, A prophet is not without honour, save in his own country, and in his own house.   *13:57*

A prophet is without honour

The saying a prophet is without honour in his own country *is based on this statement by Jesus after he was rejected in his home town of Nazareth. In contemporary usage, the expression is applied to anyone who is generally recognized as great, except by his own family, compatriots, etc.*

55.100   And she, being before instructed of her mother, said, Give me here John Baptist's head in a charger.   *14:8*

55.101   And they say unto him, We have here but five loaves, and two fishes. *14:17*

55.102   And in the fourth watch of the night Jesus went unto them, walking on the sea. And when the disciples saw him walking on the sea, they were troubled, saying, It is a spirit; and they cried out for fear. But straightway Jesus spake unto them, saying, Be of good cheer; it is I; be not afraid.   *14:25-27*

55.103   And immediately Jesus stretched forth his hand, and caught him, and said unto him, O thou of little faith, wherefore didst thou doubt?   *14:31*

55.104   Not that which goeth into the mouth defileth a man; but that which cometh out of the mouth, this defileth a man.   *15:11*

The blind leading the blind

The saying the blind leading the blind *refers to inexperienced people who try to guide others who are similarly inexperienced. The result is that neither group is helped. The expression derives from this comment by Jesus about his critics, the Pharisees.*

55.105   Let them alone: they be blind leaders of the blind. And if the blind lead the blind, both shall fall into the ditch. *15:14*

55.106   And she said, Truth, Lord: yet the dogs eat of the crumbs which fall from their masters' table.   *15:27*

55.107   He answered and said unto them, When it is evening, ye say, It will be fair weather: for the sky is red. And in the morning, It will be foul weather to day: for the sky is red and lowring. O ye hypocrites, ye can discern the face of the sky; but can ye not discern the signs of the times?   *16:2-3*

55.108   And Simon Peter answered and said, Thou art the Christ, the Son of the living God. And Jesus answered and said unto him, Blessed art thou, Simon Barjona: for flesh and blood hath not revealed it unto thee, but my Father which is in heaven. And I say also unto thee, That thou art Peter, and upon this rock I will build my church; and the gates of hell shall not prevail against it. And I will give unto thee the keys of the kingdom of heaven: and whatsoever thou shalt loose on earth shall be loosed in heaven. *16:16-19*

55.109   From that time forth began Jesus to shew unto his disciples, how that he must go unto Jerusalem, and suffer many things of the elders and chief priests and scribes, and be killed, and be raised again the third day. Then Peter took him, and began to rebuke him, saying, Be it far from thee, Lord: this shall not be unto thee. But he turned, and said unto Peter, Get thee behind me, Satan: thou art an offence unto me: for thou savourest not the things that be of God, but those that be of men.   *16:21-23*

55.110   Then said Jesus unto his disciples, If any man will come after me, let him deny himself, and take up his cross, and follow me. For whosoever will save his life shall lose it: and whosoever will lose his life for my sake shall find it. For what is a man profited, if he shall gain the whole world, and lose his own soul?

or what shall a man give in exchange for his soul?   *16:24-26*

55.111   And was transfigured before them: and his face did shine as the sun, and his raiment was white as the light. *17:2*

55.112   And Jesus said unto them, Because of your unbelief: for verily I say unto you, If ye have faith as a grain of mustard seed, ye shall say unto this mountain, Remove hence to yonder place; and it shall remove; and nothing shall be impossible unto you.   *17:20*

55.113   And said, Verily I say unto you, Except ye be converted, and become as little children, ye shall not enter into the kingdom of heaven.   *18:3*

55.114   And whoso shall receive one such little child in my name receiveth me. But whoso shall offend one of these little ones which believe in me, it were better for him that a millstone were hanged about his neck, and that he were drowned in the depth of the sea.   *18:5-6*

55.115   Wherefore if thy hand or thy foot offend thee, cut them off, and cast them from thee: it is better for thee to enter into life halt or maimed, rather than having two hands or two feet to be cast into everlasting fire. And if thine eye offend thee, pluck it out, and cast it from thee: it is better for thee to enter into life with one eye, rather than having two eyes to be cast into hell fire.   *18:8-9*

55.116   Moreover if thy brother shall trespass against thee, go and tell him his fault between thee and him alone: if he shall hear thee, thou hast gained thy brother. But if he will not hear thee, then take with thee one or two more, that in the mouth of two or three witnesses every word may be established. And if he shall neglect to hear them, tell it unto the church: but if he neglect to hear the church, let him be unto thee as an heathen man and a publican. Verily I say unto you, Whatsoever ye shall bind on earth shall be

bound in heaven: and whatsoever ye shall loose on earth shall be loosed in heaven. *18:15-18*

55.117   Again I say unto you, That if two of you shall agree on earth as touching any thing that they shall ask, it shall be done for them of my Father which is in heaven. For where two or three are gathered together in my name, there am I in the midst of them.   *18:19-20*

55.118   Then came Peter to him, and said, Lord, how oft shall my brother sin against me, and I forgive him? till seven times? Jesus saith unto him, I say not unto thee, Until seven times: but, Until seventy times seven.   *18:21-22*

55.119   But the same servant went out, and found one of his fellowservants, which owed him an hundred pence: and he laid hands on him, and took him by the throat, saying, Pay me that thou owest. *18:28*

55.120   And said, For this cause shall a man leave father and mother, and shall cleave to his wife: and they twain shall be one flesh? Wherefore they are no more twain, but one flesh What therefore God hath joined together, let not man put asunder.   *19:5-6*

55.121   And I say unto you, Whosoever shall put away his wife, except it be for fornication, and shall marry another, committeth adultery: and whoso marrieth her which is put away doth commit adultery.   *19:9*

55.122   Then were there brought unto him little children, that he should put his hands on them, and pray: and the disciples rebuked them. But Jesus said, Suffer little children, and forbid them not, to come unto me: for of such is the kingdom of heaven. And he laid his hands on them, and departed thence.   *19:13-15*

55.123   And he said unto him, Why callest thou me good? there is none good but one, that is, God: but if thou wilt enter into life, keep the commandments.   *19:17*

55.124   He saith unto him, Which? Jesus said, Thou shalt do no murder, Thou shalt not commit adultery, Thou shalt not steal, Thou shalt not bear false witness, Honour thy father and thy mother: and, Thou shalt love thy neighbour as thyself.   *19:18-19*

55.125   Jesus said unto him, If thou wilt be perfect, go and sell that thou hast, and give to the poor, and thou shalt have treasure in heaven: and come and follow me. But when the young man heard that saying, he went away sorrowful: for he had great possessions.   *19:21-22*

55.126   And again I say unto you, It is easier for a camel to go through the eye of a needle, than for a rich man to enter into the kingdom of God.   *19:24*

55.127   When his disciples heard it, they were exceedingly amazed, saying, Who then can be saved? But Jesus beheld them, and said unto them, With men this is impossible; but with God all things are possible.   *19:25-26*

55.128   But many that are first shall be last; and the last shall be first.   *19:30*

55.129   And about the eleventh hour he went out, and found others standing idle, and saith unto them, Why stand ye here all the day idle?   *20:6*

At the eleventh hour

At the eleventh hour *means at the last possible moment; nearly, but just not, too late for something to happen. The expression refers to the time of the hiring of the final workers in Jesus' parable about the labourers in the vineyard.*

55.130   Is it not lawful for me to do what I will with mine own? Is thine eye evil, because I am good? So the last shall be

first, and the first last: for many be called, but few chosen.   *20:15-16*

55.131   But Jesus answered and said, Ye know not what ye ask. Are ye able to drink of the cup that I shall drink of, and to be baptized with the baptism that I am baptized with? They say unto him, We are able. And he saith unto the, Ye shall drink indeed of my cup, and be baptized with the baptism that I am baptized with: but to sit on my right hand, and on my left, is not mine to give, but it shall be given to them for whom it is prepared of my Father.   *20:22-23*

55.132   All this was done, that it might be fulfilled which was spoken by the prophet, saying, Tell ye the daughter of Sion, Behold, thy King cometh unto thee, meek, and sitting upon an ass, and a colt the foal of an ass.   *21:4-5*

55.133   And a very great multitude spread their garments in the way; others cut down branches from the trees, and strawed them in the way. And the multitudes that went before, and that followed, cried, saying, Hosanna to the Son of David: Blessed is he that cometh in the name of the Lord; Hosanna in the highest.   *21:8-9*

55.134   And Jesus went into the temple of God, and cast out all them that sold and bought in the temple, and overthrew the tables of the moneychangers, and the seats of them that sold doves, And said unto them, It is written, My house shall be called the house of prayer; but ye have made it a den of thieves.   *21:12-13*

55.135   And when he saw a fig tree in the way, he came to it, and found nothing thereon, but leaves only, and said unto it, Let no fruit grown on thee henceforward for ever. And presently the fig tree withered away.   *21:19*

55.136   Jesus answered and said unto them, Verily I say unto you, If ye have faith, and doubt not, ye shall not only do this which is done to the fig tree, but also if ye shall say unto this mountain, Be thou removed, and be thou cast into the sea; it shall be done. And all things, whatsoever ye shall ask in prayer, believing, ye shall receive.   *21:21-22*

55.137   Go ye therefore into the highways, and as many as ye shall find, bid to the marriage.   *22:9*

55.138   They say unto him, Caesar's. Then saith he unto them, Render therefore unto Caesar the things which are Caesar's; and unto God the things that are God's.   *22:21*

55.139   For in the resurrection they neither marry, nor are given in marriage, but are as the angels of God in heaven. *22:30*

55.140   Jesus said unto him, Thou shalt love the Lord thy God with all thy heart, and with all thy soul, and with all thy mind. This is the first and great commandment. And the second is like unto it, Thou shalt love thy neighbour as thyself. On these two commandments hang all the law and the prophets. *22:37-40*

55.141   But he that is greatest among you shall be your servant.   *23:11*

55.142   Ye blind guides, which strain at a gnat, and swallow a camel.   *23:24*

55.143   Woe unto you, scribes and Pharisees, hypocrites! for ye are like unto whited sepulchres, which indeed appear beautiful outward, but are within full of dead men's bones, and of all uncleanness.   *23:27*

55.144   O Jerusalem, Jerusalem, thou that killest the prophets, and stonest them which are sent unto thee, how often would I have gathered thy children together, even as a hen gathereth her chickens under her wings, and ye would not!   *23:37*

55.145   And ye shall hear of wars and rumours of wars: see that ye be not troubled: for all these things must come to pass, but the end is not yet. For nation shall rise against nation, and kingdom against kingdom: and there shall be famines, and pestilences, and earthquakes, in divers places.   *24:6-7*

55.146   And this gospel of the kingdom shall be preached in all the world for a witness unto all nations; and then shall the end come.   *24:14*

55.147   For as the lightning cometh out of the east, and shineth even unto the west; so shall also the coming of the Son of man be.   *24:27*

55.148   Immediately after the tribulation of those days shall the sun be darkened, and the moon shall not give her light, and the stars shall fall from heaven, and the powers of the heavens shall be shaken: And then shall appear the sign of the Son of man in heaven: and then shall all the tribes of the earth mourn, and they shall see the Son of man coming in the clouds of heaven with power and great glory. And he shall send his angels with a great sound of a trumpet, and they shall gather together his elect from the four winds, from one end of heaven to the other. *24:29-31*

55.149   Verily I say unto you, This generation shall not pass, till all these things be fulfilled. Heaven and earth shall pass away, but my words shall not pass away.   *24:34-35*

55.150   But of that day and hour knoweth no man, no, not the angels of heaven, but my Father only.   *24:36*

55.151   For as in the days that were before the flood they were eating and drinking, marrying and giving in marriage, until the day that Noe entered into the ark. *24:38*

55.152   Watch therefore: for ye know not what hour your Lord doth come. But know this, that if the goodman of the house had known in what watch the thief would come, he would have watched, and would not have suffered his house to be broken up. *24:42-43*

55.153   And at midnight there was a cry made, Behold, the bridegroom cometh; go ye out to meet him. Then all those virgins arose, and trimmed their lamps. And the foolish said unto the wise, Give us of your oil; for our lamps are gone out. *25:6-8*

55.154   Afterward came also the other virgins, saying, Lord, Lord, open to us. But he answered and said, Verily I say unto you, I know you not. Watch therefore, for ye know neither the day nor the hour wherein the Son of man cometh. *25:11-13*

55.155   For the kingdom of heaven is as a man travelling into a far country, who called his own servants, and delivered unto them his goods. And unto one he gave five talents, to another two, and another one; to every man according to his several ability; and straightway took his journey. *25:14-15*

55.156   His lord said unto him, Well done, thou good and faithful servant: thou hast been faithful over a few things, I will make thee ruler over many things: enter thou into the joy of thy lord. *25:21*

55.157   His lord said unto him, Well done, good and faithful servant; thou hast been faithful over a few things, I will make thee ruler over many things: enter thou into the joy of thy lord. *25:23*

55.158   Then he which had received the one talent came and said, Lord, I knew thee that thou art an hard man, reaping where thou hast not sown, and gathering where thou hast not strawed: And I was afraid, and went and hid thy talent in the earth: lo, there thou hast that is thine. *25:24-25*

55.159   For unto every one that hath shall be given, and he shall have abundance: but from him that hath not shall be taken away even that which he hath. And cast ye the unprofitable servant into outer darkness: there shall be weeping and gnashing of teeth. *25:29-30*

55.160   When the Son of man shall come in his glory, and all the holy angels with him, then shall he sit upon the throne of his glory: And before him shall be gathered all nations: and he shall separate them one from another, as a shepherd divideth his sheep from the goats: And he shall set the sheep on his right hand, but the goats on the left. *25:31-33*

55.161   Then shall the King say unto them on his right hand, Come, ye blessed of my Father, inherit the kingdom prepared for you from the foundation of the world: For I was an hungred, and ye gave me meat: I was thirsty, and ye gave me drink: I was a stranger, and ye took me in: Naked, and ye clothed me: I was sick, and ye visited me: I was in prison, and ye came unto me. *25:34-36*

55.162   And the King shall answer and say unto them, Verily I say unto you, Inasmuch as ye have done it unto one of the least of these my brethren, ye have done it unto me. *25:40*

55.163   Then shall he say also unto them on the left hand, Depart from me, ye cursed, into everlasting fire, prepared for the devil and his angels: For I was an hungred, and ye gave me no meat: I was thirsty, and ye gave me no drink: I was a stranger, and ye took me not in: naked, and ye clothed me not: sick, and in prison, and ye visited me not. *25:41-43*

55.164   There came unto him a woman having an alabaster box of very precious ointment, and poured it on his head, as he sat at meat. But when his disciples saw it, they had indignation, saying, To what purpose is this waste? For this ointment might have been sold for much, and given to the poor. *26:7-9*

55.165 For ye have the poor always with you; but me ye have not always. *26:11*

55.166 Then one of the twelve, called Judas Isacariot, went unto the chief priests, And said unto them, What will ye give me, and I will deliver him unto you? And they covenanted with him for thirty pieces of silver. *26:14-15*

55.167 And as they were eating, Jesus took bread, and blessed it, and brake it, and gave it to the disciples, and said, Take, eat; this is my body. And he took the cup, and gave thanks, and gave it to them, saying, Drink ye all of it; For this is my blood of the new testament, which is shed for many for the remission of sins. *26:26-28*

55.168 Jesus said unto him, Verily I say unto thee, That this night, before the cock crow, thou shalt deny me thrice. Peter said unto him, Though I should die with thee yet will I not deny thee. Likewise also said all the disciples. *26:34-35*

55.169 And he took with him Peter and the two sons of Zebedee, and began to be sorrowful and very heavy. Then saith he unto them, My soul is exceeding sorrowful, even unto death: tarry ye here, and watch with me. *26:37-38*

The spirit is willing

The saying the spirit is willing but the flesh is weak *is used to show that someone lacks the ability, energy, or will-power to put his or her good intentions into practice. The expression is often used as an explanation of someone's failure to do something. The phrase derives from this warning by Jesus to his disciples to remain alert and not to yield to temptation.*

55.170 And he went a little further, and fell on his face, and prayed, saying, O my Father, if it be possible, let this cup pass from me: nevertheless not as I will, but as thou wilt. *26:39*

55.171 Watch and pray, that ye enter not into temptation: the spirit indeed is willing, but the flesh is weak. *26:41*

55.172 And forthwith he came to Jesus, and said, Hail, master; and kissed him. *26:49*

55.173 Then said Jesus unto him, Put up again thy sword into his place: for all they that take the sword shall perish with the sword. *26:52*

55.174 But Jesus held his peace. And the high priest answered and said unto him, I adjure thee by the living God, that thou tell us whether thou be the Christ, the Son of God. Jesus saith unto him, Thou hast said: nevertheless I say unto you, Hereafter shall ye see the Son of man sitting on the right hand of power, and coming in the clouds of heaven. *26:63-64*

55.175 And after a while came unto him they that stood by, and said to Peter, Surely thou also art one of them; for thy speech bewrayeth thee. Then began he to curse and to swear, saying, I know not the man. And immediately the cock crew. And Peter remembered the word of Jesus, which said unto him, Before the cock crow, thou shalt deny me thrice. And he went out, and wept bitterly. *26:73-75*

55.176 Then Judas, which had betrayed him, when he saw that he was condemned, repented himself, and brought again the thirty pieces of silver to the chief priests and elders. *27:3*

55.177 Pilate saith unto them, What shall I do then with Jesus which is called Christ? They all say unto him, Let him be crucified. And the governor said, Why, what evil hath he done? But they cried out the more, saying, Let him be crucified. *27:22-23*

55.178 When Pilate saw that he could prevail nothing, but that rather a tumult was made, he took water, and washed his hands before the multitude, saying I am innocent of the blood of this just person: see ye to it. Then answered all the people, and said, His blood be on us, and on our children.   *27:24-25*

Wash one's hands of

The expression wash one's hands of something *means to say or show that one no longer wants to be responsible for or involved in an action. This idiomatic phrase has its origins in this verse: Pilate washed his hands, symbolizing his dissociation from the desire of the people to crucify Jesus. He refused to assume responsibility for Jesus' death.*

55.179   Then released he Barabbas unto them: and when he had scourged Jesus, he delivered him to be crucified.   *27:26*

55.180   And they stripped him, and put on him a scarlet robe. And when they had platted a crown of thorns, they put it upon his head, and a reed in his right hand: and they bowed the knee before him, and mocked him, saying, Hail, King of the Jews! And they spit upon him, and took the reed, and smote him on the head. And after that they had mocked him, they took the robe off from him, and put his own raiment on him, and led him away to crucify him.   *27:28.31*

55.181   They gave him vinegar to drink mingled with gall: and when he had tasted thereof, he would not drink. And they crucified him, and parted his garments, casting lots: that it might be fulfilled which was spoken by the prophet, They parted my garments among them, and upon my vesture did they cast lots.   *27:34-35*

55.182   And set up over his head his accusation written, THIS IS JESUS THE KING OF THE JEWS.   *27:37*

55.183   And saying, Thou that destroyest the temple, and buildest it in three days, save thyself. If thou be the Son of God, come down from the cross.   *27:40*

55.184   He saved others; himself he cannot save. If he be the King of Israel, let him now come down from the cross, and we will believe him.   *27:42*

55.185   Now from the sixth hour there was darkness over all the land unto the ninth hour.   *27:45*

55.186   And about the ninth hour Jesus cried with a loud voice, saying Eli, Eli, lama sabachthani? that is to say, My God, my God, why hast thou forsaken me? *27:46*

55.187   Jesus, when he had cried again with a loud voice, yielded up the ghost. And behold, the veil of the temple was rent in twain from the top to the bottom; and the earth did quake, and the rocks rent; And the graves were opened; and many bodies of the saints which slept arose.   *27:50-52*

55.188   He is not here: for he is risen, as he said. Come, see the place where the Lord lay. And go quickly, and tell his disciples that he is risen from the dead; and, behold, he goeth before you into Galilee; there shall ye see him: lo, I have told you.   *28:6-7*

55.189   And Jesus came and spake unto them, saying, All power is given unto me in heaven and in earth. Go ye therefore, and teach all nations, baptizing them in the name of the Father, and of the Son, and of the Holy Ghost: Teaching them to observe all things whatsoever I have commanded you: and, lo, I am with you alway, even unto the end of the world. Amen.   *28:18-20*

ST MARK

56.1   The beginning of the gospel of Jesus Christ, the Son of God.   *1:1*

56.2　And preached, saying, There cometh one mightier than I after me, the latchet of whose shoes I am not worthy to stoop down and unloose. I indeed have baptized you with water: but he shall baptize you with the Holy Ghost.   *1:7-8*

56.3　Now after that John was put in prison, Jesus came into Galilee, preaching the gospel of the kingdom of God, And saying, The time is fulfilled, and the kingdom of God is at hand: repent ye, and believe the gospel.   *1:14-15*

56.4　Whether is it easier to say to the sick of the palsy, Thy sins be forgiven thee; or to say, Arise, and take up thy bed, and walk? But that ye may know that the Son of man hath power on earth to forgive sins, (he saith to the sick of the palsy,) I say unto thee, Arise, and take up thy bed, and go thy way into thine house. And immediately he arose, took up the bed, and went forth before them all; insomuch that they were all amazed, and glorified God, saying, We never saw it on this fashion.   *2:9-12*

56.5　When Jesus heard it, he saith unto them, They that are whole have no need of the physician, but they that are sick: I came not to call the righteous, but sinners to repentance.   *2:17*

56.6　And he said unto them, The sabbath was made for man, and not man for the sabbath: Therefore the Son of man is Lord also of the sabbath.   *2:27-28*

56.7　And if a kingdom be divided against itself, that kingdom cannot stand. And if a house be divided against itself, that house cannot stand. And if Satan rise up against himself, and be divided, he cannot stand, but hath an end. No man can enter into a strong man's house, and spoil his goods, except he will first bind the strong man; and then he will spoil his house.   *3:24-27*

56.8　And he said unto them, He that hath ears to hear, let him hear.   *4:9*

56.9　And he said unto them, Take heed what ye hear: with what measure ye mete, it shall be measured to you: and unto you that hear shall more be given.   *4:24*

56.10　And he asked him, What is thy name? And he answered, saying, My name is Legion: for we are many.   *5:9*

56.11　And they come to Jesus, and see him that was possessed with the devil, and had the legion, sitting, and clothed, and in his right mind: and they were afraid.   *5:15*

56.12　And Jesus, immediately knowing in himself that virtue had gone out of him, turned him about in the press, and said, Who touched my clothes?   *5:30*

56.13　And he said unto them, Come ye yourselves apart into a desert place, and rest a while: for there were many coming and going, and they had no leisure so much as to eat.   *6:31*

56.14　And were beyond measure astonished, saying, He hath done all things well: he maketh both the deaf to hear, and the dumb to speak.   *7:37*

56.15　And he looked up, and said, I see men as trees, walking.   *8:24*

56.16　And straightway the father of the child cried out, and said with tears, Lord, I believe; help thou mine unbelief.   *9:24*

56.17　But when Jesus saw it, he was much displeased, and said unto them, Suffer the little children to come unto me, and forbid them not: for of such is the kingdom of God.   *10:14*

56.18　For even the Son of man came not to be ministered unto, but to minister, and to give his life a ransom for many.   *10:45*

56.19　And there came a certain poor widow, and she threw in two mites, which make a farthing. And he called unto him his disciples, and saith unto them, Verily I say unto you, That this poor widow hath cast more in, than all they which have cast into the treasury: For all they did cast in of their abundance; but she of her want did cast in all that she had, even all her living.   *12:42-44*

The widow's mite

A widow's mite *is a small gift of money that is more than the giver can afford. The phrase alludes to the offering by the widow whose commitment to God was total: she gave all she had to live on.*

56.20   And he said, Abba, Father, all things are possible unto thee; take away this cup from me: nevertheless not what I will, but what thou wilt.   *14:36*

56.21   And he cometh the third time, and saith unto them, Sleep on now, and take your rest: it is enough, the hour is come; behold, the Son of man is betrayed into the hands of sinners. Rise up, let us go; lo, he that betrayeth me is at hand. *14:51-52*

56.22   And when the centurion, which stood over against him, saw that he so cried out, and gave up the ghost, he said, Truly this man was the Son of God. *15:39*

56.23   But go your way, tell his disciples and Peter that he goeth before you into Galilee: there shall ye see him, as he said unto you.   *16:7*

56.24   And he said unto them, Go ye into all the world, and preach the gospel to every creature.   *16:15*

ST LUKE

57.1   It seemed good to me also, having had perfect understanding of all things from the very first, to write unto thee in order, most excellent Theophilus.   *1:3*

57.2   For he shall be great in the sight of the Lord, and shall drink neither wine nor strong drink; and he shall be filled with the Holy Ghost, even from his mother's womb.   *1:15*

57.3   And he shall go before him in the spirit and power of Elias, to turn the hearts of the fathers to the children, and the disobedient to the wisdom of the just; to make ready a people prepared for the Lord.   *1:17*

57.4   And the angel came in unto her, and said, Hail, thou that art highly favoured, the Lord is with thee: blessed art thou among women. And when she saw him, she was troubled at his saying, and cast in her mind what manner of salutation this should be.   *1:28-29*

57.5   And the angel said unto her, Fear not, Mary: for thou hast found favour with God. And, behold, thou shalt conceive in thy womb, and bring forth a son, and shalt call his name JESUS. He shall be great, and shall be called the Son of the Highest; and the Lord God shall give unto him the throne of his father David: And he shall reign over the house of Jacob for ever; and of his kingdom there shall be no end.   *1:30-33*

57.6   And the angel answered and said unto her, The Holy Ghost shall come upon thee, and the power of the Highest shall overshadow thee: therefore also that holy thing which shall be born of thee shall be called the Son of God.   *1:35*

57.7   For with God nothing shall be impossible.   *1:37*

57.8   And Mary said, Behold the handmaid of the Lord; be it unto me according to thy word. And the angel departed from her.   *1:38*

57.9   And she spake out with a loud voice, and said, Blessed art thou among women, and blessed is the fruit of thy womb.   *1:42*

57.10   And Mary said, My soul doth magnify the Lord, And my spirit hath rejoiced in God my Saviour. For he hath regarded the low estate of his handmaiden: for, behold, from henceforth all generations shall call me blessed. For he that is mighty hath done to me great things; and holy is his name. And his mercy is on them that fear him from generation to generation. He hath shewed strength with his arm; he hath scattered the proud in the imagination of their hearts. He hath put down the mighty from their seats, and exalted them of low degree. He hath filled the hungry with good things; and the rich he hath sent empty away. He hath holpen his servant Israel, in remembrance of his mercy; As he spake to our fathers, to Abraham, and to his seed for ever. *1:46-55*

57.11   And thou, child, shalt be called the prophet of the Highest: for thou shalt go before the face of the Lord to prepare his ways; To give knowledge of salvation unto his people by the remission of their sins, Through the tender mercy of our God; whereby the dayspring from on high hath visited us, To give light to them that sit in darkness and in the shadow of death, to guide our feet into the way of peace.   *1:76-79*

57.12   And it came to pass in those days, that there went out a decree from Caesar Augustus, that all the world should be taxed.   *2:1*

57.13   And so it was, that, while they were there, the days were accomplished that she should be delivered. And she brought forth her firstborn son, and wrapped him in swaddling clothes, and laid him in a manger; because there was no room for them in the inn.   *2:6-7*

57.14   And there were in the same country shepherds abiding in the field,

keeping watch over their flock by night. And, lo, the angel of the Lord came upon them, and the glory of the Lord shone round about them: and they were sore afraid. And the angel said unto them, Fear not: for, behold, I bring you good tidings of great joy, which shall be to all people. For unto you is born this day in the city of David a Saviour, which is Christ the Lord. And this shall be a sign unto you; Ye shall find the babe wrapped in swaddling clothes, lying in a manger. And suddenly there was with the angel a multitude of the heavenly host praising God, and saying, Glory to God in the highest, and on earth peace, good will toward men. And it came to pass, as the angels were gone away from them into heaven, the shepherds said one to another, Let us now go even unto Bethlehem, and see this thing which is come to pass, which the Lord hath made known unto us.   *2:8-15*

57.15   But Mary kept all these things, and pondered them in her heart.   *2:19*

57.16   And, behold, there was a man in Jerusalem, whose name was Simeon; and the same man was just and devout, waiting for the consolation of Israel: and the Holy Ghost was upon him.   *2:25*

57.17   Lord, now lettest thou thy servant depart in peace, according to thy word: For mine eyes have seen thy salvation, Which thou hast prepared before the face of all people; A light to lighten the Gentiles, and the glory of thy people Israel.   *2:29-32*

57.18   And the child grew, and waxed strong in spirit, filled with wisdom: and the grace of God was upon him.   *2:40*

57.19   And he said unto them, How is it that ye sought me? wist ye not that I must be about my Father's business?   *2:49*

57.20   And Jesus increased in wisdom and stature, and in favour with God and man.   *2:52*

57.21   The Spirit of the Lord is upon me, because he hath anointed me to preach the gospel to the poor; he hath sent me to heal the brokenhearted, to preach deliverance to the captives, and recovering of sight to the blind, to set at liberty them that are bruised, To preach the acceptable year of the Lord.   *4:18-19*

57.22   And he said unto them, Ye will surely say unto me this proverb, Physician, heal thyself: whatsoever we have heard done in Capernaum, do also here in thy country.   *4:23*

57.23   And Simon answering said unto him, Master, we have toiled all the night, and have taken nothing: nevertheless at thy word I will let down the net.   *5:5*

57.24   When Simon Peter saw it, he fell down at Jesus' knees, saying, Depart from me; for I am a sinful man, O Lord. For he was astonished, and all that were with him, at the draught of the fishes which they had taken.   *5:8-9*

57.25   Woe unto you, when all men shall speak well of you! for so did their fathers to the false prophets.   *6:26*

57.26   Give, and it shall be given unto you; good measure, pressed down, and shaken together, and running over, shall men give into your bosom. For with the same measure that ye mete withal it shall be measured to you again.   *6:38*

57.27   And he turned to the woman, and said unto Simon, Seest thou this woman? I entered into thine house, thou gavest me no water for my feet: but she hath washed my feet with tears, and wiped them with the hairs of her head.   *7:44*

57.28   Wherefore I say unto thee, Her sins, which are many, are forgiven; for she loved much: but to whom little is forgiven, the same loveth little.   *7:47*

57.29   And he said to them all, If any man will come after me, let him deny himself, and take up his cross daily, and follow me.   *9:23*

57.30   And Jesus said unto him, No man, having put his hand to the plough, and looking back, is fit for the kingdom of God.   *9:62*

57.31   And into whatsoever house ye enter, first say, Peace be to this house. And if the son of peace be there, your peace shall rest upon it: if not, it shall turn to you again. And in the same house remain, eating and drinking such things as they give: for the labourer is worthy of his hire. Go not from house to house.   *10:5-7*

57.32   And he said unto them, I beheld Satan as lightning fall from heaven.   *10:18*

57.33   Notwithstanding in this rejoice not, that the spirits are subject unto you; but rather rejoice, because your names are written in heaven.   *10:20*

57.34   In that hour Jesus rejoiced in spirit, and said, I thank thee, O Father, Lord of heaven and earth, that thou hast hid these things from the wise and prudent, and hast revealed them unto babes: even so, Father; for so it seemed good in thy sight.   *10:21*

57.35   And Jesus answering said, A certain man went down from Jerusalem to Jericho, and fell among thieves, which stripped him of his raiment, and wounded him, and departed, leaving him half dead. And by chance there came down a certain priest that way: and when he saw him, he passed by on the other side.   *10:30-31*

57.36   But a certain Samaritan, as he journeyed, came where he was: and when he saw him, he had compassion on him, And went to him, and bound up his wounds, pouring in oil and wine, and set him on his own beast, and brought him to an inn, and took care of him. And on the morrow when he departed, he took out two pence, and gave them to the host, and said unto him, Take care of him; and whatsoever thou spendest more, when I come again, I will repay thee.   *10:33-35*

The good Samaritan

A good Samaritan *is someone who helps others who are in need. The expression alludes to the parable Jesus told of the Samaritan who rescued and helped the injured man who had been attacked and robbed. A priest and a Levite went by,* 'passed by on the other side', *without taking any action. It was a Samaritan - and the story is all the more pointed because Jews regarded Samaritans with contempt - who helped the man and looked after him personally and generously. It is the good Samaritan's kind and selfless actions to the person in distress that are remembered in the expression which has become part of the language.*

57.37   And he said, He that shewed mercy on him. Then said Jesus unto him, Go, and do thou likewise.   *10:37*

57.38   But Martha was cumbered about much serving, and came to him, and said, Lord, dost thou not care that my sister hath left me to serve alone? bid her therefore that she help me. And Jesus answered and said unto her, Martha, Martha, thou art careful and troubled about many things: But one thing is needful: and Mary hath chosen that good part, which shall not be taken away from her.   *10:40-42*

57.39   And it came to pass, that, as he was praying in a certain place, when he ceased, one of his disciples said unto him, Lord, teach us to pray, as John also taught his disciples.   *11:1*

57.40   He that is not with me is against me: and he that gathereth not with me scattereth.   *11:23*

57.41   In the mean time, when there were gathered together an innumerable

multitude of people, insomuch that they trode one upon another, he began to say unto his disciples first of all, Beware ye of the leaven of the Pharisees, which is hypocrisy.   *12:1*

57.42   And he said, This will I do: I will pull down my barns, and build greater; and there will I bestow all my fruits and my goods. And I will say to my soul, Soul, thou hast much goods laid up for many years; take thine ease, eat, drink, and be merry. But God said unto him, Thou fool, this night thy soul shall be required of thee: then whose shall those things be, which thou hast provided? So is he that layeth up treasure for himself, and is not rich toward God.   *12:18-21*

57.43   Let your loins be girded about, and your lights burning.   *12:35*

57.44   But when thou art bidden, go and sit down in the lowest room; that when he that bade thee cometh, he may say unto thee, Friend, go up higher: then shalt thou have worship in the presence of them that sit at meat with thee.   *14:10*

57.45   And they all with one consent began to make excuse. The first said unto him, I have bought a piece of ground, and I must needs go and see it: I pray thee have me excused. And another said, I have bought five yoke of oxen, and I go to prove them: I pray thee have me excused. And another said, I have married a wife, and therefore I cannot come. So that servant came, and shewed his lord these things. Then the master of the house being angry said to his servant, Go out quickly into the streets and lanes of the city, and bring in hither the poor, and the maimed, and the halt, and the blind.   *14:18-21*

57.46   And the lord said unto the servant, Go out into the highways and hedges, and compel them to come in, that my house may be filled.   *14:23*

57.47   For which of you, intending to build a tower, sitteth not down first, and counteth the cost, whether he have sufficient to finish it?   *14.28*

57.48   What man of you, having an hundred sheep, if he lose one of them, doth not leave the ninety and nine in the wilderness, and go after that which is lost, until he find it? And when he hath found it, he layeth it on his shoulders, rejoicing.   *15:4-5*

57.49   Either what woman having ten pieces of silver, if she lose one piece, doth not light a candle, and sweep the house, and seek diligently till she find it? And when she hath found it, she calleth her friends and her neighbours together, saying, Rejoice with me; for I have found the piece which I had lost. Likewise, I say unto you, there is joy in the presence of the angels of God over one sinner that repenteth.   *15:8-10*

57.50   And not many days after the younger son gathered all together, and took his journey into a far country, and there wasted his substance with riotous living.   *15:13*

The prodigal son

A prodigal *or a* prodigal son *is a reformed spendthrift - for example someone who leaves his family early and spends all his money carelessly but later returns home sorry for his actions. The expression alludes to this parable of Jesus. When the son returned, he was welcomed home by his father, who celebrated his home-coming by holding a feast. They* killed the fatted calf *in his honour - they gave him the best possible food and treatment.*

57.51   And he would fain have filled his belly with the husks that the swine did eat: and no man gave unto him. And when he came to himself, he said, How many hired servants of my father's have bread enough and to spare, and I perish with hunger! I will arise and go to my father, and will say unto him, Father, I

have sinned against heaven, and before thee, And am no more worthy to be called thy son: make me as one of thy hired servants.   *15:16-19*

57.52   And he arose, and came to his father. But when he was yet a great way off, his father saw him, and had compassion, and ran, and fell on his neck, and kissed him. And the son said unto him, Father, I have sinned against heaven, and in thy sight, and am no more worthy to be called thy son. But the father said to his servants, Bring forth the best robe, and put it on him; and put a ring on his hand, and shoes on his feet: And bring hither the fatted calf, and kill it: and let us eat, and be merry;: For this my son was dead, and is alive again; he was lost, and is found. And they began to be merry. *15:20-24*

57.53   But as soon as this thy son was come, which hath devoured thy living with harlots, thou hast killed for him the fatted calf.   *15:30*

57.54   It was meet that we should make merry, and be glad: for this thy brother was dead, and is alive again; and was lost, and is found.   *15:32*

57.55   And the lord commended the unjust steward, because he had done wisely: for the children of this world are in their generation wiser than the children of light.   *16:8*

57.56   And I say unto you, Make to yourselves friends of the mammon of unrighteousness; that, when ye fail, they may receive you into everlasting habitations.   *16:9*

57.57   He that is faithful in that which is least is faithful also in much: and he that is unjust in the least is unjust also in much.   *16:10*

57.58   There was a certain rich man, which was clothed in purple and fine linen, and fared sumptuously every day: And there was a certain beggar named

Lazarus, which was laid at his gate, full of sores, And desiring to be fed with the crumbs which fell from the rich man's table: moreover the dogs came and licked his sores. *16:19-21*

57.59 And it came to pass, that the beggar died, and was carried by the angels into Abraham's bosom: the rich man also died, and was buried; And in hell he lift up his eyes, being in torments, and seeth Abraham afar off, and Lazarus in his bosom. And he cried and said, Father Abraham, have mercy on me, and send Lazarus, that he may dip the tip of his finger in water, and cool my tongue; for I am tormented in this flame. *16:22-24*

57.60 And beside all this, between us and you there is a great gulf fixed: so that they which would pass from hence to you cannot; neither can they pass to us, that would come from thence. *16:26*

57.61 Abraham saith unto him, They have Moses and the prophets; let them hear them. And he said, Nay, father Abraham: but if one went unto them from the dead, they will repent. And he said unto him, If they hear not Moses and the prophets, neither will they be persuaded, though one rose from the dead. *16:29-31*

57.62 And the apostles said unto the Lord, Increase our faith. *17:5*

57.63 So likewise ye, when ye shall have done all those things which are commanded you, say, We are unprofitable servants: we have done that which was our duty to do. *17:10*

57.64 And Jesus answering said, Were there not ten cleansed? but where are the nine? *17:17*

57.65 Neither shall they say, Lo here! or, lo there! for, behold, the kingdom of God is within you. *17:21*

57.66 Remember Lot's wife. *17:32*

57.67 Two men went up into the temple to pray, the one a Pharisee, and the other a publican. The Pharisee stood and prayed thus with himself, God, I thank thee, that I am not as other men are, extortioners, unjust, adulterers, or even as this publican. I fast twice in the week, I give tithes of all that I possess. And the publican, standing afar off, would not lift up so much as his eyes unto heaven, but smote upon his breast, saying, God be merciful to me a sinner. I tell you, this man went down to his house justified rather than the other: for every one that exalteth himself shall be abased; and he that humbleth himself shall be exalted. *18:10-14*

57.68 And Jesus said unto him, This day is salvation come to this house, forsomuch as he also is a son of Abraham. *19:9*

57.69 And he answered and said unto them, I tell you that, if these should hold their peace, the stones would immediately cry out. *19:40*

57.70 And when he was come near, he beheld the city, and wept over it, Saying, If thou hadst known, even thou, at least in this thy day, the things which belong unto thy peace! but now they are hid from thine eyes. *19:41-42*

57.71 In your patience possess ye your souls. *21:19*

57.72 And the Lord said, Simon, Simon, behold, Satan hath desired to have you, that he may sift you as wheat: But I have prayed for thee, that thy faith fail not: and when thou art converted, strengthen thy brethren. *22:31-32*

57.73 Saying, Father, if thou be willing, remove this cup from me: nevertheless not my will, but thine, be done. *22:42*

57.74 And there appeared an angel unto him from heaven, strengthening him. And being in an agony he prayed more earnestly: and his sweat was as it were

57.75   And the Lord turned, and looked upon Peter. And Peter remembered the word of the Lord, how he had said unto him, Before the cock crow, thou shalt deny me thrice.   *22:61*

57.76   Then said Jesus, Father, forgive them; for they know not what they do. And they parted his raiment, and cast lots.   *23:34*

57.77   And he said unto Jesus, Lord, remember me when thou comest into thy kingdom. And Jesus said unto him, Verily I say unto thee, To day shalt thou be with me in paradise.   *23:42-43*

57.78   And the sun was darkened, and the veil of the temple was rent in the midst.   *23:45*

57.79   And when Jesus had cried with a loud voice, he said, Father, into thy hands I commend my spirit: and having said thus, he gave up the ghost.   *23:46*

57.80   And, behold, there was a man named Joseph, a counseller; and he was a good man, and a just.   *23:50*

57.81   And as they were afraid, and bowed down their faces to the earth, they said unto them, Why seek ye the living among the dead? He is not here, but is risen: remember how he spake unto you when he was yet in Galilee.   *24:5-6*

57.82   And their words seemed to them as idle tales, and they believed them not.   *24:11*

57.83   And beginning at Moses and all the prophets, he expounded unto them in all the scriptures the things concerning himself.   *24:27*

57.84   But they constrained him, saying, Abide with us: for it is toward evening, and the day is far spent. And he went in to tarry with them.   *24:29*

57.85   And they said one to another, Did not our heart burn within us, while he talked with us by the way, and while he opened to us the scriptures?   *24:32*

57.86   Behold my hands and my feet, that it is I myself: handle me, and see; for a spirit hath not flesh and bones, as ye see me have.   *24:39*

57.87   And they gave him a piece of a broiled fish, and of an honeycomb. *24:42*

57.88   And that repentance and remission of sins should be preached in his name among all nations, beginning at Jerusalem.   *24:47*

57.89   And, behold, I send the promise of my Father upon you: but tarry ye in the city of Jerusalem, until ye be endued with power from on high.   *24:49*

ST JOHN

58.1   In the beginning was the Word, and the Word was with God, and the Word was God. The same was in the beginning with God. All things were made by him; and without him was not anything made that was made.   *1:1-3*

58.2   In him was life; and the life was the light of men. And the light shineth in darkness; and the darkness comprehended it not.   *1:4-5*

58.3   There was a man sent from God, whose name was John. The same came for a witness, to bear witness of the Light, that all men through him might believe. He was not that Light, but was sent to bear witness of that Light.   *1:6-8*

58.4   That was the true Light, which lighteth every man that cometh into the world. He was in the world, and the world was made by him, and the world knew him not.   *1:9-10*

58.5   He came unto his own, and his own received him not. But as many as received him, to them gave he power to become the sons of God, even to them that believe on his name: Which were born, not of blood, nor of the will of the flesh, nor of the will of man, but of God.   *1:11-13*

58.6   And the Word was made flesh, and dwelt among us, (and we beheld his glory, the glory as of the only begotten of the Father,) full of grace and truth.   *1:14*

58.7   For the law was given by Moses, but grace and truth came by Jesus Christ. No man hath seen God at any time; the only begotten Son, which is in the bosom of the Father, he hath declared him.   *1:17-18*

58.8   He it is, who coming after me is preferred before me, whose shoe's latchet I am not worthy to unloose.   *1:27*

58.9   The next day John seeth Jesus coming unto him, and saith, Behold the Lamb of God, which taketh away the sin of the world.   *1:29*

58.10   And Nathanael said unto him, Can there any good thing come out of Nazareth? Philip saith unto him, Come and see.   *1:46*

58.11   Jesus saith unto her, Woman, what have I to do with thee? mine hour is not yet come.   *2:4*

58.12   When the ruler of the feast had tasted the water that was made wine, and knew not whence it was: (but the servants which drew the water knew;) the governor of the feast called the bridegroom, And saith unto him, Every man at the beginning doth set forth good wine; and when men have well drunk, then that which is worse: but thou hast kept the good wine until now.   *2:9-10*

58.13   This beginning of miracles did Jesus in Cana of Galilee, and manifested forth his glory; and his disciples believed on him.   *2:11*

58.14   Jesus answered and said unto him, Verily, verily, I say unto thee, Except a man be born again, he cannot see the kingdom of God. Nicodemus saith unto him, How can a man be born when he is old? can he enter the second time into his mother's womb, and be born?   *3:3-4*

58.15   Jesus answered, Verily, verily, I say unto thee, Except a man be born of water and of the Spirit, he cannot enter into the kingdom of God. That which is born of the flesh is flesh; and that which is born of the Spirit is spirit.   *3:5-6*

Born again

Born again *in contemporary English is sometimes used to describe an enthusiastic conversion to a particular cause (*a born-again monetarist*), or even as a synonym for 'renewed; fresh or new'. The origin of the expression is Jesus' explanation to Nicodemus that unless he was reborn spiritually - was radically changed by the Spirit of God in his inner being - he could not see the kingdom of God.*

58.16   Marvel not that I said unto thee, Ye must be born again. The wind bloweth where it listeth, and thou hearest the sound thereof, but canst not tell whence it cometh, and whither it goeth: so is every one that is born of the Spirit.   *3:7-8*

58.17   For God so loved the world, that he gave his only begotten Son, that whosoever believeth in him should not perish, but have everlasting life.   *3:16*

58.18   For God sent not his Son into the world to condemn the world; but that the world through him might be saved. He that believeth on him is not condemned: but he that believeth not is condemned already, because he hath not believed in the name of the only begotten Son of

God. And this is the condemnation, that light is come into the world, and men loved darkness rather than light, because their deeds were evil. *3:17-19*

58.19   He must increase, but I must decrease. *3:30*

58.20   The Father loveth the Son, and hath given all things into his hand. He that believeth on the Son hath everlasting life: and he that believeth not the Son shall not see life; but the wrath of God abideth on him. *3:35-36*

58.21   Jesus answered and said unto her, Whosoever drinketh of this water shall thirst again: But whosoever drinketh of the water that I shall give him shall never thirst; but the water that I shall give him shall be in him a well of water springing up into everlasting life. *4:13-14*

58.22   But the hour cometh, and now is, when the true worshippers shall worship the Father in spirit and in truth: for the Father seeketh such to worship him. God is a Spirit: and they that worship him must worship him in spirit and in truth. *4:23-24*

58.23   The woman saith unto him, I know that Messias cometh, which is called Christ: when he is come, he will tell us all things. Jesus saith unto her, I that speak unto thee am he. *4:25-26*

58.24   Say not ye, There are yet four months, and then cometh harvest? behold, I say unto you, Lift up your eyes, and look on the fields; for they are white already to harvest. *4:35*

58.25   I sent you to reap that whereon ye bestowed no labour: other men laboured, and ye are entered into their labours. *4:38*

58.26   Jesus saith unto him, Rise, take up thy bed, and walk. *5:8*

58.27   Verily, verily, I say unto you, He that heareth my word, and believeth on him that sent me, hath everlasting life, and shall not come into condemnation; but is passed from death unto life. Verily, verily, I say unto you, The hour is coming, and now is, when the dead shall hear the voice of the Son of God: and they that hear shall live. *5:24-25*

58.28   For as the Father hath life in himself; so hath he given to the Son to have life in himself. *5:26*

58.29   He *[John the Baptist]* was a burning and a shining light: and ye were willing for a season to rejoice in his light. *5:35*

58.30   Search the scriptures; for in them ye think ye have eternal life: and they are they which testify of me. *5:39*

58.31   There is a lad here, which hath five barley loaves, and two small fishes: but what are they among so many? *6:9*

58.32   And Jesus said unto them, I am the bread of life: he that cometh to me shall never hunger; and he that believeth on me shall never thirst. *6:35*

58.33   All that the Father giveth me shall come to me; and him that cometh to me I will in no wise cast out. *6:37*

58.34   Verily, verily, I say unto you, He that believeth on me hath everlasting life. I am that bread of life. Your fathers did eat manna in the wilderness, and are dead. This is the bread which cometh down from heaven, that a man may eat thereof, and not die. I am the living bread which came down from heaven: if any man eat of this bread, he shall live for ever: and the bread that I will give is my flesh, which I will give for the life of the world. *6:47-51*

58.35   It is the spirit that quickeneth; the flesh profiteth nothing: the words that I speak unto you, they are spirit, and they are life.   *6:63*

58.36   Then Simon Peter answered him, Lord, to whom shall we go? thou hast the words of eternal life.   *6:68*

58.37   In the last day, that great day of the feast, Jesus stood and cried, saying, If any man thirst, let him come unto me, and drink. He that believeth on me, as the scripture hath said, out of his belly shall flow rivers of living water.   *7:37-38*

58.38   So when they continued asking him, he lifted up himself, and said unto them, He that is without sin among you, let him first cast a stone at her.   *8:7*

58.39   She said, No man, Lord. And Jesus said unto her, Neither do I condemn thee: go, and sin no more.   *8:11*

58.40   Then spake Jesus again unto them, saying, I am the light of the world: he that followeth me shall not walk in darkness, but shall have the light of life. *8:12*

58.41   And ye shall know the truth, and the truth shall make you free.   *8:32*

58.42   If the Son therefore shall make you free, ye shall be free indeed.   *8:36*

58.43   Ye are of your father the devil, and the lusts of your father ye will do. He was a murderer from the beginning, and abode not in the truth, because there is no truth in him. When he speaketh a lie, he speaketh of his own: for he is a liar, and the father of it.   *8:44*

58.44   Verily, verily, I say unto you, If a man keep my saying, he shall never see death.   *8:51*

58.45   Jesus said unto them, Verily, verily, I say unto you, Before Abraham was, I am.   *8:58*

58.46   But by what means he now seeth, we know not; or who hath opened his eyes, we know not: he is of age; ask him: he shall speak for himself.   *9:21*

58.47   He answered and said, Whether he be a sinner or no, I know not: one thing I know, that, whereas I was blind, now I see.   *9:25*

58.48   I am the door: by me if any man enter in, he shall be saved, and shall go in and out, and find pasture.   *10:9*

58.49   The thief cometh not, but for to steal, and to kill, and to destroy: I am come that they might have life, and that they might have it more abundantly. *10:10*

58.50   I am the good shepherd: the good shepherd giveth his life for the sheep. But he that is an hireling, and not the shepherd, whose own the sheep are not, seeth the wolf coming, and leaveth the sheep, and fleeth: and the wolf catcheth them, and scattereth the sheep. The hireling fleeth, because he is an hireling, and careth not for the sheep. I am the good shepherd, and know my sheep, and am known of mine. As the Father knoweth me, even so know I the Father: and I lay down my life for the sheep. And other sheep I have which are not of this fold: them also I must bring, and they shall hear my voice; and there shall be one fold, and one shepherd.   *10:11-16*

58.51   My sheep hear my voice, and I know them, and they follow me: And I give unto them eternal life; and they shall never perish, neither shall any man pluck them out of my hand. My Father, which gave them me, is greater than all; and no man is able to pluck them out of my Father's hand.   *10:27-29*

58.52   Jesus said unto her, I am the resurrection, and the life: he that believeth in me, though he were dead, yet shall he live.   *11:25*

58.53   And whosoever liveth and believeth in me shall never die. Believest thou this? She saith unto him, Yea, Lord: I believe that thou art the Christ, the Son of God, which should come into the world.   *11:26-27*

58.54   Jesus wept.   *11:35*

Jesus wept

This verse is the shortest verse in the Bible. Its two words describe Jesus' grief at the death of Lazarus and his sympathy with the tears of others. The longest verse in the Bible is Esther 8:9. This is a 90-word description of the edict of the Persian king Ahasuerus (Xerxes) on behalf of the Jews.

58.55   And when he thus had spoken, he cried with a loud voice, Lazarus, come forth.   *11:43*

58.56   For the poor always ye have with you; but me ye have not always.   *12:8*

58.57   The same came therefore to Philip, which was of Bethsaida of Galilee, and desired him, saying, Sir, we would see Jesus.   *12:21*

58.58   Verily, verily, I say unto you, Except a corn of wheat fall into the ground and die, it abideth alone: but if it die, it bringeth forth much fruit.   *12:24*

58.59   Now is my soul troubled; and what shall I say? Father, save me from this hour: but for this cause came I unto this hour.   *12:27*

58.60   Now is the judgment of this world: now shall the prince of this world be cast out. And I, if I be lifted up from the earth, will draw all men unto me. *12:31-32*

58.61   Now before the feast of the passover, when Jesus knew that his hour was come that he should depart out of this world unto the Father, having loved his own which were in the world, he loved them unto the end.   *13:1*

58.62   He riseth from supper, and laid aside his garments; and took a towel, and girded himself. After that he poureth water into a bason, and began to wash the disciples' feet, and to wipe them with the towel wherewith he was girded.   *13:4-5*

58.63   Then cometh he to Simon Peter: and Peter saith unto him, Lord, dost thou wash my feet?   *13:6*

58.64   Simon Peter saith unto him, Lord, not my feet only, but also my hands and my head.   *13:9*

58.65   Now there was leaning on Jesus' bosom one of his disciples, whom Jesus loved.   *13:23*

58.66   And after the sop Satan entered into him. Then said Jesus unto him, That thou doest, do quickly.   *13:27*

58.67   A new commandment I give unto you, That ye love one another; as I have loved you, that ye also love one another. By this shall all men know that ye are my disciples, if ye have love one to another. *13:34-35*

58.68   Simon Peter said unto him, Lord, whither goest thou? Jesus answered him, Whither I go, thou canst not follow me now; but thou shalt follow me afterwards.   *13:36*

58.69   Let not your heart be troubled: ye believe in God, believe also in me.   *14:1*

58.70   In my Father's house are many mansions: if it were not so, I would have told you. I go to prepare a place for you. And if I go and prepare a place for you, I will come again, and receive you unto myself; that where I am, there ye may be also.   *14:2-3*

58.71   Jesus saith unto him, I am the way, the truth, and the life: no man cometh unto the Father, but by me.   *14:6*

58.72   If ye love me, keep my commandments. And I will pray the

Father, and he shall give you another Comforter, that he may abide with you for ever; Even the Spirit of truth; whom the world cannot receive, because it seeth him not, neither knoweth him: by ye know him; for he dwelleth with you and shall be in you. *14:15-17*

58.73 Jesus answered and said unto him, If a man love me, he will keep my words: and my Father will love him, and we will come unto him, and make our abode with him. *14:23*

58.74 But the Comforter, which is the Holy Ghost, whom the Father will send in my name, he shall teach you all things, and bring all things to your remembrance, whatsoever I have said unto you. *14:26*

58.75 Peace I leave with you, my peace I give unto you: not as the world giveth, give I unto you, Let not your heart be troubled, neither let it be afraid. *14:27*

58.76 I am the true vine, and my Father is the husbandman. *15:1*

58.77 Abide in me, and I in you. As the branch cannot bear fruit of itself, except it abide in the vine; no more can ye, except ye abide in me. I am the vine, ye are the branches: He that abideth in me, and I in him, the same bringeth forth much fruit: for without me ye can do nothing. *15:4-5*

58.78 This is my commandment, That ye love one another, as I have loved you. Greater love hath no man than this, that a man lay down his life for his friends. *15:12-13*

58.79 Ye are my friends, if ye do whatsoever I command you. Henceforth I call you not servants; for the servant knoweth not what his lord doeth: but I have called you friends; for all things that I have heard of my Father I have made known unto you. Ye have not chosen me, but I have chosen you, and ordained you, that ye should go and bring forth fruit,

and that your fruit should remain: that whatsoever ye shall ask of the Father in my name, he may give it you. *15:14-16*

58.80 But now I go my way to him that sent me; and none of you asketh me, Whither goest thou? But because I have said these things unto you, sorrow hath filled your heart. Nevertheless I tell you the truth; It is expedient for you that I go away: for if I go not away, the Comforter will not come unto you; but if I depart, I will send him unto you. *16:5-7*

58.81 And when he is come, he will reprove the world of sin, and of righteousness, and of judgment. *16:8*

58.82 Howbeit when he, the Spirit of truth, is come, he will guide you into all truth: for he shall not speak of himself; but whatsoever he shall hear, that shall he speak: and he will shew you things to come. *16:13*

58.83 These things I have spoken unto you, that in me ye might have peace. In the world ye shall have tribulation: but be of good cheer; I have overcome the world. *16:33*

58.84 And this is life eternal, that they might know thee the only true God, and Jesus Christ, whom thou hast sent. *17:3*

58.85 I have glorified thee on the earth: I have finished the work which thou gavest me to do. And now, O Father, glorify thou me with thine own self with the glory which I had with thee before the world was. *17:4-5*

58.86 I pray for them: I pray not for the world, but for them which thou hast given me; for they are thine. *17:9*

58.87 While I was with them in the world, I kept them in thy name: those that thou gavest me I have kept, and none of them is lost, but the son of perdition; that the scripture might be fulfilled. *17:12*

58.88   Sanctify them through thy truth: thy word is truth.   *17:17*

58.89   That they all may be one; as thou, Father, art in me, and I in thee, that they also may be one in us: that the world may believe that thou hast sent me. And the glory which thou gavest me I have given them; that they may be one, even as we are one: I in them, and thou in me, that they may be made perfect in one; and that the world may know that thou hast sent me, and hast loved them, as thou hast loved me.   *17:21-23*

58.90   Father, I will that they also, whom thou hast given me, be with me where I am; that they may behold my glory, which thou hast given me: for thou lovedst me before the foundation of the world.   *17:24*

58.91   Jesus answered, My kingdom is not of this world: if my kingdom were of this world, then would my servants fight, that I should not be delivered to the Jews: but now is my kingdom not from hence. Pilate therefore said unto him, Art thou a king then? Jesus answered, Thou sayest that I am a king. To this end was I born, and for this cause came I into the world, that I should bear witness unto the truth. Every one that is of the truth heareth my voice.   *18:36-37*

58.92   Pilate saith unto him, What is truth? And when he had said this, he went out again unto the Jews, and saith unto them, I find in him no fault at all.   *18:38*

58.93   Then said the chief priests of the Jews to Pilate, Write not, The King of the Jews; but that he said, I am King of the Jews. Pilate answered, What I have written I have written.   *19:21-22*

58.94   When Jesus therefore saw his mother, and the disciple standing by, whom he loved, he saith unto his mother, Woman, behold thy son! Then saith he to the disciple, Behold thy mother! And from that hour that disciple took her unto his own home.   *19:26-27*

58.95   After this, Jesus knowing that sll things were now accomplished, that the scripture might be fulfilled, saith, I thirst. Now there was set a vessel full of vinegar: and they filled a spunge with vinegar, and put it upon hyssop, and put it to his mouth. When Jesus therefore had received the vinegar, he said, It is finished: and he bowed his head, and gave up the ghost.   *19:28-30*

58.96   But one of the soldiers with a spear pierced his side, and forthwith came there out blood and water.   *19:34*

58.97   The first day of the week cometh Mary Magdalene early, when it was yet dark, unto the sepulchre, and seeth the stone taken away from the sepulchre. Then she runneth, and cometh to Simon Peter, and to the other disciple, whom Jesus loved, and saith unto them, They have taken away the Lord out of the sepulchre, and we know not where they have laid him.   *20:1-2*

58.98   So they ran both together: and the other disciple did outrun Peter, and came first to the sepulchre.   *20:4*

58.99   Jesus saith unto her, Woman, why weepest thou? whom seekest thou? She, supposing him to be the gardener, saith unto him, Sir, if thou have borne him hence, tell me where thou hast laid him, and I will take him away. Jesus saith unto her, Mary. She turned herself, and saith unto him, Rabboni; which is to say, Master. Jesus saith unto her, Touch me not; for I am not yet ascended to my Father: but go to my brethren, and say unto them, I ascend unto my Father, and your Father; and to my God, and your God.   *20:15-17*

58.100   And when he had said this, he breathed on them, and saith unto them, Receive ye the Holy Ghost.   *20:22*

58.101   But Thomas, one of the twelve, called Didymus, was not with them when Jesus came. The other disciples therefore said unto him, We have seen the

Lord. But he said unto them, Except I shall see in his hands the print of the nails, and put my finger into the print of the nails, and thrust my hand into his side, I will not believe. *20:24-25*

A doubting Thomas

A doubting Thomas *is a sceptical person, one who refuses to believe something until he or she has actually seen complete proof or evidence for it. The expression derives from Thomas, one of the 12 disciples who at first did not believe in Jesus' resurrection. Jesus then satisfied his doubts and Thomas in belief confessed Jesus to be his Lord and his God.*

58.102 Then saith he to Thomas, Reach hither thy finger, and behold my hands; and reach hither thy hand, and thrust it into my side: and be not faithless, but believing. And Thomas answered and said unto him, My Lord and my God. Jesus saith unto him, Thomas, because thou hast seen me, thou hast believed: blessed are they that have not seen, and yet have believed. *20:27-29*

58.103 And many other signs truly did Jesus in the presence of his disciples, which are not written in this book: But these are written, that ye might believe that Jesus is the Christ, the Son of God; and that believing ye might have life through his name. *20:30-31*

58.104 So when they had dined, Jesus saith to Simon Peter, Simon, son of Jonas, lovest thou me more than these? He saith unto him, Yea, Lord; thou knowest that I love thee. He saith unto him, Feed my lambs. He saith to him again the second time, Simon, son of Jonas, lovest thou me? He saith unto him, Yea, Lord; thou knowest that I love thee. He saith unto him, Feed my sheep. He saith unto him the third time, Simon, son of Jonas, lovest thou me? Peter was grieved because he said unto him the third time, Lovest thou me? And he said unto him, Lord, thou knowest all things; thou

knowest that I love thee. Jesus saith unto him, Feed my sheep. *21:15-17*

58.105 And there are also many other things which Jesus did, the which, if they should be written every one, I suppose that even the world itself could not contain the books that should be written. Amen. *21:25*

ACTS OF THE APOSTLES

59.1 The former treatise have I made, O Theophilus, of all that Jesus began both to do and teach. *1:1*

59.2 And he said unto them, It is not for you to know the times or the seasons, which the Father hath put in his own power. But ye shall receive power, after that the Holy Ghost is come upon you: and ye shall be witnesses unto me both in Jerusalem, and in all Judaea, and in Samaria, and unto the uttermost part of the earth. *1:7-8*

59.3 Which also said, Ye men of Galilee, why stand ye gazing up into heaven? this same Jesus, which is taken up from you into heaven, shall so come in like manner as ye have seen him go into heaven. *1:11*

59.4 And when the day of Pentecost was fully come, they were all with one accord in one place. And suddenly there came a sound from heaven as of a rushing mighty wind, and it filled all the house where they were sitting. And there appeared unto them cloven tongues like as of fire, and it sat upon each of them. And they were all filled with the Holy Ghost, and began to speak with other tongues, as the Spirit gave them utterance. *2:1-4*

59.5 And they were all amazed and, marvelled, saying one to another, Behold, are not all these which speak Galilaeans? And how hear we every man in our own tongue, wherin we were born? Parthians, and Medes, and Elamites, and the dwellers in Mesopotamia, and in Judaea, and Cappadocia, in Pontus, and Asia, Phrygia, and Pamphylia, in Egypt, and into parts of Libya about Cyrene, and strangers of Rome, Jews and proselytes, Cretes and Arabians, we do hear them speak in our tongues the wonderful works of God.   *2:7-11*

59.6   And it shall come to pass in the last days, saith God, I will pour out of my Spirit upon all flesh: and your sons and your daughters shall prophesy, and your young men shall see visions, and your old men shall dream dreams.   *2:17*

59.7   Ye men of Israel, hear these words; Jesus of Nazareth, a man approved of God among you by miracles and wonders and signs, which God did by him in the midst of you, as ye yourselves also know: Him, being delivered by the determinate counsel and foreknowledge of God, ye have taken, and by wicked hands have crucified and slain; Whom God hath raised up, having loosed the pains of death: because it was not possible that he should be holden of it.   *2:22-24*

59.8   Now when they heard this, they were pricked in their heart, and said unto Peter and to the rest of the apostles, Men and brethren, what shall we do? Then Peter said unto them, Repent, and be baptized every one of you in the name of Jesus Christ for the remission of sins, and ye shall receive the gift of the Holy Ghost.   *2:37-38*

59.9   And they continued stedfastly in the apostles' doctrine and fellowship, and in breaking of bread, and in prayers.   *2:42*

59.10   Then Peter said, Silver and gold have I none; but such as I have give I thee: In the name of Jesus Christ of Nazareth rise up and walk.   *3:6*

59.11   And he leaping up stood, and walked, and entered with them into the temple, walking, and leaping, and praising God.   *3:8*

59.12   But ye denied the Holy One and the Just, and desired a murderer to be granted unto you; And killed the Prince of life, whom God hath raised from the dead; whereof we are witnesses.   *3:14-15*

59.13   Neither is there salvation in any other: for there is none other name under heaven given among men, whereby we must be saved.   *4:12*

59.14   Now when they saw the boldness of Peter and John, and perceived that they were unlearned and ignorant men, they marvelled; and they took knowledge of them, that they had been with Jesus.   *4:13*

59.15   But Peter said, Ananias, why hath Satan filled thine heart to lie to the Holy Ghost, and to keep back part of the price of the land? Whiles it remained, was it not thine own? and after it was sold, was it not in thine own power? why hast thou conceived this thing in thine heart? thou hast not lied unto men, but unto God.   *5:3-4*

59.16   Then Peter and the other apostles answered and said, We ought to obey God rather than men.   *5:29*

59.17   Then the twelve called the multitude of the disciples unto them, and said, It is not reason that we should leave the word of God, and serve tables. Wherefore, brethren, look ye out among you seven men of honest report, full of the Holy Ghost and wisdom, whom we may appoint over this business. But we will give ourseves continually to prayer, and to the ministry of the word.   *6:2-4*

59.18   Then they cried out with a loud voice, and stopped their ears, and ran upon him with one accord, And cast him out of the city, and stoned him: and the witnesses laid down their clothes at a young man's feet, whose name was Saul.   *7:57-58*

59.19   And Saul was consenting unto his death. And at that time there was a great persecution against the church which was at Jerusalem; and they were all scattered abroad throughout the regions of Judaea and Samaria, except the apostles.   *8:1*

59.20   And Philip ran thither to him, and heard him read the prophet Esaias, and said, Understandest thou what thou readest? And he said, How can I, except some man should guide me? And he desired Philip that he would come up and sit with him.   *8:30-31*

59.21   And Saul, yet breathing out threatenings and slaughter against the disciples of the Lord, went unto the high priest, And desired of him letters to Damascus to the synagogues, that if he found any of this way, whether they were men or women, he might bring them bound unto Jerusalem.   *9:1-2*

59.22   And as he journeyed, he came near Damascus: and suddenly there shined round about him a light from heaven: And he fell to the earth, and heard a voice saying unto him, Saul, Saul, why persecutest thou me? And he said, Who art thou, Lord? And the Lord said, I am Jesus whom thou persecutest: it is hard for thee to kick against the pricks.   *9:3-5*

59.23   And he trembling and astonished said, Lord, what wilt thou have me to do? And the Lord said unto him, Arise, and go into the city, and it shall be told thee what thou must do.   *9:6*

59.24   And the Lord said unto him, Arise, and go into the street which is called Straight, and inquire in the house of Judas for one called Saul, of Tarsus: for, behold, he prayeth.   *9:11*

59.25   But the Lord said unto him, Go thy way: for he is a chosen vessel unto me, to bear my name before the Gentiles, and kings, and the children of Israel.   *9:15*

59.26   Now there was at Joppa a certain disciple named Tabitha, which by interpretation is called Dorcas: this woman was full of good works and almsdeeds which she did.   *9:36*

59.27   And saw heaven opened, and a certain vessel descending unto him, as it had been a great sheet knit at the four corners, and let down to the earth: Wherein were all manner of fourfooted beasts of the earth, and wild beasts, and creeping things, and fowls of the air. And there came a voice to him, Rise, Peter; kill, and eat.   *10:11-13*

59.28   And the voice spake unto him again the second time, What God hath cleansed, that call not thou common.   *10:15*

59.29   Then Peter opened him mouth, and said, Of a truth I perceive that God is no respecter of persons: But in every nation he that feareth him, and worketh righteousness, is accepted with him.   *10:34-35*

No respecter of persons

The expression no respecter of persons *describes an attitude that treats all the people involved in the same way, regardless of their wealth, fame, class, etc.:* The epidemic was no respecter of persons – young and old, rich and poor – thousands died as the plague swept across the country. *This verse is the origin of the phrase God 'had no favourites' between one nation and another. He accepted all, Jews and Gentiles, who feared him and acted in the right way.*

59.30   And they of the circumcision which believed were astonished, as many as came with Peter, because that on the Gentiles also was poured out the gift of the Holy Ghost.   *10:45*

59.31   And when he had found him, he brought him unto Antioch, And it came to pass, that a whole year they assembled themselves with the church, and taught much people. And the disciples were called Christians first in Antioch.   *11:26*

59.32   Now there were in the church that was at Antioch certain prophets and teachers; as Barnabas, and Simeon that was called Niger, and Lucius of Cyrene, and Manaen, which had been brought up with Herod the tetrarch, and Saul. As they ministered to the Lord, and fasted, the Holy Ghost said, Separate me Barnabas and Saul for the work whereunto I have called them. And when they had fasted and prayed, and laid their hands on them, they sent them away. *13:1-3*

59.33   And saying, Sirs, why do ye these things? We also are men of like passions with you, and preach unto you that ye should turn from these vanities unto the living God, which made heaven, and earth, and the sea, and all things that are therein. *14:15*

59.34   Confirming the souls of the disciples, and exhorting them to continue in the faith, and that we must through much tribulation enter into the kingdom of God. *14:22*

59.35   For it seemed good to the Holy Ghost, and to us, to lay upon you no greater burden than these necessary things; That ye abstain from meats offered to idols, and from blood, and from things strangled, and from fornication: from which if ye keep yourselves, ye shall do well. Fare ye well. *15:28-29*

59.36   And a vision appeared to Paul in the night; There stood a man of Macedonia, and prayed him, saying, Come over into Macedonia, and help us. *16:9*

59.37   And a certain woman named Lydia, a seller of purple, of the city of Thyatira, which worshipped God, heard us: whose heart the Lord opened, that she attended unto the things which were spoken of Paul. *16:14*

59.38   And brought them out, and said, Sirs, what must I do to be saved? And they said, Believe on the Lord Jesus Christ, and thou shalt be saved, and thy house. *16:30-31*

59.39   But the Jews which believed not, moved with envy, took unto them certain lewd fellows of the baser sort, and gathered a company, and set all the city on an uproar, and assaulted the house of Jason, and sought to bring them out to the people. And when they found them not, they drew Jason and certain brethren unto the rulers of the city, crying, These that have turned the world upside down are come hither also. *17:5-6*

59.40   These were more noble than those in Thessalonica, in that they received the word with all readiness of mind, and searched the scriptures daily, whether those things were so. *17:11*

59.41   Then certain philosophers of the Epicureans, and of the Stoicks, encountered him, And some said, what will this babbler say? other some, He seemeth to be a setter forth of strange gods: because he preached unto them Jesus, and the resurrection. *17:18*

59.42   Then Paul stood in the midst of Mars' hill, and said, Ye men of Athens, I perceive that in all things ye are too superstitious. For as I passed by, and beheld your devotions, I found an altar with this inscription, TO THE UNKNOWN GOD. Whom therefore ye ignorantly worship, him declare I unto you. *17:22-23*

59.43   God that made the world and all things therein, seeing that he is Lord of heaven and earth, dwelleth not in temples made with hands; Neither is worshipped with men's hands, as though he needed any thing, seeing he giveth to all life, and breath, and all things. *17:24-25*

59.44   For in him we live, and move and have our being; as certain also of your own poets have said, For we are also his offspring. *17:28*

59.45   And the times of this ignorance God winked at; but now commandeth all men every where to repent: Because he hath appointed a day, in the which he will judge the world in righteousness by that man whom he hath ordained; whereof he hath given assurance unto all men, in that he hath raised him from the dead. *17:30-31*

59.46   He said unto them, Have ye received the Holy Ghost since ye believed? And they said unto him, We have not so much as heard whether there be any Holy Ghost. *19:2*

59.47   Some therefore cried one thing, and some another: for the assembly was confused; and the more part knew not wherefore they were come together. *19:32*

59.48   Testifying both to the Jews, and also to the Greeks, repentance toward God, and faith toward our Lord Jesus Christ. *20:21*

59.49   Take heed therefore unto yourselves, and to all the flock, over the which the Holy Ghost hath made you overseers, to feed the church of God, which he hath purchased with his own blood. *20:28*

59.50   And now, brethren, I commend you to God, and to the word of his grace, which is able to build you up, and to give you an inheritance among all them which are sanctified. *20:32*

59.51   I have shewed you all things, how that so labouring ye ought to support the weak, and to remember the words of the Lord Jesus, how he said, It is more blessed to give than to receive. *20:35*

59.52   But Paul said, I am a man which am a Jew of Tarsus, a city in Cilicia, a citizen of no mean city: and, I beseech thee, suffer me to speak unto the people. *21:39*

59.53   I am verily a man which am a Jew, born in Tarsus, a city in Cilicia, yet brought up in this city at the feet of Gamaliel, and taught according to the perfect manner of the law of the fathers, and was zealous toward God, as ye all are this day. *22:3*

59.54   Then the chief captain came, and said unto him, Tell me, art thou a Roman? He said, Yea. And the chief captain answered, With a great sum obtained I this freedom. And Paul said, But I was free born. *22:27-28*

59.55   But when Paul perceived that the one part were Sadducees, and the other Pharisees, he cried out in the council, Men and brethren, I am a Pharisee, the son of a Pharisee: of the hope and resurrection of the dead I am called in question. *23:6*

59.56   And the night following the Lord stood by him, and said, Be of good cheer, Paul: for as thou hast testified of me in Jerusalem, so must thou bear witness also at Rome. *23:11*

59.57   For if I be an offender, or have committed any thing worthy of death, I refuse not to die: but if there be none of these things whereof these accuse me, no man may deliver me unto them. I appeal unto Caesar. *25:11*

59.58   And as he thus spake for himself, Festus said with a loud voice, Paul, thou art beside thyself; much learning doth make thee mad. *26:24*

59.59   Then Agrippa said unto Paul, Almost thou persuadest me to be a Christian. *26:28*

59.60   And Paul dwelt two whole years in his own hired house, and received all that came in unto him. *28:30*

THE LETTERS

The Church was helped in its early years by apostles who set down in their letters teaching about God and the gospel, with instructions on practical aspects of the Christian life.

The letters can be grouped in this way: *Romans, 1 and 2 Corinthians*, and *Galatians* emphasize the nature of the gospel that Paul preached. *Ephesians, Philippians, Colossians*, and *Philemon*, all written while Paul was a prisoner in Rome, contain important teaching on what it means to be Christian believers. *1 and 2 Thessalonians* were probably Paul's earliest letters and are especially concerned about Christ's Second Coming. *1 and 2 Timothy* and *Titus* contain practical advice on church leadership and organization.

Hebrews shows that not only was Jesus better than the Old Testament priesthood and system of sacrifices, but also that he was the perfect fulfilment of all that they had stood for. *James* is a letter about practical Christianity; *1 Peter* a letter to Christians who were persecuted for their faith; *2 Peter* and *Jude* warn against false teachers. *1 John* was written to help Christians be sure of their faith; the very brief *2 and 3 John* show some of the implications of the life of love and truth.

ROMANS

60.1   Paul, a servant of Jesus Christ, called to be an apostle, separated unto the gospel of God.   *1:1*

60.2   Concerning his Son Jesus Christ our Lord, which was made of the seed of David according to the flesh; And declared to be the Son of God with power, according to the spirit of holiness, by the resurrection from the dead.   *1:3-4*

60.3   For God is my witness, whom I serve with my spirit in the gospel of his Son, that without ceasing I make mention of you always in my prayers.   *1:9*

60.4   For I am not ashamed of the gospel of Christ: for it is the power of God unto

salvation to every one that believeth; to the Jew first, and also to the Greek. For therein is the righteousness of God revealed from faith to faith: as it is written, The just shall live by faith.   *1:16-17*

60.5   Professing themselves to be wise, they became fools.   *1:22*

60.6   Who changed the truth of God into a lie, and worshipped and served the creature more than the Creator, who is blessed for ever. Amen.   *1:25*

60.7   Or despisest thou the riches of his goodness and forbearance and longsuffering; not knowing that the goodness of God leadeth thee to repentance?   *2:4*

60.8   To them who by patient continuance in well doing seek for glory and honour and immortality, eternal life.   *2:7*

60.9   For there is no respect of persons with God.   *2:11*

60.10   For when the Gentiles, which have not the law, do by nature the things contained in the law, these, having not the law, are a law unto themselves.   *2:14*

A law unto themselves

To be a law unto oneself *means that someone does what he or she wants, sets his or her own guidelines as to what is right and wrong, without considering the usual rules or conventions of society or the advice of others. The expression derives from this verse, which shows that the moral nature of Gentiles serves in place of the law of Moses to show God's demands. In this sense, the Gentiles are 'a law unto themselves'.*

60.11   God forbid: yea, let God be true, but every man a liar; as it is written, That thou mightest be justified in thy sayings, and mightest overcome when thou art judged.   *3:4*

60.12   Now we know that what things soever the law saith, it saith to them who are under the law: that every mouth may be stopped, and all the world may become guilty before God. Therefore by the deeds of the law there shall no flesh be justified in his sight: for by the law is the knowledge of sin.   *3:19-20*

60.13   But now the righteousness of God without the law is manifested, being witnessed by the law and the prophets; Even the righteousness of God which is by faith of Jesus Christ unto all and upon all them that believe: for there is no difference.   *3:21-22*

60.14   For all have sinned, and come short of the glory of God; Being justified freely by his grace through the redemption that is in Christ Jesus: Whom God hath set forth to be a propitiation

through faith in his blood, to declare his righteousness for the remission of sins that are past, through the forbearance of God.   *3:23-25*

60.15   Because the law worketh wrath: for where no law is, there is no transgression.   *4:15*

60.16   Who against hope believed in hope, that he might become the father of many nations; according to that which was spoken, So shall thy seed be.   *4:18*

60.17   And therefore it was imputed to him for righteousness.   *4:22*

60.18   Therefore being justified by faith, we have peace with God through our Lord Jesus Christ: By whom also we have access by faith into this grace wherein we stand, and rejoice in hope of the glory of God. And not only so, but we glory in tribulations also: knowing that tribulation worketh patience; And patience, experience; and experience, hope: And hope maketh not ashamed; because the love of God is shed abroad in our hearts by the Holy Ghost which is given unto us.   *5:1-5*

60.19   But God commendeth his love toward us, in that, while we were yet sinners, Christ died for us.   *5:8*

60.20   Wherefore, as by one man sin entered into the world, and death by sin; and so death passed upon all men, for that all have sinned.   *5:12*

60.21   Moreover the law entered, that the offence might abound. But where sin abounded, grace did much more abound.   *5:20*

60.22   What shall we say then? Shall we continue in sin, that grace may abound? God forbid. How shall we, that are dead to sin, live any longer therein?   *6:1-2*

60.23   Know ye not, that so many of us as were baptized into Jesus Christ were baptized into his death? Therefore we are buried with him by baptism into death: that like as Christ was raised up from the dead by the glory of the Father, even so we also should walk in newness of life. *6:3-4*

60.24   Knowing this, that our old man is crucified with him, that the body of sin might be destroyed, that henceforth we should not serve sin.   *6:6*

60.25   Knowing that Christ being raised from the dead dieth no more; death hath no more dominion over him.   *6:9*

60.26   Likewise reckon ye also yourselves to be dead indeed unto sin, but alive unto God through Jesus Christ our Lord. Let not sin therefore reign in your mortal body, that ye should obey it in the lusts thereof. Neither yield ye your members as instruments of unrighteousness unto sin: but yield yourselves unto God, as those that are alive from the dead, and your members as instruments of righteousness unto God.   *6:11-13*

60.27   For sin shall not have dominion over you: for ye are not under the law, but under grace.   *6:14*

60.28   For the wages of sin is death; but the gift of God is eternal life through Jesus Christ our Lord.   *6:23*

60.29   For I know that in me (that is, in my flesh,) dwelleth no good thing: for to will is present with me; but how to perform that which is good I find not. For the good that I would I do not: but the evil which I would not, that I do. Now if I do that I would not, it is no more I that do it, but sin that dwelleth in me. I find then a law, that, when I would do good, evil is present with me.   *7:18-21*

60.30   For I delight in the law of God after the inward man: But I see another law in my members, warring against the law of my mind, and bringing me into captivity to the law of sin which is in my members. O wretched man that I am!

who shall deliver me from the body of this death? I thank God through Jesus Christ our Lord. So then with the mind I myself serve the law of God; but with the flesh the law of sin.   *7:22-25*

60.31   There is therefore now no condemnation to them which are in Christ Jesus, who walk not after the flesh, but after the Spirit. For the law of the Spirit of life in Christ Jesus hath made me free from the law of sin and death.   *8:1-2*

60.32   For what the law could not do, in that it was weak through the flesh, God sending his own Son in the likeness of sinful flesh, and for sin, condemned sin in the flesh: That the righteousness of the law might be fulfilled in us, who walk not after the flesh, but after the Spirit.   *8:3-4*

60.33   For they that are after the flesh do mind the things of the flesh; but they that are after the Spirit the things of the Spirit. For to be carnally minded is death; but to be spiritually minded is life and peace. *8:5-6*

60.34   But ye are not in the flesh, but in the Spirit, if so be that the Spirit of God dwell in you. Now if any man have not the Spirit of Christ, he is none of his.   *8:9*

60.35   For as many as are led by the Spirit of God, they are the sons of God. For ye have not received the spirit of bondage again to fear; but ye have received the Spirit of adoption, whereby we cry, Abba, Father. The Spirit itself beareth witness with our spirit, that we are the children of God: And if children, then heirs; heirs of God, and joint-heirs with Christ; if so be that we suffer with him, that we may be also glorified together. *8:14-17*

60.36   For we know that the whole creation groaneth and travaileth in pain together until now.   *8:22*

60.37   And we know that all things work together for good to them that love God, to them who are the called according to his purpose.   *8:28*

60.38   What shall we then say to these things? If God be for us, who can be against us? He that spared not his own Son, but delivered him up for us all, how shall he not with him also freely give us all things? Who shall lay any thing to the charge of God's elect? It is God that justifieth. Who is he that condemneth? It is Christ that died, yea rather, that is risen again, who is even at the right hand of God, who also maketh intercession for us. Who shall separate us from the love of Christ? shall tribulation, or distress, or persecution, or famine, or nakedness, or peril, or sword? As it is written, For thy sake we are killed all the day long; we are accounted as sheep for the slaughter. Nay, in all these things we are more than conquerors through him that loved us. For I am persuaded, that neither death, nor life, nor angels, nor principalities, nor powers, nor things present, nor things to come, Nor height, nor depth, nor any other creature, shall be able to separate us from the love of God, which is in Christ Jesus our Lord.   *8:31-39*

60.39   Nay but, O man, who art thou that repliest against God? Shall the thing formed say to him that formed it, Why hast thou made me thus? Hath not the potter power over the clay, of the same lump to make one vessel unto honour, and another unto dishonour?   *9:20-21*

60.40   Brethren, my heart's desire and prayer to God for Israel is, that they might be saved.   *10:1*

60.41   That if thou shalt confess with thy mouth the Lord Jesus, and shalt believe in thine heart that God hath raised him from the dead, thou shalt be saved. For with the heart man believeth unto righteousness; and with the mouth confession is made unto salvation.   *10:9-10*

60.42   For whosoever shall call upon the name of the Lord shall be saved.   *10:13*

60.43   How then shall they call on him in whom they have not believed? and how shall they believe in him of whom they have not heard? and how shall they hear without a preacher? And how shall they preach, except they be sent? as it is written, How beautiful are the feet of them that preach the gospel of peace, and bring glad tidings of good things!   *10:14-15*

60.44   So then faith cometh by hearing, and hearing by the word of God.   *10:17*

60.45   And so all Israel shall be saved: as it is written, There shall come out of Sion the Deliverer, and shall turn away ungodliness from Jacob.   *11:26*

60.46   O the depth of the riches both of the wisdom and knowledge of God! how unsearchable are his judgments, and his ways past finding out! For who hath known the mind of the Lord? or who hath been his counseller? Or who hath first given to him, and it shall be recompensed unto him again? For of him, and through him, and to him, are all things: to whom be glory for ever. Amen.   *11:33-36*

60.47   I beseech you therefore, brethren, by the mercies of God, that ye present your bodies a living sacrifice, holy, acceptable unto God, which is your reasonable service. And be not conformed to this world: but be ye transformed by the renewing of your mind, that ye may prove what is that good, and acceptable, and perfect, will of God.   *12:1-2*

60.48   Let love be without dissimulation. Abhor that which is evil; cleave to that which is good. Be kindly affectioned one to another with brotherly love; in honour preferring one another.   *12:9-10*

60.49   Not slothful in business; fervent in spirit; serving the Lord.   *12:11*

60.50   Bless them which persecute you: bless, and curse not.   *12:14*

60.51   Rejoice with them that do rejoice, and weep with them that weep.   *12:15*

60.52   Be of the same mind one toward another. Mind not high things, but condescend to men of low estate. Be not wise in your own conceits. Recompense to no man evil for evil. Provide things honest in the sight of all men. If it be possible, as much as lieth in you, live peaceably with all men. Dearly beloved, avenge not yourselves, but rather give place unto wrath: for it is written, Vengeance is mine; I will repay, saith the Lord.   *12:16-19*

60.53   Be not overcome of evil, but overcome evil with good.   *12:21*

60.54   Let every soul be subject unto the higher powers. For there is no power but of God: the powers that be are ordained of God.   *13:1*

The powers that be

The expression the powers that be *refers to the controlling authority or the governing body; in other words, the Establishment. The phrase comes from this verse, which teaches subjection to the governing authorities because they are instituted by God.*

60.55   Render therefore to all their dues: tribute to whom tribute is due; custom to whom custom; fear to whom fear; honour to whom honour. Owe no man any thing, but to love one another: for he that loveth another hath fulfilled the law.   *13:7-8*

60.56   Love worketh no ill to his neighbour: therefore love is the fulfilling of the law.   *13:10*

60.57   But put ye on the Lord Jesus Christ, and make not provision for the flesh, to fulfil the lusts thereof.   *13:14*

60.58   One man esteemeth one day above another: another esteemeth every day alike. Let every man be fully persuaded in his own mind.   *14:5*

60.59   For none of us liveth to himself, and no man dieth to himself. For whether we live, we live unto the Lord; and whether we die, we die unto the Lord: whether we live therefore, or die, we are the Lord's.   *14:7-8*

60.60   Now the God of hope fill you with all joy and peace in believing, that ye may abound in hope, through the power of the Holy Ghost.   *15:13*

60.61   Salute one another with an holy kiss. The churches of Christ salute you.   *16:16*

---

1 CORINTHIANS

61.1   For the preaching of the cross is to them that perish foolishness; but unto us which are saved it is the power of God.   *1:18*

61.2   For after that in the wisdom of God the world by wisdom knew not God, it pleased God by the foolishness of preaching to save them that believe.   *1:21*

61.3   For the Jews require a sign, and the Greeks seek after wisdom: But we preach Christ crucified, unto the Jews a stumblingblock, and unto the Greeks foolishness; But unto them which are called, both Jews and Greeks, Christ the power of God, and the wisdom of God.   *1:22-24*

61.4   But God hath chosen the foolish things of the world to confound the wise; and God hath chosen the weak things of the world to confound the things which are mighty.   *1:27*

61.5   But of him are ye in Christ Jesus, who of God is made unto us wisdom, and righteousness, and sanctification, and redemption: That, according as it is written, He that glorieth, let him glory in the Lord. *1:30-31*

61.6   And I, brethren, when I came to you, came not with excellency of speech or of wisdom, declaring unto you the testimony of God. For I determined not to know any thing among you, save Jesus Christ, and him crucified. *2:1-2*

61.7   And I was with you in weakness, and in fear, and in much trembling. And my speech and my preaching was not with enticing words of man's wisdom, but in demonstration of the Spirit and of power: That your faith should not stand in the wisdom of men, but in the power of God. *2:3-5*

61.8   But as it is written, Eye hath not seen, nor ear heard, neither have entered into the heart of man, the things which God hath prepared for them that love him. But God hath revealed them unto us by his Spirit: for the Spirit searcheth all things, yea, the deep things of God. *2:9-10*

61.9   I have planted, Apollos watered; but God gave the increase. *3:6*

61.10   For other foundation can no man lay than that is laid, which is Jesus Christ. *3:11*

61.11   Every man's work shall be made manifest: for the day shall declare it, because it shall be revealed by fire; and the fire shall try every man's work of what sort it is. *3:13*

61.12   Know ye not that ye are the temple of God, and that the Spirit of God dwelleth in you? *3:16*

61.13   Whether Paul, or Apollos, or Cephas, or the world, or life, or death, or things present, or things to come; all are yours; And ye are Christ's; and Christ is God's. *3:22-23*

61.14   For I think that God hath set forth us the apostles last, as it were appointed to death: for we are made a spectacle unto the world, and to angels, and to men. *4:9*

61.15   For the kingdom of God is not in word, but in power. *4:20*

61.16   For I verily, as absent in body, but present in spirit, have judged already, as though I were present, concerning him that hath so done this deed. *5:3*

61.17   Your glorying is not good. Know ye not that a little leaven leaveneth the whole lump? Purge out therefore the old leaven, that ye may be a new lump, as ye are unleavened. For even Christ our passover is sacrificed for us: Therefore let us keep the feast, not with old leaven, neither with the leaven of malice and wickedness; but with the unleavened bread of sincerity and truth. *5:6-8*

61.18   What? know ye not that your body is the temple of the Holy Ghost which is in you, which ye have of God, and ye are not your own? For ye are bought with a price: therefore glorify God in your body, and in your spirit, which are God's. *6:19-20*

61.19   But if they cannot contain, let them marry: for it is better to marry than to burn. *7:9*

61.20   For the unbelieving husband is sanctified by the wife, and the unbelieving wife is sanctified by the husband: else were your children unclean; but now are they holy. *7:14*

61.21   Circumcision is nothing, and uncircumcision is nothing, but keeping of the commandments of God. Let every man abide in the same calling wherein he was called. *7:19-20*

61.22   Brethren, let every man, wherein he is called, therein abide with God. *7:24*

61.23　But he that is married careth for the things that are of the world, how he may please his wife.　*7:33*

61.24　The wife is bound by the law as long as her husband liveth; but if her husband be dead, she is at liberty to be married to whom she will; only in the Lord.　*7:39*

61.25　Now as touching things offered unto idols, we know that we all have knowledge. Knowledge puffeth up, but charity edifieth.　*8:1*

61.26　For though I preach the gospel, I have nothing to glory of: for necessity is laid upon me; yea, woe is unto me, if I preach not the gospel!　*9:16*

61.27　To the weak became I as weak, that I might gain the weak: I am made all things to all men, that I might by all means save some.　*9:22*

All things to all men

People who are all things to all men try *to please everyone, modifying their behaviour to adapt to those whom they are with. The expression has its source in this verse. Paul was willing to be completely versatile to fit in with different groups of people in an attempt to bring about their salvation.*

61.28　Know ye not that they which run in a race run all, but one receiveth the prize? So run, that ye may obtain.　*9:24*

61.29　But I keep under my body, and bring it into subjection: lest that by any means, when I have preached to others, I myself should be a castaway.　*9:27*

61.30　Wherefore let him that thinketh he standeth take heed lest he fall.　*10:12*

61.31　There hath no temptation taken you but such as is common to man: but God is faithful, who will not suffer you to be tempted above that ye are able; but will with the temptation also make a way to escape, that ye may be able to bear it.　*10:13*

61.32　All things are lawful for me, but all things are not expedient: all things are lawful for me, but all things edify not.　*10:23*

61.33　For the earth is the Lord's, and the fulness thereof.　*10:26*

61.34　Whether therefore ye eat, or drink, or whatsoever ye do, do all to the glory of God.　*10:31*

61.35　But if a woman have long hair, it is a glory to her: for her hair is given her for a covering.　*11:15*

61.36　For I have received of the Lord that which also I delivered unto you, That the Lord Jesus the same night in which he was betrayed took bread: And when he had given thanks, he brake it, and said, Take, eat: this is my body, which is broken for you: this do in remembrance of me. After the same manner also he took the cup, when he had supped, saying, This cup is the new testament in my blood: this do ye, as oft as ye drink it, in remembrance of me. For as often as ye eat this bread, and drink this cup, ye do shew the Lord's death till he come.　*11:23-26*

61.37　Wherefore whosoever shall eat this bread, and drink this cup of the Lord, unworthily, shall be guilty of the body and blood of the Lord.　*11:27*

61.38　Wherefore I give you to understand, that no man speaking by the Spirit of God calleth Jesus accursed: and that no man can say that Jesus is the Lord, but by the Holy Ghost.　*12:3*

61.39　Now there are diversities of gifts, but the same Spirit.　*12:4*

61.40　And there are differences of administrations, but the same Lord. And there are diversities of operations, but it is the same God which worketh all in all. But the manifestation of the Spirit is given to every man to profit withal.   *12:5-7*

61.41   For as the body is one, and hath many members, and all the members of that one body, being many, are one body: so also is Christ. For by one Spirit are we all baptized into one body, whether we be Jews or Gentiles, whether we be bond or free; and have been all made to drink into one Spirit. For the body is not one member, but many.   *12:12-14*

61.42   Though I speak with the tongues of men and of angels, and have not charity, I am become as sounding brass, or a tinkling cymbal. And though I have the gift of prophecy, and understand all mysteries, and all knowledge; and though I have all faith, so that I could remove mountains, and have not charity, I am nothing. And though I bestow all my goods to feed the poor, and though I give my body to be burned, and have not charity, it profiteth me nothing. Charity suffereth long, and is kind; charity envieth not; charity vaunteth not itself, is not puffed up, Doth not behave itself unseemly, seeketh not her own, is not easily provoked, thinketh no evil; Rejoiceth not in iniquity, but rejoiceth in the truth; Beareth all things, believeth all things, hopeth all things, endureth all things. Charity never faileth: but whether there be prophecies, they shall fail; whether there be tongues, they shall cease; whether there be knowledge, it shall vanish away. For we know in part, and we prophesy in part. But when that which is perfect is come, then that which is in part shall be done away. When I was a child, I spake as a child, I understood as a child, I thought as a child: but when I became a man, I put away childish things. For now we see through a glass, darkly; but then face to face: now I know in part; but then shall I know even as also I am known. And now abideth faith, hope, charity, these three; but the greatest of these is charity.   *13:1-13*

61.43   For if the trumpet give an uncertain sound, who shall prepare himself to the battle?   *14:8*

61.44   Brethren, be not children in understanding: howbeit in malice be ye children, but in understanding be men.   *14:20*

61.45   For God is not the author of confusion, but of peace, as in all churches of the saints.   *14:33*

61.46   Let all things be done decently and in order.   *14:40*

61.47   For I delivered unto you first of all that which I also received, how that Christ died for our sins according to the scriptures; And that he was buried, and that he rose again the third day according to the scriptures.   *15:3-4*

61.48   And last of all he was seen of me also, as of one born out of due time. For I am the least of the apostles, that am not meet to be called an apostle, because I persecuted the church of God. But by the grace of God I am what I am: and his grace which was bestowed upon me was not in vain; but I laboured more abundantly than they all: yet not I, but the grace of God which was with me.   *15:8-10*

61.49   If in this life only we have hope in Christ, we are of all men most miserable.   *15:19*

61.50   But now is Christ risen from the dead, and become the firstfruits of them that slept. For since by man came death, by man came also the resurrection of the dead. For as in Adam all die, even so in Christ shall all be made alive.   *15:20-22*

61.51   But every man in his own order: Christ the firstfruits; afterward they that are Christ's at his coming.   *15:23*

61.52   Then cometh the end, when he shall have delivered up the kingdom to God, even the Father; when he shall have put down all rule and all authority and power. For he must reign, till he hath put all enemies under his feet. The last enemy that shall be destroyed is death. *15:24-26*

61.53   There is one glory of the sun, and another glory of the moon, and another glory of the stars: for one star differeth from another star in glory. So also is the resurrection of the dead. It is sown in corruption; it is raised in incorruption. *15:41-42*

61.54   The first man is of the earth, earthy: the second man is the Lord from heaven. *15:47*

61.55   Now this I say, brethren, that flesh and blood cannot inherit the kingdom of God; neither doth corruption inherit incorruption. *15:50*

61.56   Behold, I shew you a mystery; We shall not all sleep, but we shall all be changed, In a moment, in the twinkling of an eye, at the last trump: for the trumpet shall sound, and the dead shall be raised incorruptible, and we shall be changed. For this corruptible must put on incorruption, and this mortal must put on immortality. So when this corruptible shall have put on incorruption, and this mortal shall have put on immortality, then shall be brought to pass the saying that is written, Death is swallowed up in victory. *15:51-54*

61.57   O death, where is thy sting? O grave, where is thy victory? The sting of death is sin; and the strength of sin is the law. But thanks be to God, which giveth us the victory through our Lord Jesus Christ. *15:55-57*

61.58   Therefore, my beloved brethren, be ye stedfast, unmoveable, always abounding in the work of the Lord, forasmuch as ye know that your labour is not in vain in the Lord. *15:58*

61.59   Watch ye, stand fast in the faith, quit you like men, be strong. *16:13*

2 CORINTHIANS

62.1   For all the promises of God in him are yea, and in him Amen, unto the glory of God by us. *1:20*

62.2   Now thanks be unto God, which always causeth us to triumph in Christ, and maketh manifest the savour of his knowledge by us in every place. *2:14*

62.3   Forasmuch as ye are manifestly declared to be the epistle of Christ ministered by us, written not with ink, but with the Spirit of the living God; not in tables of stone, but in fleshy tables of the heart. *3:3*

62.4   Not that we are sufficient of ourselves to think any thing as of ourselves; but our sufficiency is of God; Who also hath made us able ministers of the new testament; not of the letter, but of the spirit: for the letter killeth, but the spirit giveth life. *3:5-6*

The letter of the law

The letter of the law *is a literal understanding of the law as it is expressed. This phrase is often used in contrast with the* spirit of the law, *the law's general purpose or effect. Both expressions derive from this verse.*

62.5   But their minds were blinded: for until this day remaineth the same vail untaken away in the reading of the old testament; which vail is done away in Christ. But even unto this day, when Moses is read, the vail is upon their heart. Nevertheless when it shall turn to the Lord, the vail shall be taken away. *3:14-16*

62.6   Now the Lord is that Spirit: and where the Spirit of the Lord is, there is liberty. But we all, with open face beholding as in a glass the glory of the Lord, are changed into the same image from glory to glory, even as by the Spirit of the Lord.   *3:17-18*

62.7   In whom the god of this world hath blinded the minds of them which believe not, lest the light of the glorious gospel of Christ, who is the image of God, should shine unto them.   *4:4*

62.8   For God, who commanded the light to shine out of darkness, hath shined in our hearts, to give the light of the knowledge of the glory of God in the face of Jesus Christ.   *4:6*

62.9   But we have this treasure in earthen vessels, that the excellency of the power may be of God, and not of us.   *4:7*

62.10   We are troubled on every side, yet not distressed; we are perplexed, but not in despair.   *4:8*

62.11   For our light affliction, which is but for a moment, worketh for us a far more exceeding and eternal weight of glory; While we look not at the things which are seen, but at the things which are not seen: for the things which are seen are temporal; but the things which are not seen are eternal.   *4:17-18*

62.12   For we know that if our earthly house of this tabernacle were dissolved, we have a building of God, an house not made with hands, eternal in the heavens.   *5:1*

62.13   For in this we groan, earnestly desiring to be clothed upon with our house which is from heaven: If so be that being clothed we shall not be found naked. For we that are in this tabernacle do groan, being burdened: not for that we would be unclothed, but clothed upon, that mortality might be swallowed up of life.   *5:2-4*

62.14   For we walk by faith, not by sight.   *5:7*

62.15   We are confident, I say, and willing rather to be absent from the body, and to be present with the Lord.   *5:8*

62.16   For we must all appear before the judgment seat of Christ; that every one may receive the things done in his body, according to that he hath done, whether it be good or bad.   *5:10*

62.17   For the love of Christ constraineth us; because we thus judge, that if one died for all, then were all dead.   *5:14*

62.18   Therefore if any man be in Christ, he is a new creature: old things are passed away; behold, all things are become new.   *5:17*

62.19   Now then we are ambassadors for Christ, as though God did beseech you by us: we pray you in Christ's stead, be ye reconciled to God. For he hath made him to be sin for us, who knew no sin; that we might be made the righteousness of God in him.   *5:20-21*

62.20   For he saith, I have heard thee in a time accepted, and in the day of salvation have I succoured thee: behold, now is the accepted time; behold, now is the day of salvation.   *6:2*

62.21   As unknown, and yet well known; as dying, and, behold, we live; as chastened, and not killed; As sorrowful, yet alway rejoicing; as poor, yet making many rich; as having nothing, and yet possessing all things.   *6:9-10*

62.22   Be ye not unequally yoked together with unbelievers: for what fellowship hath righteousness with unrighteousness? and what communion hath light with darkness? And what concord hath Christ with Belial? or what part hath he that believeth with an infidel?   *6:14-15*

62.23   For, when we were come into Macedonia, our flesh had no rest, but we were troubled on every side; without were fightings, within were fears.   *7:5*

62.24   And this they did, not as we hoped, but first gave their own selves to the Lord, and unto us by the will of God.   *8:5*

62.25   For ye know the grace of our Lord Jesus Christ, that, though he was rich, yet for your sakes he became poor, that ye through his poverty might be rich.   *8:9*

62.26   Every man according as he purposeth in his heart, so let him give; not grudgingly, or of necessity: for God loveth a cheerful giver.   *9:7*

62.27   Thanks be unto God for his unspeakable gift.   *9:15*

62.28   For though we walk in the flesh, we do not war after the flesh: (For the weapons of our warfare are not carnal, but mighty through God to the pulling down of strong holds.)   *10:3-4*

62.29   But he that glorieth, let him glory in the Lord.   *10:17*

62.30   For ye suffer fools gladly, seeing ye yourselves are wise.   *11:19*

Not suffer fools gladly

A person who does not suffer fools gladly is impatient and unsympathetic towards foolish people. The expression derives from this verse: the Corinthians thought themselves to be wise and so respected and submitted themselves naively to false teachers.

62.31   Of the Jews five times received I forty stripes save one. Thrice was I beaten with rods, once was I stoned, thrice I suffered shipwreck, a night and a day I have been in the deep; In journeyings often, in perils of waters, in perils of robbers, in perils by mine own countrymen, in perils by the heathen, in perils in the city, in perils in the wilderness, in perils in the sea, in perils among false brethren; In weariness and painfulness, in watchings often, in

hunger and thirst, in fastings often, in cold and nakedness.   *11:24-27*

62.32   I knew a man in Christ above fourteen years ago, (whether in the body, I cannot tell; or whether out of the body, I cannot tell: God knoweth;) such an one caught up the third heaven.   *12:2*

62.33   And lest I should be exalted above measure through the abundance of the revelations, there was given to me a thorn in the flesh, the messenger of Satan to buffet me, lest I should be exalted above measure.   *12:7*

62.34   For this thing I besought the Lord thrice, that it might depart from me. And he said unto me, My grace is sufficient for thee: for my strength is made perfect in weakness. Most gladly therefore will I rather glory in my infirmities, that the power of Christ may rest upon me. Therefore I take pleasure in infirmities, in reproaches, in necessities, in persecutions, in distresses for Christ's sake: for when I am weak, then am I strong.   *12:8-10*

62.35   The grace of the Lord Jesus Christ, and the love of God, and the communion of the Holy Ghost, be with you all. Amen.   *13:14*

GALATIANS

63.1   I marvel that ye are so soon removed from him that called you into the grace of Christ unto another gospel: Which is not another; but there be some that trouble you, and would pervert the gospel of Christ. But though we, or an angel from heaven, preach any other gospel unto you than that which we have preached unto you, let him be accursed.   *1:6-8*

63.2   But I certify you, brethren, that the gospel which was preached of me is not after man. For I neither received it of man, neither was I taught it, but by the revelation of Jesus Christ.   *1:11-12*

63.3   To reveal his Son in me, that I might preach him among the heathen; immediately I conferred not with flesh and blood.   *1:16*

63.4   And when James, Cephas, and John, who seemed to be pillars, perceived the grace that was given unto me, they gave to me and Barnabas the right hands of fellowship; that we should go unto the heathen, and they unto the circumcision.   *2:9*

63.5   Knowing that a man is not justified by the works of the law, but by the faith of Jesus Christ, even we have believed in Jesus Christ, that we might be justified by the faith of Christ, and not by the works of the law: for by the works of the law shall no flesh be justified.   *2:16*

63.6   I am crucified with Christ: nevertheless I live; yet not I, but Christ liveth in me: and the life which I now live in the flesh I live by the faith of the Son of God, who loved me, and gave himself for me.   *2:20*

63.7   Christ hath redeemed us from the curse of the law, being made a curse for us: for it is written, Cursed is every one that hangeth on a tree.   *3:13*

63.8   Wherefore the law was our schoolmaster to bring us unto Christ, that we might be justified by faith.   *3:24*

63.9   There is neither Jew nor Greek, there is neither bond nor free, there is neither male nor female: for ye are all one in Christ Jesus.   *3:28*

63.10   But when the fulness of the time was come, God sent forth his Son, made of a woman, made under tha law, To redeem them that were under the law, that we might receive the adoption of sons. *4:4-5*

63.11   And because ye are sons, God hath sent forth the Spirit of his Son into your hearts, crying, Abba, Father.   *4:6*

63.12   My little children, of whom I travail in birth again until Christ be formed in you.   *4:19*

63.13   Stand fast therefore in the liberty wherewith Christ hath made us free, and be not entangled again with the yoke of bondage.   *5:1*

63.14   Christ is become of no effect unto you, whosoever of you are justified by the law; ye are fallen from grace.   *5:4*

Fall from grace

The idiomatic expression to fall from grace*, to lose one's privileged and favoured position, has its origin in this verse. The meaning in the biblical text is different, however, from its contemporary meaning. The Galatians were trying to put themselves right with God by relying on their own efforts to keep the law. They were therefore falling away from receiving God's favour only by grace - his love and kindness - and so were rejecting Christ.*

63.15   For in Jesus Christ neither circumcision availeth any thing, nor uncircumcision; but faith which worketh by love.   *5:6*

63.16   For, brethren, ye have been called unto liberty; only use not liberty for an occasion to the flesh, but by love serve one another.   *5:13*

63.17   For the flesh lusteth against the Spirit, and the Spirit against the flesh: and these are contrary the one to the other: so that ye cannot do the things that ye would.   *5:17*

63.18   But if ye be led of the Spirit, ye are not under the law.   *5:18*

63.19   Now the works of the flesh are manifest, which are these; Adultery, fornication, uncleanness, lasciviousness, Idolatry, witchcraft, hatred, variance, emulations, wrath, strife, seditions, heresies, Envyings, murders, drunkenness, revellings, and such like: of the which I tell you before, as I have also told you in time past, that they which do such things shall not inherit the kingdom of God.   *5:19-21*

63.20   But the fruit of the Spirit is love, joy, peace, longsuffering, gentleness, goodness, faith, Meekness, temperance: against such there is no law.   *5:22-23*

63.21   If we live in the Spirit, let us also walk in the Spirit.   *5:25*

63.22   Bear ye one another's burdens, and so fulfil the law of Christ.   *6:2*

63.23   Be not deceived; God is not mocked: for whatsoever a man soweth, that shall he also reap. For he that soweth to his flesh shall of the flesh reap corruption; but he that soweth to the Spirit shall of the Spirit reap life everlasting. And let us not be weary in well doing: for in due season we shall reap, if we faint not.   *6:7-9*

EPHESIANS

64.1   Blessed be the God and Father of our Lord Jesus Christ, who hath blessed us with all spiritual blessings in heavenly places in Christ: According as he hath chosen us in him before the foundation of the world, that we should be holy and without blame before him in love: Having predestinated us unto the adoption of children by Jesus Christ to himself, according to the good pleasure of his will, To the praise of the glory of his grace, wherein he hath made us accepted in the beloved. In who, we have redemption through his blood, the forgiveness of sins, according to the riches of his grace.   *1:3-7*

64.2   The eyes of your understanding being enlightened; that ye may know what is the hope of his calling, and what the riches of the glory of his inheritance in the saints, And what is the exceeding greatness of his power to usward who believe, according to the working of his mighty power, Which he wrought in Christ, when he raised him from the dead, and set him at his own right hand in the heavenly places.   *1:18-19*

64.3   And you hath he quickened, who were dead in trespasses and sins; Wherein in time past ye walked according to the course of this world, according to the prince of the power of the air, the spirit that now worketh in the children of disobedience: Among whom also we all had our conversation in times past in the lusts of our flesh, fulfilling the desires of the flesh and of the mind; and were by nature the children of wrath, even as others. But God, who is rich in mercy, for his great love wherewith he loved us, Even when we were dead in sins, hath quickened us together with Christ, (by grace ye are saved).   *2:1-5*

64.4   And hath raised us up together, and made us sit together in heavenly places in Christ Jesus: That in the ages to come he might shew the exceeding riches of his grace in his kindness toward us through Christ Jesus.   *2:6-7*

64.5   For by grace are ye saved through faith; and that not of yourselves: it is the gift of God: Not the works, lest any man should boast. For we are his workmanship, created in Christ Jesus unto good works, which God hath before ordained that we should walk in them. *2:8-10*

64.6   And came and preached peace to you which were afar off, and to them that were nigh.   *2:17*

64.7   Now therefore ye are no more strangers and foreigners, but fellow citizens with the saints, and of the household of God.   *2:19*

64.8   And are built upon the foundation of the apostles and prophets, Jesus Christ himself being the chief corner stone. *2:20*

64.9   Unto me, who am less than the least of all saints, is this grace given, that I should preach among the Gentiles the unsearchable riches of Christ.   *3:8*

64.10   For this cause I bow my knees unto the Father of our Lord Jesus Christ, Of whom the whole family in heaven and earth is named, That he would grant you, according to the riches of his glory, to be strengthened with might by his Spirit in the inner man; That Christ may dwell in your hearts by faith; that ye, being rooted and grounded in love, May be able to comprehend with all saints what is the breadth, and length, and depth, and height; And to know the love of Christ, which passeth knowledge, that ye might be filled with all the fulness of God. *3:14-19*

64.11   Now unto him that is able to do exceeding abundantly above all that we ask or think, according to the power that worketh in us, Unto him be glory in the church by Christ Jesus throughout all ages, world without end. Amen. *3:20-21*

64.12   I therefore, the prisoner of the Lord, beseech you that ye walk worthy of the vocation wherewith ye are called. *4:1*

64.13   There is one body, and one Spirit, even as ye are called in one hope of your calling; One Lord, one faith, one baptism, One God and Father of all, who is above all, and through all, and in you all.   *4:4-6*

64.14   And he gave some, apostles; and some, prophets; and some, evangelists; and some, pastors and teachers; For the perfecting of the saints, for the work of the ministry, for the edifying of the body of Christ: Till we all come in the unity of the faith, and of the knowledge of the Son of God, unto a perfect man, unto the measure of the stature of the fulness of Christ.   *4:11-13*

64.15   But speaking the truth in love, may grow up into him in all things, which is the head, even Christ: From whom the whole body fitly joined together and compacted by that which every joint supplieth, according to the effectual working in the measure of every part, maketh increase of the body unto the edifying of itself in love.   *4:15-16*

64.16   Wherefore putting away lying, speak every man truth with his neighbour: for we are members one of another. Be ye angry, and sin not: let not the sun go down upon your wrath: Neither give place to the devil. Let him that stole steal no more: but rather let him labour, working with his hands the thing which is good, that he may have to give to him that needeth.   *4:25-28*

64.17   And grieve not the holy Spirit of God, whereby ye are sealed unto the day of redemption.   *4:30*

64.18   And walk in love, as Christ also hath loved us, and hath given himself for us an offering and a sacrifice to God for a sweetsmelling savour.   *5:2*

64.19   Redeeming the time, because the days are evil.   *5:16*

64.20   And be not drunk with wine, wherein is excess; but be filled with the Spirit; Speaking to yourselves in psalms and hymns and spiritual songs, singing and making melody in your heart to the Lord; Giving thanks always for all things unto God and the Father in the name of our Lord Jesus Christ.   *5:18-20*

64.21   Submitting yourselves one to another in the fear of God.   *5:21*

64.22   Wives, submit yourselves unto your own husbands, as unto the Lord. For the husband is the head of the wife, even as Christ is the head of the church: and he is the saviour of the body.   *5:22-23*

64.23   Husbands, love your wives, even as Christ also loved the church, and gave himself for it.   *5:25*

64.24   For this cause shall a man leave his father and mother, and shall be joined unto his wife, and they two shall be one flesh. This is a great mystery: but I speak concerning Christ and the church. *5:31-32*

64.25   Children, obey your parents in the Lord: for this is right.   *6:1*

64.26   Honour thy father and mother; (which is the first commandment with promise;) That it may be well with thee, and thou mayest live long on the earth. *6:2-3*

64.27   Servants, be obedient to them that are your masters according to the flesh, with fear and trembling, in singleness of your heart, as unto Christ; Not with eyeservice, as menpleasers; but as the servants of Christ, doing the will of God from the heart; With good will doing service, as to the Lord, and not to men. *6:5-7*

64.28   Finally, my brethren, be strong in the Lord, and in the power of his might. Put on the whole armour of God, that ye may be able to stand against the wiles of the devil. For we wrestle not against flesh and blood, but against principalities, against powers, against the rulers of the darkness of this world, against spiritual wickedness in high places. Wherefore take unto you the whole armour of God, that ye may be able to withstand in the evil day, and having done all, to stand. Stand therefore, having your loins girt about with truth, and having on the breastplate of righteousness; And your feet shod with the preparation of the gospel of peace; Above all, taking the shield of faith, wherewith ye shall be able to quench all the fiery darts of the wicked. And take the helmet of salvation, and the sword of the Spirit, which is the word of God: Praying always with all prayer and supplication in the Spirit, and watching thereunto with all perseverance and supplication for all saints.   *6:10-18*

PHILIPPIANS

65.1   I thank my God upon every remembrance of you, Always in every prayer of mine for you all making request with joy.   *1:3-4*

65.2   Being confident of this very thing, that he which hath begun a good work in you will perform it until the day of Jesus Christ.   *1:6*

65.3   For to me to live is Christ, and to die is gain. But if I live in the flesh, this is the fruit of my labour: yet what I shall choose I wot not.   *1:21-22*

65.4   Only let your conversation be as it becometh the gospel of Christ: that whether I come and see you, or else be absent, I may hear of your affairs, that ye stand fast in one spirit, with one mind striving together for the faith of the gospel.   *1:27*

65.5   Let this mind be in you, which was also in Christ Jesus: Who, being in the form of God, thought it not robbery to be equal with God: But made himself of no reputation, and took upon him the form of a servant, and was made in the likeness of men: And being found in fashion as a man, he humbled himself, and became obedient unto death, even the death of the cross. Wherefore God also hath highly exalted him, and given him a name which is above every name: That at the name of Jesus every knee should bow, of things in heaven, and things in earth, and things under the earth; And that every tongue should confess that Jesus Christ is Lord, to the glory of God the Father.   *2:5-11*

65.6   Wherefore, my beloved, as ye have always obeyed, not as in my presence only, but now much more in my absence, work out your own salvation with fear and trembling. For it is God which worketh in you both to will and to do of his good pleasure.   *2:12-13*

The example of Christ

These verses may well be a quotation from an early Christian hymn, describing Christ's humbling of himself and his exaltation by God the Father. The climax comes in verse 11: the statement of belief that Jesus Christ is Lord. Paul's purpose in quoting these lines is to encourage his readers to imitate Christ's self-sacrificial humility.

65.7   Holding forth the word of life; that I may rejoice in the day of Christ, that I have not run in vain, neither laboured in vain.   *2:16*

65.8   Circumcised the eighth day, of the stock of Israel, of the tribe of Benjamin, an Hebrew of the Hebrews; as touching the law, a Pharisee.   *3:5*

65.9   But what things were gain to me, those I counted loss for Christ. Yea doubtless, and I count all things but loss for the excellency of the knowledge of Christ Jesus my Lord: for whom I have suffered the loss of all things, and do count them but dung, that I may win Christ.   *3:7-8*

65.10   And be found in him, not having mine own righteousness, which is of the law, but that which is through the faith of Christ, the righteousness which is of God by faith: That I may know him, and the power of his resurrection, and the fellowship of his sufferings, being made conformable unto his death; If by any means I might attain unto the resurrection of the dead.   *3:9-11*

65.11   Not as though I had already attained, either were already perfect: but I follow after, if that I may apprehend that

for which also I am apprehended of Christ Jesus.   *3:12*

65.12   Brethren, I count not myself to have apprehended: but this one thing I do, forgetting those things which are behind, and reaching forth unto those things which are before, I press toward the mark for the prize of the high calling of God in Christ Jesus.   *3:13-14*

65.13   Whose end is destruction, whose God is their belly, and whose glory is in their shame, who mind earthly things. *3:19*

65.14   For our conversation is in heaven; from whence also we look for the Saviour, the Lord Jesus Christ.   *3:20*

65.15   Therefore, my brethren dearly beloved and longed for, my joy and crown, so stand fast in the Lord, my dearly beloved.   *4:1*

65.16   Rejoice in the Lord alway: and again I say, Rejoice. Let your moderation be known unto all men. The Lord is at hand. Be careful for nothing; but in every thing by prayer and supplication with thanksgiving let your requests be made known unto God. And the peace of God, which passeth all understanding, shall keep your hearts and minds through Christ Jesus.   *4:4-7*

65.17   Finally, brethren, whatsoever things are true, whatsoever things are honest, whatsoever things are just, whatsoever things are pure, whatsoever things are lovely, whatsoever things are of good report; if there be any virtue, and if there be any praise, think on these things.   *4:8*

65.18   Not that I speak in respect of want: for I have learned, in whatsoever state I am, therewith to be content. I know both how to be abased, and I know how to abound: every where and in all things I am instructed both to be full and to be hungry, both to abound and to suffer need.   *4:11-12*

65.19   I can do all things through Christ which strengtheneth me.   *4:13*

65.20   But my God shall supply all your need according to his riches in glory by Christ Jesus.   *4:19*

COLOSSIANS

66.1   That ye might walk worthy of the Lord unto all pleasing, being fruitful in every good work, and increasing in the knowledge of God; Strengthened with all might, according to his glorious power, unto all patience and longsuffering with joyfulness.   *1:10-11*

66.2   Who hath delivered us from the power of darkness, and hath translated us into the kingdom of his dear Son: In whom we have redemption through his blood, even the forgiveness of sins: Who is the image of the invisible God, the firstborn of every creature: For by him were all things created, that are in heaven, and that are in earth, visible and invisible, whether they be thrones, or dominions, or principalities, or powers: all things were created by him, and for him: And he is before all things, and by him all things consist. And he is the head of the body, the church: who is the beginning, the firstborn from the dead; that in all things he might have the preeminence. For it pleased the Father that in him should all fulness dwell; And, having made peace through the blood of his cross, by him to reconcile all things unto himself; by him, I say, whether they be things in earth, or things in heaven.   *1:13-20*

66.3   To whom God would make known what is the riches of the glory of this mystery among the Gentiles; which is Christ in you, the hope of glory.   *1:27*

66.4   Whom we preach, warning every man, and teaching every man in all wisdom; that we may present every man perfect in Christ Jesus.   *1:28*

66.5   Beware lest any man spoil you through philosophy and vain deceit, after the tradition of men, after the rudiments of the world, and not after Christ.   *2:8*

66.6   For in him dwelleth all the fulness of the Godhead bodily.   *2:9*

66.7   Wherefore if ye be dead with Christ from the rudiments of the world, why, as though living in the world, are ye subject to ordinances, (Touch not; taste not; handle not; Which all are to perish with the using;) after the commmandments and doctrines of men?   *2:20-22*

66.8   If ye then be risen with Christ, seek those things which are above, where Christ sitteth on the right hand of God. Set your affection on things above, not on things on the earth.   *3:1-2*

66.9   When Christ, who is our life, shall appear, then shall ye also appear with him in glory.   *3:4*

66.10   Lie not one to another, seeing that ye have put off the old man with his deeds; And have put on the new man, which is renewed in knowledge after the image of him that created him: Where there is neither Greek nor Jew, circumcision nor uncircumcision, Barbarian, Scythian, bond nor free: but Christ is all, and in all.   *3:9-11*

66.11   And let the peace of God rule in your hearts, to the which also ye are called in one body; and be ye thankful.   *3:15*

66.12   And whatsoever ye do, do it heartily, as to the Lord, and not unto men.   *3:23*

66.13   Let your speech be alway with grace, seasoned with salt, that ye may know how ye ought to answer every man.   *4:6*

66.14   Luke, the beloved physician, and Demas, greet you.   *4:14*

1 THESSALONIANS

67.1   Remembering without ceasing your work of faith, and labour of love, and patience of hope in our Lord Jesus Christ, in the sight of God and our Father.   *1:3*

67.2   For our gospel came not unto you in word only, but also in power, and in the Holy Ghost, and in much assurance; as ye know what manner of men we were among you for your sake.   *1:5*

67.3   But we were gentle among you, even as a nurse cherisheth her children: So being affectionately desirous of you, we were willing to have imparted unto you, not the gospel of God only, but also our own souls, because ye were dear unto us.   *2:7-8*

67.4   For this cause also thank we God without ceasing, because, when ye received the word of God which ye heard of us, ye received if not as the word of men, but as it is in truth, the word of God, which effectually worketh also in you that believe.   *2:13*

67.5   For this is the will of God, even your sanctification, that ye should abstain from fornication.   *4:3*

67.6   And that ye study to be quiet, and to do your own business, and to work with your own hands, as we commanded you.   *4:11*

67.7   But I would not have you to be ignorant, brethren, concerning them which are asleep, that ye sorrow not, even as others which have no hope. For if we believe that Jesus died and rose again, even so them also which sleep in Jesus will God bring with him.   *4:13-14*

67.8   For the Lord himself shall descend from heaven with a shout, with the voice of the archangel, and with the trump of God: and the dead in Christ shall rise first:

Then we which are alive and reamin shall be caught up together with them in the clouds, to meet the Lord in the air: and so shall we ever be with the Lord. Wherefore comfort one another with these words.   *4:16-18*

67.9   For yourselves know perfectly that the day of the Lord so cometh as a thief in the night. For when they shall say, Peace and safety; then sudden destruction cometh upon them, as travail upon a woman with child; and they shall not escape.   *5:2-3*

A thief in the night

If something happens like a thief in the night, *it comes unexpectedly. The expression derives from this verse. The day of the Lord - Christ's Second Coming - will take place at a sudden, unforeseen time.*

67.10   Now we exhort you, brethren, warn them that are unruly, comfort the feebleminded, support the weak, be patient toward all men.   *5:14*

67.11   Quench not the Spirit.   *5:19*

67.12   Prove all things; hold fast that which is good.   *5:21*

---

2 THESSALONIANS

68.1   Now we beseech you, brethren, by the coming or our Lord Jesus Christ, and by our gathering together unto him, That ye be not soon shaken in mind, or be troubled, neither by spirit, nor by word, nor by letter as from us, as that the day of Christ is at hand. Let no man deceive you by any means: for that day shall not come, except there come a falling away first, and that man of sin be revealed, the son of perdition.   *2:1-3*

68.2   For even when we were with you, this we commanded you, that if any would not work, neither should he eat. *3:10*

68.3   But ye, brethren, be not weary in well doing.   *3:13*

1 TIMOTHY

69.1   Neither give heed to fables and endless genealogies, which minister questions, rather than godly edifying which is in faith: so do.   *1:4*

69.2   This is a faithful saying, and worthy of all acceptation, that Christ Jesus came into the world to save sinners; of whom I am chief.   *1:15*

69.3   Howbeit for this cause I obtained mercy, that in me first Jesus Christ might shew forth all longsuffering, for a pattern to them which should hereafter believe on him to life everlasting. Now unto the King eternal, immortal, invisible, the only wise God, be honour and glory for ever and ever. Amen.   *1:16-17*

69.4   I exhort therefore, that, first of all, supplications, prayers, intercessions, and giving of thanks, be made for all men; For kings, and for all that are in authority; that we may lead a quiet and peaceable life in all godliness and honesty.   *2:1-2*

69.5   For there is one God, and one mediator between God and men, the man Christ Jesus.   *2:5*

69.6   This is a true saying, If a man desire the office of a bishop, he desireth a good work. A bishop then must be blameless, the husband of one wife, vigilant, sober, of good behaviour, given to hospitality, apt to teach; Not given to wine, no striker, not greedy of filthy lucre; but patient, not a brawler, not covetous. *3:1-3*

69.7   And without controversy great is the mystery of godliness: God was manifest in the flesh, justified in the Spirit, seen of angels, preached unto the Gentiles, believed on in the world, received up into glory.   *3:16*

69.8   For every creature of God is good, and nothing to be refused, if it be received with thanksgiving.   *4:4*

69.9   But refuse profane and old wives' fables, and exercise thyself rather unto godliness. For bodily exercise profiteth little: but godliness is profitable unto all things, having promise of the life that now is, and of that which is to come. *4:7-8*

69.10   Let no man despise thy youth; but be thou an example of the believers, in word, in conversation, in charity, in spirit, in faith, in purity. Till I come, give attendance to reading, to exhortation, to doctrine. Neglect not the gift that is in thee, which was given thee by prophecy, with the laying on of the hands of the presbytery.   *4:12-14*

69.11   But if any provide not for his own, and specially for those of his own house, he hath denied the faith, and is worse than an infidel.   *5:8*

69.12   Drink no longer water, but use a little wine for thy stomach's sake and thine often infirmities.   *5:23*

69.13   But godliness with contentment is great gain. For we brought nothing into this world, and it is certain we can carry nothing out. And having food and raiment let us be therewith content. *6:6-8*

69.14   For the love of money is the root of all evil: which while some coveted after, they have erred from the faith, and pierced themselves through with many sorrows.   *6:10*

69.15   But thou, O man of God, flee these things; and follow after righteousness, godliness, faith, love, patience, meekness. Fight the good fight of faith, lay hold on eternal life, whereunto thou art also called, and hast professed a good profession before many witnesses.   *6:11-12*

Money is the root of all evil

The saying money is the root of all evil *is a misquotation of the biblical text of this verse. It is not money itself, but the love of money that is condemned by Paul in this letter.*

69.16   Charge them that are rich in this world, that they be not highminded, nor trust in uncertain riches, but in the living God, who giveth us richly all things to enjoy.   *6:17*

---

2 TIMOTHY

70.1   For God hath not given us the spirit of fear; but of power, and of love, and of a sound mind.   *1:7*

70.2   But is now made manifest by the appearing of our Saviour Jesus Christ, who hath abolished death, and hath brought life and immortality to light through the gospel.   *1:10*

70.3   For the which cause I also suffer the things: nevertheless I am not ashamed: for I know whom I have believed, and am persuaded that he is able to keep that which I have committed unto him against that day.   *1:12*

70.4   Hold fast the form of sound words, which thou hast heard of me, in faith and love which is in Christ Jesus.   *1:13*

70.5   Thou therefore, my son, be strong in the grace that is in Christ Jesus. And the things that thou hast heard of me among many witnesses, the same commit thou to faithful men, who shall be able to teach others also. Thou therefore endure hardness, as a good soldier of Jesus Christ.   *2:1-3*

70.6   It is a faithful saying: For if we be dead with him, we shall also live with him: If we suffer, we shall also reign with him: if we deny him, he also will deny us: If we believe not, yet he abideth faithful: he cannot deny himself.   *2:11-13*

70.7   Persecutions, afflictions, which came unto me at Antioch, at Iconium, at Lystra; what persecutions I endured: but out of them all the Lord delivered me. Yea, and all that will live godly in Christ Jesus shall suffer persecution.   *3:11-12*

70.8   And that from a child thou hast known the holy scriptures, which are able to make thee wise unto salvation through faith which is in Christ Jesus. All scripture is given by inspiration of God, and is profitable for doctrine, for reproof, for correction, for instruction in righteousness: That the man of God may be perfect, throughly furnished unto all good works.   *3:15-17*

70.9   I charge thee therefore before God, and the Lord Jesus Christ, who shall judge the quick and the dead at his appearing and his kingdom; Preach the word; be instant in season, out of season; reprove, rebuke, exhort with all longsuffering and doctrine.   *4:1-2*

70.10   For I am now ready to be offered, and the time of my departure is at hand. I have fought a good fight, I have finished my course, I have kept the faith: Henceforth there is laid up for me a crown of righteousness, which the Lord, the righteous judge, shall give me at that day: and not to me only, but unto all them also that love his appearing.   *4:6-8*

70.11   For Demas hath forsaken me, having loved this present world, and is departed unto Thessalonica; Crescens to Galatia, Titus unto Dalmatia.   *4:10*

TITUS

71.1   One of themselves, even a prophet of their own, said, The Cretans are alway liars, evil beasts, slow bellies.   *1:12*

71.2   Unto the pure all things are pure: but unto them that are defiled and unbelieving is nothing pure; but even their mind and conscience is defiled. *1:15*

71.3   Teaching us that, denying ungodliness and worldly lusts, we should live soberly, righteously, and godly, in this present world; Looking for that blessed hope, and the glorious appearing of the great God and our Saviour Jesus Christ.   *2:12-13*

71.4   But after that the kindness and love of God our Saviour toward man appeared, Not by works of righteousness which we have done, but according to his mercy he saved us, by the washing of regeneration, and renewing of the Holy Ghost; Which he shed on us abundantly through Jesus Christ our Saviour; That being justified by his grace, we should be made heirs according to the hope of eternal life.   *3:4-7*

PHILEMON

72.1   Yet for love's sake I rather beseech thee, being such an one as Paul the aged, and now also a prisoner of Jesus Christ. I beseech thee for my son Onesimus, whom I have begotten in my bonds. *9-10*

72.2   For perhaps he therefore departed for a season, that thou shouldest receive him for ever.   *15*

HEBREWS

73.1   God, who at sundry times and in divers manners spake in time past unto the fathers by the prophets, Hath in these last days spoken unto us by his Son, whom he hath appointed heir of all things, by whom also he made worlds; Who being the brightness of his glory, and the express image of his person, and upholding all things by the word of his power, when he had by himself purged our sins, sat down on the right hand of the Majesty on high.   *1:1-3*

73.2   Being made so much better than the angels, as he hath by inheritance obtained a more excellent name than they.   *1:4*

73.3   But to which of the angels said he at any time, Sit on my right hand, until I make thine enemies thy footstool? Are they not all ministering spirits, sent forth to minister for them who shall be heirs of salvation?   *1:13-14*

73.4   How shall we escape, if we neglect so great salvation; which at the first began to be spoken by the Lord, and was confirmed unto us by them that heard him.   *2:3*

73.5   But we see Jesus, who was made a little lower than the angels for the suffering of death, crowned with glory and honour; that he by the grace of God should taste death for every man.   *2:9*

73.6   Forasmuch then as the children are partakers of flesh and blood, he also himself likewise took part of the same; that through death he might destroy him that had the power of death, that is, the devil; And deliver them who through fear of death were all their lifetime subject to bondage.   *2:14-15*

73.7   But exhort one another daily, while it is called To day; lest any of you be hardened through the deceitfulness of sin. *3:13*

73.8   For the word of God is quick, and powerful, and sharper than any twoedged sword, piercing even to the dividing asunder of soul and spirit, and of the joints and marrow, and is a discerner of the thoughts and intents of the heart. Neither is there any creature that is not manifest in his sight: but all things are naked and opened unto the eyes of him with whom we have to do.   *4:12-13*

73.9   Seeing then that we have a great high priest, that is passed into the heavens, Jesus the Son of God, let us hold fast our profession. For we have not an high priest which cannot be touched with the feeling of our infirmities; but was in all points tempted like as we are, yet without sin. Let us therefore come boldly unto the throne of grace, that we may obtain mercy, and find grace to help in time of need.   *4:14-16*

73.10   Who in the days of his flesh, when he had offered up prayers and supplications with strong crying and tears unto him that was able to save him from death, and was heard in that he feared; Though he were a Son, yet learned he obedience by the things which he suffered.   *5:7-8*

Strong meat

If something is strong meat, *it is thought not to be suitable for people who are easily distressed or upset. The expression comes from this verse. The Hebrews needed someone to teach them again the 'milk' of the elementary truths of God's word. They were not yet ready for the 'solid food' of more advanced teaching.*

73.11   For when for the time ye ought to be teachers, ye have need that one teach you again which be the first principles of the oracles of God; and are become such as have need of milk, and not of strong meat.   *5:12*

73.12   For it is impossible for those who were once enlightened, and have tasted of the heavenly gift, and were made partakers of the Holy Ghost, And have tasted the good word of God, and the powers of the world to come, If they fall away, to renew them again unto repentance; seeing they crucify to themselves the Son of God afresh, and put him to an open shame.   *6:4-6*

73.13   Wherefore he is able also to save them to the uttermost that come unto God by him, seeing he ever liveth to make intercession for them.   *7:25*

73.14   For this is the covenant that I will make with the house of Israel after those days, saith the Lord; I will put my laws into their mind, and write them in their hearts: and I will be to them a God, and they shall be to me a people.   *8:10*

73.15   And almost all things are by the law purged with blood; and without shedding of blood is no remission.   *9:22*

73.16   And as it is appointed unto men once to die, but after this the judgment. *9:27*

73.17   And every priest standeth daily ministering and offering oftentimes the same sacrifices, which can never take away sins: But this man, after he had offered one sacrifice for sins for ever, sat down on the right hand of God. *10:11-12*

73.18   Having therefore, brethren, boldness to enter into the holiest by the blood of Jesus, By a new and living way, which he hath consecrated for us, through the veil, that is to say, his flesh; And having an high priest over the house of God; Let us draw near with a true heart in full assurance of faith, having our hearts sprinkled from an evil conscience, and our bodies washed with pure water. Let us hold fast the profession of our faith without wavering; (for he is faithful that promised;) And let us consider one another to provoke unto love and to good works: Not forsaking the assembling of ourselves together, as the manner of some is; but exhorting one another: and so much the more, as ye see the day approaching.   *10:19-25*

73.19   It is a fearful thing to fall into the hands of the living God.   *10:31*

73.20   Now faith is the substance of things hoped for, the evidence of things not seen.   *11:1*

73.21   But without faith it is impossible to please him: for he that cometh to God must believe that he is, and that he is a rewarder of them that diligently seek him.   *11:6*

73.22   These all died in faith, not having received the promises, but having seen them afar off, and were persuaded of them, and embraced them, and confessed that they were strangers and pilgrims on the earth.   *11:13*

73.23   But now they desire a better country, that is, an heavenly: wherefore God is not ashamed to be called their God: for he hath prepared for them a city.   *11:16*

73.24   Esteeming the reproach of Christ greater riches than the treasures in Egypt: for he had respect unto the recompence of the reward.   *11:26*

73.25   (Of whom the world was not worthy:) they wandered in deserts, and in mountains, and in dens and caves of the earth.   *11:38*

73.26   Wherefore seeing we also are compassed about with so great a cloud of witnesses, let us lay aside every weight, and the sin which doth so easily beset us, and let us run with patience the race that is set before us, Looking unto Jesus the author and finisher of our faith; who for the joy that was set before him endured the cross, despising the shame, and is set down at the right hand of the throne of God.   *12:1-2*

73.27   For consider him that endured such contradiction of sinners against himself, lest ye be wearied and faint in your minds.   *12:3*

73.28   For whom the Lord loveth he chasteneth, and scourgeth every son whom he receiveth.   *12:6*

73.29   Now no chastening for the present seemeth to be joyous, but grievous: nevertheless afterward it yieldeth the peaceable fruit of righteousness unto them which are exercised thereby. Wherefore lift up the hands which hang down, and the feeble knees; And make straight paths for your feet, lest that which is lame be turned out of the way; but let it rather be healed.   *12:11-13*

73.30   Lest there be any fornicator, or profane person, as Esau, who for one morsel of meat sold his birthright. For ye know how that afterward, when he would have inherited the blessing, he was rejected: for he found no place of repentance, though he sought it carefully with tears.   *12:16-17*

73.31   For ye are not come unto the mount that might be touched, and that burned with fire, nor unto blackness, and darkness, and tempest.   *12:18*

73.32   But ye are come unto mount Sion, and unto the city of the living God, the heavenly Jerusalem, and to an innumerable company of angels.   *12:22*

73.33   To the general assembly and church of the firstborn, which are written in heaven, and to God the Judge of all, and to the spirits of just men made perfect.   *12:23*

73.34   For our God is a consuming fire.   *12:29*

73.35   Let brotherly love continue. Be not forgetful to entertain strangers: for thereby some have entertained angels unawares.   *13:1-2*

73.36   Let your conversation be without covetousness; and be content with such things as ye have: for he hath said, I will never leave thee, nor forsake thee.   *13:5*

73.37   Jesus Christ the same yesterday, and to day, and for ever.   *13:8*

73.38   For here have we no continuing city, but we seek one to come.   *13:14*

73.39   Now the God of peace, that brought again from the dead our Lord Jesus, that great shepherd of the sheep, through the blood of the everlasting convenant, Make you perfect in every good work to do his will, working in you that which is wellpleasing in his sight, through Jesus Christ; to whom be glory for ever and ever. Amen.   *13:20-21*

JAMES

74.1   My brethren, count it all joy when ye fall into divers temptations; Knowing this, that the trying of your faith worketh patience. But let patience have her perfect work, that ye may be perfect and entire, wanting nothing.   *1:2-4*

74.2   If any of you lack wisdom, let him ask of God, that giveth to all men liberally, and upbraideth not, and is shall be given him. But let him ask in faith, nothing wavering. For he that wavereth is like a wave of the sea driven with the wind and tossed. For let not that man think that he shall receive any thing of the Lord. A double minded man is unstable in all his ways.   *1:5-8*

74.3   Blessed is the man that endureth temptation: for when he is tried, he shall receive the crown of life, which the Lord hath promised to them that love him.   *1:12*

74.4   Every good gift and every perfect gift is from above, and cometh down from the Father of lights, with whom is no variableness, neither shadow of turning.   *1:17*

74.5   But be ye doers of the word, and not hearers only, deceiving your own selves. For if any be a hearer of the word, and not a doer, he is like unto a man beholding his natural face in a glass.   *1:22-23*

74.6   But whoso looketh into the perfect law of liberty, and continueth therein, he being not a forgetful hearer, but a doer of the work, this man shall be blessed in his deed.   *1:25*

74.7   If any man among you seem to be religious, and bridleth not his tongue, but deceiveth his own heart, this man's religion is vain.   *1:26*

74.8   Pure religion and undefiled before God and the Father is this, To visit the fatherless and widows in their affliction, and to keep himself unspotted from the world.   *1:27*

74.9   Even so faith, if it hath not works, is dead, being alone.   *2:17*

74.10   Thou believest that there is one God; thou doest well: the devils also believe, and tremble.   *2:19*

74.11   Ye see then how that by works a man is justified, and not by faith only.   *2:24*

74.12   Even so the tongue is a little member, and boasteth great things. Behold, how great a matter a little fire kindleth!   *3:5*

74.13   And the tongue is a fire, a world of iniquity: so is the tongue among our members, that it defileth the whole body, and setteth on fire the course of nature; and it is set on fire of hell.   *3:6*

74.14   Out of the same mouth proceedeth blessing and cursing. My brethren, these things ought not so to be. Doth a fountain send forth at the same place sweet water and bitter?   *3:10-11*

74.15   This wisdom descendeth not from above, but is earthly, sensual, devilish.   *3:15*

74.16   But the wisdom that is from above is first pure, then peaceable, gentle, and easy to be intreated, full of mercy and good fruits, without partiality, and without hypocrisy.   *3:17*

74.17   Submit yourselves therefore to God, Resist the devil, and he will flee from you. Draw nigh to God, and he will draw nigh to you. Cleanse your hands, ye sinners; and purify your hearts, ye double minded.   *4:7-8*

74.18   Go to now, ye that say, To day or to morrow we will go into such a city, and continue there a year, and buy and sell, and get gain: Whereas ye know not what shall be on the morrow. For what is your life? It is even a vapour, that appeareth for a little time, and then vanisheth away. For that ye ought to say, If the Lord will, we shall live, and do this, or that.   *4:13-15*

74.19   Be patient therefore, brethren, unto the coming of the Lord. Behold, the husbandman waiteth for the precious fruit of the earth, and hath long patience for it, until he receive the early and latter rain.   *5:7*

74.20   But above all things, my brethren, swear not, neither by heaven, neither by the earth, neither by any other oath: but let your yea be yea; and your nay, nay; lest ye fall into comdemnation.   *5:12*

74.21   And the prayer of faith shall save the sick, and the Lord shall raise him up; and if he have committed sins, they shall be forgiven him. Confess your faults one to another, and pray one for another, that ye may be healed. The effectual fervent prayer of a righteous man availeth much.   *5:15-16*

74.22   Let him know, that he which converteth the sinner from the error of his way shall save a soul from death, and shall hide a multitude of sins.   *5:20*

---

1 PETER

75.1   Elect according to the foreknowledge of God the Father, through sanctification of the Spirit, unto obedience and sprinkling of the blood of Jesus Christ: Grace unto you, and peace, be multiplied.   *1:2*

75.2   Blessed be the God and Father of our Lord Jesus Christ, which according to his abundant mercy hath begotten us again unto a lively hope by the resurrection of Jesus Christ from the dead, To an inheritance incorruptible, and undefiled, and that fadeth not away, reserved in heaven for you, Who are kept by the power of God through faith unto salvation ready to be revealed in the last time.   *1:3-5*

75.3   Wherein ye greatly rejoice, though now for a season, if need be, ye are in heaviness through manifold temptations: That the trial of your faith, being much more precious than of gold that perisheth, though it be tried with fire, might be found unto praise and honour and glory at the appearing of Jesus Christ: Whom having not seen, ye love; in whom, though now ye see him not, yet believing, ye rejoice with joy unspeakable and full of glory.   *1:6-8*

75.4   Wherefore gird up the loins of your mind, be sober, and hope to the end for the grace that is to be brought unto you at the revelation of Jesus Christ.   *1:13*

75.5   Forasmuch as ye know that ye were not redeemed with corruptible things, as silver and gold, from your vain conversation received by tradition from your fathers; But with the precious blood of Christ, as of a lamb without blemish and without spot.   *1:18-19*

75.6   For all flesh is as grass, and all the glory of man as the flower of grass. The grass withereth, and the flower thereof falleth away.   *1:24*

75.7   As newborn babes, desire the sincere milk of the word, that ye may grow thereby.   *2:2*

75.8   To whom coming, as unto a living stone, disallowed indeed of men, but chosen of God, and precious, Ye also, as lively stones, are built up a spiritual house, an holy priesthood, to offer up spiritual sacrifices, acceptable to God by Jesus Christ. Wherefore also it is contained in the scripture, Behold, I lay in Sion a chief corner stone, elect, precious: and he that believeth on him shall not be confounded. Unto you therefore which believe he is precious: but unto them which be disobedient, the stone which the builders disallowed, the same is made the head of the corner, And a stone of stumbling, and a rock of offence, even to them which stumble at the word, being disobedient: whereunto also they were appointed. But ye are a chosen generation, a royal priesthood, an holy nation, a peculiar people; that ye should shew forth the praises of him who hath called you out of darkness into his marvellous light.   *2:4-9*

75.9   Honour all men. Love the brotherhood. Fear God. Honour the king.   *2:17*

75.10   For even hereunto were ye called: because Christ also suffered for us, leaving us an example, that ye should follow his steps.   *2:21*

75.11   Who his own self bare our sins in his own body on the tree, that we, being dead to sins, should live unto righteousness: by whose stripes ye were healed.   *2:24*

75.12   For ye were as sheep going astray; but are now returned unto the Shepherd and Bishop of your souls.   *2:25*

75.13   Likewise, ye husbands, dwell with them according to knowledge, giving honour unto the wife, as unto the weaker vessel, and as being heirs together of the grace of life; that your prayers be not hindered.   *3:7*

75.14   For he that will love life, and see good days, let him refrain his tongue from evil, and his lips that they speak no guile.   *3:10*

75.15   For the eyes of the Lord are over the righteous, and his ears are open unto their prayers: but the face of the Lord is against them that do evil.   *3:12*

75.16   But sanctify the Lord God in your hearts: and be ready always to give an answer to every man that asketh you a reason of the hope that is in you with meekness and fear.   *3:15*

75.17   For Christ also hath once suffered for sins, the just for the unjust, that he might bring us to God, being put to death in the flesh, but quickened by the Spirit.   *3:18*

75.18   But the end of all things is at hand: be ye therefore sober, and watch unto prayer.   *4:7*

75.19   And above all things have fervent charity among yourselves: for charity shall cover the multitude of sins.   *4:8*

75.20   Humble yourselves therefore under the mighty hand of God, that he may exalt you in due time: Casting all your care upon him; for he careth for you.   *5:6-7*

75.21   Be sober, be vigilant; because your adversary the devil, as a roaring lion, walketh about, seeking whom he may devour: Whom resist stedfast in the faith, knowing that the same afflictions are accomplished in your brethren that are in the world.   *5:8-9*

> ### Cover a multitude of sins
> *If something covers a multitude of sins, it deliberately hides many different things, especially faults and weaknesses. The phrase has its origin in this verse: charity (love) in the Christian community forgives again and again.*

2 PETER

76.1   Whereby are given unto us exceeding great and precious promises: that by these ye might be partakers of the divine nature, having escaped the corruption that is in the world through lust.   *1:4*

76.2   Wherefore the rather, brethren, give diligence to make your calling and election sure: for if ye do these things, ye shall never fall.   *1:10*

76.3   Knowing this first, that no prophecy of the scripture is of any private interpretation. For the prophecy came not in old time by the will of man: but holy men of God spake as they were moved by the Holy Ghost.   *1:20-21*

76.4   But there were false prophets also among the people, even as there shall be false teachers among you, who privily shall bring in damnable heresies, even denying the Lord that bought them, and bring upon themselves swift destruction.   *2:1*

76.5   But chiefly them that walk after the flesh in the lust of uncleanness, and despise government. Presumptuous are they, selfwilled, they are not afraid to speak evil of dignities.   *2:10*

76.6   But it is happened unto them according to the true proverb, The dog is turned to his own vomit again; and the sow that was washed to her wallowing in the mire.   *2:22*

76.7   But, beloved, be not ignorant of this one thing, that one day is with the Lord as a thousand years, and a thousand years as one day. The Lord is not slack concerning his promise, as some men count slackness; but is longsuffering to us-ward, not willing that any should perish, but that all should come to repentance.   *3:8-9*

76.8   But the day of the Lord will come as a thief in the night; in the which the heavens shall pass away with a great noise, and the elements shall melt with fervent heat, the earth also and the works that are therein shall be burned up. Seeing then that all these things shall be dissolved, what manner of persons ought ye to be in all holy conversation and godliness. *3:10-11*

76.9   Nevertheless we, according to his promise, look for new heavens and a new earth, wherein dwelleth righteousness. Wherefore, beloved, seeing that ye look for such things, be diligent that ye may be found of him in peace, without spot, and blameless.   *3:13-14*

1 JOHN

77.1   That which we have seen and heard declare we unto you, that ye also may have fellowship with us: and truly our fellowship is with the Father, and with his Son Jesus Christ.   *1:3*

77.2   This then is the message which we have heard of him, and declare unto you, that God is light, and in him is no darkness at all.   *1:5*

77.3   If we say that we have fellowship with him, and walk in darkness, we lie, and do not the truth: But if we walk in the light, as he is in the light, we have fellowship one with another, and the blood of Jesus Christ his Son cleanseth us from all sin. If we say that we have no sin, we deceive ourselves, and the truth is not in us. If we confess our sins, he is faithful and just to forgive us our sins, and to cleanse us from all unrighteousness. *1:6-9*

77.4   My little children, these things write I unto you, that ye sin not. And if any man sin, we have an advocate with the Father, Jesus Christ the righteous: And he is the propitiation for our sins: and not for ours only, but also for the sins of the whole world. *2:1-2*

77.5   Love not the world, neither the things that are in the world. If any man love the world, the love of the Father is not in him. *2:15*

77.6   For all that is in the world, the lust of the flesh, and the lust of the eyes, and the pride of life, is not of the Father, but is of the world. *2:16*

77.7   And the world passeth away, and the lust thereof: but he that doeth the will of God abideth for ever. *2:17*

77.8   Behold, what manner of love the Father hath bestowed upon us, that we should be called the sons of God: therefore the world knoweth us not, because it knew him not. Beloved, now are we the sons of God, and it doth not yet appear what we shall be: but we know that, when he shall appear, we shall be like him; for we shall see him as he is. *3:1-2*

77.9   He that committeth sin is of the devil; for the devil sinneth from the beginning. For this purpose the Son of God was manifested, that he might destroy the works of the devil. *3:8*

77.10   We know that we have passed from death unto life, because we love the brethren. He that loveth not his brother abideth death. *3:14*

77.11   But whoso hath this world's good, and seeth his brother have need, and shutteth up his bowels of compassion from him, how dwelleth the love of God in him? *3:17*

77.12   My little children, let us not love in word, neither in tongue; but in deed and in truth. *3:18*

77.13   And this is his commandment, That we should believe on the name of his Son Jesus Christ, and love one another, as he gave us commandment. *3:23*

77.14   Ye are of God, little children, and have overcome them: because greater is he that is in you, than he that is in the world. *4:4*

77.15   Beloved, let us love one another: for love is of God; and every one that loveth is born of God, and knoweth God. He that loveth not knoweth not God; for God is love. In this was manifested the love of God toward us, because that God sent his only begotten Son into the world, that we might live through him. *4:7-9*

77.16   Herein is love, not that we loved God, but that he loved us, and sent his Son to be the propitiation for our sins. Beloved, if God so loved us, we ought also to love one another. *4:10-11*

77.17   No man hath seen God at any time. If we love one another, God dwelleth in us, and his love is perfected in us. *4:12*

77.18   And we have seen and do testify that the Father sent the Son to be the Saviour of the world. *4:14*

77.19   And we have known and believed the love that God hath to us. God is love; and he that dwelleth in love dwelleth in God, and God in him. *4:16*

77.20   There is no fear in love; but perfect love casteth out fear: because fear hath torment. He that feareth is not made perfect in love.   *4:18*

77.21   If a man say, I love God, and hateth his brother, he is a liar: for he that loveth not his brother whom he hath seen, how can he love God whom he hath not seen?   *4:20*

77.22   For whatsoever is born of God overcometh the world: and this is the victory that overcometh the world, even our faith.   *5:4*

77.23   He that hath the Son hath life; and he that hath not the Son of God hath not life.   *5:12*

77.24   And this is the confidence that we have in him, that, if we ask any thing according to his will, he heareth us. *5:14*

77.25   Little children, keep yourselves from idols. Amen.   *5:21*

2 JOHN

78.1   The elder unto the elect lady and her children, whom I love in the truth; and not I only, but also all they that have known the truth.   *1*

78.2   I rejoiced greatly that I found of thy children walking in truth, as we have received a commandment from the Father. And now I beseech thee, lady, not as though I wrote a new commandment unto thee, but that which we had from the beginning, that we love one another. *4-5*

78.3   Look to yourselves, that we lose not those things which we have wrought, but that we receive a full reward.   *8*

3 JOHN

79.1   I have no greater joy than to hear that my children walk in truth.   *4*

79.2   I wrote unto the church: but Diotrephes, who loveth to have the preeminence among them receiveth us not.   *9*

79.3   Beloved, follow not that which is evil, but that which is good. He that doeth good is of God: but he that doeth evil hath not seen God.   *11*

JUDE

80.1   Beloved, when I gave all diligence to write unto you of the common salvation, it was needful for me to write unto you, and exhort you that ye should earnestly contend for the faith which was once delivered unto the saints. For there are certain men crept in unawares, who were before of old ordained to this condemnation, ungodly men, turning the grace of our God into lasciviousness, and denying the only Lord God, and our Lord Jesus Christ.   *3-4*

80.2   Likewise also these filthy dreamers defile the flesh, despise dominion, and speak evil of dignities. Yet Michael the archangel, when contending with the devil he disputed about the body of Moses, durst not bring against him a railing accusation, but said, The Lord rebuke thee.   *8-9*

80.3   These are spots in your feasts of charity, when they feast with you, feeding themselves without fear: clouds they are without water, carried about of winds; trees whose fruit withereth, without fruit, twice dead, plucked up by the roots; Raging waves of the sea, foaming out their own shame; wandering stars, to whom, is reserved the blackness of darkness for ever.   *12:13*

80.4   But ye, beloved, building up yourselves on your most holy faith, praying in the Holy Ghost, Keep yourselves in the love of God, looking for the mercy of our Lord Jesus Christ unto eternal life. And of some have compassion, making a difference: And

others save with fear, pulling them out of the fire; hating even the garment spotted by the flesh.   *20:23*

80.5   Now unto him that is able to keep you from falling, and to present you faultless before the presence of his glory with exceeding joy, To the only wise God our Saviour, be glory and majesty, dominion and power, both now and ever. Amen.   *24–25*

REVELATION

The final book in the Bible is *Revelation,* a prophetic book of visions and symbols, written at a time when Christians were being persecuted. It opens with a vision of Christ in glory; then come letters to seven churches. Visions of judgment and victory follow, showing God's sovereignty and his ultimate triumph through Christ over evil. The book closes with a picture of a new heaven and a new earth.

81.1   Blessed is he that readeth, and they that hear the words of this prophecy, and keep those things which are written therein: for the time is at hand.   *1:3*

81.2   John to the seven churches which are in Asia: Grace be unto you, and peace, from him which is, and which was, and which is to come; and from the seven Spirits which are before his throne; And from Jesus Christ, who is the faithful witness, and the first begotten of the dead, and the prince of the kings of the earth. Unto him that loved us, and washed us from our sins in his own blood, And hath made us kings and priests unto God and his Father; to him be glory and dominion for ever and ever. Amen. *1:4-6*

81.3   Behold, he cometh with clouds; and every eye shall see him, and they also which pierced him: and all kindreds of the earth shall wail because of him. Even so, Amen. I am Alpha and Omega, the beginning and the ending, saith the Lord, which is, and which was, and which is to come, the Almighty.   *1:7-8*

81.4   I John, who also am your brother, and companion in tribulation, and in the kingdom and patience of Jesus Christ, was in the isle that is called Patmos, for the word of God, and for the testimony of Jesus Christ. I was in the Spirit on the Lord's day, and heard behind me a great voice, as of a trumpet, Saying, I am Alpha and Omega, the first and the last: and, What thou seest, write in a book, and send it unto the seven churches which are in Asia; unto Ephesus, and unto Smyrna, and unto Pergamos, and unto Thyatira, and unto Sardis, and unto Philadelphia, and unto Laodicea. And I turned to see the voice that spake with me. And being turned, I saw seven golden candlesticks; And in the midst of the seven candlesticks one like unto the Son of man, clothed with a garment down to the foot, and girt about the paps with golden girdle. His head and his hairs were white like wool, as white as snow; and his eyes were as a flame of fire; And his feet like unto fine brass, as if they burned in a furnace; and his voice as the sound of many waters. And he had in his right hand seven stars: and out of his mouth went a sharp two-edged sword: and his countenance was as the sun shineth in his strength. And when I saw him, I fell at his feet as dead. And he laid his right hand upon me, saying unto me, Fear not; I am the first and the last: I am he that liveth, and was dead; and, behold, I am alive for evermore, Amen; and have the keys of hell and of death. *1:9-18*

81.5   And hast borne, and hast patience, and for my name's sake hast laboured, and hast not fainted. Nevertheless I have somewhat against thee, because thou hast left thy first love. Remember therefore from whence thou art fallen, and repent, and do the first works; or else I will come unto thee quickly, and will remove thy candlestick out of his place, except thou repent.   *2:3-5*

81.6   He that hath an ear, let him hear what the Spirit saith unto the churches; To him that overcometh will I give to eat of the tree of life, which is in the midst of the paradise of God.   *2:7*

81.7   Fear none of those things which thou shalt suffer: behold, the devil shall cast some of you into prison, that ye may be tried; and ye shall have tribulation ten days: be thou faithful unto death, and I will give thee a crown of life.   *2:10*

81.8   Repent; or else I will come unto thee quickly, and will fight against them with the sword of my mouth.   *2:16*

81.9   And he shall rule them with a rod of iron; as the vessels of a potter shall they be broken to shivers: even as I received of my Father.   *2:27*

81.10   He that overcometh, the same shall be clothed in white raiment; and I will not blot out his name out of the book of life, but I will confess his name before my Father, and before his angels.   *3:5*

81.11   I know thy works: behold, I have set before thee an open door, and no man can shut it: for thou hast a little strength, and hast kept my word, and hast not denied my name.   *3:8*

81.12   And unto the angel of the church of the Laodiceans write; These things saith the Amen, the faithful and true witness, the beginning of the creation of God; I know thy works, that thou art neither cold nor hot: I would thou wert cold or hot. So then because thou art lukewarm, and neither cold nor hot, I will spue thee out of my mouth.   *3:14-16*

81.13   Behold, I stand at the door, and knock: if any man hear my voice, and open the door, I will come in to him, and will sup with him, and he with me.   *3:20*

Laodicean

Laodicean *is used to describe someone who is lukewarm and indifferent, especially in religious or political matters. The application of this word comes from the criticism expressed by Christ of the church at Laodicea. The believers there were neither cold nor hot, but showed a tepid, half-hearted commitment.*

81.14   To him that overcometh will I grant to sit with me in my throne, even as I also overcame, and am set down with my Father in his throne.   *3:21*

81.15   After this I looked, and, behold, a door was opened in heaven: and the first voice which I heard was as it were of a trumpet talking with me; which said, Come up hither, and I will shew thee things which must be hereafter. And immediately I was in the spirit: and, behold, a throne was set in heaven, and one sat on the throne. And he that sat was to look upon like a jasper and a sardine stone: and there was a rainbow round about the throne, in sight like unto an emerald. And round about the throne were four and twenty seats: and upon the seats I saw four and twenty elders sitting, clothed in white raiment; and they had on their heads crowns of gold. And out of the throne proceeded lightnings and thunderings and voices: and there were seven lamps of fire burning before the throne, which are the seven Spirits of God.   *4:1-5*

81.16   And before the throne there was a sea of glass like unto crystal: and in the midst of the throne, and round about the throne, were four beasts full of eyes before and behind. And the first beast was like a lion, and the second beast like a calf, and the third beast had a face as man, and the

fourth beast was like a flying eagle.
4:6-7

81.17   And the four beasts had each of
them six wings about him; and they were
full of eyes within: and they rest not day
and night, saying, Holy, holy, holy, Lord
God Almighty, which was, and is, and is
to come.   *4:8*

81.18   The four and twenty elders fall
down before him that sat on the throne,
and worship him that liveth for ever and
ever, and cast their crowns before the
throne, saying, Thou art worthy, O Lord,
to receive glory and honour and power:
for thou hast created all things, and for thy
pleasure they are and were created.
4:10-11

81.19   And I saw in the right hand of him
that sat on the throne a book written
within and on the backside, sealed with
seven seals. And I saw a strong angel
proclaiming with a loud voice, Who is
worthy to open the book, and to loose the
seals thereof? And no man in heaven, nor
in earth, neither under the earth, was able
to open the book, neither to look
thereon. And I wept much, because no
man was found worthy to open and to
read the book, neither to look thereon.
5:1-4

81.20   And I beheld, and, lo, in the midst
of the throne and of the four beasts, and in
the midst of the elders, stood a Lamb as it
had been slain, having seven horns and
seven eyes, which are the seven Spirits of
God went forth into all the earth.   *5:6*

81.21   And when he had taken the book,
the four beasts and four and twenty elders
fell down before the Lamb, having every
one of them harps, and golden vials full
of odours, which are the prayers of
saints.   *5:8*

81.22   And I beheld, and I heard the
voice of many angels round about the
throne and the beasts and the elders: and
the number of them was ten thousand
times ten thousand, and thousands of

thousands; Saying with a loud voice,
Worthy is the Lamb that was slain to
receive power, and riches, and wisdom,
and strength, and honour, and glory, and
blessing.   *5:11-12*

81.23   And I saw when the Lamb opened
one of the seals, and I heard, as it were the
noise of thunder, one of the four beasts
saying, Come and see. And I saw, and
behold a white horse: and he that sat on
him had a bow; and crown was given unto
him: and he went forth conquering, and
to conquer.   *6:1-2*

81.24   And I looked, and behold a pale
horse: and his name that sat on him was
Death, and Hell followed with him. And
power was given unto them over the
fourth part of the earth, to kill with
sword, and with hunger, and with death,
and with the beasts of the earth.   *6:8*

81.25   And they cried with loud voice,
saying, How long, O Lord, holy and
true, dost thou not judge and avenge our
blood on them that dwell on the earth?
6:10

81.26   And the stars of heaven fell unto
the earth, even as a fig tree casteth her
untimely figs, when she is shaken of a
mighty wind. And the heaven departed
as a scroll when it is rolled together; and
every mountain and island were moved
out of their places.   *6:13-14*

81.27   And said to the mountains and
rocks, Fall on us, and hide us from the
face of him that sitteth on the throne, and
from the wrath of the Lamb: For the great
day of his wrath is come; and who shall be
able to stand?   *6:16-17*

81.28   After this I beheld, and, lo, a great
multitude, which no man could number,
of all nations, and kindreds, and people,
and tongues, stood before the throne, and
before the Lamb, clothed with white
robes, and palms in their hands; And
cried with a loud voice, saying, Salvation
to our God which sitteth upon the
throne, and unto the Lamb. And all the

angels stood round about the throne, and about the elders and the four beasts, and fell before the throne on their faces, and worshipped God, Saying, Amen: Blessing, and glory, and wisdom, and thanksgiving, and honour, and power, and might, be unto our God for ever and ever. Amen. *7:9-12*

81.29   And one of the elders answered, saying unto me, What are these which are arrayed in white robes? and whence came they? And I said unto him, Sir, thou knowest. And he said to me, These are they which came out of great tribulation, and have washed their robes, and made the white in the blood of the Lamb. Therefore are they before the throne of God, and serve him day and night in his temple: and he that sitteth on the throne shall dwell among them. They shall hunger no more, neither thirst any more; neither shall the sun light on them nor any heat. For the Lamb which is in the midst of the throne shall feed them, and shall lead them unto living fountains of waters: and God shall wipe away all tears from their eyes. *7:13-17*

81.30   And when he had opened the seventh seal, there was silence in heaven about the space of half an hour. *8:1*

81.31   And the smoke of the incense, which came with the prayers of the saints, ascended up before God out of the angel's hand. *8:4*

81.32   And the fifth angel sounded, and I saw a star fall from heaven unto the earth: and to him was given the key of the bottomless pit. *9:1*

81.33   And I went unto the angel, and said unto him, Give me the little book. And he said unto me, Take it, and eat it up; and it shall make thy belly bitter, but it shall be in thy mouth sweet as honey. And I took the little book out of the angel's hand, and ate it up; and it was in my mouth sweet as honey: and as soon as I had eaten it, my belly was bitter. *10:9-10*

81.34   And the seventh angel sounded; and there were great voices in heaven, saying, The kingdoms of this world are become the kingdoms of our Lord, and of his Christ; and he shall reign for ever and ever. *11:15*

81.35   Saying, We give thee thanks, O Lord God Almighty, which art, and wast, and art to come; because thou hast taken to thee thy great power, and hast reigned. *11:17*

81.36   And there appeared a great wonder in heaven; a woman clothed with the sun, and the moon under her feet, and upon her head a crown of twelve stars. *12:1*

81.37   And she brought forth a man child, who was to rule all nations with a rod of iron: and her child was caught up unto God, and to his throne. *12:5*

81.38   And there was war in heaven: Michael and his angels fought against the dragon; and the dragon fought and his angels, And prevailed not; neither was their place found any more in heaven. And the great dragon was cast out, that old serpent, called the Devil, and Satan, which deceiveth the whole world: he was cast out into the earth, and his angels were cast out with him. *12:7-9*

81.39   And they overcame him by the blood of the Lamb, and by the word of their testimony; and they loved not their lives unto the death. *12:11*

81.40   Therefore rejoice, ye heavens, and ye that dwell in them. Woe to the inhabiters of the earth and of the sea! for the devil is come down unto you, having great wrath, because he knoweth that he hath but a short time. *12:12*

81.41   And they worshipped the dragon which gave power unto the beast: and they worshipped the beast, saying, Who is like unto the beast? who is able to make war with him? *13:4*

81.42   And all that dwell upon the earth shall worship him, whose names are not written in the book of life of the Lamb slain from the foundation of the world. *13:8*

81.43   And that no man might buy or sell, save he that had the mark, or the name of the beast, or the number of his name. Here is wisdom. Let him that hath understanding count the number of the beast: for it is the number of a man; and his number is Six hundred threescore and six. *13:17-18*

81.44   And I looked, and, lo, a Lamb stood on the mount Sion, and with him an hundred forty and four thousand, having his Father's name written in their foreheads. And I heard a voice from heaven, as the voice of many waters, and as the voice of a great thunder: and I heard the voice of harpers harping with their harps: And they sung as it were a new song before the throne, and before the four beasts, and the elders: and not man could learn that song but the hundred and forty and four thousand, which were redeemed from the earth. *14:1-3*

81.45   And in their mouth was found no guile: for they are without fault before the throne of God. *14:5*

81.46   And I saw another angel fly in the midst of heaven, having the everlasting gospel to preach unto them that dwell on the earth, and to every nation, and kindred, and tongue, and people, Saying with a loud voice, Fear God, and give glory to him; for the hour of his judgment is come: and worship him that made heaven, and earth, and the sea, and the fountains of waters. *14:6-7*

81.47   The same shall drink of the wine of the wrath of God, which is poured out without mixture into the cup of his indignation; and he shall be tormented with fire and brimstone in the presence of the holy angels, and in the presence of the Lamb: And the smoke of their torment ascendeth up for ever and ever: and they have no rest day nor night, who worship the beast and his image, and whosoever receiveth the mark of his name. *14:10-11*

81.48   And I heard a voice from heaven saying unto me, Write, Blessed are the dead which die in the Lord from henceforth: Yea, saith the Spirit, that they may rest from their labours; and their works do follow them. *14:13*

81.49   And I looked, and behold a white cloud, and upon the cloud one sat like unto the Son of man, having on his head a golden crown, and in his hand a sharp sickle. And another angel came out of the temple, crying with a loud voice to him that sat on the cloud, Thrust in thy sickle, and reap: for the time is come for thee to reap; for the harvest of the earth is ripe. *14:14-15*

81.50   And the angel thrust in his sickle into the earth, and gathered the vine of the earth, and cast it into the great winepress of the wrath of God. *14:19*

81.51   And I saw as it were a sea of glass mingled with fire: and them that had gotten the victory over the beast, and over his image, and over his mark, and over the number of his name, stand on the sea of glass, having the harps of God. *15:2*

81.52   And I heard a great voice out of the temple saying to the seven angels, Go your ways, and pour out the vials of the wrath of God upon the earth. *16:1*

81.53   Behold, I come as a thief. Blessed is he that watcheth, and keepeth his garments, lest he walk naked, and they see his shame. And he gathered them together into a place called in the Hebrew tongue Armageddon. *16:15-16*

81.54   And every island fled away, and the mountains were not found. *16:20*

81.55   And there came one of the seven angels which had the seven vials, and talked with me, saying unto me, Come hither; I will shew unto thee the judgment of the great whore that sitteth upon many waters.   *17:1*

81.56   So he carried me away in the spirit into the wilderness: and I saw a woman sit upon a scarlet coloured beast, full of names of blasphemy, having seven heads and ten horns. And the woman was arrayed in purple and scarlet colour, and decked with gold and precious stones and pearls, having a golden cup in her hand full of abominations and filthiness of her fornication: And upon her forehead was a name written, MYSTERY, BABYLON THE GREAT, THE MOTHER OF HARLOTS AND ABOMINATIONS OF THE EARTH. And I saw the woman drunken with the blood of the saints, and with the blood of the martyrs of Jesus: and when I saw her, I wondered with great admiration.   *17:3-6*

A scarlet woman

A scarlet woman *is a sexually promiscuous woman, especially a prostitute. The expression has its origin in these verses, which describe the sinful woman dressed in scarlet. The term has been variously applied to pagan Rome, Papal Rome, or the world in its anti-Christian sense.*

81.57   These shall make war with the Lamb, and the Lamb shall overcome them: for he is Lord of lords, and King of kings: and they that are with him are called, and chosen, and faithful.   *17:14*

81.58   And a mighty angel took up a stone like a great millstone, and cast it into the sea, saying, Thus with violence shall that great city Babylon be thrown down, and shall be found no more at all.   *18:21*

81.59   And a voice came out of the throne, saying, Praise our God, all ye his servants, and ye that fear him, both small and great. And I heard as it were the voice of a great multitude, and as the voice of many waters, and as the voice of mighty thunderings, saying, Alleluia: for the

Lord God omnipotent reigneth. Let us be glad and rejoice, and give honour to him: for the marriage of the Lamb is come, and his wife hath made herself ready.   *19:5-7*

81.60   And he saith unto me, Write, Blessed, are they which are called unto the marriage supper of the Lamb. And he saith unto me, These are the true sayings of God. And I fell at his feet to worship him. And he said unto me, See thou do it not: I am thy fellowservant, and of thy brethren that have the testimony of Jesus: worship God: for the testimony of Jesus is the spirit of prophecy.   *19:9-10*

81.61   And I saw heaven opened, and behold a white horse; and he that sat upon him was called Faithful and True, and in righteousness he doth judge and make war. His eyes were as a flame of fire, and on his head were many crowns; and he had a name written, that no man knew, but he himself. And he was clothed with a vesture dipped in blood: and his name is called The Word of God.   *19:11-13*

81.62   And he hath on his vesture and on his thigh a name written, KING OF KINGS, AND LORD OF LORDS.   *19:16*

81.63   And I saw an angel come down from heaven, having the key of the bottomless pit and a great chain in his hand. And he laid hold on the dragon, that old serpent, which is the Devil, and Satan, and bound him a thousand years, And cast him into the bottomless pit, and shut him up, and set a seal upon him, that he should deceive the nations no more, till the thousand years should be fulfilled: and after that he must be loosed a little season. And I saw thrones, and they sat upon them, and judgment was given unto them: and I saw the souls of them that were beheaded for the witness of Jesus, and for the word of God, and which had not worshipped the beast, neither his image, neither had received his mark upon their foreheads, or in their hands; and they lived and reigned with Christ a thousand years.   *20:1-4*

81.64   And when the thousand years are expired, Satan shall be loosed out of his prison, And shall go out to deceive the nations which are in the four quarters of the earth, Gog and Magog, to gather them together to battle: the number of whom is as the sand of the sea. And they went up on the breadth of the earth, and compassed the camp of the saints about, and the beloved city: and fire came down from God out of heaven, and devoured them. And the devil that deceived them was cast into the lake of fire and brimstone, where the beast and the false prophet are, and shall be tormented day and night for ever and ever.   *20:7-10*

81.65   And I saw a great white throne, and him that sat on it, from whose face the earth and the heaven fled away; and there was found no place for them. And I saw the dead, small and great, stand before God; and the books were opened: and another book was opened, which is the book of life: and the dead were judged out of those things which were written in the books, according to their works. And the sea gave up the dead which were in it; and death and hell delivered up the dead which were in them: and they were judged every man according to their works. And death and hell were cast into the lake of fire. This is the second death. And whosoever was not found written in the book of life was cast into the lake of fire.   *20:11-15*

81.66   And I saw a new heaven and a new earth: for the first heaven and the first earth were passed away; and there was no more sea. And I John saw the holy city, new Jerusalem, coming down from God out of heaven, prepared as a bride adorned for her husband. And I heard a great voice out of heaven saying, Behold, the tabernacle of God is with men, and he will dwell with them, and they shall be his people, and God himself shall be with them, and be their God. And God shall wipe away all tears from their eyes; and there shall be no more death, neither sorrow, nor crying, neither shall there be any more pain: for the former things are passed away. And he that sat upon the throne said, Behold, I make all things new. And he said unto me, Write: for these words are true and faithful.   *21:1-5*

81.67   And he said unto me, It is done. I am Alpha and Omega, the beginning and the end. I will give unto him that is athirst of the fountain of the water of life freely.   *21:6*

81.68   And he carried me away in the spirit to a great and high mountain, and shewed me that great city, the holy Jerusalem, descending out of heaven from God, Having the glory of God: and her light was like unto a stone most precious, even like a jasper stone, clear as crystal.   *21:10-11*

81.69   And the foundations of the wall of the city were garnished with all manner of precious stones. The first foundation was jasper; the second, sapphire; the third, a chalcedony; the fourth, an emerald; The fifth, sardonyx; the sixth, sardius; the seventh, chrysolite; the eighth, beryl; the ninth, a topaz; the tenth, a chrysoprasus; the eleventh, a jacinth; the twelfth, an amethyst. And the twelve gates were twelve pearls; every several gate was of one pearl: and the street of the city was pure gold, as it were transparent glass. And I saw no temple therein: for the Lord God Almighty and the Lamb are the temple of it. And the city had no need of the sun, neither of the moon, to shine in it: for the glory of God did lighten it, and the Lamb is the light thereof.   *21:19-23*

81.70   And the nations of them which are saved shall walk in the light of it: and the kings of the earth do bring their glory and honour into it. And the gates of it shall not be shut at all by day: for there shall be no night there.   *21:24-25*

81.71   And there shall in no wise enter into it any thing that defileth, neither whatsoever worketh abomination, or maketh a lie: but they which are written in the Lamb's book of life.   *21:27*

81.72   And he shewed me a pure river of water of life, clear as crystal, proceeding out of the throne of God and of the Lamb. In the midst of the street of it, and on either side of the river, was there the tree of life, which bare twelve manner of fruits, and yielded her fruit every month: and the leaves of the tree were for the healing of the nations. And there shall be no more curse: but the throne of God and of the Lamb shall be in it; and his servants shall serve him: And they shall see his face; and his name shall be in their foreheads. And there shall be no night there; and they need no candle, neither light of the sun; for the Lord God giveth them light: and they shall reign for ever and ever.   *22:1-5*

81.73   Behold, I come quickly: blessed is he that keepeth the sayings of the prophecy of this book.   *22:7*

81.74   And the Spirit and the bride say, Come. And let him that heareth say, Come. And let him that is athirst come. And whosoever will, let him take the water of life freely.   *22:17*

81.75   For I testify unto every man that heareth the words of the prophecy of this book, If any man shall add unto these things, God shall add unto him the plagues that are written in this book: And if any man shall take away from the words of the book of this prophecy, God shall take away his part out of the book of life, and out of the holy city, and from the things which are written in this book. *22:18-19*

81.76   He which testifieth these things saith, Surely I come quickly. Amen. Even so, come, Lord Jesus. The grace of our Lord Jesus Christ be with you all. Amen.   *22:20-21*

THE BOOK
OF COMMON PRAYER

The Book of Common Prayer is the traditional service book of the Church of England. After the Reformation, Cranmer and others began to formulate an order of worship in English. The first Prayer Book was published in 1549, with revisions in 1552 and 1559. The 1662 book - almost unchanged until modern times - introduced the Authorized (King James) Version for the Epistles and Gospels. The version of the Bible used in the Psalms is the translation by Miles Coverdale (1488-1568).

82.1   A Table of the Moveable Feasts. *Introductory Pages*

82.2   Dearly beloved brethren, the Scripture moveth us in sundry places to acknowledge and confess our manifold sins and wickedness.   *Morning Prayer*

82.3   We have erred and strayed from thy ways like lost sheep. We have followed too much the devices and desires of our own hearts. We have offended against thy holy laws. We have left undone those things which we ought to have done. And we have done those things which we ought not to have done. And there is no health in us.   *Morning Prayer, General Confession*

82.4   A godly, righteous, and sober life.   *Morning Prayer, General Confession*

82.5   And forgive us our trespasses, As we forgive them that trespass against us.   *Morning Prayer, the Lord's Prayer*

82.6   *Priest.* O Lord, open thou our lips.

Answer. And our mouth shall shew forth thy praise.

Priest. O God, make speed to save us.

Answer. O Lord, make haste to help us. *Morning Prayer*

82.7   *Priest.* Glory be to the Father, and to the Son: and to the Holy Ghost;

Answer. As it was in the beginning, is now and ever shall be: world without end. Amen.   *Morning Prayer, Gloria*

82.8   Lord God of Sabaoth.   *Morning Prayer, Te Deum*

82.9   The noble army of Martyrs. *Morning Prayer, Te Deum*

82.10   Of an infinite Majesty.   *Morning Prayer, Te Deum*

82.11   O Lord, in thee have I trusted: let me never be confounded.   *Morning Prayer, Te Deum*

82.12   O all ye Works of the Lord, bless ye the Lord: praise him, and magnify him for ever.   *Morning Prayer, Benedicite*

82.13   I believe in God the Father Almighty, Maker of heaven and earth: And in Jesus Christ his only Son our Lord, Who was conceived by the Holy Ghost, Born of the Virgin Mary, Suffered under Pontius Pilate, Was crucified, dead, and buried: He descended into hell; The third day he rose again from the dead; He ascended into heaven, And sitteth on the right hand of God the Father Almighty; From thence he shall come to judge the quick and the dead. I believe in the Holy Ghost; The holy Catholick Church; The Communion of Saints; The Forgiveness of sins; The Resurrection of the body, And the life everlasting. Amen.
Morning Prayer, Apostles' Creed

82.14   *Minister.* Lord, have mercy upon us.
(Response). Christ, have mercy upon us.   *Morning Prayer*

82.15   Give peace in our time, O Lord. *Morning Prayer*

82.16   The author of peace and lover of concord, in knowledge of whom standeth our eternal life, whose service is perfect freedom.   *Morning Prayer, Second Collect, for Peace*

82.17   Neither run into any kind of danger.   *Morning Prayer, Third Collect, for Grace*

82.18   Almighty God, the fountain of all goodness.   *Morning Prayer, Prayer for the Royal Family*

82.19   Pour upon them the continual dew of thy blessing.   *Morning Prayer, Prayer for the Clergy and People*

82.20   O God, from whom all holy desires, all good counsels, and all just works do proceed: Give unto thy servants that peace which the world cannot give.   *Evening Prayer, Second Collect*

82.21   Lighten our darkness, we beseech thee, O Lord; and by thy great mercy defend us from all perils and dangers of this night.   *Evening Prayer, Third Collect, for Aid against Perils*

82.22   Whosoever will be saved: before all things it is necessary that he hold the Catholick Faith.   *Athanasian Creed*

82.23   Neither confounding the Persons: nor dividing the Substance. *Athanasian Creed*

82.24   And yet they are not three Gods: but one God.   *Athanasian Creed*

82.25   O God the Father of heaven: have mercy upon us miserable sinners. *Litany*

82.26   From envy, hatred, and malice, and all uncharitableness, Good Lord, deliver us.   *Litany*

82.27   The deceits of the world, the flesh, and the devil.   *Litany*

82.28   In the hour of death, and the day of judgement.   *Litany*

82.29   Unity, peace, and concord. *Litany*

82.30   To bring forth the fruits of the Spirit.   *Litany*

82.31   The kindly fruits of the earth, so as in due time we may enjoy them. *Litany*

82.32   *Priest.* O Lord, deal not with us after our sins.

Answer. Neither reward us after our iniquities.   *Litany*

82.33   The safety, honour, and welfare of our Sovereign and her Dominions. *Prayer for the High Court of Parliament*

82.34   All sorts and conditions of men.   *Prayer for all Conditions of Men*

82.35   All who profess and call themselves Christians.   *Prayer for all Conditions of Men*

82.36   We bless thee for our creation, preservation, and all the blessings of this life; but above all for thine inestimable, love in the redemption of the world by our Lord Jesus Christ, for the means of grace, and for the hope of glory.   *General Thanksgiving*

82.37   Almighty God, give us grace that we may cast away the works of darkness, and put upon us the armour of light, now in the time of this mortal life.   *Collect, 1st Sunday in Advent*

82.38   *[Of all the holy Scriptures]* hear them, read, mark, learn, and inwardly digest them.   *Collect, 2nd Sunday in Advent*

82.39   The glory that shall be revealed.   *Collect, St Stephen's Day*

82.40   Send thy Holy Ghost, and pour into our hearts that most excellent gift of charity.   *Collect, Quinquagesima Sunday*

82.41   Have mercy upon all Jews, Turks, Infidels, and Hereticks, and take from them all ignorance, hardness of heart, and contempt of thy word.   *Third Collect, Good Friday*

82.42   Lord of all power and might, who art the author and giver of all good things.   *Collect, 7th Sunday after Trinity*

82.43   Serve thee with a quiet mind.   *Collect, 21st Sunday after Trinity*

82.44   Lord, we beseech thee to keep thy household the Church in continual godliness.   *Collect, 22nd Sunday after Trinity*

82.45   O almighty God, whom truly to know is everlasting life.   *Collect, St Philip and St James's Day*

82.46   Almighty God, unto whom all hearts be open, all desires known, and from whom no secrets are hid: Cleanse the thoughts of our hearts by the inspiration of thy Holy Spirit, that we may perfectly love thee, and worthily magnify thy holy Name; through Christ our Lord. Amen.   *Holy Communion, Collect*

82.47   For I the Lord thy God am a jealous God, and visit the sins of the fathers upon the children unto the third and fourth generation of them that hate me, and shew mercy unto thousands in them that love me and keep my commandments.   *Holy Communion, Second Commandment*

The sins of the fathers

The expression the sins of the fathers, *sometimes with the additional words* are visited upon the children *has its origin in this quotation from the Book of Common Prayer. Based on Exodus 20:5, the meaning of the contemporary phrase is that the crimes, errors, and misdemeanours of a generation have an effect upon that generation's descendants.*

82.48   All things visible and invisible.   *Holy Communion, Nicene Creed*

82.49   Very God of very God, Begotten, not made, Being of one substance with the Father, By whom all things were made: Who for us men and for our salvation came down from heaven.   *Holy Communion, Nicene Creed*

82.50   And I believe in the Holy Ghost, The Lord and giver of life, Who proceedeth from the Father and Son, Who with the Father and the Son together is worshipped and glorified, Who spake by the Prophets.   *Holy Communion, Nicene Creed*

82.51   And I believe one Catholick and Apostolick Church.   *Holy Communion, Nicene Creed*

82.52 Let us pray for the whole state of Christ's Church militant here in earth. *Holy Communion, Introduction to Prayer for the Church militant*

82.53 We eat and drink our own damnation. *Holy Communion, Third Exhortation*

82.54 To the end that we should alway remember the exceeding great love of our Master and only Saviour Jesus Christ, thus dying for us, and the innumerable benefits which by his precious blood-shedding he hath obtained to us; he hath instituted and ordained holy mysteries, as pledges of his love, and for a continual remembrance of his death, to our great and endless comfort. *Holy Communion, Third Exhortation*

82.55 Ye that do truly and earnestly repent you of your sins, and are in love and charity with your neighbours, and intend to lead a new life. *Holy Communion, Invitation*

82.56 Draw near with faith. *Holy Communion, Invitation*

82.57 We acknowledge and bewail our manifold sins and wickedness, Which we from time to time most grievously have committed, By thought, word, and deed, Against thy Divine Majesty, Provoking most justly thy wrath and indignation against us. *Holy Communion, General Confession*

82.58 Hear what comfortable words our Saviour Christ saith unto all that truly turn to him. *Holy Communion, Words of Encouragement*

82.59 It is meet and right so to do. *Holy Communion*

82.60 Therefore with Angels, and Archangels, and with all the company of heaven, we laud and magnify thy glorious Name; evermore praising thee, and saying: Holy, holy, holy, Lord God of hosts, heaven and earth are full of thy glory: Glory be to thee, O Lord most High. Amen. *Holy Communion, Praise*

82.61 We do not presume to come to this thy Table, O merciful Lord, trusting in our own righteousness, but in thy manifold and great mercies. We are not worthy so much as to gather up the crumbs under thy Table. But thou art the same Lord, whose property is always to have mercy: Grant us therefore, gracious Lord, so to eat the flesh of thy dear Son Jesus Christ, and to drink his blood, that our sinful bodies may be made clean by his body, and our souls washed through his most precious blood, and that we may evermore dwell in him, and he in us. Amen. *Holy Communion*

82.62 A full, perfect, and sufficient sacrifice, oblation, and satisfaction, for the sins of the whole world. *Holy Communion, Prayer of Consecration*

82.63 The Body of our Lord Jesus Christ, which was given for thee, preserve thy body and soul unto everlasting life: Take and eat this in remembrance that Christ died for thee, and feed on him in thy heart by faith with thanksgiving. *Holy Communion*

82.64 The Blood of our Lord Jesus Christ, which was shed for thee, preserve thy body and soul unto everlasting life: Drink this in remembrance that Christ's Blood was shed for thee, and be thankful. *Holy Communion*

82.65 The peace of God, which passeth all understanding, keep your hearts and minds in the knowledge and love of God, and of his Son Jesus Christ our Lord: And the blessing of God Almighty, the Father, the Son, and the Holy Ghost, be amongst you and remain with you always. Amen. *Holy Communion, Blessing*

82.66 All our works, begun, continued, and ended in thee. *Holy Communion, Collects after the Offertory*

82.67 Dost thou, in the name of this Child, renounce the devil and all his works, the vain pomp and glory of the world. *Publick Baptism of Infants*

82.68 O merciful God, grant that the old Adam in this Child may be so buried, that the new man may be raised up in him. Amen. *Publick Baptism of Infants, Blessing*

82.69 We receive this Child into the Congregation of Christ's flock, and do sign him with the sign of the Cross, in token that hereafter he shall not be ashamed to confess the faith of Christ crucified, and manfully to fight under his banner against sin, the world, and the devil, and to continue Christ's faithful soldier and servant unto his life's end. Amen. *Publick Baptism of Infants, Reception of the Child*

82.70 Dead unto sin, and living unto righteousness. *Publick Baptism of Infants*

82.71 Crucify the old man. *Publick Baptism of Infants*

82.72 The Ministration of Baptism to Such as are of Riper years. *Publick Baptism of Such as are of Riper Years, Title*

82.73 The pomps and vanity of this wicked world. *Catechism*

82.74 To keep my hands from picking and stealing, and my tongue from evil-speaking, lying, and slandering. *Catechism*

82.75 To learn and labour truly to get mine own living, and to do my duty in that state of life, unto which it shall please God to call me. *Catechism*

82.76 An outward and visible sign of an inward and spiritual grace given unto us. *Catechism*

82.77 In their mother tongue. *Catechism*

82.78 The Order of Confirmation or Laying on of Hands. *Confirmation*

82.79 Children being now come to the years of discretion. *Confirmation, Preface*

82.80 If any of you know cause or just impediment, why these two persons should not be joined together in holy Matrimony, ye are to declare it. This is the first time of asking. *Solemnization of Matrimony, the Banns*

82.81 Dearly beloved, we are gathered together here in the sight of God, and in the face of this Congregation, to join together this man and this woman in holy Matrimony; which is an honourable estate, instituted of God. *Solemnization of Matrimony, Exhortation*

82.82 Therefore is not by any to be enterprized, nor taken in hand, unadvisedly, lightly, or wantonly, to satisfy men's carnal lusts and appetites, like brute beasts that have no understanding; but reverently, discreetly, advisedly, soberly, and in the fear of God. *Solemnization of Marriage, Exhortation*

82.83 First, It was ordained for the procreation of children, to be brought up in the fear and nurture of the Lord, and to the praise of his holy Name. *Solemnization of Marriage, Exhortation*

82.84 Secondly, It was ordained for a remedy against sin, and to avoid fornication; that such persons as have not the gift of continency might marry, and keep themselves undefiled members of Christ's body. *Solemnization of Marriage, Exhortation*

82.85 Thirdly, It was ordained for the mutual society, help, and comfort, that the one ought to have of the other, both in prosperity and adversity. Into which holy estate these two persons present come now to be joined. *Solemnization of Marriage, Exhortation*

82.86   Therfore if any man can shew any just cause, why they may not lawfully be joined together, let him now speak, or else hereafter for ever hold his peace. *Solemnization of Marriage, Exhortation*

Speak now or forever hold you peace

The expression speak now or forever hold your peace *is used to show that the present time is the only or last opportunity when a request, objection, etc., may be made. The phrase is based on this quotation from the marriage ceremony in the Book of Common Prayer.*

82.87   I require and charge you both, as ye will answer at the dreadful day of judgement, when the secrets of all hearts shall be disclosed, that if either of you know any impediment, why ye may not be lawfully joined together in Matrimony, ye do now confess it. *Solemnization of Marriage*

82.88   Wilt thou have this woman to thy wedded wife, to live together after God's ordinance in the holy estate of Matrimony? Wilt thou love her, comfort her, honour, and keep her, in sickness and in health; and, forsaking all other, keep thee only unto her, so long as ye both shall live? *Solemnization of Marriage*

82.89   Wilt thou have this man to thy wedded husband, to live together after God's ordinance in the holy estate of Matrimony? Wilt thou obey him, and serve him, love, honour and keep him, in sickness and in health; and, forsaking all other, keep thee only unto him, so long as ye both shall live? *Solemnization of Marriage*

82.90   To have and to hold from this day forward, for better for worse, for richer for poorer, in sickness and in health, to love and to cherish, till death us do part, according to God's holy ordinance; and thereto I plight thee my troth. *Solemnization of Marriage*

82.91   To love, cherish, and to obey. *Solemnization of Marriage*

82.92   With this ring I thee wed, with my body I thee worship, and with all my worldly goods I thee endow. *Solemnization of Marriage*

82.93   Those whom God hath joined together let no man put asunder. *Solemnization of Marriage, Priest's Declaration*

82.94   Consented together in holy wedlock. *Solemnization of Marriage, Minister's Declaration*

82.95   Peace be to this house. *Visitation of the Sick*

82.96   Look graciously upon him, O Lord; and the more the outward man decayeth, strengthen him, we beseech thee, so much the more continually with thy grace and Holy Spirit in the inner man. *Visitation of the Sick, Prayer for a sick person when there appeareth small hope of recovery*

82.97   Laid violent hands upon themselves. *Burial of the Dead, Introductory Note*

82.98   Man that is born of a woman hath but a short time to live, and is full of misery. *Burial of the Dead, Anthem*

82.99   In the midst of life we are in death. *Burial of the Dead, Anthem*

82.100   We therefore commit his body to the ground; earth to earth, ashes to ashes, dust to dust; in sure and certain hope of the Resurrection to eternal life, through our Lord Jesus Christ. *Burial of the Dead, Committal*

82.101   Why do the heathen so furiously rage together, and why do the people imagine a vain thing? The kings of the earth stand up, and the rulers take counsel together, against the Lord, and against his Anointed. *Psalm 2:1-2*

82.102   I will lay me down in peace, and take my rest: for it is thou, Lord, only, that makest me dwell in safety.   *Psalm 4:9*

82.103   Thou shalt destroy them that speak leasing: the Lord will abhor both the blood-thirsty and deceitful man. *Psalm 5:6*

82.104   Make thy way plain before my face.   *Psalm 5:8*

82.105   Let them perish through their own imaginations.   *Psalm 5:11*

82.106   God is a righteous Judge, strong and patient: and God is provoked every day.   *Psalm 7:12*

82.107   Up, Lord, and let not man have the upper hand.   *Psalm 9:19*

82.108   They do but flatter with their lips, and dissemble in their double heart.   *Psalm 12:2*

82.109   But they are all gone out of the way, they are altogether become abominable: there is none that doeth good, no not one.   *Psalm 14:4*

82.110   Whoso doeth these things shall never fall.   *Psalm 15:7*

82.111   The lot is fallen unto me in a fair ground: yea, I have a goodly heritage. *Psalm 16:7*

82.112   The heavens declare the glory of God: and the firmament sheweth his handywork. One day telleth another: and one night certifieth another. There is neither speech nor language: but their voices are heard among them. Their sound in gone out into all lands: and their words into the ends of the world.   *Psalm 19:1-4*

82.113   Thou shalt prepare a table before me against them that trouble me: thou hast anointed my head with oil, and my cup shall be full.   *Psalm 23:5*

82.114   I should utterly have fainted: but that I believe verily to see the goodness of the Lord in the land of the living.   *Psalm 27:15*

82.115   Into thy hands I commend my spirit.   *Psalm 31:6*

82.116   For while I held my tongue, my bones consumed away through my daily complaining.   *Psalm 32:3*

82.117   Sing unto the Lord a new song: sing praises lustily unto him with a good courage.   *Psalm 33:3*

82.118   Fret not thyself because of the ungodly; neither be thou envious against the evildoers.   *Psalm 37:1*

82.119   I myself have seen the ungodly in great power, and flourishing like a green bay-tree. I went by, and lo, he was gone: I sought him, but his place could no where be found. Keep innocency, and take heed unto the thing that is right: for that shall bring a man peace at the last.   *Psalm 37:36-38*

Flourish like the green bay tree
The expression flourish like the green bay tree *means to be exuberantly prosperous and healthy. The phrase, which sometimes has the implication that the success is short-lived or not deserved, has its origins in this quotation from the Book of Common Prayer.*

82.120   Lord, let me know mine end, and the number of my days: that I may be certified how long I have to live.   *Psalm 39:5*

82.121   When thou with rebukes dost chasten man for sin, thou makest his beauty to consume away, like as it were a moth fretting a garment: every man therefore is but vanity.   *Psalm 39:12*

82.122   My bones are smitten asunder as with a sword: while mine enemies that trouble me cast me in the teeth; Namely, while they say daily unto me: Where is now thy God?   *Psalm 42:12-13*

82.123   Instead of thy fathers thou shalt have children, whom thou mayest make princes in all lands.   *Psalm 45:17*

82.124   He maketh wars to cease in all the world: he breaketh the bow, and knappeth the spear in sunder, and burneth the chariots in the fire. Be still then, and know that I am God.   *Psalm 46:9-10*

82.125   God is gone up with a merry noise: and the Lord with the sound of the trump.   *Psalm 47:5*

82.126   For lo, the kings of the earth are gathered, and gone by together. They marvelled to see such things: they were astonished, and suddenly cast down. *Psalm 48:3-4*

82.127   And I said, O that I had wings like a dove: for then would I flee away, and be at rest.   *Psalm 55:6*

82.128   Be merciful unto me, O God, be merciful unto me, for my soul trusteth in thee: and under the shadow of thy wings shall be my refuge, until this tyranny be over-past.   *Psalm 57:1*

82.129   They are as venomous as the poison of a serpent: even like the deaf adder that stoppeth her ears; Which refuseth to hear the voice of the charmer: charm he never so wisely.   *Psalm 58:4-5*

82.130   They go to and fro in the evening: they grin like a dog, and run about through the city.   *Psalm 59:6*

82.131   As for the children of men, they are but vanity: the children of men are deceitful upon the weights, they are altogether lighter than vanity itself. *Psalm 62:9*

82.132   Have I not remembered thee in my bed: and thought upon thee when I was waking?   *Psalm 63:7*

82.133   Let them fall upon the edge of the sword: that they may be a portion for foxes.   *Psalm 63:11*

82.134   Thou, O God, art praised in Sion: and unto thee shall the vow be performed in Jerusalem.   *Psalm 65:1*

82.135   God be merciful unto us, and bless us: and shew us the light of his countenance, and be merciful unto us. *Psalm 67:1*

82.136   He is the God that meketh men to be of one mind in an house, and bringeth the prisoners out of captivity: but letteth the runagates continue in scarceness.   *Psalm 68:6*

82.137   Why hop ye so, ye high hills? this is God's hill, in the which it pleaseth him to dwell: yea, the Lord will abide in it for ever.   *Psalm 68:16*

82.138   Thou art gone up on high, thou hast led captivity captive, and received gifts for men.   *Psalm 68:18*

82.139   For the zeal of thine house hath even eaten me; and the rebukes of them that rebuked thee are fallen upon me. *Psalm 69:9*

82.140   They that sit in the gate speak against me: and the drunkards make songs upon me.   *Psalm 69:12*

82.141   Thy rebuke hath broken my heart; I am full of heaviness: I looked for some to have pity on me, but there was no man, neither found I any to comfort me. They gave me gall to eat: and when I was thirsty they gave me vinegar to drink. *Psalm 69:21-22*

82.142   Let them for their reward be soon brought to shame: that cry over me, There, there.   *Psalm 70.3*

82.143   So the Lord awaked as one out of sleep: and like a giant refreshed with wine.   *Psalm 78:66*

82.144   O how amiable are thy dwellings, thou Lord of hosts!   *Psalm 84:1*

82.145   Lord, thou hast been our refuge from one generation to another. Before the mountains were brought forth, or ever the earth and the world were made: thou art God from everlasting, and world without end.   *Psalm 90:1-2*

82.146   O come, let us sing unto the Lord; let us heartily rejoice in the strength of our salvation. Let us come before his presence with thanksgiving; and shew ourselves glad in him with psalms. For the Lord is a great God; and a great King above all gods. In his hand are all the corners of the earth; and the strength of the hills is his also. The sea is his, and he made it; and his hands prepared the dry land. O come, let us worship and fall down, and kneel before the Lord our Maker. For he is the Lord our God; and we are the people of his pasture, and the sheep of his hand.   *Psalm 95:1-7*

82.147   Today if ye will hear his voice, harden not your hearts: as in the provocation, and as in the day of temptation in the wilderness; When your fathers tempted me: proved me, and saw my works.   *Pslam 95:8-9*

82.148   O be joyful in the Lord, all ye lands: serve the Lord with gladness, and come before his presence with a song.   *Psalm 100:1*

82.149   Whose feet they hurt in the stocks: the iron entered into his soul.   *Psalm 105:18*

At death's door

If someone is at death's door, he or she is on the point of dying. The expression comes from this translation of Psalm 107:18 in the Book of Common Prayer.

82.150   Their soul abhorred all manner of meat: and they were even hard at death's door.   *Psalm 107:18*

82.151   They that go down to the sea in ships: and occupy their business in great waters; These men see the works of the Lord: and his wonders in the deep.   *Psalm 107:23-24*

82.152   Thy wife shall be as the fruitful vine upon the walls of thine house. Thy children like the olive-branches round about thy table.   *Psalm 128:3-4*

82.153   Lord, I am not high-minded: I have no proud looks.   *Psalm 131:1*

82.154   Such knowledge is too wonderful and excellent for me: I cannot attain unto it.   *Psalm 139:5*

82.155   I will give thanks unto thee, for I am fearfully and wonderfully made: marvellous are thy works, and that my soul knoweth right well.   *Psalm 139:13*

82.156   Man is like a thing of nought: his time passeth away like a shadow.   *Psalm 144:4*

82.157   That our oxen may be strong to labour, that there be no decay no leading into captivity, and no complaining in our streets.   *Psalm 144:14*

82.158   O put not your trust in princes, nor in any child of man: for there is no help in them.   *Psalm 146:2*

82.159   O praise the Lord, for it is a good thing to sing praises unto our God: yea, a joyful and pleasant thing it is to be thankful.   *Psalm 147:1*

82.160   To bind their kings in chains: and their nobles with links of iron.   *Psalm 149:8*

82.161   Praise him upon the well-tuned cymbals: praise him upon the loud cymbals. Let every thing that hath breath: praise the Lord.   *Psalm 150:5-6*

82.162   We therefore commit his body to the deep, to be turned into corruption, looking for the resurrection of the body,

(when the Sea shall give up her dead.)
Forms of Prayer to be Used at Sea, At the Burial of their Dead at Sea

82.163   Holy Scripture containeth all things necessary to salvation.   *Articles of Religion, VI Of the Sufficiency of the holy Scriptures for Salvation*

82.164   Of Works of Supererogation. *Articles of Religion, XIV, Title*

82.165   A fond thing vainly invented. *Articles of Religion, XXII Of Purgatory*

82.166   The Bishop of *Rome* hath no jurisdiction in this Realm of *England*.

Articles of Religion, XXXVII Of the Civil Magistrates

82.167   It is lawful for Christian men, at the commandment of the Magistrate, to wear weapons, and serve in the wars. *Articles of Religion, XXXVII Of the Civil Magistrates*

82.168   A Table of Kindred and Affinity.   *Title*

82.169   A Man may not marry his Grandmother.   *Table of Kindred and Affinity*

INDEX

A

Abba
And he said, A. Father 56.20
A. Father 60.35
Spirit of his Son into your hearts, crying,
A. Father 63.11

abide
who can a. in the fierceness of his anger?
34.2
But who may a. the day of his coming?
39.6
A. with us: for it is toward 57.84
A. in me, and I in you 58.77
therein a. with God 61.22

able
that is a. to keep you from falling 80.5

abominable
altogether become a. 82.109

abomination
A false balance is a. to the LORD 20.33
The sacrifice of the wicked is an a. to the
LORD 20.52

abound
sin abounded, grace did much more a.
60.21

abounded
sin a. grace did much more abound 60.21

Abraham
Before A. was, I am 58.45

absent
a. from the body 62.15

abundance
out of the a. of the heart 55.87
shall be given, and he shall have a. 55.159

abundantly
he will a. pardon 23.101
life ... more a. 58.49

acceptable
prove what is ..a. and perfect, will of God
60.47

accomplish
it shall a. that which I please 23.103

accursed
let him be a. 63.1

acknowledge
For I a. my transgressions 19.91
thy ways a. him 20.5

acknowledged
I a. my sin 19.54

adoption
received the Spirit of a. 60.35
we might receive the a. of sons 63.10
predestinated us unto the a. of children
64.1

adultery
Thou shalt not commit a. 2.44
hath committed a. with her already 55.23

and shall marry another, committeth a.
55.121

afflict
he doth not a. willingly 25.9

afflicted
the Almighty hath a. me? 8.3
It is good for me that I have been a. 19.198

afraid
I was a. 1.19
he was a. to look upon God 2.11
of whom shall I be a. 19.41
Thou shalt not be a. for the terror by night
19.143
it is I; be not a. 55.102

again
Ye must be born a. 58.16

age
he is of a. ask him 58.46

agree
if two of you shall a. on earth 55.117

agreed
Can two walk together, except they be a.
30.3

aha
their shame that say, A. a. 19.116

all
a. that is within me 19.159
a. is vanity 21.1
For a. have sinned, and come short of the
glory of God 60.14
a. things to all men 61.27
do a. to the glory of God 61.34
Christ is a. and in a. 66.10

Almighty
shall abide under the shadow of the A.
19.142

alone
It is not good that the man should be a. 1.12

alpha
I am A. and Omega 81.3
I am A. and Omega 81.4
I am A. and Omega 81.67

altar
Noah builded an a. unto the LORD 1.44
there builded he an a. unto the LORD 1.52
taken with the tongs from off the a. 23.14

ambassadors
we are a. for Christ 62.19

amiable
How a. are thy tabernacles 19.129
how a. are thy dwellings 82.144

ancient
the A. of days did sit 27.27
and came to the A. of days 27.28

angel
the a. of the LORD appeared 2.10
who hath sent his a. and delivered his
servants 27.15

B

Babel
Therefore is the name of it called B.   1.49

babes
Out of the mouth of b. and sucklings   19.9
hast revealed them unto b.   57.34

backsliding
I will heal their b.   28.14

backslidings
thy b. shall reprove thee   24.5

balance
A false b. is abomination to the LORD
20.33

balances
Thou art weighed in the b. and art found
wanting   27.21

bald
Go up, thou b. head   12.4

balm
Is there no b. in Gilead   24.18

banner
his b. over me was love   22.7

banqueting
He brought me to the b. house   22.7

baptize
shall b. you with the Holy Ghost   55.9
but he shall b. you with the Holy Ghost
56.2

baptized
Jesus, when he was b.   55.10
Repent, and be b. every one of you   59.8
by one Spirit are we all b. into one body
61.41

baptizing
b. them in the name of the Father ... Holy
Ghost   55.189

battle
the b. is not yours, but God's   14.10
nor the b. to the strong   21.41

bay-tree
flourishing like green b.   82.119

beam
considerest not the b. that is in thine own
55.39

bear
I am not able to b. all this people alone   4.8

beast
God formed every b. of the field   1.13
b. was like a lion   81.16
mark ... of the b.   81.43
worship the b.   81.47

beat
B. your plowshares into swords   29.9
they shall b. their swords into plowshares
33.3

beautiful
the woman was very b.   10.6
He hath made every thing b. in his time
21.12
How b. upon the mountains are the feet
23.92

beauty
worship the LORD in the b. of holiness   13.3
to behold the b. of the LORD   19.42
worship the LORD in the b. of holiness
19.46
O worship the LORD in the b. of holiness
19.155
Thine eyes shall see the king in his b.   23.49
there is no b. that we should desire him
23.95
to give unto them b. for ashes   23.120

bed
Rise, take up thy b. and walk   58.26
remembered thee in my b.   82.132

begat
Noah b. Shem, Ham, and Japheth   1.33

beginning
In the b. God created the heaven and the
earth   1.1
The fear of the LORD is the b. of wisdom
19.181
The fear of the LORD is the b. of
knowledge   20.2
The fear of the LORD is the b. of wisdom
20.24
Better is the end of a thing than the b.
thereof   21.29
In the b. was the Word   58.1
As it was in the b.   82.7

begotten
this day have I b. thee   19.5
he gave his only b. Son   58.17

begotten
B. not made   82.49

begun
he which hath b. a good work   65.2

behemoth
Behold now b.   18.55

behold
B. your God!   23.57
Thou art of purer eyes than to b. evil   35.2

believe
repent ye, and b. the gospel   56.3
Lord, I b. help thou mine unbelief   56.16
I will not b.   58.101
these are written, that ye might b. that
58.103
B. on the Lord Jesus Christ   59.38
shalt b. in thine heart that God   60.41
cometh to God must b. that he   73.21
the devils also b.   74.10
I b. in God   82.13

believed
he b. in the LORD   1.56
Who hath b. our report?   23.95
believest
B. thou this?   58.53
believeth
he that b. shall not make haste   23.40
whosoever b. in him should not perish
58.17
He that b. on the Son hath everlasting life
58.20
and b. on him that sent me   58.27
believing
be not faithless, but b.   58.102
that b. ye might have life through   58.103
belly
upon thy b. shalt thou go   1.21
Jonah was in the b. of the fish   32.3
out of his b. shall flow rivers of living
water   58.37
whose God is their b.   65.13
make thy b. bitter   81.33
beloved
My b. is mine   22.12
Let my b. come into his garden   22.17
I opened to my b.   22.20
My b. is white and ruddy   22.21
I am my beloved's, and my b. is mine   22.22
Dearly b. brethren   82.2
beloved's
I am my b. and my beloved is mine   22.22
I am my b. and his desire is   22.26
Bethlehem
B. Ephratah, though thou be little   33.4
better
that there is nothing b. than that a man
should rejoice   21.16
a b. country   73.23
for b. for worse   82.90
bind
B. up the testimony   23.18
whatsoever thou shalt b. on earth   55.108
Whatsoever ye shall b. on earth   55.116
birthright
sell me this day thy b.   1.74
he took away my b.   1.78
morsel of meat sold his b.   73.30
bishop
A b. then must be   69.6
desire the office of a b.   69.6
The B. of *Rome*   82.166
bitten
every one that is b.   4.20
bitter
they made their lives b. with hard
bondage   2.3
bitterly
for the Almighty hath dealt very b. with
me   8.3

black
I am b. but comely, O ye daughters of
Jerusalem   22.2
blasphemy
the b. against the Holy Ghost   55.86
blemish
Your lamb shall be without b.   2.29
a young bullock without b.   3.2
Children in whom was no b.   27.1
bless
I will b. thee   1.50
not let thee go, except thou b. me   1.82
The LORD b. thee, and keep thee   4.2
b. the LORD your God   16.11
I will b. the LORD at all times   19.57
blessed
God b. the seventh day   1.8
the LORD b. the latter end of Job   18.63
B. is the man that walketh not in the counsel
of the ungodly   19.1
B. is he whose transgression is forgiven
19.53
I b. the most High   27.18
B. are the poor in spirit   55.17
b. is the fruit of thy womb   57.9
B. art thou among women   57.9
blessing
The b. of the LORD, it maketh rich   20.32
and pour you out a b. that there shall not be
room   39.8
blind
Then the eyes of the b. shall be opened
23.52
To open the b. eyes   23.70
The b. receive their sight   55.75
the b. lead the b.   55.105
recovering of sight to the b.   57.21
whereas I was b. now I see   58.47
blood
the voice of thy brother's b. crieth unto me
1.28
Whoso sheddeth man's b. by man shall his
b. be shed   1.45
the b. shall be to you for a token upon the
houses   2.30
when I see the b. I will pass over you   2.30
the life of the flesh is in the b.   3.11
it is the b. that maketh an atonement for the
soul   3.11
for flesh and b. hath not revealed it   55.108
this is my b. of the new testament   55.167
his sweat was as it were great drops of b.
falling   57.74
came there out b. and water   58.96
church of God ... purchased with his own
b.   59.49
Whom God hath ... through faith in his b.
60.14

This cup is the new testament in my b. 61.36

flesh and b. cannot inherit the kingdom of God   61.55

we have redemption through his b.   64.1

redemption through his b.   66.2

without shedding of b. is no remission 73.15

to enter into the holiest by the b.   73.18

through the b. of the everlasting convenant   73.39

the precious b. of Christ   75.5

b. of Jesus Christ his Son cleanseth   77.3

overcame him by the b. of the Lamb   81.39

drink his b. that   82.61

The B. of our Lord Jesus Christ   82.64

blossom

Although the fig tree shall not b.   35.7

bodies

present your b. a living sacrifice   60.47

body

Take, eat; this is my b.   55.167

not sin therefore reign in your mortal b. 60.26

who shall deliver me from the b. of this death?   60.30

Take, eat: this is my b.   61.36

as the b. is one, and hath many members 61.41

absent from the b.   62.15

There is one b. and one Spirit   64.13

The B. of our Lord Jesus Christ   82.63

boils

smote Job with sore b.   18.6

boldly

come b. unto the throne of grace   73.9

boldness

the b. of Peter and John   59.14

Having ... b. to enter into the holiest   73.18

bone

This is now b. of my bones   1.14

My b. cleaveth to my skin and to my flesh 18.28

bones

my b. waxed old   19.53

his word was in mine heart as a burning fire shut up in my b.   24.27

the valley which was full of b.   26.33

b. consumed away   82.116

My b. are smitten asunder   82.122

book

all the people were attentive unto the b. of the law   16.8

in the volume of the b. it is written of me 19.71

the b. of life   81.10

names are not written in the b.   81.42

which is the b. of life   81.65

books

of making many b. there is no end   21.54

b. were opened   81.65

born

A time to be b.   21.11

For unto us a child is b.   23.20

Except a man be b. again   58.14

Ye must be b. again   58.16

borne

Surely he hath b. our griefs   23.95

bosom

carried by the angels into Abraham's b. 57.59

bottomless

the key of the b. pit   81.32

bought

ye are b. with a price   61.18

bow

I do set my b. in the cloud   1.46

name of Jesus every knee should b.   65.5

bowels

shutteth up his b. of compassion   77.11

branch

a B. shall grow out of his roots   23.23

will I cause the B. of righteousness to grow up unto David   24.37

brass

become as sounding b.   61.42

brawling

than with a b. woman in a wide house 20.77

bread

In the sweat of thy face shalt thou eat b. 1.24

man doth not live by b.   5.13

eat thy b. with joy   21.39

Cast thy b. upon the waters   21.48

Is it not to deal thy b. to the hungry   23.111

command that these stones be made b. 55.11

Man shall not live by b. alone   55.11

Give us this day our daily b.   55.33

if his son ask b.   55.42

Jesus took b. and blessed it   55.167

I am the b. of life   58.22

the b. that I will give is my flesh   58.34

continued stedfastly ... in breaking of b. 59.9

break

Thou shalt b. them with a rod of iron   19.5

breastplate

he put on righteousness as a b.   23.116

the b. of righteousness   64.28

breasts

he shall lie all night betwixt my b.   22.4

Thy two b. are like two young roes   22.15

breath

breathed into his nostrils the b. of life   1.9

breathe
b. upon these slain, that they may live
26.33
breathing
yet b. out threatenings and slaughter
against   59.21
brethren
Behold my mother and my b.   55.91
unto one of the least of these my b.   55.162
bride
as a b. adorned for her husband   81.66
brier
instead of the b. shall come up the myrtle
ree   23.105
brightness
the b. of his glory   73.1
brimstone
the LORD rained upon Sodom and upon
Gomorrah b. and fire   1.66
bring
that he might b. us to God   75.17
broken
The sacrifices of God are a b. spirit   19.94
a b. and a contrite heart   19.94
a threefold cord is not quickly b.   21.20
the staff of this b. reed   23.55
brokenhearted
sent me to heal the b.   57.21
brother
there is a friend that sticketh closer than a
b.   20.69
brotherly
kindly affectioned one to another with b.
love   60.48
brother's
Am I my b. keeper?   1.28
the voice of thy b. blood crieth unto me
1.28
bruise
it shall b. thy head   1.21
thou shalt b. his heel   1.21
Yet it pleased the LORD to b. him   23.96
bruised
A b. reed shall he not break   23.69
he was b. for our iniquities   23.95
A b. reed shall he not break   55.84
to set at liberty them that are b.   57.21
bucket
Behold, the nations are as a drop of a b.
23.60
budded
rod of Aaron for the house of Levi was b.
4.16
build
Except the LORD b. the house   19.214
thou art Peter, and upon this rock I will b.
my church   55.108
intending to b. a tower   57.47

bulrushes
she took for him an ark of b.   2.5
burden
Cast thy b. upon the LORD   19.97
burdens
Bear ye one another's b.   63.22
burn
the day that cometh shall b. them up   39.10
better to marry than to b.   61.19
burned
his clothes not be b.   20.18
burning
cast them into the b. fiery furnace   27.13
bury
let the dead b. their dead   55.52
bush
a flame of fire out of the midst of a b.   2.10
bushel
put it under a b.   55.19
business
do b. in great waters   19.175
about my Father's b.   57.19

C

Caesar
Render therefore unto C.   55.138
calf
after he had made it a molten c.   2.59
he saw the c. and the dancing   2.62
the c. and the young lion   23.24
the fatted c. and kill it   57.52
call
unto Adam to see what he would c. them
1.13
c. ye upon him while he is near   23.100
thou shalt c. his name JESUS   55.2
c. ... sinners to repentance   55.57
shall c. upon the name of the Lord shall be
saved   60.42
How then shall they c. on him   60.43
called
and c. my son out of Egypt   28.9
for many be c. but few chosen   55.130
calledst
Here am I; for thou c. me   9.5
calleth
he c. them all by names   23.65
camel
It is easier for a c. to go through the eye
55.126
candle
c. of understanding in thine heart   41.6
candlesticks
in the midst of the seven c.   81.4
captives
to proclaim liberty to the c.   23.120
to preach deliverance to the c.   57.21

correction
profitable for c.   70.8

counsellor
his name shall be called ... C.   23.20
being his c. hath taught him?   23.59

counsellers
in the multitude of c. there is safety   20.35

countenance
The LORD lift up his c. upon thee   4.2
A merry heart maketh a cheerful c.   20.53

counteth
c. the cost   57.47

courage
Be strong and of a good c.   5.39
Be strong and of a good c.   6.1

courageous
Be strong and c.   14.12

course
finished my c.   70.10

covenant
with thee will I establish my c.   1.38
it shall be for a token of a c.   1.46
I will establish my c. between me and thee 1.61
an everlasting c.   1.61
God remembered his c.   2.9
the faithful God, which keepeth c. and mercy   5.12
he will shew them his c.   19.38
He hath remembered his c.   19.170
I will make a new c. with the house of Israel   24.35
I will make an everlasting c. with them 24.36
this is the c. that I will make   73.14

cover
He shall c. thee with his feathers   19.143
c. the multitude of sins   75.19

covereth
love c. all sins   20.28
He that c. a transgression   20.63

covet
Thou shalt not c. thy neighbour's house 2.44

create
I c. new heavens and a new earth   23.129

created
God c. man in his own image   1.6
thou hast c. all things   81.18

creation
whole c. groaneth and travaileth in pain 60.36

creator
Remember now thy C. in the days of thy youth   21.53
the C. of the ends of the earth, fainteth not, neither is weary?   23.67

creature
and preach the gospel to every c.   56.24
in Christ, he is a new c.   62.18

creeping
dominion over every c. thing   1.6
every c. thing that creepeth upon the earth

crib
the ass his master's c.   23.1

cross
taketh not his c.   55.71
and take up his c.   55.110
take up his c. daily   57.29
For the preaching of the c. is to them that perish   61.1

crown
Children's children are the c. of old men 20.62
platted a c. of thorns   55.180
my joy and c.   65.15
a c. of righteousness   70.10
I will give thee a c. of life   81.7

crownest
Thou c. the year with thy goodness   19.103

crowns
on his head were many c.   81.61

crucified
Let him be c.   55.177
old man is c. with him   60.24
we preach Christ c.   61.3
Jesus Christ, and him c.   61.6
I am c. with Christ   63.6

crucify
they c. to themselves the Son   73.12
led him away to c. him   55.180

cruel
jealousy is c. as the grave   22.27

crumbs
the dogs eat of the c. which fall   55.106
the c. which fell from the rich man's table 57.58

cruse
a little oil in a c.   11.31

crying
The voice of one c. in the wilderness   55.6

crystal
sea of glass like unto c.   81.16

cup
I will take the c. of salvation   19.187
Are ye able to drink of the c. that I   55.131
let this c. pass from me   55.170
if thou be willing, remove this c.   57.73
and my c. shall be full   82.113

cups
they are in their c.   40.3

curse
I called thee to c. mine enemies   4.25
he will c. thee to thy face   18.4
c. God, and die   18.7
every one of them doth c. me   24.23
Christ hath redeemed us from the c.   63.7

cursed
 thou art c. above all cattle 1.21
 c. is the ground 1.23
 C. shalt thou be in the city 5.35
 C. be the day wherein I was born 24.28
cut
 for he was c. off out of the land of the
 living 23.95

D

daily
 Give us this day our d. bread 55.33
 take up his cross d. 57.29
damnation
 drink our own d. 82.53
dance
 a time to mourn, and a time to d. 21.11
danced
 David d. before the LORD 10.3
 ye have not d. 55.79
dancing
 turned for me my mourning into d. 19.48
danger
 run into any kind of d. 82.17
dangers
 perils and d. of this night 82.21
darkly
 now we see through a glass, d. 61.42
darkness
 d. was upon the face 1.1
 the d. he called Night 1.3
 that there may be d. over the land of Egypt
 2.27
 the thick d. where God was 2.46
 Surely the d. shall cover 19.225
 The people that walked in d. have seen a
 great light 23.19
 The sun shall be turned into d. 29.7
 sat in d. saw great light 55.14
 there was d. over all the land 55.185
 To give light to them that sit in d. 57.11
 men loved d. rather than light 58.18
 shall not walk in d. but 58.40
 delivered us from the power of d. 66.2
 Lighten our d. 82.21
daughters
 your sons and your d. shall prophesy 29.7
David
 Jesus Christ, the son of D. 55.1
 and the Lord God shall give unto him the
 throne of his father D. 57.5
 in the city of D. a Saviour 57.14
day
 God called the light D. 1.3
 Let the d. perish wherein I was born 18.8
 D. unto d. uttereth speech 19.24
 call upon me in the d. of trouble 19.89

 a d. in thy courts is better 19.131
 This is the d. which the LORD hath made
 19.191
 thou knowest not what a d. may bring
 forth 20.95
 the d. of the LORD 29.2
 the great and the terrible d. of the LORD
 29.7
 For who hath despised the d. of small
 things? 38.8
 But who may abide the d. of his coming?
 39.6
 Give us this d. our daily bread 55.33
 unto the d. is the evil thereof 55.37
 more, as ye see the d. approaching 73.18
 at the dreadful d. of judgement 82.87
days
 as thy d. so shall thy strength be 5.47
 in length of d. understanding 18.22
 all the d. of my life 19.31
 So teach us to number our d. 19.141
 for thou shalt find it after many d. 21.48
 Remember now thy Creator in the d. of thy
 youth 21.53
 the Ancient of d. did sit 27.27
 and came to the Ancient of d. 27.28
 Hath in these last d. 73.1
dayspring
 the d. from on high 57.11
dead
 Thy d. men shall live 23.38
 let the d. bury their d. 55.52
 raise the d. 55.64
 the d. are raised up 55.75
 Why seek ye the living among the d. 57.81
 the d. shall hear the voice of the Son 58.27
 d. to sin 60.22
 reckon ye also yourselves to be d. indeed
 unto sin 60.26
 quickened, who were d. in trespasses 64.3
 judge the quick and the d. 82.13
deaf
 the ears of the d. shall be unstopped 23.52
 the d. hear 55.75
deal
 Is it not to d. thy bread to the hungry
 23.111
dealt
 He hath not d. with us after our sins 19.160
dearly
 D. beloved brethren 82.2
 D. beloved 82.81
death
 I have set before you life and d. 5.38
 So the dead which he slew at his d. 7.28
 the valley of the shadow of d. 19.31
 sight of the LORD is the d. of his saints
 19.188

the end thereof are the ways of d. 20.46
Love is strong as d. 22.27
they that dwell in the land of the shadow of
d. 23.19
he hath poured out his soul unto d. 23.96
he shall never see d. 58.44
d. passed upon all men 60.20
the wages of sin is d. 60.28
who shall deliver me from the body of this
d. 60.30
neither d. ... shall be able to separate us
60.38
shew the Lord's d. till he come 61.36
last enemy that shall be destroyed is d.
61.52
D. is swallowed up in victory 61.56
O d. where is thy sting? 61.57
taste d. for every man 73.5
through d. he might destroy him 73.6
loved not their lives unto the d. 81.39
This is the second d. 81.65
no more d. 81.66

death's
hard at d. door 82.150

debts
forgive us our d. as we forgive our debtors
55.33

decay
that there be no d. 82.157

deceit
neither was any d. in his mouth 23.95

deceitfulness
the d. of riches 55.93

deceits
The d. of the world 82.27

deceiveth
Satan, which d. the whole world 81.38

decree
a d. from Caesar Augustus 57.12

deed
love ... in d. and in truth 77.12
By thought, word, and d. 82.57

deep
D. calleth unto d. 19.76
He revealeth the d. and secret things 27.6

defile
he would not d. himself with the portion of
the king's 27.2

delight
his d. is in the law of the LORD 19.1
D. thyself also in the LORD 19.64
I d. to do thy will, O my God 19.71
I was daily his d. 20.21
call the sabbath a d. the holy of the LORD
23.114
Then shalt thou d. thyself in the LORD
23.114
I d. in the law of God 60.30

deliver
he shall d. thee from the snare 19.143
lead us not into temptation, but d. us from
evil 55.33
who shall d. me from the body of this
death? 60.30

deliverance
to preach d. to the captives 57.21

den
become a d. of robbers 24.15
a d. of thieves 55.134

deny
let him d. himself 55.110
thou shalt d. me thrice 55.168
let him d. himself 57.29

depart
when he is old, he will not d. from it 20.78
D. from me; for I am a sinful man 57.24

depths
thou wilt cast all their sins into the d. of the
sea 33.8

descending
the Spirit of God d. like a dove 55.10

desert
He found him in a d. land 5.42
make straight in the d. a highway for our
God 23.56

desire
thy d. shall be to thy husband 1.22
I am my beloved's and his d. is 22.26
there is no beauty that we should d. him
23.95

desires
devices and d. of our own hearts 82.3
from whom all holy d. 82.20

despised
He is d. and rejected of men 23.95
For who hath d. the day of small things?
38.8
Wherein have we d. thy name? 39.1

destroy
Wilt thou also d. the righteous with the
wicked? 1.64
he might d. the works of the devil 77.9

destruction
Pride goeth before d. 20.58
broad is the way, that leadeth to d. 55.44

devices
d. and desires of our own hearts 82.3

devil
into the wilderness to be tempted of the d.
55.11
are of your father the d. 58.43
he might destroy the works of the d. 77.9
the flesh, and the d. 82.27
renounce the d. 82.67
See also **Satan**

dreamer

Behold, this d. cometh 1.85

dreams

Joseph remembered the d. which he dreamed 1.94

a dreamer of d. 5.21

Daniel had understanding in all visions and d. 27.3

drink

no better thing ...than to eat, and to d. and to be merry 21.36

d. thy wine with a merry heart 21.39

that they may follow strong d. 23.12

let us eat and d. for to morrow we shall die 23.29

Are ye able to d. of the cup that I 55.131

D. ye all of it 55.167

They gave him vinegar to d. mingled with gall 55.181

shall d. neither wine nor strong d. 57.2

drop

Behold, the nations are as a d. of a bucket 23.60

dropping

A continual d. in a very rainy day 20.98

drunkard

The earth shall reel to and fro like a d. 23.31

dry

the midst of the sea upon the d. ground 2.35

O ye d. bones, hear the word of the LORD 26.33

dumb

the tongue of the d. sing 23.52

dust

God formed man of the d. of the ground 1.9

for d. thou art 1.24

unto d. shalt thou return 1.24

am but d. and ashes 1.65

repent in d. and ashes 18.60

he remembereth that we are d. 19.162

many of them that sleep in the d. of the earth shall awake 27.33

shake off the d. of your feet 55.65

d. to d. 82.100

duty

this is the whole d. of man 21.55

dwell

that I may d. in the house of the LORD 19.42

I d. in the midst of a people of unclean lips 23.14

dwellings

how amiable are thy d. 82.144

E

eagles

they shall mount up with wings as e. 23.67

ear

The Lord GOD hath opened mine e. 23.89

O my God, incline thine e. and hear 27.30

the e. of jealousy 45.3

He that hath an e. let him hear 81.6

ears

the e. of every one that heareth it shall tingle 9.7

the e. of the deaf shall be unstopped 23.52

He that hath e. to hear 55.78

He that hath e. to hear 56.8

earth

God created the heaven and the e. 1.1

the e. was without form 1.1

dominion over ... all the e. 1.6

and in thee shall all families of the e. be blessed 1.50

Shall not the Judge of all the e. do right? 1.64

I am going the way of all the e. 6.15

go the way of all the e. 11.2

all that is in the heaven and in the e. is thine 13.9

The e. is the LORD'S 19.32

the whole e. is full of his glory 23.13

for the e. shall be full of the knowledge of the LORD 23.24

The e. shall reel to and fro like a drunkard 23.31

all the ends of the e. 23.76

all the ends of the e. shall see the salvation 23.93

I create new heavens and a new e. 23.129

The e. shall quake before them 29.4

wonders in the heavens and in the e. 29.7

meek ... inherit the e. 55.17

Ye are the salt of the e. 55.18

Thy will be done in e. as it is in heaven 55.33

whatsoever thou shalt bind on e. 55.108

Heaven and e. shall pass away 55.149

All power is given unto me in heaven and in e. 55.189

on e. peace, goodwill toward men 57.14

the uttermost part of the e. 59.2

the e. is the Lord's 61.33

new heaven and a new e. 81.66

earthen

this treasure in e. vessels 62.9

earthquake

the LORD was not in the e. 11.43

ease

Woe to them that are at e. in Zion 30.14

east

the e. is from the west, so far 19.161

there came wise men from the e. to
Jerusalem 55.4

easy

my yoke is e. 55.83

eat

thou shalt not e. of it 1.11

Ye shall not e. of it … lest ye die 1.16

she … did eat 1.18

In the sweat of thy face shalt thou e. bread
1.24

no better thing … than to e. and to drink,
and to be merry 21.36

e. thy bread with joy 21.39

let us e. and drink; for to morrow we shall
die 23.29

open thy mouth, and e. that I give thee
26.5

Take, e. this is my body 55.167

Rise, Peter; kill, and e. 59.27

Take, e. this is my body 61.36

eaten

Hast thou e. of the tree 1.19

I will restore to you the years that the locust
hath e. 29.6

Eden

God planted a garden eastward in E.
1.10

put him into the garden of E. 1.11

effectual

The e. fervent prayer of a righteous man
74.21

elders

the discourse of the e. 46.10

saw four and twenty e. 81.15

elect

E. according to the foreknowledge 75.1

election

make your calling and e. sure 76.2

eleventh

about the e. hour he went out 55.129

eloquent

I am not e. 2.15

embrace

a time to e. 21.11

Emmanuel

E. … God with us 55.3

See also **Immanuel**

end

at their wit's e. 19.176

the e. thereof are the ways of death 20.46

Better is the e. of a thing than the beginning
thereof 21.29

Of the increase of his government and peace
there shall be no e. 23.20

he that endureth to the e. 55.67

the e. is not yet 55.145

and then shall the e. come 55.146

even unto the e. of the world 55.189

the e. of all things 75.18

world without e. 82.7

ended

on the seventh day God e. his work 1.8

ends

all the e. of the earth 23.76

all the e. of the earth shall see the salvation
23.93

enemies

preparest a table before me in the presence of
mine e. 19.31

Love your e. 55.27

enemy

If thine e. be hungry, give him bread 20.88

An e. hath done this 55.96

enjoy

God, who giveth us richly all things to e.
69.16

enlarge

E. the place of thy tent 23.97

enmity

I will put e. between thee and the woman
1.21

enter

Having … boldness to e. into the holiest
73.18

envious

I was e. at the foolish 19.123

erred

We have e. and strayed 82.3

escape

How shall we e. if 73.4

escaped

I am e. with the skin of my teeth 18.28

estate

For he hath regarded the low e. of his
handmaiden 57.10

an honourable e. 82.81

holy e. these two persons 82.85

eternal

The e. God is thy refuge 5.48

things which are not seen are e. 62.11

Ethiopian

Can the E. change his skin, or the leopard
his spots? 24.21

Eve

Adam called his wife's name E. 1.25

evening

to his labour until the e. 19.166

everlasting

underneath are the e. arms 5.48

from e. to e. thou art God 19.138

lead me in the way e. 19.228

his name shall be called … The e. Father
23.20

the LORD shall be unto thee an e. light
23.119

Behold, thou art f. my love   22.15
Thou art all f. my love   22.15
How f. and how pleasant art thou, O love
22.25
unto me in a f. ground   82.111

fairest
O thou f. among women?   22.21

faith
the just shall live by his f.   35.3
I have not found so great f.   55.49
O ye of little f.   55.53
they f. hath made thee whole   55.59
O thou of little f.   55.103
f. as a grain of mustard seed   55.112
Increase our f.   57.62
f. toward our Lord Jesus Christ   59.48
the righteousness of God revealed from f. to
f.   60.4
righteousness of God which is by f. of
Jesus   60.13
Whom God ... to be a propitiation through
f. in his blood   60.14
Therefore being justified by f. we have peace
with God   60.18
So then f. cometh by hearing   60.44
now abideth f. hope, charity   61.42
we walk by f. not by sight   62.14
but f. which worketh by love   63.15
by grace are ye saved through f.   64.5
That Christ may dwell in your hearts by f.
64.10
the shield of f.   64.28
striving together for the f. of the gospel
65.4
f. is the substance of things hoped for
73.20
Even so f. if it hath not   74.9
earnestly contend for the f.   80.1
Draw near with f.   82.56
confess the f. of Christ crucified   82.69

faithful
the f. God, which keepeth covenent and
mercy   5.12
F. are the wounds of a friend   20.97
A f. friend is the medicine of life   46.8
Well done, thou good and f. servant   55.156
f. in that which is least   57.57
This is a f. saying   69.2
commit thou to f. men   70.5
for he is f. that promised   73.18

faithfulness
great is thy f.   25.5

faithless
be not f. but believing   58.102

fall
an haughty spirit before a f.   20.58
young men shall utterly f.   23.67
if thou wilt f. down and worship me   55.13

shall not f. on the ground   55.69
things shall never f.   82.110
worship and f. down   82.146

fallen
ye are f. from grace   63.14
from whence thou art f.   81.5

false
Thou shalt not bear f. witness against thy
neighbour   2.44
A f. witness that speaketh lies   20.16
A f. balance is abomination to the LORD
20.33
borne f. witness against me   50.2

families
and in thee shall all f. of the earth be
blessed   1.50
God setteth the solitary in f.   19.107

famine
the f. was sore in the land   1.96
that I will send a f. in the land   30.18

famous
Let us now praise f. men   46.36

far
Be it f. from thee, Lord   55.109

fast
and f. ye for me   17.6
Is it such a f. that I have chosen?   23.110
Is not this the f. that I have chosen?   23.111
people of Nineveh believed God, and
proclaimed a f.   32.7

fasted
f. and prayed before the God of heaven   16.1

fat
ye shall eat the f. of the land   1.98

father
a man leave his f. and his mother   1.14
Honour thy f. and thy mother   2.44
a f. pitieth his children   19.162
his name shall be called ... The everlasting
F.   23.20
Have we not all one f.   39.4
Our F. which art in heaven   55.33
it shall be done for them of my F.   55.117
but my F. only   55.150
O my F. if it be possible   55.170
baptizing them in the name of the F. and
55.189
F. into thy hands I commend my spirit
57.79
no man cometh unto the F. but   58.71
I ascend unto my F. and your F.   58.99
Honour thy f. and mother   64.26

fatherless
it shall be ... for the f.   5.31

fathers
he shall turn the heart of the f. to the
children   39.11
to turn the hearts of the f. to the children
57.3

find

thou shalt f. him   5.5

a man cannot f. out the work that is done under the sun   21.37

for thou shalt f. it after many days   21.48

ye shall seek me, and f. me   24.31

run ... to seek the word of the LORD, and shall not f. it   30.18

seek, and ye shall f.   55.41

findeth

He that f. his life   55.71

fingers

came forth f. of a man's hand   27.20

finished

It is f.   58.95

fire

the LORD rained upon Sodom and upon Gomorrah brimstone and f.   1.66

a flame of f. out of the midst of a bush   2.10

and by night in a pillar of f. to give them light   2.34

Then the f. of the LORD fell   11.37

Can a man take f. in his bosom   20.18

all ye that kindle a f.   23.90

walk in the light of your f.   23.90

his word was in mine heart as a burning f. shut up in my bones   24.27

Is not my word like as a f.   24.30

walked in the midst of the f.   49.1

everlasting f. prepared for the devil   55.163

the f. shall try every man's   61.11

our God is a consuming f.   73.34

lake of f. and brimstone   81.64

cast into the lake of f.   81.65

first

f. shall be last   55.128

So the last shall be f.   55.130

thou hast left thy f. love   81.5

firstfruits

The first of the f. of thy land   2.48

fish

let them have dominion over the f. of the sea   1.6

the LORD had prepared a great f. to swallow up Jonah   32.3

fishers

make you f. of men   55.16

five

f. loaves, and two fishes   55.101

flax

the smoking f. shall he not quench   23.69

fled

earth and the heaven f.   81.65

flee

But Jonah rose up to f. unto Tarshish   32.1

f. from the wrath to come?   55.8

fleece

I will put a f. of wool in the floor   7.12

flesh

f. of my flesh   1.14

they shall be one f.   1.14

when we sat by the f. pots   2.39

the life of the f. is in the blood   3.11

the hair of my f. stood up   18.10

yet in my f. shall I see God   18.30

my heart and my f. crieth out for the living God   19.129

much study is a weariness of the f.   21.54

I will take the stony heart out of their f.   26.10

I will give you an heart of f.   26.32

I will pour out my spirit upon all f.   29.7

for f. and blood hath not revealed it   55.108

and they twain shall be one f.   55.120

the f. is weak   55.171

the Word was made f.   58.6

born of the f. is f.   58.15

I will pour out of my Spirit upon all f.   59.6

his own Son in the likeness of sinful f.   60.32

f. and blood cannot inherit the kingdom of God   61.55

a thorn in the f.   62.33

two shall be one f.   64.24

the f. and the devil   82.27

eat the f. of thy dear Son   82.61

flies

Dead f. cause the ointment of the apothecary   21.44

flint

have I set my face like a f.   23.89

flock

He shall feed his f. like a shepherd   23.58

therefore unto yourselves, and to all the f.   59.49

flood

I, do bring a f. of waters upon the earth   1.38

flourishing

f. like green bay-tree   82.119

follow

if the LORD be God, f. him   11.34

F. me, and I will   55.16

he saith unto him, F. me   55.55

ye should f. his steps   75.10

followeth

f. after me   55.71

folly

a fool returneth to his f.   20.91

fond

A f. thing   82.165

fool

I have played the f.   9.33

The f. hath said in his heart   19.13

The way of a f. is right in his own eyes   20.39

a f. returneth to his folly   20.91
Thou f. this night thy soul   57.42

foolish
I was envious at the f.   19.123
shall be likened unto a f. man   55.48
And the f. said unto the wise   55.153
chosen the f. things of the world   61.4

foolishness
by the f. of preaching to save   61.2

fools
a companion of f. shall be destroyed   20.44
For ye suffer f. gladly   62.30

foot
He will not suffer thy f. to be moved   19.206
Keep thy f. when thou goest to the house of God   21.22
the sole of the f. even unto the head   23.2
if thy hand or thy f. offend thee   55.115

foreheads
Father's name written in their f.   81.44

forget
thou f. the LORD thy God   5.15
f. not all his benefits   19.159

forgive
if thou wilt f. their sin   2.64
will f. their sin and will heal their land   14.2
f. us our debts, as we f. our debtors   55.33
oft shall my brother sin against me, and I f.   55.118
the Son of man hath power on earth to f. sins   56.4
Father, f. them   57.76
f. us our trespasses   82.5

forgiven
as concerning his sin, and it shall be f. him   3.3
Blessed is he whose transgression is f.   19.53
Her sins, which are many, are f.   57.28

forgiveness
the f. of sins   64.1

forgiveth
Who f. all thine iniquities   19.159

form
he hath no f. nor comeliness   23.95

formed
Before I f. thee in the belly I knew thee   24.1

forsake
he will not fail thee, nor f. thee   5.39
I will not fail thee, nor f. thee   6.1
Let the wicked f. his way   23.101
F. not an old friend   46.13

forsaken
hast thou f. me?   19.27
Thou shalt no more be termed F.   23.122
they have f. me   24.4
My God, my God, why hast thou f. me?   55.186

Demas hath f. me   70.11

forsaking
f. all other   82.88

fortress
He is my refuge and my f.   19.142

forty
fasted f. days and f. nights   55.11

found
Seek ye the LORD while he may be f.   23.100
Thou art weighed in the balances, and art f. wanting   27.21

foundation
Behold, I lay in Zion for a f. a stone   23.40
other f. can no man lay   61.10
the f. of the apostles and prophets   64.8

foundations
when I laid the f. of the earth?   18.46

fowl
dominion over … the f. of the air   1.6

fowls
Behold the f. of the air   55.36

foxes
The f. have holes   55.51

frankincense
gold, and f. and myrrh   55.5

free
the truth shall make you f.   58.41
ye shall be f. indeed   58.42
But I was f. born   59.54
Spirit of life in Christ Jesus hath made me f. from   60.31

freedom
service is perfect f.   82.16

freely
f. ye have received   55.64

fret
F. not thyself because of evildoers   19.63
F. not thyself because of the ungodly   82.118

friend
a man speaketh unto his f.   2.66
A f. loveth at all times   20.65
there is a f. that sticketh closer than a brother   20.69
Faithful are the wounds of a f.   20.97
A faithful f. is the medicine of life   46.8
Forsake not an old f.   46.13
a f. of publicans and sinners   55.80

friends
when he prayed for his f.   18.62
but the rich hath many f.   20.47
that a man lay down his life for his f.   58.78
I have called you f.   58.79

frogs
the f. came up   2.24

fruit
she took of the f.   1.18
neither shall f. be in the vines   35.7
which also beareth f.   55.94

blessed is the f. of thy womb 57.9
ye should go and bring forth f. 58.79
the f. of the Spirit is love 63.20
the f. of my labour 65.3

fruitful
Be f. and multiply 1.6
the children of Israel were f. 2.1

fruits
by their f. ye shall know them 55.46
the f. of the Spirit 82.30

full
and my cup shall be f. 82.113

fulness
in thy presence is f. of joy 19.17
be filled with all the f. of God 64.10
in him should all f. dwell 66.2
in him dwelleth all the f. of the Godhead 66.6

furnace
heat the f. one seven times more 27.13
cast them into the burning fiery f. 27.13

G

gain
if he shall g. the whole world 55.110
to die is g. 65.3
godliness with contentment is great g. 69.13

gall
They gave me also g. for my meat em *19.114*
the wormwood and the g. 25.4
They gave him vinegar to drink mingled with g. 55.181
They gave me g. to eat 82.141

garden
God planted a g. eastward in Eden 1.10
put him into the g. of Eden 1.11
God sent him forth from the g. 1.26
Let my beloved come into his g. 22.17

gardener
She, supposing him to be the g. 58.99

garment
hating even the g. spotted by the flesh 80.4

garments
They part my g. among them 19.30
he hath clothed me with the g. of salvation 23.121
parted his g. casting lots 55.181
and laid aside his g. 58.62

gasp
he was at the last g. 54.2

gates
Lift up your heads, O ye g. 19.34
and the g. of hell shall not prevail 55.108

Gath
Tell it not in G. 10.1

gather
not worthy so much as to g. up the crumbs 82.61

gave
the LORD g. and the LORD hath taken away 18.3
the LORD g. Job twice as much 18.62
he g. his only begotten Son 58.17
g. their own selves to the Lord, and unto us 62.24

Gentiles
on the G. also was poured out the gift of the Holy Ghost 59.30

gently
shall g. lead those that are with young 23.58

get
G. thee out of thy country 1.50

ghost
with a loud voice, yielded up the g. .55:
that I had given up the g. 18.18
gave up the g. 58.95

giant
g. refreshed with wine 82.143

giants
There were g. in the earth in those days 1.34
there we saw the g. 4.12

gift
ye shall receive the g. of the Holy Ghost 59.8
the g. of God is eternal life 60.28
it is the g. of God 64.5
tasted of the heavenly g. 73.12
Every good g. and every perfect g. is 74.4

gifts
hast received g. for men 19.108
know how to give good g. unto your children 55.42
diversities of g. but the same Spirit 61.39

Gilead
Is there no balm in G. 24.18

gird
G. up thy loins 12.11

give
be more ready to hear, than to g. 21.22
How shall I g. thee up, Ephraim 28.11
It is more blessed to g. than to receive 59.51

given
of thine own have we g. thee 13.10
unto us a son is g. 23.20
Ask, and it shall be g. you 55.41
shall be g. and he shall have abundance 55.159

giver
God loveth a cheerful g. 62.26
author and g. of all good things 82.42
Lord and g. of life 82.50

glad
And wine that maketh g. the heart of man
19.165
made to make men g.   46.30
and shew ourselves g. in him   82.146

gladness
the oil of g. above thy fellows   19.80
they shall obtain joy and g.   23.54

glass
now we see through a g. darkly   61.42

glorified
I have g. thee on the earth   58.85

glorify
O Father, g. thou me   58.85

glorious
who is like thee, g. in holiness   2.38
G. things are spoken of thee, O city of
God   19.135

glory
the g. of the LORD abode upon the mount
Sinai   2.50
shew me thy g.   2.68
the g. of the LORD filled the tabernacle
2.73
The g. is departed from Israel   9.10
for the g. of the LORD had filled   11.11
Give unto the LORD the g. due   13.3
crowned him with g. and honour   19.10
The heavens declare the g. of God   19.24
Who is this King of g.   19.34
afterward receive me to g.   19.125
the whole earth is full of his g.   23.13
And the g. of the LORD shall be revealed
23.56
But let him that glorieth g. in this, that he
understandeth   24.20
behold, the g. of the LORD filled the house
26.36
there was given him dominion, and g.
27.28
I will fill this house with g.   37.4
The g. of this latter house shall be greater
than of the former   37.4
thine is ... the g.   55.33
Solomon in all his g. was not arrayed   55.36
G. to God in the highest   57.14
we beheld his g.   58.6
and manifested forth his g.   58.13
g. which thou gavest me I have given them
58.89
they may behold my g.   58.90
For all have sinned, and come short of the g.
of God   60.14
to whom be g. for ever   60.46
let him g. in the Lord   61.5
do all to the g. of God   61.34
woman have long hair, it is a g.   61.35

are changed into the same image from g. to
g.   62.6
far more exceeding and eternal weight of
g.   62.11
let him g. in the Lord   62.29
g. in the church by Christ Jesus   64.11
Christ in you, the hope of g.   66.3
receive g. and honour and power   81.18
g. of God did lighten   81.69
G. be to the Father   82.7
The g. that shall be revealed   82.39

gnashing
be weeping and g. of teeth   55.50
shall be weeping and g. of teeth   55.159

gnat
strain at a g. and swallow   55.142

go
the LORD thy God, he it is that doth g. with
thee   5.39
for whither thou goest, I will g.   8.2
who will g. for us?   23.14
And he said, G. and tell this people   23.15
And g. quickly, and tell his disciples   55.188
G. ye therefore, and teach all nations
55.189
G. and do thou likewise   57.37

goat
Aaron shall lay both his hands upon the head
of the live g.   3.10

goats
divideth his sheep from the g.   55.160

god
an altar ... To the unknown g.   59.42
the g. of this world   62.7

God
In the beginning G. created the heaven and
the earth   1.1
G. created man in his own image   1.6
for G. did send me before you   1.97
but G. meant it unto good   1.103
will be your G. and ye shall be my people
3.17
the LORD thy G. is with thee   6.1
G. his way is perfect   10.16
Now by this I that thou art a man of G.
11.33
if the LORD be G. follow him   11.34
he is a g. either he is talking   11.36
The LORD, he is the G.   11.37
I told them of the hand of my G. which was
good   16.3
Doth Job fear G. for nought?   18.2
Canst thou by searching find out G.   18.20
yet in my flesh shall I see G.   18.30
There is no G.   19.13
by my G. have I leaped   19.22
The heavens declare the glory of G.   19.24

My G. my G. why   19.27
Blessed is the nation whose G. is the LORD
19.56
G. is our refuge and strength   19.81
Be still, and know that I am G.   19.83
G. is the strength of my heart   19.125
my heart and my flesh crieth out for the
living G.   19.129
from everlasting to everlasting, thou art
G.   19.138
For the LORD is a great G.   19.152
For he is our G. and we are the people
19.152
Keep thy foot when thou goest to the house
of G.   21.22
for G. is in heaven, and thou   21.23
Fear G. and keep his commandments   21.55
his name shall be called … The mighty G.
23.20
but the word of our G. shall stand for ever
23.56
Behold your G.   23.57
be not dismayed; for I am thy G.   23.68
smitten of G. and afflicted   23.95
will be their G. and they shall be my
people   24.35
G. gave them knowledge and skill in all
learning and wisdom   27.3
there is a G. in heaven that revealeth secrets
27.7
your G. is a God of gods   27.10
to walk humbly with thy G.   33.7
a G. like unto thee, that pardoneth
iniquity   33.8
G. with us   55.3
pure in heart … see G.   55.17
Ye cannot serve G. and mammon   55.35
What therefore G. hath joined together
55.120
Thou shalt love the Lord thy G. with all thy
heart   55.140
My G. my God, why hast thou forsaken
me?   55.186
the kingdom of G. is at hand   56.3
For with G. nothing shall be impossible
57.7
my spirit hath rejoiced in G. my Saviour
57.10
he cannot see the kingdom of G.   58.14
For G. so loved the world   58.17
G. is a Spirit   58.22
My Lord and my G.   58.102
hast not lied unto men, but unto G.   59.15
For all have sinned, and come short of the
glory of G.   60.14
Therefore being justified by faith, we have
peace with G.   60.18
the gift of G. is eternal life   60.28

If G. be for us   60.38
hearing by the word of G.   60.44
do all to the glory of G.   61.34
by the grace of G. I am what I am   61.48
flesh and blood cannot inherit the kingdom
of G.   61.55
be filled with all the fulness of G.   64.10
Put on the whole armour of G.   64.28
G. who at sundry times   73.1
Fear G.   75.9
be unto our G. for ever   81.28
one G.   82.24
G. hath joined together   82.93

godliness
g. with contentment is great gain   69.13
godly
A g. righteous, and sober life   82.4
gods
ye shall be as g.   1.17
Thou shalt have no other g. before me   2.44
Ye shall not go after other g.   5.10
Let us go and serve other g.   5.23
his wives turned away his heart after
other g.   11.22
Gog
G. and Magog   81.64
gold
More to be desired are they than g.   19.25
The silver is mine, and the g. is mine   37.4
g. and frankincense, and myrrh   55.5
golden
worship the g. image that
Nebuchadnezzar   27.11
good
God saw that it was g.   1.4
behold, it was very g.   1.7
the tree of knowledge of g. and evil   1.10
It is not g. that the man should be alone
1.12
the woman saw that the tree was g. for
food   1.18
to know g. and evil   1.26
but God meant it unto g.   1.103
thy God bringeth thee into a g. land   5.14
For he is g.   14.1
O taste and see that the LORD is g.   19.59
no g. thing will he withhold from them
19.132
It is a g. thing to give thanks   19.145
g. news from a far country   20.89
a portion with the g.   23.96
g. tidings unto the meek   23.120
And seekest thou g. things for thyself?
24.39
g. is thy faithfulness   25.5
He hath shewed thee, O man, what is g.
33.7
none g. but one, that is, G.   55.123

He shall be g. and shall be called the Son of the Highest   57.5

he that is mighty hath done to me g. things   57.10

filled the hungry with g. things   57.10

g. tidings of great joy   57.14

any g. thing come out of Nazareth?   58.10

thou hast kept the g. wine until now   58.12

this woman was full of g. works   59.26

dwelleth no g. thing   60.29

all things work together for g. to them that love God   60.37

prove what is that g.   60.47

whatsoever things are of g. report   65.17

Fight the g. fight   69.15

came out of g. tribulation   81.29

G. Lord, deliver us   82.26

goodly

he was a g. child   2.5

How g. are thy tents, O Jacob   4.24

goodness

Surely g. and mercy shall follow me   19.31

fountain of all g.   82.18

goods

with all my worldly g.   82.92

good will

on earth peace, g. toward men   57.14

gospel

the poor have the g.   55.75

this g. of the kingdom shall be preached in all   55.146

The beginning of the g. of Jesus   56.1

and preach the g. to every creature   56.24

he hath anointed me to preach the g. to the poor   57.21

I am not ashamed of the g. of Christ   60.4

woe is unto me, if I preach not the g.   61.26

gourd

the LORD God prepared a g.   32.10

government

the g. shall be upon his shoulder   23.20

Of the increase of his g. and peace there shall be no end   23.20

grace

Noah found g. in the eyes of the LORD   1.36

she obtained g. and favour in his sight   17.2

full of g. and truth   58.6

sin abounded, g. did much more abound   60.21

not under the law, but under g.   60.27

by the g. of God I am what I am   61.48

g. of our Lord Jesus Christ, that, though he was rich   62.25

My g. is sufficient for thee   62.34

The g. of the Lord Jesus Christ, and   62.35

ye are fallen from g.   63.14

by g. ye are saved   64.3

by g. are ye saved through faith   64.5

g. to help in time of need   73.9

come boldly unto the throne of g.   73.9

gracious

will be g. to whom I will be g.   2.69

The LORD ... will be g. unto thee   4.2

The LORD is merciful and g.   19.160

grain

The kingdom of heaven is like to a g. of mustard seed   55.97

faith as a g. of mustard seed   55.112

grandmother

A Man may not marry his G.   82.169

grapes

he looked that it should bring forth g.   23.10

The fathers have eaten sour g.   26.15

grass

man, his days are as g.   19.163

The g. withereth, the flower fadeth   23.56

did eat g. as oxen   27.17

grasshoppers

we were in our own sight as g.   4.12

the inhabitants thereof are as g.   23.63

grave

jealousy is cruel as the g.   22.27

And he made his g. with the wicked   23.95

graven

Thou shalt not make unto thee any g. image   2.44

graves

And the g. were opened   .55:

great

a portion with the g.   23.96

And seekest thou g. things for thyself?   24.39

g. is thy faithfulness   25.5

He shall be g. and shall be called the Son of the Highest   57.5

he that is mighty hath done to me g. things   57.10

came out of g. tribulation   81.29

greater

a g. than John the Baptist   55.77

a g. than Solomon is here   55.89

g. is he that is in you   77.14

greatness

Thine, O LORD, is the g.   13.9

Greek

neither Jew nor G.   63.9

griefs

Surely he hath borne our g.   23.95

grieve

And g. not the holy Spirit of God   64.17

grieved

it g. him at his heart   1.35

grind

g. the faces of the poor?   23.9

groaning

God heard their g.   2.9

ground

God formed man of the dust of the g.   1.9
to till the g.   1.26
sat down upon the g.   46.14

guide

I will g. thee with mine eye   19.55
And the LORD shall g. thee continually
23.113

guilty

shall be g. of the body and blood of the
Lord   61.37

gulf

there is a great g. fixed   57.60

H

hair

the h. of my flesh stood up   18.10

hairs

the very h. of your head are all numbered
55.69

hairy

Esau my brother is a h. man   1.75

hallowed

H. be thy name   55.33

halt

How long h. ye between two opinions?
11.34

hammer

like a h. that breaketh the rock   24.30

hand

when Moses held up his h.   2.42
the h. of the LORD was on Elijah   11.40
Uzza put forth his h. to hold the ark   13.1
the h. of the LORD his God upon him   15.3
the h. of our God was upon us   15.5
I told them of the h. of my God which was
good   16.3
only upon himself put not forth thine h.
18.2
he is at my right h.   19.16
at thy right h. there are pleasures   19.17
My times are in thy h.   19.51
In his h. are the deep places   19.152
Sit thou at my right h.   19.179
Even there shall thy h. lead me   19.225
Whatsoever thy h. findeth to do   21.40
My beloved put in his h. by the hole of the
door   22.19
I will uphold thee with the right h. of my
righteousness   23.68
Behold, the LORD's h. is not shortened, that
it cannot save   23.115
none can stay his h.   27.18
came forth fingers of a man's h.   27.20

let not thy left h. know what thy right h.
doeth   55.30
if thy h. or thy foot offend thee   55.115
shall any man pluck them out of my h.
58.51
under the mighty h. of God   75.20

handle

h. me, and see   57.86
Touch not; taste not; h. not   66.7

handmaid

Behold the h. of the Lord   57.8

hands

Aaron shall lay both his h. upon the head of
the live goat   3.10
O Clap your h.   19.84
I will lift up my h. in thy name   19.101
Strengthen ye the weak h.   23.51
I have graven thee upon the palms of my h.
23.86
fall into the h. of the Lord   46.4
washed his h.   55.178
Behold my h. and my feet   57.86
laid their h. on them   59.32
into the h. of the living God   73.19
lift up the h. which hang down   73.29

hanged

a millstone were h. about his neck   55.114

hap

her h. was to light on a part of the field   8.4

happy

H. is the man that findeth wisdom   20.8

hard

Is any thing too h. for the LORD?   1.63
they made their lives bitter with h.
bondage   2.3
that thou art an h. man   55.158

harden

H. not your heart   19.153

hardened

Pharaoh's heart was h.   2.25

harmless

h. as doves   55.66

hart

As the h. panteth after the water   19.75

harvest

While the earth remaineth, seedtime and
h.   1.44
The h. truly is plenteous   55.61
h. of the earth is ripe   81.49

haste

I said in my h. All men   19.186
make h. to help us   82.6

hate

They that h. me without a cause   19.111
A time to love, and a time to h.   21.11

hatred

than a stalled ox and h. therewith   20.54

haughty

an h. spirit before a fall   20.58

have

To h. and to hold   82.90

head

it shall bruise thy h.   1.21
thou anointest my h. with oil   19.31
my h. is filled with dew   22.18
His h. is as the most fine gold   22.21
the whole h. is sick   23.2
she took the h. out of the bag   43.3
Son of man hath not where to lay his h.   55.51

heads

Lift up your h. O ye gates   19.34

heal

will forgive their sin and will h. their land   14.2
I will h. their backsliding   28.14
H. the sick   55.64
sent me to h. the brokenhearted   57.21
Physician, h. thyself   57.22

healed

with his stripes we are h.   23.95

healeth

who h. all thy diseases   19.159

healing

with h. in his wings   39.10

health

no h. in us   82.3
in sickness and in h.   82.88

heap

For thou shalt h. coals of fire upon his head   20.88

hear

H. O Israel: The LORD our God is one LORD   5.8
be more ready to h. than to give   21.22
H. ye indeed, but understand not   23.15
the deaf h.   55.75
Take heed what ye h.   56.9
and how shall they h. without a preacher?   60.43

heareth

Speak, LORD; for thy servant h.   9.6

hearing

of h. the words of the LORD   30.18
So then faith cometh by h.   60.44
h. by the word of God   60.44

hearken

Now therefore h. O Israel   5.2

heart

Pharaoh's h. was hardened   2.25
every one whose h. stirred him up   2.71
if thou seek him with all thy h. and with all thy soul   5.5
that your h. be not deceived   5.17
shall ye lay up these my words in your h.   5.18

sought him a man after his own h.   9.18
but the LORD looketh on the h.   9.23
his wives turned away his h. after other gods   11.22
Ezra had prepared his h. to seek the law   15.4
commune with your own h. upon your bed   19.7
the meditation of my h. be acceptable   19.25
Create in me a clean h. O God   19.93
I commune with mine own h.   19.126
my h. and my flesh crieth out for the living God   19.129
Harden not your h.   19.153
And wine that maketh glad the h. of man   19.165
know my h.   19.228
Trust in the LORD with all thine h.   20.5
I gave my h. to seek and search out   21.6
he hath set the world in their h.   21.12
I applied mine h. to know wisdom   21.37
drink thy wine with a merry h.   21.
the whole h. faint   23.2
Make the h. of this people fat   23.15
but have removed their h. far from me   23.41
this people hath a revolting and a rebellious h.   24.11
The h. is deceitful above all things   24.24
his word was in mine h. as a burning fire shut up in my bones   24.27
when ye shall search for me with all your h.   24.31
give them one h. and I will put a new spirit within you   26.10
A new h. also will I give you   26.32
I will give you an h. of flesh   26.32
Daniel purposed in his h.   27.2
And rend your h. and not your garments   29.5
he shall turn the h. of the fathers to the children   39.11
candle of understanding in thine h.   41.6
turn to him with your whole h.   42.4
Blessed are the pure in h.   55.17
there will your h. be also   55.34
I am meek and lowly in h.   55.83
out of the abundance of the h.   55.87
Thou shalt love the Lord thy God with all thy h.   55.140
pondered them in her h.   57.15
Did not our h. burn within us   57.85
Let not your h. be troubled   58.69
Let not your h. be troubled   58.75
they were pricked in their h.   59.8
whose h. the Lord opened   59.37

heartily

let us h. rejoice in the   82.146

hearts

and write it in their h.   24.35

to turn the h. of the fathers to the children 57.3

he hath scattered the proud in the imagination of their h.   57.10

That Christ may dwell in your h. by faith 64.10

devices and desires of our own h.   82.3

unto whom all h. be open   82.46

heathen

Why do the h. rage   19.3

Ask of me, and I shall give thee the h.   19.5

the h. so furiously rage together   82.101

heaven

God created the h. and the earth   1.1

behold, the h. and h. of heavens cannot contain thee   11.13

all that is in the h. and in the earth is thine 13.9

then will I hear from h.   14.2

Whom have I in h. but thee?   19.125

as the h. is high above the earth   19.161

If I ascend up into h.   19.225

for God is in h. and thou   21.23

How art thou fallen from h. O Lucifer 23.27

the kingdom of h. is at hand   55.6

Repent: for the kingdom of h. is at hand 55.15

poor in spirit ... kingdom of h.   55.17

for righteousness' sake ... kingdom of h. 55.17

Thy will be done in earth, as it is in h. 55.33

The kingdom of h. is like to a grain of mustard seed   55.97

Again the kingdom of h. is like unto a merchant   55.98

the keys of the kingdom of h.   55.108

ye shall not enter into the kingdom of h. 55.113

shall be bound in h.   55.116

H. and earth shall pass away   55.149

All power is given unto me in h. and in earth   55.189

Lord himself shall descend from h.   67.8

a door was opened in h.   81.15

I saw h. opened   81.61

new h. and a new earth   81.66

heavens

behold, the heaven and heaven of h. cannot contain thee   11.13

When I consider thy h.   19.10

The h. declare the glory of God   19.24

as the h. are higher than the earth   23.102

Oh that thou wouldest rend the h.   23.125

I create new h. and a new earth   23.129

wonders in the h. and in the earth   29.7

the h. were opened unto him   55.10

new h. and a new earth   76.9

The h. declare   82.112

heaviness

the garment of praise for the spirit of h. 23.120

heed

take h. lest he fall   61.30

take h. unto the thing   82.119

heel

thou shalt bruise his h.   1.21

heir

hath appointed h. of all things   73.1

hell

thou wilt not leave my soul in h.   19.17

and the gates of h. shall not prevail   55.108

descended into h.   82.13

helmet

an h. of salvation upon his head   23.116

the h. of salvation   64.28

help

a very present h. in trouble   19.81

My h. cometh from the LORD   19.206

helped

Hitherto hath the LORD h. us   9.11

help meet

I will make him an h. for him   1.12

hem

touched the h. of his garment   55.59

hen

a h. gathereth her chickens   55.144

here

he answered, H. am I   9.5

H. am I; send me   23.14

hereticks

Infidels, and H.   82.41

heritage

children are an h. of the LORD   19.215

hewed

h. them out cisterns, broken cisterns   24.4

hewers

h. of wood and drawers of water   6.9

hid

Adam and his wife h. themselves from the presence of the LORD   1.18

My way is h. from the LORD   23.66

we h. as it were our faces from him   23.95

hide

h. us from the face   81.27

high

the h. places were not removed   12.18

get thee up into the h. mountain   23.57

I dwell in the h. and holy place   23.107

tread upon the h. places of the earth   33.1

gone up on h.   82.138

they that plow i.   18.9

Wash me throughly from mine i.   19.90

I was shapen in i.   19.91

thine i. is taken away   23.14

her i. is pardoned   23.56

the LORD hath laid on him the i. of us all
23.95

a God like unto thee, that pardoneth i.   33.8

Thou ... canst not look on i.   35.2

inn

no room for them in the i.   57.13

innocency

Keep i.   82.119

inspiration

All scripture is given by i.   70.8

instruct

I will i. thee and teach thee in the way   19.55

interpretation

we will shew the i.   27.4

iron

Thou shalt break them with a rod of i.   19.5

I. sharpeneth i.   20.99

rule them with a rod of i.   81.9

island

every i. fled away   81.54

Israel

no more Jacob, but I.   1.82

the Egyptians made the children of I. to
serve with rigour   2.3

arose a mother in I.   7.6

The glory is departed from I.   9.10

And all I. heard of the judgment   11.9

what one nation in the earth is like thy
people I.   13.7

O thou that inhabitest the praises of I.
19.28

he that keepeth I. shall neither slumber nor
sleep   19.206

Let I. hope in the LORD   19.219

I. doth not know, my people doth not
consider   23.1

the Holy One of I.   23.22

why will ye die, O house of I.   26.26

When I. was a child   28.9

hath holpen his servant I.   57.10

I. is, that they might be saved   60.40

And so all I. shall be saved   60.45

ivory

Thy neck is as a tower of i.   22.24

J

jawbone

he found a new j. of an ass   7.24

jealous

I the LORD thy God am a j. God   2.44

I have been very j.   11.42

am a j. God   82.47

jealousy

j. is cruel as the grave   22.27

Jerusalem

Pray for the peace of J.   19.209

Speak ye comfortably to J.   23.56

shout, O daughter of J.   38.11

O J. J. thou that   55.144

the holy city, new J.   81.66

Jesse

a rod out of the stem of J.   23.23

Jesus

the generation of J. Christ   55.1

J. ... save his people from their sins   55.2

J. the King of the Jews   55.182

J. wept   58.54

this same J. which is taken up   59.3

In the name of J. Christ of Nazareth rise
59.10

that they had been with J.   59.14

But put ye on the Lord J. Christ   60.57

J. Christ, and him crucified   61.6

by the faith of J. Christ   63.5

name of J. every knee should bow   65.5

But we see J.   73.5

J. the author and finisher   73.26

blood of J. Christ his Son cleanseth   77.3

See also **Christ**

Jew

neither J. nor Greek   63.9

Jews

Where is he that is born King of the J.   55.4

Jesus the King of the J.   55.182

joined

What therefore God hath j. together   55.120

God hath j. together   82.93

jot

one j. or one tittle shall in no wise   55.20

journeyings

In j. often   62.31

joy

for the j. of the LORD is your strength   16.10

in thy presence is fulness of j.   19.17

They that sow in tears shall reap in j.   19.213

with j. shall ye draw water out of the wells of
salvation   23.25

come to Zion with songs and everlasting j.
23.54

they shall obtain j. and gladness   23.54

the oil of j. for mourninng   23.120

enter thou into the j. of thy lord   55.156

good tidings of great j.   57.14

my j. and crown   65.15

for the j. that was set before   73.26

count it all j. when   74.1

rejoice with j. unspeakable   75.3

no greater j. than to hear   79.1

joyful

Make a j. noise unto God, all ye lands 19.104

let us make a j. noise to the rock of our salvation 19.151

Make a j. noise unto the LORD 19.157

Make a j. noise unto the LORD 19.158

In the day of prosperity be j. 21.32

be j. in the Lord 82.148

j. and pleasant thing it is 82.159

jubile

A j. shall that fiftieth year be 3.16

judge

Shall not the J. of all the earth do right? 1.64

Who made thee a prince and a j. over us? 2.7

God shall j. the righteous and the wicked 21.14

J. not, that ye be not judged 55.38

he will j. the world in righteousness 59.45

j. the quick and the dead 82.13

judged

Judge not, that ye be not j. 55.38

judgement

To do justice and j. is more acceptable to the LORD 20.74

he looked for j. but behold oppression 23.11

But let j. run down as waters 30.13

Now is the j. of this world 58.60

all appear before the j. seat 62.16

but after this the j. 73.16

at the dreadful day of j. 82.87

judgements

how unsearchable are his j. 60.46

judges

when the LORD raised them up j. 7.2

just

how should man be j. with God? 18.15

the j. shall live by his faith 35.3

sendeth rain on the j. and on the unjust 55.28

whatsoever things are j. 65.17

the j. for the unjust 75.17

justice

To do j. and judgment is more acceptable to the LORD 20.74

justified

went down to his house j. rather than 57.67

Being j. freely by his grace 60.14

Therefore being j. by faith, we have peace with God 60.18

by works a man is j. 74.11

justify

shall my righteous servant j. many 23.96

justly

to do j. 33.7

K

keeper

Am I my brother's k. 1.28

The LORD is thy k. 19.206

kept

I k. them in thy name 58.87

keys

the k. of the kingdom of heaven 55.108

have the k. of hell and of death 81.4

kick

it is hard for thee to k. against the pricks 59.22

kid

the leopard shall lie down with the k. 23.24

kill

Thou shalt not k. 2.44

Rise, Peter; k. and eat 59.27

killed

and be k. and be raised again the third day 55.109

kin

The man is near of k. unto us 8.6

kindle

all ye that k. a fire 23.90

kindred

A Table of K. and Affinity 82.168

king

there arose up a new k. over Egypt 2.2

there was no k. in Israel 7.29

God save the k. 9.16

Who is this K. of glory? 19.34

mine eyes have seen the K. 23.14

Thine eyes shall see the k. in his beauty 23.49

behold, thy K. cometh unto thee 38.11

Where is he that is born K. of the Jews? 55.4

Jesus the K. of the Jews 55.182

Art thou a k. then? 58.91

unto the K. eternal 69.3

Honour the k. 75.9

kingdom

his k. that which shall not be destroyed 27.28

the k. of heaven is at hand 55.6

Repent: for the k. of heaven is at hand 55.15

Thy k. come 55.33

thine is the k. 55.33

But seek ye first the k. of God 55.37

The k. of heaven is like to a grain of mustard seed 55.97

Again the k. of heaven is like unto a merchant 55.98

the keys of the k. of heaven 55.108

ye shall not enter into the k. of heaven 55.113

brought us up out of a l. that floweth with milk and honey   4.15

will forgive their sin and will heal their l.   14.2

for he was cut off out of the l. of the living   23.95

landmark

Cursed be he that removeth his neighbour's l.   5.33

Remove not the old l.   20.80

language

And the whole earth was of one l.   1.48

they have all one l.   1.49

last

first shall be l.   55.128

So the l. shall be first   55.130

Hath in these l. days   73.1

late

to rise up early, to sit up l.   19.214

laugh

He that sitteth in the heavens shall l.   19.4

A time to weep, and a time to l.   21.11

laughter

of l. It is mad   21.9

law

This book of the l. shall not depart out of thy mouth   6.1

all the people were attentive unto the book of the l.   16.8

his delight is in the l. of the LORD   19.1

The l. of the LORD is perfect   19.25

wondrous things out of thy l.   19.195

Great peace have they which love thy l.   19.205

seal the l.   23.18

I will put my l. in their inward parts   24.35

the l. of the Medes and Persians   27.23

are a l. unto themselves   60.10

not under the l. but under grace   60.27

the l. was our schoolmaster to bring us unto Christ   63.8

perfect l. of liberty   74.6

lawful

It is l. for Christian men   82.167

laying

L. on of Hands   82.78

lead

shall gently l. those that are with young   23.58

the blind l. the blind   55.105

leadeth

he l. me beside the still waters   19.31

lean

and l. not unto thine own understanding   20.5

leap

Then shall the lame man l.   23.52

leaping

he cometh l. upon the mountains   22.10

learn

that I might l. thy statutes   19.198

read, mark, l.   82.38

learned

to hear as the l.   23.88

wisdom of a l. man   46.34

least

unto one of the l. of these my brethren   55.162

leave

I will never l. thee   73.36

leaven

Beware ye of the l. of the Pharisees   57.41

a little l. leaveneth the whole lump?   61.17

Purge out therefore the old l.   61.17

led

l. by the Spirit of God   60.35

left

let not thy l. hand know what thy right hand doeth   55.30

legion

My name is L.   56.10

legs

His l. are as pillars of marble   22.21

lendeth

He that hath pity upon the poor l. unto the LORD   20.71

lengthen

l. thy cords   23.97

leopard

the l. shall lie down with the kid   23.24

Can the Ethiopian change his skin, or the l. his spots?   24.21

leper

l. … shall cry, unclean, unclean   3.7

lepers

cleanse the l.   55.64

the l. are cleansed   55.75

let

neither will I l. Israel go   2.17

letter

not of the l. but of the spirit   62.4

leviathan

Canst thou draw out l.   18.57

there is that l.   19.167

liberty

to proclaim l. to the captives   23.120

to set at l. them that are bruised   57.21

Spirit of the Lord is, there is l.   62.6

the l. wherewith Christ hath made us free   63.13

lie

God is not a man, that he should l.   4.33

He maketh me to l. down in green pastures   19.31

life
breathed into his nostrils the breath of l. 1.9
the tree of l. also in the midst of the garden 1.10
the l. of the flesh is in the blood   3.11
l. shall go for l.   5.30
I have set before you l. and death   5.38
choose l.   5.38
take away my l.   11.41
Thou wilt shew me the path of l.   19.17
all the days of my l.   19.31
For with thee is the fountain of l.   19.62
With long l. will I satisfy him   19.144
Who redeemeth thy l. from destruction 19.159
whoso findeth me findeth l.   20.22
some to everlasting l. and some to shame and everlasting contempt   27.33
He that findeth his l.   55.71
and he that loseth his l. for my sake   55.71
and to give his l. a ransom for many   56.18
In him was l.   58.2
but have everlasting l.   58.17
He that believeth on the Son hath everlasting l.   58.20
hath he given to the Son to have l. in himself   58.28
thou hast the words of eternal l.   58.36
I come that they might have l.   58.49
I am the resurrection, and the l.   58.52
I am the way, the truth, and the l.   58.71
that a man lay down his l. for his friends 58.78
he giveth to all l. and breath   59.43
walk in newness of l.   60.23
the gift of God is eternal l.   60.28
Christ, who is our l.   66.9
hath the Son hath l.   77.23
the l. everlasting   82.13
Lord and giver of l.   82.50
intend to lead a new l.   82.55

lift
L. up your heads, O ye gates   19.34
I will l. up mine eyes unto the hills   19.206
L. up your eyes on high, and behold   23.65

lifted
if I be l. up from the earth   58.60

light
Let there be l. and there was l.   1.2
God called the l. Day   1.3
a l. unto my path   19.202
entrance of thy words giveth l.   19.204
The people that walked in darkness have seen a great l.   23.19
upon them hath the l. shined   23.19
a l. to the Gentiles   23.82

that walketh in darkness, and hath no l. 23.90
walk in the l. of your fire   23.90
Then shall thy l. break forth as the morning   23.112
for thy l. is come   23.118
the LORD shall be unto thee an everlasting l.   23.119
sat in darkness saw great l.   55.14
Ye are the l. of the world   55.19
Let your l. so shine   55.19
To give l. to them that sit in darkness   57.11
And the l. shineth in darkness   58.2
to bear witness of the L.   58.3
men loved darkness rather than l.   58.18
a burning and a shining l.   58.29
I am the l. of the world   58.40
shined round about him a l.   59.22
to give the l. of the knowledge of the glory of God   62.8
God is l.   77.2
walk in the l.   77.3

lighten
L. our darkness   82.21

lightning
beheld Satan as l. fall from heaven   57.32

lights
the Father of l.   74.4

likeness
what l. will ye compare unto him?   23.61
they had the l. of a man   26.1
his own Son in the l. of sinful flesh   60.32

lilies
Consider the l. of the field   55.36

lily
the l. of the valleys   22.5

line
l. upon l.   23.39

linen
She maketh fine l. and selleth it   20.105

lines
The l. are fallen unto me in pleasant places 19.15

lion
LORD that delivered me out of the paw of the l.   9.27
the calf and the young l.   23.24
The l. hath roared   30.5
devil, as a roaring l.   75.21

lips
O Lord, open thou my l.   19.94
he that refraineth his l. is wise   20.30
Thy l. are like a thread of scarlet   22.15
I am a man of unclean l.   23.14
For with stammering l. and another tongue will he speak   23.39
and with their l. do honour me   23.41
open thou our l.   82.6

lowly

I am meek and l. in heart   55.83

Lucifer

How art thou fallen from heaven, O L.
23.27

lucre

not greedy of filthy l.   69.6

lukewarm

because thou art l.   81.12

lump

a little leaven leaveneth the whole l.   61.17

lust

the l. of the flesh   77.6

M

magnify

O m. the LORD with me   19.57

make

Let us m. man in our image   1.6
I m. all things new   81.66

maker

M. of heaven and   82.13

male

m. and female created he them   1.6
neither m. nor female   63.9

mammon

Ye cannot serve God and m.   55.35
friends of the m. of unrighteousness   57.56

man

Let us make m. in our image   1.6
God created m. in his own image   1.6
God formed m. of the dust of the ground
1.9
m. became a living soul   1.9
It is not good that the m. should be alone
1.12
she was taken out of M.   1.14
sought him a m. after his own heart   9.18
Thou art the m.   10.10
Now by this I know that thou art a m. of
God   11.33
m. is born unto trouble, as the sparks fly
upward   18.12
God will not cast away a perfect m.   18.14
how should m. be just with God?   18.15
M. that is born of a woman   18.26
there is a spirit in m.   18.34
Blessed is the m. that walketh not in the
counsel of the ungodly   19.1
What is m. that thou art mindful of him?
19.10
m. his days are as grass   19.163
one m. among a thousand have I found
21.33
keep his commandments ... whole duty of
m.   21.55

they had the likeness of a m.   26.1
one like the Son of m.   27.28
But they shall sit every m. under his vine
33.3
wisdom of a learned m.   46.34
M. shall not live by bread alone   55.11
shall be likened unto a foolish m.   55.48
a m. under authority   55.49
What manner of m. is this   55.53
a m. leave father and mother   55.120
let not m. put asunder   55.120
The sabbath was made for m.   56.6
a m. leave his father and mother   64.24
let no m. put asunder   82.93

manger

laid him in a m.   57.13

manifest

the works of the flesh are m.   63.19

manna

It is m. for they wist not what it was   2.40
fed thee with m.   5.13

manner

What m. of man is this   55.53
what m. of persons ought ye   76.8

mansions

In my Father's house are many m.   58.70

mantle

Elijah passed by him and cast his m. upon
him   11.44

mark

And the LORD set a m. upon Cain   1.29
m. ... of the beast   81.43
read, m. learn   82.38

marriage

marrying and giving in m.   55.151
m. of the Lamb is come   81.59

married

I have m. a wife   57.45

marry

better to m. than to burn   61.19

marrying

m. and giving in marriage   55.151

martyrs

noble army of M.   82.9

marvelled

m. to see such things   82.126

master

The disciple is not above his m.   55.68
Rabboni; which is to say, M.   58.99

masters

No man can serve two m.   55.35

matrimony

joined together in holy M.   82.80

measured

Who hath m. the waters in the hollow of his
hand   23.59

meat

They gave me also gall for my m.   19.114
not of strong m.   73.11

Medes

the law of the M. and Persians   27.23

mediator

one m. between God   69.5

medicine

A merry heart doeth good like a m.   20.66
A faithful friend is the m. of life   46.8

meditate

but thou shalt m. therein day and night   6.1
but thou shalt m. therein day and night   7.1
in his law doth he m.   19.1

meditation

the m. of my heart, be acceptable   19.25
it is my m. all the day   19.199

meek

Now the man Moses was very m.   4.10
the m. shall inherit the earth   19.65
he will beautify the m. with salvation   19.242
· good tidings unto the m.   23.120
Blessed are the m.   55.17
I am m. and lowly in heart   55.83

meet

m. the Lord in the air   67.8
It is m. and right so to do   82.59

members

as the body is one, and hath many m.   61.41

men

He is despised and rejected of m.   23.95
all m. have one entrance into life   45.9
Let us now praise famous m.   46.36
I am not as other m. are   57.67
hast not lied unto m. but unto God   59.15
but in understanding be m.   61.44
quit you like m.   61.59
us m. and for our salvation   82.49

merciful

For the LORD thy God is a m. God   5.6
The LORD is m. and gracious   19.160
Blessed are the m.   55.17
God be m. to me a sinner   57.67

mercy

sprinkle it with his finger upon the m. seat   3.9
for his m. endureth for ever   13.5
his m. endureth for ever   14.1
Surely goodness and m. shall follow me   19.31
Have m. upon me, O God   19.90
his m. endureth for ever   19.189
his m. endureth for ever   19.221
and he will have m. upon him   23.101
to love m.   33.7
in wrath remember m.   35.5
full of compassion and m.   46.3
merciful ... obtain m.   55.17
his m. is on them that fear him   57.10

God, who is rich in m.   64.3
Lord, have m. upon us   82.14

merry

A m. heart maketh a cheerful countenance   20.53
A m. heart doeth good like a medicine   20.66
gone up with a m. noise   82.125

messenger

Behold, I will send my m.   39.6
Behold, I send my m. before thy face   55.76

might

with all thy m.   5.8
My power and the m. of mine hand hath gotten me this wealth   5.15
do it with thy m.   21.40
no m. he increaseth strength   23.67
Not by m. nor by power ... saith the LORD of hosts   38.7

mightier

cometh after me is m. than I   55.9

mighty

how are the m. fallen!   10.1
his name shall be called ... The m. God   23.20
The LORD thy God in the midst of thee is m.   36.8
Truth ... m. above all things   40.7
put down the m. from their seats   57.10

mile

to go a m. go with him twain   55.26

militant

Church m.   82.52

milk

a land flowing with m. and honey   2.12
a land flowing with m. and honey   2.65
brought us up out of a land that floweth with m. and honey   4.15
buy wine and m. without money and without price   23.99
sincere m. of the word   75.7

millstone

a m. were hanged about his neck   55.114
stone like a great m.   81.58

mind

Thou wilt keep him in perfect peace, whose m. is stayed on thee   23.37
This I recall to my m. therefore have I hope   25.5
with all thy soul, and with all thy m.   55.140
clothed, and in his right m.   56.11
but be ye transformed by the renewing of your m.   60.47
Let this m. be in you   65.5
spirit ... of a sound m.   70.1

ministering

Are they not all m. spirits   73.3

In the n. of Jesus Christ of Nazareth rise
59.10

none other n. under heaven given among
men   59.13

shall call upon the n. of the Lord shall be
saved   60.42

Father's n. written in their foreheads   81.44

names

he calleth them all by n.   23.65

n. are not written in the book   81.42

narrow

n. is the way, which leadeth unto life   55.44

nation

I will make of thee a great n.   1.50

Blessed is the n. whose God is the LORD
19.56

Righteousness exalteth a n.   20.50

n. shall not lift up sword against n.   23.6

n. shall not lift up a sword against n.   33.3

n. shall rise against n.   55.145

an holy n.   75.8

nations

Behold, the n. are as a drop of a bucket
23.60

Go ye therefore, and teach all n.   55.189

nature

partakers of the divine n.   76.1

Nazarite

for I have been a N. unto God   7.26

near

call ye upon him while he is n.   23.100

neck

Thy n. is like the tower of David   22.15

Thy n. is as a tower of ivory   22.24

a millstone were hanged about his n.   55.114

need

God shall supply all your n.   65.20

grace to help in time of n.   73.9

needful

But one thing is n.   57.38

neglect

we n. so great salvation   73.4

neighbour

Thou shalt not bear false witness against to
thy n.   2.44

thou shalt love thy n. as thyself   3.12

Thou shalt love thy n. as thyself   55.140

new

there is no n. thing under the sun   21.4

I create n. heavens and a n. earth   23.129

They are n. every morning   25.5

give them one heart, and I will put a n. spirit
within you   26.10

A n. heart also will I give you   26.32

a n. spirit will I put within you   26.32

n. wine into old bottles   55.58

all things are become n.   62.18

n. heavens and a n. earth   76.9

n. heaven and a n. earth   81.66

I make all things n.   81.66

newness

walk in n. of life   60.23

news

good n. from a far country   20.89

night

the darkness he called N.   1.3

he shall lie all n. betwixt my breasts   22.4

cometh as a thief in the n.   67.9

perils and dangers of this n.   82.21

one n. certifieth another   82.112

noise

Make a joyful n. unto God, all ye lands
19.104

let us make a joyful n. to the rock of our
salvation   19.151

Make a joyful n. unto the LORD   19.157

Make a joyful n. unto the LORD   19.158

as I prophesied, there was a n. and behold a
shaking   26.33

gone up with a merry n.   82.125

nothing

that there is n. better, than that a man should
rejoice   21.16

For with God n. shall be impossible   57.7

for without me ye can do n.   58.77

now

n. is the day of salvation   62.20

n. is the accepted time   62.20

number

no man could n.   81.28

his n. is Six hundred   81.43

the n. of my days   82.120

numbered

those which were n. of the children of
Israel   4.1

he was n. with the transgressors   23.96

nurture

the fear and n. of the Lord   82.83

O

obedience

learned he o. by the things   73.10

obey

if ye will o. my voice indeed   2.43

to o. is better than sacrifice   9.21

even the winds and the sea o. him!   55.53

We ought to o. God rather than men   59.16

Children, o. your parents in the Lord
64.25

Wilt thou o. him   82.89

To love, cherish, and to o.   82.91

obeyed

thou hast o. my voice   1.72

persecuted

they which are p. for righteousness' 55.17
so p. they the prophets 55.17

persecutest

Saul, Saul, why p. thou me? 59.22

persecution

a great p. against the church 59.19
shall suffer p. 70.7

Persians

the law of the Medes and P. 27.23

persons

God is no respecter of p. 59.29

persuaded

am p. that he is able to keep 70.3

persuasions

popular p. and commotions 40.9

Pharisee

the one a P. and the other a publican 57.67
I am a P. the son of a Pharisee 59.55

Pharisees

Woe unto you, scribes and P. 55.143

physician

is there no p. there? 24.18
Honour a p. with the honour 46.33
be whole need not a p. 55.57
P. heal thyself 57.22

pieces

they weighed for my price thirty p. of
silver 38.13
And they covenanted with him for thirty p.
of silver 55.166
the thirty p. of silver 55.176

pierced

they shall look upon me whom they have
p. 38.14

pillar

in a p. of a cloud, to lead them the way 2.34
and by night in a p. of fire, to give them
light 2.34

pillars

Samson took hold of the two middle p.
7.28

piped

We have p. unto you 55.79

pit

He will deliver his soul from going into the
p. 18.39
the key of the bottomless p. 81.32
cast him into the bottomless p. 81.63

place

I go and prepare a p. for you 58.70

plain

Write the vision, and make it p. upon
tables 35.3
Make thy way p. before my face 82.104

pleasant

The lines are fallen unto me in p. places
19.15

joyful and p. thing it is 82.159

pleasantness

ways of p. 20.8

please

without faith it is impossible to p. him
73.21

pleased

Yet it p. the LORD to bruise him 23.96

pleasure

Have I any p. at all that the wicked should
die? 26.17
I have no p. in the death of the wicked
26.26

plenteous

The harvest truly is p. 55.61

plough

having put his hand to the p. 57.30

plowshares

they shall beat their swords into p. 23.6
Beat your p. into swords 29.9
they shall beat their swords into p. 33.3

pluck

shall any man p. them out of my hand
58.51

plumbline

the Lord stood upon a wall made by a p.
30.16

pole

Make thee a fiery serpent, and set it upon a
p. 4.20

pomegranate

thy temples are like a piece of a p. 22.15

pondered

p. them in her heart 57.15

poor

This p. man cried 19.58
grind the faces of the p. 23.9
Blessed are the p. in spirit 55.17
the p. have the gospel 55.75
For ye have the p. always with you 55.165
he hath anointed me to preach the gospel to
the p. 57.21
For the p. always ye have with you 58.56
as p. yet making many rich 62.21
he became p. that ye 62.25

portion

a p. with the great 23.96
The LORD is my p. saith my soul 25.6

possessed

The LORD p. me in the beginning 20.21

possible

with God all things are p. 55.127

potsherd

he took him a p. to scrape himself 18.7

pottage

Feed me I pray thee, with that same red p.
1.74

potter

Hath not the p. power over the clay 60.39

pour

I will p. out my spirit upon all flesh 29.7

poured

he hath p. out his soul unto death 23.96

power

My p. and the might of mine hand hath gotten me this wealth 5.15

he that giveth thee p. to get wealth 5.15

all that he hath is in thy p. 18.2

He giveth p. to the faint 23.67

Not by might, nor by p. but by my spirit, saith the LORD of hosts 38.7

thine is ... the p. 55.33

All p. is given unto me in heaven and in earth 55.189

the Son of man hath p. on earth to forgive sins 56.4

But ye shall receive p. after that the Holy Ghost is come upon you 59.2

it is the p. of God unto salvation 60.4

it is the p. of God 61.1

Christ the p. of God, and the wisdom of God 61.3

Christ the p. of God, and the wisdom of God 61.6

kingdom of God is not in word, but in p. 61.15

the excellency of the p. may be of God 62.9

the exceeding greatness of his p. 64.2

spirit ... of p. 70.1

powers

the p. that be are ordained 60.54

principalities, against p. 64.28

praise

my mouth shall shew forth thy p. 19.94

I will sing p. to my God 19.168

P. ye the LORD 19.234

P. ye him, all his angels 19.239

Let us now p. famous men 46.36

our mouth shall shew forth thy p. 82.6

praised

art p. in Sion 82.134

praises

O thou that inhabitest the p. of Israel 19.28

Let the high p. of God be in their mouth 19.243

praising

walking, and leaping, and p. God 59.11

pray

If my people ... shall ... p. and seek my face 14.2

P. for the peace of Jerusalem 19.209

P. ye therefore the Lord 55.61

Watch and p. that ye enter not into temptation 55.171

Lord, teach us to p. as John also taught his disciples 57.39

I p. for them: I p. not for the world 58.86

prayed

So I p. to the God of heaven 16.2

when he p. for his friends 18.62

But I have p. for thee, that thy faith fail not 57.72

prayer

we made our p. unto our God 16.4

p. also shall be made for him continually 19.121

the p. of the upright is his delight 20.52

my p. came in unto thee 32.5

My house shall be called the house of p. 55.134

ye shall ask in p. believing 55.136

give ourseves continually to p. 59.17

The effectual fervent p. of a righteous man 74.21

p. of faith shall save the sick 74.21

prayers

continued stedfastly ... in p. 59.9

which are the p. of saints 81.21

prayeth

for, behold, he p. 59.24

preach

the LORD hath anointed me to p. 23.120

and p. the gospel to every creature 56.24

he hath anointed me to p. the gospel to the poor 57.21

to p. deliverance to the captives 57.21

To p. the acceptable year of the Lord 57.21

And how shall they p. 60.43

we p. Christ crucified 61.3

woe is unto me, if I p. not the gospel! 61.26

P. the word 70.9

preacher

and how shall they hear without a p. 60.43

preaching

For the p. of the cross is to them that perish 61.1

by the foolishness of p. to save 61.2

precept

For p. must be upon p. 23.39

precious

How p. also are thy thoughts 19.227

alabaster box of very p. ointment 55.164

which believe he is p. 75.8

preeminence

all things he might have the p. 66.2

prepare

P. ye the way of the LORD 23.56

presence

My p. shall go with thee 2.67

So Satan went forth from the p. of the LORD 18.2

come before his p. with thanksgiving 19.151

pressed
p. down, and shaken together   57.26

presume
We do not p.   82.61

price
one pearl of great p.   55.98

pricks
it is hard for thee to kick against the p.   59.22

pride
P. goeth before destruction   20.58

priest
he was the p. of the most high God   1.54
Thou art a p. for ever   19.180
a great high p. that is passed   73.9

priesthood
an holy p. to offer   75.8

prince
Who made thee a p. and a judge over us?   2.7
his name shall be called ... The P. of Peace   23.20
casteth out devils through the p. of the devils   55.60
p. of the power of the air   64.3

princes
That bringeth the p. to nothing   23.63

prison
I was in p. and ye came   55.161

prize
mark for the p. of the high calling   65.12

proclaim
to p. liberty to the captives   23.120
To p. the acceptable year of the LORD   23.120

profitable
p. for doctrine   70.8

promise
the p. of my Father   57.89
not slack concerning his p.   76.7

promised
for he is faithful that p.   73.18

promises
all the p. of God in him are yea   62.1
great and precious p.   76.1

prophecy
p. came not in old time   76.3

prophesy
The prophets p. falsely   24.12
p. against the shepherds of Israel   26.28
P. upon these bones   26.33
your sons and your daughters shall p.   29.7

prophet
If there arise among you a p.   5.21
thy God will raise up unto thee a P.   5.28
I will raise them up a P. from among their brethren   5.29
he shall know that there is a p. in Israel   12.7

A p. is not without honour   55.99
child, shalt be called the p. of the Highest   57.11

prophets
would God that all the LORD'S people were p.   4.9
Is Saul also among the p.   9.14
believe his p. so shall ye prosper   14.11
The p. prophesy falsely   24.12
so persecuted they the p.   55.17
the foundation of the apostles and p.   64.8
spake ... by the p.   73.1

propitiation
a p. through faith in his blood   60.14
the p. for our sins   77.4
to be the p. for our sins   77.16

prosper
it shall p. in the thing whereto I sent it   23.103

prosperity
I saw the p. of the wicked   19.123
In the day pf p. be joyful   21.32

proud
A p. look   20.16
he hath scattered the p. in the imagination of their hearts   57.10

prove
and p. me now herewith   39.8
p. what is that good   60.47
P. all things   67.12

provide
My son, God will p. himself a lamb   1.69

psalms
make a joyful noise unto him with p.   19.151

pure
Blessed are the p. in heart   55.17
whatsoever things are p.   65.17
Unto the p. all things are p.   71.2
wisdom that is from above is first p.   74.16

purer
Thou art of p. eyes than to behold evil   35.2

purged
when he had by himself p. our sins   73.1

Purim
called these days P.   17.9

Q

queen
the q. of Sheba heard of the fame of Solomon   11.18

quench
Many waters cannot q. love   22.27
the smoking flax shall he not q.   23.69
Q. not the Spirit   67.11

quick
judge the q. and the dead   82.13

quiet
lead a q. and peaceable life   69.4
Serve thee with a q. mind   82.43

quietness
in q. and in confidence shall be your
strength   23.44

quit
q. you like men   61.59

quiver
the man that hath his q.   19.215

R

race
let us run with patience the r.   73.26

rags
all our righteousnesses are as filthy r.
23.126

rain
If the clouds be full of r. they empty
themselves   21.49
sendeth r. on the just and on the unjust
55.28

raise
I r. up the Chaldeans   35.1
r. the dead   55.64

raised
the dead are r. up   55.75
and be killed, and be r. again the third day
55.109

ram
behold behind him a r. caught in a thicket
1.70

ransom
and to give his life a r. for many   56.18

ransomed
the r. of the LORD shall return   23.54

rash
Be not r. with thy mouth   21.23

rasor
There hath not come a r. upon mine head
7.26

ravens
I have commanded the r. to feed thee there
11.29

read
r. mark, learn   82.38

readeth
that he may run that r. it   35.3

ready
r. always to give an answer   75.16

reap
They that sow in tears shall r. in joy   19.213
sown the wind, and they shall r. the
whirlwind   28.8
a man soweth, that shall he also r.   63.23

reaping
r. where thou hast not sown   55.158

reason
let us r. together   23.5

rebellion
r. is as the sin of witchcraft   9.22

rebellious
I was not r.   23.89
this people hath a revolting and a r. heart
24.11

rebuke
Thy r. hath broken   82.141

receive
afterward r. me to glory   19.125
It is more blessed to give than to r.   59.51

received
hast r. gifts for men   19.108
as many as r. him   58.5

red
fair weather: for the sky is r.   55.107

redeemed
Fear not: for I have r. thee   23.71
Christ hath r. us from the curse   63.7

redeemer
I know that my r. liveth   18.30

redeemeth
Who r. thy life from dest   19.159

redemption
through the r. that is in Christ Jesus   60.14
we have r. through his blood   64.1
r. through his blood   66.2

reed
the staff of this broken r.   23.55
A bruised r. shall he not break   23.69
A r. shaken with the wind?   55.76
A bruised r. shall he not break   55.84

refiner
he shall sit as a r. and purifier of silver   39.6

refuge
The eternal God is thy r.   5.48
God is our r. and strength   19.81
He is my r. and my fortress   19.142
hast been our r.   82.145

reign
not sin therefore r. in your mortal body
60.26
they shall r. for ever   81.72

reigned
lived and r. with Christ a thousand   81.63

rejected
He is despised and r. of men   23.95

rejoice
Yet I will r. in the LORD   35.7
R. greatly, O daughter of Zion   38.11
rather r. because your names   57.33
R. with them that do r.   60.51
R. in the Lord alway   65.16
let us heartily r. in the   82.146

rejoicing
As sorrowful, yet alway r.   62.21

religion
Pure r. and undefiled before God   74.8

remember
thou shalt r. the LORD thy God   5.15
R. now thy Creator in the days of thy
youth   21.53
in wrath r. mercy   35.5
R. Lot's wife   57.66

remembrance
this do in r. of me   61.36

remission
blood ... shed for many for the r. of sins
55.167

remnant
the r. whom the LORD shall call   29.7

rend
Oh that thou wouldest r. the heavens
23.125

render
R. therefore unto Caesar   55.138

renew
But they that wait upon the LORD
shall r. their strength   23.67

renewing
but be ye transformed by the r. of your
mind   60.47

renounce
r. the devil   82.67

repay
I will r. saith the Lord   60.52

repeateth
he that r. a matter separateth very friends
20.63

repent
neither the son of man, that he should r.
4.33
r. in dust and ashes   18.60
R. ye   55.6
R. for the kingdom of heaven is at hand
55.15
r. ye, and believe the gospel   56.3
R. and be baptized every one of you   59.8
but now commandeth all men every where
to r.   59.45
truly and earnestly r.   82.55

repentance
call ... sinners to r.   55.57
r. and remission of sins should be
preached   57.88
r. toward God   59.48
that all should come to r.   76.7

repented
r. the LORD that he had made man on the
earth   1.35
God r. of the evil, that he had said that he
would do unto them   32.8

they would have r. long ago   55.81

report
they brought up an evil r. of the land   4.12
Who hath believed our r.   23.95
seven men of honest r. full   59.17

reproof
profitable ... for r.   70.8

require
what doth the LORD r. of thee   33.7

resist
R. the devil   74.17

respecter
God is no r. of persons   59.29

rest
I will give thee r.   2.67
And the spirit of the LORD shall r.   23.23
returning and r. shall ye be saved   23.44
I will give you r.   55.83
ye shall find r. unto your souls   55.83
Come ye yourselves apart into a desert place,
and r.   56.13
no r. day nor night   81.47
may r. from their labours   81.48

rested
he r. on the seventh day   1.8

restore
I will r. to you the years that the locust hath
eaten   29.6

resurrection
For in the r. they neither marry   55.139
I am the r. and the life   58.52

return
Go, r. each to her mother's house   8.1
the ransomed of the LORD shall r.   23.54
it shall not r. unto me void   23.103
that he should r. from his ways, and live?
26.17
Come, and let us r. unto the LORD   28.6
I will r. into my house   55.90

returning
r. and rest shall ye be saved   23.44

revealed
those things which are r. belong unto us and
our children   5.37
for flesh and blood hath not r. it   55.108
hast r. them unto babes   57.34

revive
r. thy work in the midst of the years   35.5

reward
They have their r.   55.31

rewarder
a r. of them   73.21

rib
the r. ... made he a woman   1.14

ribs
he took one of his r.   1.14

summer is ended, and we are not s.   24.17
but that the world through him might
be s.   58.18
name … whereby we must be s.   59.13
what must I do to be s.   59.38
Israel is, that they might be s.   60.40
shall call upon the name of the Lord shall
be s.   60.42
by grace are ye s. through faith   64.5

Saviour
my spirit hath rejoiced in God my S.   57.10
in the city of David a S.   57.14
to be the S. of the world   77.18

savour
the LORD smelled a sweet s.   1.44
maketh manifest the s. of his knowledge
62.2

saw
I s. the prosperity of the wicked   19.123

scapegoat
the lot fell to be the s.   3.8
let him go for a s. into the wilderness   3.8

scarlet
though your sins be as s.   23.5
arrayed in purple and s.   81.56

scattered
So the LORD s. them abroad   1.49
smite the shepherd, and the sheep shall be
s.   38.16

sceptre
The s. shall not depart from Judah   1.101

schoolmaster
the law was our s. to bring us unto Christ
63.8

scorn
Laugh no man to s.   46.9

scripture
All s. is given by inspiration   70.8
Holy S. containeth all things   82.163

scriptures
Search the s.   58.30
and searched the s. daily   59.40
a child thou hast known the holy s.   70.8

sea
the LORD caused the s. to go back by a strong
east wind   2.35
The s. is his   19.152
They that go down to the s. in ships   19.175
dwell in the uttermost parts of the s.
19.225
as the waters cover the s.   23.24
thou wilt cast all their sins into the depths of
the s.   33.8
s. gave up the dead   81.65

seal
s. the law   23.18

search
S. me, O God   19.228
when ye shall s. for me with all your heart
24.31

searched
and s. the scriptures daily   59.40

searching
Canst thou by s. find out God?   18.20

season
To every thing there is a s.   21.11
I should know how to speak a word in s. to
him that is weary   23.88
be instant in s. out of s.   70.9

secret
The s. things belong unto the LORD our
God   5.37
He that dwelleth in the s. place of the most
High   19.142
He revealeth the deep and s. things   27.6
but he revealeth his s. unto his servants
30.5

see
there shall no man s. me, and live   2.69
yet in my flesh shall I s. God   18.30
lest they s. with their eyes   23.15
pure in heart … s. God   55.17
whereas I was blind, now I s.   58.47
Sir, we would s. Jesus   58.57
But we s. Jesus   73.5

seed
enmity … between thy s. and her s.   1.21
Unto thy s. will I give this land   1.52
I will multiply thy s. as the stars   1.72
in thy s. shall all the nations of the earth be
blessed   1.72
In the morning sow thy s.   21.50
The kingdom of heaven is like to a grain of
mustard s.   55.97
faith as a grain of mustard s.   55.112

seek
if from thence thou shalt s. the LORD thy
God   5.5
S. the LORD and his strength   13.2
If my people … shall … pray and s. my face
14.2
S. ye the LORD while he may be found
23.100
ye shall s. me, and find me   24.31
S. ye me, and ye shall live   30.9
run to and fro to s. the word of the LORD
30.18
S. ye the LORD   36.5
But s. ye first the kingdom of God   55.37
s. and ye shall find   55.41
Why s. ye the living among the dead?   57.81
risen with Christ, s. those things   66.8

seen
blessed are they that have not s. and yet 58.102
things which are not s. are eternal 62.11
No man hath s. God 77.17

send
Whom shall I s. 23.14
Here am I; s. me 23.14
he will s. forth labourers 55.61

sent
God s. him forth from the garden 1.26
except they be s. 60.43

separate
shall s. us from the love of Christ? 60.38

separated
your iniquities have s. between you and your God 23.115

sepulchres
like unto whited s. 55.143

seraphims
Above it stood the s. 23.13

serpent
the s. was more subtil 1.15
The s. beguiled me 1.20
and it became a s. 2.14
Make thee a fiery s. and set it upon a pole 4.20

servant
Speak, LORD; for thy s. heareth 9.6
among you shall be your s. 55.141
hath holpen his s. Israel 57.10
thy s. depart in peace 57.17
took upon him the form of a s. 65.5

servants
Henceforth I call you not s. 58.79

serve
S. the LORD with gladness 19.158
Ye cannot s. God and mammon 55.35

service
s. is perfect freedom 82.16

set
have I s. my face like a flint 23.89

seven
the s. thin ears devoured the s. rank and full ears 1.89
heat the furnace one s. times more 27.13
Until seventy times s. 55.118
in the midst of the s. candlesticks 81.4

seventh
on the s. day God ended his work 1.8
God blessed the s. day 1.8

seventy
S. weeks are determined upon thy people 27.31
Until s. times seven 55.118

shadow
the valley of the s. of death 19.31
shall abide under the s. of the Almighty 19.142

the s. of a great rock in a weary land 23.47

shake
I will s. the heavens 37.3
s. off the dust of your feet 55.65

shaking
as I prophesied, there was a noise, and behold a s. 26.33

shame
some to everlasting life, and some to s. and everlasting contempt 27.33

shave
she caused him to s. off the seven locks of his head 7.27

sheep
we are counted as s. for the slaughter 19.78
All we like s. have gone astray 23.95
I, will both search my s. 26.30
as s. having no shepherd 55.61
the lost s. of the house of Israel 55.63
s. in the midst of wolves 55.66
divideth his s. from the goats 55.160
the good shepherd, and know my s. 58.50
My s. hear my voice 58.51

sheep's
come to you in s. clothing 55.45

shepherd
The LORD is my s. 19.31
He shall feed his flock like a s. 23.58
And I will set up one s. over them 26.31
they all shall have one s. 26.35
smite the s. and the sheep shall be scattered 38.16
I am the good s. 58.50
Jesus, that great s. of 73.39
S. and Bishop of 75.12

shepherds
prophesy against the s. of Israel 26.28
country s. abiding in the field 57.14

shibboleth
Say now S. 7.17

shield
I am thy s. 1.55
the s. of faith 64.28

shine
Let your light so s. 55.19

shined
upon them hath the light s. 23.19

ships
They that go down to the sea in s. 19.175

shoes
put off thy s. from off thy feet 2.11

short
being made perfect in a s. time 45.7

shortened
Behold, the LORD's hand is not s. that it cannot save 23.115

shoulder
the government shall be upon his s. 23.20

shout
gone up with a s.   19.85
sick
I am s. of love   22.8
but they that are s.   55.57
Heal the s.   55.64
I was s. and ye visited   55.161
sickness
in s. and in health   82.88
side
passed by on the other s.   57.35
sighing
sorrow and s. shall flee away   23.54
sight
The blind receive their s.   55.75
recovering of s. to the blind   57.21
we walk by faith, not by s.   62.14
sign
adulterous generation seeketh after a s.
55.88
outward and visible s.   82.76
silence
a time to keep s. and a time to speak   21.11
let all the earth keep s. before him   35.4
s. in heaven   81.30
silver
The s. is mine, and the gold is mine   37.4
they weighed for my price thirty pieces
of s.   38.13
And they covenanted with him for thirty
pieces of s.   55.166
the thirty pieces of s.   55.176
simple
making wise the s.   19.25

sin
if thou wilt forgive their s.   2.64
forgiving iniquity and transgression
and s.   2.70
unto the LORD for a s. offering   3.2
as concerning his s. and it shall be forgiven
him   3.3
Be sure your s. will find you out   4.27
rebellion is as the s. of witchcraft   9.22
will forgive their s. and will heal their land
14.2
I acknowledged my s.   19.54
cleanse me from my s.   19.90
s. is a reproach to any people   20.50
he bare the s. of many   23.96
taketh away the s. of the world   58.9
without s. among you, let him first cast a
stone   58.38
go, and s. no more   58.39
he will reprove the world of s.   58.81
s. abounded, grace did much more
abound   60.21
dead to s.   60.22
s. shall not have dominion   60.27

the wages of s. is death   60.28
he hath made him to be s. for us, who knew
no s.   62.19
yet without s.   73.9
say that we have no s.   77.3
blood of Jesus ... cleanseth us from all s.
77.3
See also **sins**
sinews
I will lay s. upon you   26.33
sinful
Depart from me; for I am a s. man   57.24
his own Son in the likeness of s. flesh   60.32
sing
O come let us s. unto the LORD   19.151
O s. unto the LORD a new song   19.156
the tongue of the dumb s.   23.52
S. unto the Lord a new song   82.117
let us s. unto the Lord   82.146
sinned
Against thee, thee only, have I s.   19.91
Father, I have s. against heaven   57.51
For all have s. and come short of the glory of
God   60.14
sinner
angels of God over one s. that repenteth
57.49
sinners
call ... s. to repentance   55.57
a friend of publicans and s.   55.80
while we were yet s. Christ died for us
60.19
Christ Jesus came into the world to save s.
69.2
sinneth
the soul that s. it shall die   26.16
sins
He hath not dealt with us after our s.   19.160
love covereth all s.   20.28
though your s. be as scarlet   23.5
thou wilt cast all their s. into the depths
of the sea   33.8
save his people from their s.   55.2
blood ... shed for many for the remission
of s.   55.167
Her s. which are many, are forgiven   57.28
repentance and remission of s. should be
preached   57.88
Christ died for our s. according to the
scriptures   61.47
the forgiveness of s.   64.1
when he had by himself purged our s.   73.1
hide a multitude of s.   74.22
bare our s. in his own body   75.11
cover the multitude of s.   75.19
we confess our s. he   77.3
visit the s. of the fathers   82.47
See also **sin**

the s. entered into me when he spake unto me   26.4

give them one heart, and I will put a new s. within you   26.10

a new s. will I put within you   26.32

I will put my s. within you   26.32

shall put my s. in you, and ye shall live 26.34

I will pour out my s. upon all flesh   29.7

so my s. remaineth among you: fear ye not 37.3

Not by might … but by my s. saith the LORD of hosts   38.7

the S. of God descending like a dove   55.10

Blessed are the poor in s.   55.17

the s. indeed is willing   55.171

my s. hath rejoiced in God my Saviour 57.10

The S. of the Lord is upon me   57.21

Father, into thy hands I commend my s. 57.79

born of the S. is s.   58.15

shall worship the Father in s. and in truth 58.22

God is a S.   58.22

the s. that quickeneth   58.35

the S. of truth   58.72

I will pour out of my S. upon all flesh   59.6

led by the S. of God   60.35

received the S. of adoption   60.35

S. searcheth all things   61.8

diversities of gifts, but the same S.   61.39

manifestation of the S. is given to every man to profit withal   61.40

not of the letter, but of the s.   62.4

the fruit of the S. is love   63.20

And grieve not the holy S. of God   64.17

be filled with the S.   64.20

the sword of the S.   64.28

Quench not the S.   67.11

hath not given us the s. of fear   70.1

dividing asunder of soul and s.   73.8

I was in the S.   81.4

the fruits of the S.   82.30

See also **Holy Ghost**

spirits
Are they not all ministering s.   73.3
the s. of just men made   73.33

spit
they s. upon him   55.180

spoken
hath … s. unto us by his Son   73.1

spotted
hating even the garment s. by the flesh 80.4

spue
I will s. thee out of my mouth   81.12

spy
Moses sent to s. out the land   4.11

stand
and having done all, to s.   64.28
who shall be able to s.   81.27

star
we have seen his s. in the east   55.4

stars
he made the s. also   1.5
I will multiply thy seed as the s.   1.72
the s. in their courses fought   7.8
He telleth the number of the s.   19.237

stature
increased in wisdom and s.   57.20

statutes
The s. of the LORD are right   19.25
the way of thy s.   19.196

stay
none can s. his hand   27.18

steal
Thou shalt not s.   2.44

stiffnecked
it is a s. people   2.61

still
Be s. and know that I am God   19.83

sting
O death, where is thy s.   61.57

stolen
S. waters are sweet   20.25

stomach's
use a little wine for thy s. sake   69.12

stone
I will give thee tables of s.   2.49
The s. which the builders refused   19.191
without sin among you, let him first cast a s.   58.38

stones
the s. shall be with the names of the children of Israel   2.53
five smooth s. out of the brook   9.28
command that these s. be made bread 55.11
the s. would immediately cry out   57.69
lively s. are built up   75.8

stony
I will take the s. heart out of their flesh 26.10

straight
make thy way s. before my face   19.8

strain
s. at a gnat, and swallow   55.142

strait
Enter ye in at the s.   55.44

strange
I have been a stranger in a s. land   2.8
king Solomon loved many s. women   11.21
sing the LORD'S song in a s. land?   19.222

no good t. will he withhold from them 19.132

It is a good t. to give thanks   19.145

every t. that hath breath   19.244

there is no new t. under the sun   21.4

To every t. there is a season   21.11

He hath made every t. beautiful in his time 21.12

things

for all t. come of thee   13.10

The LORD hath done great t. for us   19.212

six t. doth the LORD hate   20.16

And seekest thou great t. for thyself?   24.39

For who hath despised the day of small t. 38.8

all these t. shall be added   55.37

with God all t. are possible   55.127

All t. were made by him   58.1

all t. work together for good to them that love God   60.37

all t. to all men   61.27

all t. be done decently and in order   61.46

all t. are become new   62.18

can do all t. through Christ   65.19

God, who giveth us richly all t. to enjoy 69.16

Unto the pure all t. are pure   71.2

left undone those t.   82.3

done those t. which ought not   82.3

third

and be killed, and be raised again the t. day 55.109

thirst

in my t. they gave me vinegar   19.114

hunger and t. after righteousness   55.17

If any man t.   58.37

I t.   58.95

thirsteth

Ho, every one that t.   23.99

thirsty

I was t. and ye gave   55.161

thirty

they weighed for my price t. pieces of silver   38.13

And they covenanted with him for t. pieces of silver   55.166

the t. pieces of silver   55.176

thorn

Instead of the t. shall come up the fir tree 23.105

a t. in the flesh   62.33

thou

for t. art with me   19.31

thought

By t. word, and deed   82.57

thoughts

For my t. are not your thoughts   23.102

For my thoughts are not your t.   23.102

Cleanse the t. of our hearts   82.46

thousand

a t. years in thy sight are but as yesterday 19.139

A t. shall fall at thy side   19.143

one man among a t. have I found   21.33

the chiefest among ten t.   22.21

bound him a t. years   81.63

lived and reigned with Christ a t.   81.63

threefold

a t. cord is not quickly broken   21.20

threescore

The days of our years are t. years and ten 19.140

throne

come boldly unto the t. of grace   73.9

sitteth upon the t. and unto the Lamb 81.28

fell before the t.   81.28

saw a great white t.   81.65

Thummim

the Urim and the T.   2.54

thyself

Thou shalt love thy neighbour as t.   55.140

tidings

of him that bringeth good t. that publisheth peace   23.92

good t. unto the meek   23.120

time

come to the kingdom for such a t. as this? 17.5

a t. to every purpose   21.11

A t. to be born   21.11

the fulness of the t. was come   63.10

Redeeming the t.   64.19

spake in t. past unto the fathers   73.1

times

My t. are in thy hand   19.51

tingle

the ears of every one that heareth it shall t. 9.7

tithes

he gave him t. of all   1.54

Bring ye all the t. into the storehouse   39.8

tittle

one jot or one t. shall in no wise   55.20

to day

T. shalt thou be with me in paradise   57.77

tongs

taken with the t. from off the altar   23.14

tongue

a lying t.   20.16

For with stammering lips and another t. will he speak   23.39

the t. of the dumb sing   23.52

The Lord GOD hath given me the t. of the learned   23.88

every t. should confess   65.5

valley
the v. of the shadow of death   19.31
Every v. shall be exalted   23.56
the v. which was full of bones   26.33
valleys
the lily of the v.   22.5
valour
thou mighty man of v.   7.10
value
ye are of more v. than many   55.69
vanity
V. of vanities, saith the Preacher   21.1
all is v.   21.1
all is v. and vexation of spirit   21.6
vengeance
V. is mine   60.52
vessels
this treasure in earthen v.   62.9
vexation
all is vanity and v. of spirit   21.6
victory
He will swallow up death in v.   23.35
Death is swallowed up in v.   61.56
God, which giveth us the v.   61.57
v. that overcometh the world   77.22
vine
Thy wife shall be as a fruitful v.   19.216
But they shall sit every man under his v. and
under his fig tree   33.3
I am the true v.   58.76
vinegar
in my thirst they gave me v.   19.114
They gave him v. to drink mingled with
gall   55.181
gave me v. to drink   82.141
vines
neither shall fruit be in the v.   35.7
vineyard
Give me thy v.   11.46
My wellbeloved hath a v. in a very fruitful
hill   23.10
violence
because he had done no v.   23.95
violent
Laid v. hands   82.97
vipers
O generation of v.   55.8
virgin
Behold, a v. shall conceive   23.16
a v. shall be with child   55.3
virgins
Then all those v. arose   55.153
virtuous
A v. woman is a crown to her husband
20.37
Who can find a v. woman?   20.103
visage
his v. was so marred more than any man
23.94

visible
All things v. and invisible   82.48
vision
Where there is no v. the people perish
20.102
Write the v. and make it plain upon tables
35.3
visions
Daniel had understanding in all v. and
dreams   27.3
your young men shall see v.   29.7
visitation
in the time of their v.   45.6
voice
I heard thy v. in the garden   1.19
if ye will obey my v. indeed   2.43
and after the fire a still small v.   11.43
The Lord heard her v.   50.2
The v. of one crying in the wilderness   55.6
a v. from heaven   55.10
the dead shall hear the v. of the Son   58.27
My sheep hear my v.   58.51
void
it shall not return unto me v.   23.103
vomit
As a dog returneth to his v.   20.91

W

wages
the w. of sin is death   60.28
wait
W. on the LORD: be of good courage   19.45
But they that w. upon the LORD shall renew
their strength   23.67
a man should ... quietly w. for the salvation
of the LORD   25.6
though it tarry, w. for it   35.3
walk
w. before me, and be thou perfect   1.60
let us w. in the light of the LORD   23.7
This is the way, w. ye in it   23.45
they shall w. and not faint   23.67
to w. humbly with thy God?   33.7
he will make me to w. upon mine high
places   35.8
and the lame w.   55.75
w. in newness of life   60.23
let us also w. in the Spirit   63.21
ye w. worthy of the vocation   64.12
walked
Noah w. with God   1.37
walketh
Blessed is the man that w. not in the counsel
of the ungodly   19.1
walking
w. and leaping, and praising God   59.11

wood

hewers of w. and drawers of water   6.9

word

by every w. that proceedeth out of the mouth of the LORD   5.13

Thy w. have I hid in mine heart   19.194

Thy w. is a lamp unto my feet,   19.202

a w. spoken in due season   20.55

A w. fitly spoken is like apples of gold   20.86

but the w. of our God shall stand for ever   23.56

So shall my w. be that goeth forth out of my mouth   23.103

his w. was in mine heart as a burning fire shut up in my bones   24.27

Is not my w. like as a fire?   24.30

by every w. that proceedeth out of the mouth   55.11

speak the w.   55.49

be it unto me according to thy w.   57.8

at thy w. I will let down the net   57.23

In the beginning was the W.   58.1

the W. was made flesh   58.6

prayer and ... the ministry of the w.   59.17

hearing by the w. of God   60.44

Holding forth the w. of life   65.7

in truth, the w. of God   67.4

Preach the w.   70.9

w. of God is quick   73.8

ye doers of the w.   74.5

let us not love in w.   77.12

by the w. of their testimony   81.39

By thought, w. and deed   82.57

words

shall ye lay up these my w. in your heart   5.18

Let the w. of my mouth ... be acceptable   19.25

therefore let thy w. be few   21.23

I have put my w. in thy mouth   24.2

thou hast the w. of eternal life   58.36

comfortable w. our Saviour   82.58

work

Man goeth forth unto his w.   19.166

always abounding in the w. of the Lord   61.58

w. out your own salvation   65.6

works

All thy w. shall praise thee   19.231

Commit thy w. unto the LORD   20.57

O all ye w. of the Lord, bless   49.2

the wonderful w. of God   59.5

this woman was full of good w.   59.26

the w. of the flesh are manifest   63.19

Not the w.   64.5

by w. a man is justified   74.11

judged every man according to their w.   81.65

Of W. of Supererogation   82.164

world

he hath set the w. in their heart   21.12

w. hath lost his youth   41.5

Ye are the light of the w.   55.19

the care of this w.   55.93

if he shall gain the whole w.   55.110

even unto the end of the w.   55.189

Go ye into all the w.   56.24

that all the w. should be taxed   57.12

For God so loved the w.   58.17

I am the light of the w.   58.40

In the w. ye shall have tribulation   58.83

My kingdom is not of this w.   58.91

turned the w. upside down   59.39

he will judge the w. in righteousness   59.45

be not conformed to this w.   60.47

Christ Jesus came into the w. to save sinners   69.2

brought nothing into this w.   69.13

Demas ... loved this present w.   70.11

Love not the w.   77.5

w. without end   82.7

The deceits of the w.   82.27

wormwood

the w. and the gall   25.4

worse

the last state of that men is w. than   55.90

for better for w.   82.90

worship

w. the LORD in the beauty of holiness   13.3

w. the LORD in the beauty of holiness   19.46

let us w.   19.152

O w. the LORD in the beauty of holiness   19.155

if thou wilt fall down and w. me   55.13

shall w. the Father in spirit and in truth   58.22

w. him that liveth   81.18

worshipped

and fell down, and w. him   55.5

worthy

I am not w. that thou shouldest   55.49

And am no more w. to be called thy son   57.51

shoe's latchet I am not w. to   58.8

ye walk w. of the vocation   64.12

Thou art w. O Lord   81.18

found w. to open   81.19

wounded

a w. spirit who can bear?   20.68

But he was w. for our transgressions   23.95

wounds

Faithful are the w. of a friend   20.97

wrath

A soft answer turneth away w.   20.51

in w. remember mercy   35.5
flee from the w. to come?   55.8
great day of his w.   81.27
wrestled
there w. a man with him   1.82
write
and w. it in their hearts   24.35
writer
my tongue is the pen of a ready w.   19.79
written
What I have w. I have w.   58.93
names are not w. in the book   81.42

Y

year
A jubilee shall that fiftieth y. be   3.16
years
The days of our y. are threescore y. and ten   19.140
I will restore to you the y. that the locust hath eaten   29.6
Lord as a thousand y.   76.7
bound him a thousand y.   81.63
yoke
bear the y. in his youth   25.7
Take my y. upon you   55.83
my y. is easy   55.83
yoked
ye not unequally y. together with unbelievers   62.22

young
Wherewithal shall a y. man cleanse his way?   19.193
Rejoice, O y. man, in thy youth   21.52
y. men shall utterly fall   23.67
the y. man heard that saying   55.125
youth
Rejoice, O young man, in thy y.   21.52
Remember now thy Creator in the days of thy y.   21.53
world hath lost his y.   41.5
no man despise thy y.   69.10
youths
Even the y. shall faint and be weary   23.67

Z

zeal
For the z. of thine house hath eaten me up   19.112
The z. of the LORD of hosts will perform this   23.20
the z. of thine house hath   82.139
Zion
the joy of the whole earth, is mount Z.   19.86
we wept, when we remembered Z.   19.222
come to Z. with songs and everlasting joy   23.54
O Z. that bringest good tidings   23.57
that saith unto Z. Thy God reigneth!   23.92
The LORD will roar from Z.   30.1